THE
MODERN WRITER
AND HIS WORLD

BY

G. S. FRASER

DEREK VERSCHOYLE 13 PARK PLACE ST JAMES'S LONDON SW1

FIRST PUBLISHED IN 1953 BY
DEREK VERSCHOYLE LIMITED 13 PARK PLACE
ST JAMES'S LONDON SW1

MADE AND PRINTED IN GREAT BRITAIN
BY WILLIAM CLOWES AND SONS LTD, LONDON AND BECCLES

CONTENTS

PREFACE

The bulk of this book was written, or rather dictated to my wife and polished as I copied her notes on my typewriter, at Lake Chusenji in Japan in the summer of 1950. My object was to provide Japanese students of English literature, who had been cut off from contact with us during the war, with a fairly clear guide-book to modern tendencies. In Japan, where it has gone into two editions in English, and also been translated into Japanese, the book, I think, has been found reasonably useful. In England, however, I heard that some of my friends who had looked at it – and who had always, for instance, found modern poetry puzzling – also thought it useful; and I knew that, both when I was an undergraduate exploring modern English literature for the first time, and later preparing lectures for soldiers or for Adult Education classes, I myself should have been grateful for such a book. But I am not blind to the faults which, in these days of close criticism, must be found in such a sweeping and cursory survey. In covering such a wide field, one exposes very clearly gaps in one's reading, inadequacies in one's thinking, and deficiencies in one's sensibility. It is with these in mind that I have added to my chapters on modernism in general, on the drama, on fiction, and on poetry, a new chapter on criticism which has taken me, if not more pains, at least more time than all the rest of the book. I hope it will send readers who are looking here for a general picture of the lie of the land to more competent writers on many particular themes. The pattern I have had in mind, in producing this book, is that, for instance, of Dr Joad's excellent guides to philosophy and ethics, or some of Mr G.D.H.Cole's popular books on economic theory; such works no doubt bore specialists, by seeming to labour the obvious, and by avoiding the really tricky questions, but they do start the plain man off on the right road. It is the plain man and his needs that I have chiefly thought of here; in the long run, and even in the comparatively short run, the provision of an adequate popular education is the most urgent social task that lies ahead of us. I hope, however, that this purpose has not betrayed me into a tone of condescension, and I am fairly sure that, though it may sometimes have induced a fell loquacity, it has not betrayed me into over-simplification; I am, after all, like most of my readers, in most things a plain man myself.

G. S. FRASER

CHAPTER ONE

THE BACKGROUND OF IDEAS

Section 1: What Do We Mean by 'Modernity' in Literature?

This whole book is an extensive but summary (in a sense, necessarily summary *because* extensive) consideration of the set of tendencies which we call the 'modern movement' in English literature. In a book of this sort, it is impossible, of course, and it would also be undesirable, to exclude one's personal judgments, but I am at least attempting to be as objective as possible; I am trying to record the view of contemporary English literature that one thinks 'most people' take and by 'most people' there one probably means certain critics of an older generation, certain friends of one's own generation, whose judgment one respects. I am refraining from emphasising my own personal reserves about, or qualifications of, a 'generally accepted' point of view. My task, in fact, is less the final task of criticism than the preliminary task of getting a literary scene into perspective. I have attempted as it were to dig out and put tidily upon the page that rough working scheme of the development of English literature in the last fifty years which, I suppose, every practising critic has somewhere at the back of his head. I have taken the novel, the drama, and poetry as the three main kinds of literature demanding consideration and I have added a more tentative essay on the general trends of literary criticism. For each subdivision of my period, I have made no attempt at all at an exhaustive coverage, but I have directed my attention to these writers only who seemed to me vividly to express the mood of the time. Many writers whom I admire, or who would be worth considering in another context, I have omitted because they lacked the crude illustrative value I was looking for.

Illustrative of what? Roughly, I have, as I say, been directing my attention chiefly to those writers who seem to throw most light on the vast, complicated, subtle pattern of changes that has been transforming English society in the last fifty years. I ask myself if a writer mirrors some critical or questioning moment in the nation's history. There are excellent writers, on the other hand, whose significance lies in their personalities rather than in their relation to the spirit of the age; one can think, for instance, of Max Beerbohm, of Norman Douglas, or, at another level and from another point of view, Harold Monro. About such writers I have less to say. On the other hand, there are writers of less even excellence whose significance is that they mirror rather some *un*critical or *un*questioning moment in the nation's history. Their work reflects hopes or enthusiasms which the mere passing of time shows to be unfounded. H. G. Wells and Rudyard Kipling, in spite of the completely opposite and mutually hostile relation of their social philosophies, are writers of this type. Neither Kipling's militant Imperialism, nor Wells's optimistic Liberalism, has stood the test of time. But they were both men of genius. And for my own purpose the errors of great writers are as relevant as their insights. For my subject, very broadly, is the relation of the writer to his age.

I would like to make some reserves here. I do not think that literature can be 'explained' by setting it against the historical background that it springs from, any more than I think that historical background can ultimately be 'explained' itself, by reducing the operative agents involved in it to some definite set of factors. I think literature and life are both ultimately mysterious. I do think, however, that the attempt to relate the literature of a period to the more general life of a period can increase our understanding of both; we feel more at home, we find our way about better. As to *why* we should study the literature and the life even of the fairly recent past, there are a good many answers to that. One of them is that if we do, we shall feel more at home and find our way about better in the present. The more important answer is that the literature and the life of the past are interesting for their own sakes and that the disinterested curiosity we are capable of feeling about something that does not immediately practically concern us is part of our human dignity and part, also, of what refines the individual sensibility and enriches the individual life.

This then is a study of modern literature in relation to modern life – and the setting is England, but I think the study has more than a merely local relevance. What we call specifically 'modern' or 'modernist' literature has certain common characteristics in all countries; and so of course has the development of modern history in all countries. The problems which Englishmen have faced, and to which English writers have given literary expression, in the last fifty years or so are not merely local ones.

They have a general topical and contemporary interest. In this first chapter, I want to consider the question of what some of these common characteristics of 'modernity' are. For when we describe a work of literature as 'modern,' we do not merely mean that it has been published (according to the stretch of our historical perspective) in the last year or two, or since the beginning of the century, or perhaps since the Renaissance, or perhaps since the decline of the Roman Empire and the earliest poems and chronicles written in a vernacular European tongue. (For 'modern times' might be thought to begin, from some points of view, with the Christian era itself.) No, when we describe a work as 'modern,' we are ascribing certain intrinsic qualities to it, though we may be vague in our minds about what these qualities are. Thus the question of date need not rise at all. We may find Catullus or Petronius 'modern,' in a way in which we do not find Virgil 'modern'; or Villon in a way in which we do not find Ronsard, or Donne in a way in which we do not find Spenser, or Clough in a way in which we do not find Tennyson. That is to say, all through the literature of the past, there are certain works, which, in the attitudes they express and the problems they deal with, have a peculiar affinity with the spirit of our own time. It is well worth our while then (for it will increase our understanding of the world we live in) to try to isolate some of these characteristics which, wherever we come across them, give us the feeling of 'modernity.'

Section 2: The Historical Sense in Modern Literature

Paradoxically enough, one of the main marks of 'modernism' in literature is often a lively interest in the past for its own sake. We can push the beginnings of 'modern' literature indefinitely back and back, and it is as a mere matter of convenience that in this book I have started off, in my consideration of the novel, poetry, and the drama with the 1890s. On a book of a larger scale, the English romantic movement around 1800 might have seemed a more logical starting-point. One of the most important aspects of that movement was, of course, a new sense of reverence for the past. In the Augustan age, both Englishmen and Frenchmen tended to assume that, after centuries of comparative barbarism, they had at last achieved a civilisation comparable to that of Greece and Rome, and that this civilisation could be preserved, without essential alteration, for an indefinite number of years. What was the impulse that, as the eighteenth century wore on, made Horace Walpole ornament his house in a mock-Gothic manner, made Chatterton forge poems in a mock-Middle-English, caused Bishop Percy not only to collect old ballads but to add to them and alter them in what he thought was the same style, made Mrs Radcliffe set her gloomy romances in the castles of mediaeval Italy, and turned *connoisseurs* of buildings and scenery everywhere away from formal gardens and Palladian mansions towards the contemplation of ruins (they would even have ruins specially built, to set up in their parks, and would sometimes hire hermits to live in them) and the 'wild,' and the 'romantic' (the original meaning of the word is, resembling scenes or episodes in the old fantastic romances of chivalry), and the 'picturesque'? No movement so rich, complex, and various can be explained in any simple or straightforward fashion. It may be that there was in many minds a subconscious realisation that the static civilisation of the eighteenth century could not, in fact, be preserved indefinitely, that man was rather controlled by historical forces, than controlled them. If man lost, in this way, the dignity of being the master of events, at least he could enlarge himself in another sense by uniting himself with the long perspectives of history; and the new passionate interest in nature of poets like Wordsworth sprang perhaps from a similar impulse of enlargement, a wish to belong to something more invigorating and life-inspiring than some mere stiff, conventional urban social circle. The inspiring ideas of Augustan classicism had been reason and decorum. Mystery had been cast out. With the French Revolution it became clear enough, even if there had not been Edmund Burke to emphasise it with his matchless eloquence, that Tradition was a safer watchword for the ruling classes than Reason. The existence of a stable community like that of Great Britain was in essence a mystery, to be approached with reverence, not with a prying criticism or a carping superiority. There was a strange shaping wisdom in history, there was something awesome about established institutions. Our ancestors whom we had been thinking of, till the other day, as uncouth 'gothick' creatures, whose errors our new refinement had exploded, had built better than they knew. The man who tried to live by pure abstract reason was a strutting, dangerous, destructive *doctrinaire*. Man in relation to the past, like man in relation to the natural world about him, was a mystery; that was his dignity.

This new romantic interest in history was, of course, to be one of the most important factors shaping the development of English culture in the nineteenth century. One might almost say that, in many important respects, the Victorian age had no conscious style of its own and was thus for ever covering its nakedness in fancy costumes out of the past.

Thus, as the fine tradition of eighteenth-century classical architecture decayed, not only churches but railway stations and hotels were built, under the inspiration of Pugin and Ruskin, on the model of Gothic cathedrals. It was not only, often, a matter of imitation in an inappropriate context but of imitation with unworthy materials; thus an enterprising business man in the north of England invented a way of prefabricating the structural and ornamental elements of small Gothic churches out of cast iron. And certainly an air of comedy hangs about a great deal of Victorian mediaevalism; one thinks of Disraeli's 'Young England' group going to an enormous expense to reproduce all the settings and circumstances of a mediaeval tournament and being thwarted, as those who plan open-air festivities so often are in England, by a thrashing downpour of rain.

In a wider sense, one may feel that something that could be called not merely an interest in, but almost an obsession with, the past prevented many Victorian poets doing justice to their own age. Tennyson turns to classical legend and the Arthurian romances, Browning to Renaissance Italy, Rossetti and Morris, in tone as well as in theme, to the mediaeval world. Even Matthew Arnold, a poet more uneasily aware of contemporary issues than any of these, allows his mind to dally with a vision of Oxford in the seventeenth century, at a time when 'wits ran clear beside the sparkling Thames.' A writer, again, like Walter Pater, who is fundamentally, as Mr T. S. Eliot has said, a moralist rather than a critic, nevertheless, sets his moralisings against a richly evoked background of late Roman or High Renaissance life – he does not relate them directly (what might, in any case, have been tactless and dangerous) to the life around him.

This Victorian feeling for history, then, is a complicated thing. Sometimes it is not wholly a true feeling; it is less true, for instance, in Tennyson (whose Arthurian knights are too obviously sober Victorian gentlemen in disguise) than in the Browning, say, of The Ring and the Book. Yet it might be said that Browning's chief curiosity about and interest in his characters is always a psychological one, that the local colour and the historical setting are, for him, a secondary matter. In Rossetti and Morris on the other hand a highly individualised vision of the past embodies certain values of which they feel the lack, more bitterly and consciously than Tennyson or Browning, in the contemporary scene. Their feeling for the past is beginning to be almost a religious feeling, and when they look around at the actual world about them, the world that the Industrial Revolution has produced, they have a sense of

13

desecration. Yeats inherited from the Pre-Raphaelites this nobly re-actionary attitude, and it is of them that he is thinking when he writes,

> We were the last romantics – chose for theme
> Traditional sanctity and loveliness;
> Whatever's written in what poets name
> The book of the people; whatever most can bless
> The mind of man or elevate a rhyme;
> But all is changed, that high horse riderless,
> Though mounted in that saddle Homer rode
> Were the swan drifts upon a darkening flood.

For Yeats, as for Morris before him, the sense of the past has come to include an acceptance of the validity, at their own proper level, of myths and legends as well as of actual historical facts. He also sees, as Morris saw, that myths and legends spring from 'the book of the people' – that is, from traditional folk culture – and that when folk culture is destroyed, as it so largely has been by the industrial revolution, the poet is in danger of being cut off from his sources. Homer *rode* Pegasus. But the tide of change has now flooded the scene and the swan of poetry drifts weakly and without purpose, no longer controlling man's dreams, but controlled by his fate.

That sense of drift and of the darkening flood is evoked, too, but almost briskly and cheerfully, and certainly with none of Yeats's sense of foreboding, by Walter Pater in the opening pages of his *Plato and Platonism*. There he asks himself, and is perhaps the first Victorian thinker to ask himself, what is the deeper meaning of this 'historical' attitude, which he recognises to be the dominant attitude of the age. Its deeper meaning, for Pater, is that it implies an acceptance of the relativity of all values.* Can we ask, or answer the question, he demands, whether Plato's philosophical theories are 'true' or not? No, he says, we cannot ask or answer that question. We can merely try to understand Plato the man, try to understand his background, and relate the two to each other as far as we can. It was natural that such a man, at such a time, should evolve such theories, but the theories in abstraction from the man and the time are meaningless to us. Thus the historical attitude implies, in Pater's interpretation, at once a distinctly concrete approach and a permanent suspension of judgment; it also implies an acceptance of the fact that *our own* theories about life will seem meaning-

---

* Mr Graham Hough has written very brilliantly on the relation of Pater to Yeats, and in the next two or three pages I am largely summarising his ideas as I remember them.

less to future scholars except in relation to our personalities and to the age which we lived in. How far Yeats would have followed Pater in all this, it would be hard to say. He had more of a dogmatic temperament and more of a hunger for the absolute: at the same time, he does say somewhere, like Pater (but quoting Vico, if I remember, as his authority) that he is less interested in the ideas of Socrates than in Socrates the man.

Vico, a seventeenth-century Italian scholar, who was forgotten for many years after his death, but who has now become extremely fashionable once more, was the first philosopher of history. God, he said, made nature, but man made history, and therefore history was the more proper human study. He fascinated writers like Yeats and Joyce, because of his insistence that the earliest and most primitive force in human society was the concrete, intuitive poetic imagination (such imagination, for instance, as is embodied in the wonderful primitive cave-drawings of animals at Lascaux and at several other places in Europe), and that society develops, sorts itself out, specialises its functions, with the growing abstraction of language from its original, poetic concrete force; law and reason and debate are late developments. With nothing but a knowledge of philology, and a feeling for literature, to guide him Vico was nevertheless much nearer the truth in his guesses about early society than the Whig legalists who imagined primitive individuals arriving at a contract to live together under the rule of law.

He fascinated Yeats and Joyce, also, because, like Nietzsche, he believed in an eternal recurrence. It was in the nature of human society when it had reached a certain stage of civilisation to collapse into primitivism again, and then the whole scheme of human development which Vico had sketched out would start off once more. Spengler, in our time, in a crude, wordy, and popular book, has put forth a similar theory, and Yeats was to develop a recurrence-theory himself, with occult and magical trimmings, in *A Vision*. In Joyce's last very obscure and difficult work, *Finnegan's Wake*, the opening page begins in the middle of a sentence and the beginning of the sentence is the last thing in the book; so that theoretically one could turn back to the beginning from the end, and go on for ever, which, according to Joyce, is what history does.

The reasons why great poets and philosophers have accepted this theory of eternal recurrence are obviously not principally rational ones; it enables them to escape from that complete acceptance of relativity which had failed to worry Pater. It offers a kind of earthly immortality.

It is a strange illustration of the contrast between the European and the Oriental temperaments that this eternal recurrence is just the great wheel of existence from which all world-denying religions like Hinduism and Buddhism seek for the self's ultimate escape. It should be noted that Marxism, another influential historicist philosophy in our time, has more than a little in common as a pattern of ideas with the theories of Vico and Spengler (since it is never explained by Marxists why a classless society, supposing one achieved, will not sort itself out into classes again, as primitive classless societies have done in the past): it has in common too that *amor fati*, or joyful embracing of one's destiny, which is the way in which Vico and Nietzsche and Spengler and their disciples solve (or rather evade, in an emotionally satisfactory way) the old puzzles about determinism and free will. (It is not really a solution, but an embodied self-contradiction; for if my destiny is predetermined, so is the fashion in which I will embrace it; and if the latter is not wholly predetermined, then neither is the former.)

We have seen then how a mere curiosity about the past could develop in the course of a century into an elaborate and all-inclusive philosophy of history. But other attitudes to history than those of Yeats and Joyce were, of course, possible. There was, for instance, the old Victorian belief in the inevitability, given the mounting up of human assets, and every generation's addition to them, and the growing spirit of rationality among civilised peoples, of material and moral progress. This is reflected in the works of a writer like H. G. Wells. Wells, at the end of the nineteenth century, has the same curiosity about the future as Walter Scott, at the beginning, has about the past. He has not, of course, the same materials for satisfying his curiosity. Nevertheless, he is able to make good guesses about the growth of mechanical invention, and rather bad guesses about the development of human nature; and, however far off the mark he is, he can always tell a good story and keep our interest alive. There is a similar spirit in Bernard Shaw, except that Shaw, with a more religious and a less scientific turn of mind than Wells, postulates a 'life-force' – a sort of immanent deity, a divine spirit working and moving in human history – that will ensure the progress of the race, however many blunders and errors individuals may make. Shaw's rather ruthless optimism has a singularly hollow air to-day, and one might be inclined to think that if there is indeed a god shut up in history he is to-day chafing and trying to break free from his narrow bounds. And with his optimism of immanence one might contrast an attitude that could be called the pessimism of transcendence; a distinctively Christian attitude, unlike the others so far discussed.

This pessimism of transcendence is well expressed in the famous *Speculations* of T. E. Hulme. For Hulme, man is a limited, sinful creature, bitterly aware of perfection, but aware, also, of how much he falls short, and must fall short, of perfection. By strict discipline he can achieve a limited decency, but it is folly for him to dream of a world in any however distant future of 'men like gods.' This attitude was taken over, refined and elaborated by Mr T. S. Eliot, in a more orthodoxly Christian fashion. For him the meaning of history is not to be found *in* history, but outside it, in man's relation to God, and God's relation to man. In history itself, no final order is ever achieved, and it is in this, not in any absolute sense, that Mr Eliot's attitude could be called pessimistic; for if the time is always in need of redemption, it is always, also, redeemable. We are not to make sense of time and history by inventing imaginary patterns of eternal recurrence, nor, on the other hand, by boarding, like Wells and Shaw, a fast train with no known destination. We are rather to make sense of time in our own lives by relating it to eternity, by self-examination, by prayer, by the purification of our souls. In the larger sense, just as man depends on God and time on eternity, so for society at large culture depends on religion. In a civilisation *without* faith, such as our own, everything tends to disintegrate and everybody tends to drift. That is one of the meanings of the most famous poem of Mr Eliot's early period, *The Waste Land*, a poem about society, where his later poems, like *Ash Wednesday* and *Four Quartets*, are rather religious examinations of his own individual experience.

The awareness of living in a period of peculiar crisis is not, of course, confined to writers with an elaborate, esoteric philosophy of history, like Yeats and Joyce, or with a definite and orthodox religious belief, like Mr Eliot. In the 1930s many young English poets, like Mr W. H. Auden, Mr Stephen Spender, Mr Cecil Day Lewis, and Mr Louis MacNeice saw the crisis as acute but temporary, the result of a transition in society between a capitalistic and a socialistic method of organising production, and sought for a resolution of the crisis in political terms. Many, though not all, of these poets in the 1930s were veering towards Marxism, though, like Queen Gertrude with her rue, they wore their Marxism 'with a difference.' The war, and recent political developments in the world, have tended to shatter these too rosy hopes, and in their recent poetry – Mr Auden, for instance, who is now living in the United States, has become an orthodox Anglican – these poets have tended to revert to more traditional attitudes.

The title of one of Mr Auden's latest poems, *The Age of Anxiety*, suggests one of the moods of the post-war world – a mood of what is often called *angst*, a word borrowed from the Danish religious thinker of the early nineteenth century, Sören Kierkegaard. Kierkegaard is the father of what is called to-day 'existentialist' philosophy; this is not a philosophy which has had much technical influence on English literature, but some of its attitudes – particularly the awareness of a general latent anxiety, not as the product of some particular pressure of events, but as intrinsic to the human condition itself – are shared by many English writers.

Kierkegaard was especially aware of the burden and mystery of one's individual existence to oneself – a burden which he thought ambitious, speculative philosophers like Hegel tended to ignore. Philosophers talk about the movement of ideas, or the development of tendencies, but our world is not a world of ideas and tendencies, it is a world of men, each of whom is an ultimate mystery both in and to himself. The most important thing in life for Kierkegaard was the relation of the individual soul to a transcendent God, who was in a position to judge that soul; it was from the extreme loneliness, and perhaps from the over-scrupulousness, of his own religious life that his emphasis on dread, awe, and anxiety (he has little, I am afraid, to say about joy) springs. In a sense he represents a genuine religious attitude, but a crippled one.

The most successful purely artistic development of Kierkegaard's ideas is to be found probably in the strange novels and tales of Kafka. Few modern writers are more lucid than Kafka; his two most famous novels, *The Trial* and *The Castle*, invite comparison, for direct narrative simplicity, both with Bunyan and Swift. Such simplicity can be, as it is in Swift's case, deceptive; and the profound deeper ambiguity of Kafka's 'message,' or the fundamentally elusive structure of his 'allegory,' has exposed him to more various interpretations than any other modern writer. *The Trial* is about a man who finds himself condemned and in the end punished – and he accepts his punishment abjectly – for some crime which he is not aware of having committed. *The Castle* is about a man who strives to get in touch with a local source of authority, which he has been told to get in touch with, and after all sorts of humiliating misadventures does not in the end really succeed in doing so. Thus in a sense the novels are 'about' the nature of sin, or guilt, and the nature of a kind of authority that might redeem or absolve us from them. But they cannot be read as straight religious allegories either in the Christian or in Kafka's own specifically Jewish tradition. We can take Kafka, of course, as meaning that we are guilty by inheritance, by our fallen nature, of original sin, whatever actual sins we may or may not have committed; and that though we reach out to God seeking forgiveness for our sins (or forgiveness for being the fallen creatures we are) we can never be sure of having reached God, and not merely some idol or substitute, or some institution, like a Church, which claims to speak for God but, in making that claim, may be betraying us. But the effect of these narratives – like the effect, perhaps, on some readers of *The Book of Job* – is to arouse a profound sympathy with the bewildered victim or the suffering seeker and to raise two fundamental questions: is there really a final authority at all, and, if there is, is it a just one? Thus some critics have taken these two novels not as religious allegories at all but as reflections of the helplessness of the individual in an elaborate decaying bureaucracy like that of the Austrian Empire; the citizen is always wrong, and he can never reach the department that could put things right, and perhaps there is no such department. Hostile critics of Kafka have even found in his work the climate of opinion that could lead to Fascism. He makes his wide appeal to contemporary readers not, perhaps, because they are eager to give their own answer to his riddles, but because he conveys with unparalleled purity and intensity the generalised anxiety of our time; it is all too easy for almost any contemporary reader to identify his own fears and worries with those of Kafka's heroes. Whether, to a more confident age, he would appear as he does to ours a writer of central significance may be doubted. He belongs, though in time he a little preceded it, very much to our special world of organised propaganda, control of the individual by government offices, permanent crisis of one sort or another, and crowded mental hospitals. He diagnosed a disease with frightening brilliance, but it is doubtful whether, either in his work or in his rather lonely and unhappy life, overshadowed by his father, he suggested a remedy.

Some of Kierkegaard's later successors, like the French philosopher and novelist and playwright, Jean-Paul Sartre, are not men of religious belief but atheists; but they find that the dread and awe and anxiety with which they regard the prospect of their own ultimate annihilation makes them as anxious as Kierkegaard was to insist on the unique significance of every individual human life. Moreover, they insist, if there is no God, it is man who makes man (that is to say, it is individual choices that define our ideals of what human nature should be). Therefore, in every choice I make, I must be overburdened with a weight of terrible responsibility, for I am choosing not only for myself but, ideally at least, for all other men. For the existentialists, then, we are not merely living through a period of crisis, but human existence itself is, in its very nature, a permanent crisis. There is a flavour in this philosophy like that of Jansenism. It can lead both to over-scrupulousness and intolerance. But it is, at least, very interestingly symptomatic of the troubled times we are living through.

Existentialism, whether in its theist or atheist versions, transcends, like Mr Eliot's Christian piety, a *merely* historical attitude to experience and it seems possible that the period when what we can call, in a wide sense, historicism was a main mark of modern literature may be coming to an end. In a period of recurrent calamities like our own, the mere passing of time gradually comes to have less significance than it may have in more settled or more expansive epochs. The conditions of human life, sad and limiting as they are, assume a certain air of permanence; and individuals accept what periods of peace and happiness and constructive activity they are granted less as a right than as a grace. They count their blessings, and are grateful.

Thus a certain reaction against the somewhat monotonous introspection and gloom of the existentialist position can be seen, for instance, in the group of interesting young writers who are connected with the English periodicals *Nine* and *Colonnade*. It would be wrong to say that these writers, Peter Russell, Iain Fletcher, Donald Carne-Ross, and others, have a common philosophy of life, but they have a common attitude of respect towards the great traditions of art and literature, the great historical achievements, of Europe. They feel that, just because we are in a bad way just now, we ought not to write off our whole historical culture, nevertheless, as a bad debt; that the great poems and prose works of the past can still give us spiritual refreshment, and that we owe a debt to our ancestors which we ought to repay.

Some of them have been very much influenced by the American poet, Ezra Pound, whose most ambitious work, *The Cantos*, an outwardly chaotic poem, but full of wonderful evocations of the past and what Mr Wyndham Lewis calls 'grand granitic landslides' of translation, is an attempt to pay that sort of debt: a kind of personal anthology of the high moments in Greek mythology and in European, American, and Chinese history. Pound is not at all, like Mr Eliot whom he so much influenced, an essentially religious poet, though in his later *Cantos* there are some passages of 'natural piety' like this famous one,

> What thou lovest well remains,
>   the rest is dross
> What thou lov'st well shall not be reft from thee
> What thou lov'st well is thy true heritage
> Whose world, or mine or theirs
>   or is it of none?
> First came the seen, then thus the palpable
>   Elysium, though it were in the halls of hell
> What thou lovest well is thy true heritage
>
> The ant's a centaur in his dragon world.
> Pull down thy vanity, it is not man
> Made courage, or made order, or made grace,
>   Pull down thy vanity, I say pull down
> Learn of the green world what can be thy place
> In scaled invention or true artistry,
>   Paquin pull down!
> The green casque has outdone your elegance.
>
> 'Master thyself, then others shall thee beare'
>   Pull down thy vanity
> Thou art a beaten dog beneath the hail,
> A swollen magpie in a fitful sun,
> Half black half white
> Nor knowst'ou wing from tail
> Pull down thy vanity
>   How mean thy hates
> Fostered in falsity,
>   Pull down thy vanity,
> Rathe to destroy, niggard in charity,
> Pull down thy vanity,
>   I say pull down.

On the whole, however, Pound's is rather a 'human' piety; he feels that there is a great ancestral wisdom of the past, that of Confucius, of Blackstone, of the American founding fathers, which we would be impious if we turned away from and rejected. And similarly we have a duty towards the great poetry, and music, and art of the past, a duty to keep it in use, fresh and fruitful for our understanding. Pound's status, if not as a poet, at least as a teacher of the young, has been badly damaged indeed by his personal eccentricities, by an occasional noisy arrogance or pretentiousness in his prose writing, by surprising school-boy blunders in his nevertheless beautiful translations, and latterly of course by his conduct during the war when, though retaining his United States citizenship, he broadcast on behalf of Italy, a country where he had lived for very many years. But if men of action, according to Lord Acton, should be judged at their worst rather than their best, there is something to be said in taking the opposite course in regard to poets; for there, it is the best that will last. Certainly, if one were trying to instil into a young man, in our troubled times, a sane loyalty towards all that is best in our strange mixed inheritance – to instil into him, in fact, a balanced attitude to history, so that even in these bad times he would keep his courage up and not weakly or unnecessarily repine – one could hardly find better words than these of Pound's to do this in: 'What thou lovest well is thy true heritage.'

Thus we have seen that the sense of history in modern literature can take an almost incredible diversity of forms; but that nevertheless it is one of the most vital elements in very much modern literature; and that, when properly cultivated, it can be a source of moral strength in troubled times.

Section 3: Realism, Psychology, Experiment in Modern Novels

I am using 'realism' not in the narrow sense in which it is sometimes used to describe novels, like Zola's, which are based on an elaborate documentation of fact, and deal often with the rather more sordid sides of contemporary life, but rather in the way in which, in ordinary conversation, we contrast what we call a 'realistic' with an 'idealistic' attitude to life. That again is different from the technical fashions in which these two words are used in philosophy, and perhaps we might describe the 'realistic' writer as one who thinks that truth to observed facts – facts about the outer world, or facts about his own feelings – is the great thing, while the 'idealistic' writer wants rather to create a pleasant and edifying picture.

Thus Dr Johnson who, like most critics of the eighteenth century, had an 'idealistic' conception of literature could not bear to re-read the last act of Shakespeare's King Lear, because the death of Cordelia was too harrowing, and struck him as wicked and wrong. He preferred the version written by a Restoration hack writer in which Cordelia survives and so does Lear, to a happy old age under her protection. It would be no answer to his criticism of King Lear that, after all, wickedness often does triumph in real life; he would reply that it is the business of the poet to see that it does not triumph in dramatic poetry.

Though we can respect the tender feelings that lay behind Dr Johnson's criticism, we probably do not agree with it to-day; we feel about Lear, after all the torments he has gone through, with Charles Lamb and with Shakespeare himself, that

> he hates him
> That would upon the rack of this tough world
> Stretch him out longer.

We see that a 'happy ending' to *King Lear* would be a tepid and tedious anti-climax. Have we gone through so much, and only for that? . . . Thus the 'idealistic' critic, in his urgent desire for edification, may be blind not only to the outward truth of life but to what we may call the inner truth of poetry; to the inevitability of the highest tragic conceptions of a writer like Shakespeare. What I have called the 'realistic' attitude is one more bravely exposed not only to the outer shocks, but to the inner springs, of life.

The realistic attitude, in this wider sense, might be opposed to the eighteenth-century convention of decorum. In a neo-classical poem, like many of Dryden's panegyric odes, it is assumed that it is only proper for the poet to treat kings as if they were noble and gracious, and statesmen as if they were wise and prudent and far-sighted, and great ladies as if they were beautiful and chaste, and famous soldiers as if they were always brave and always successful, whatever actually may be the case; even though, in fact, as in the Restoration Court, everybody knows the case to be quite otherwise. The same tone of solemn official laudation may be seen in the funeral sermons of Bossuet. One cannot exactly call it flattery, for nobody was deceived by it; it was simply part of the routine of courtly politeness. But we can see the other side of the picture in works like the memoirs of Saint-Simon or Grammont in which what moves the writer is a curiosity, often a rather malicious one, about the real motives and actions of great men; and these works are much more 'modern' in tone, and can be read with much more pleasure, than the more formal sort of writing I have been describing.

That interest in people's real actions and real motives lay, of course, behind the rise of the novel. But where there was a formula for describing conventional 'heroic' actions, there was not one for what Fielding, attempting to describe the scope of the novel in his time, called the 'comic prose epic.' One way, which Fielding makes use of in *Tom Jones* was to take some of the formulas for the heroic poem, some of the neo-classical 'receipts to make an epic,' and burlesque them; and of course in Fielding's first novel, *Joseph Andrews*, he started off with an intention of pure burlesque. But the novel, after all, is not merely the comic antithesis of the heroic poem; Tom Jones is not Augustus or Alexander, as these might have been represented in a Restoration tragedy, but he is not a mere lay-figure of fun either. He is a young man, with his faults, but with his virtues, too, who in the end deeply engages both Fielding's sympathy and the reader's. He represents mixed, average human nature and it is with that, in future, that the novelist will deal. Fielding, however, has not found the final formula for the novel; George Moore observed that in *Tom Jones* there is no psychology and no description in the modern sense, 'no inner or outer world.' There is not, but there is perhaps a firmer grasp of action and character than in many later novels, like Moore's own, which are full of psychology and description. It was in these directions, however, that the novel was to develop. If we compare Dickens with Smollett or Fielding we notice how much more vividly he evokes the outer scene, and how much more definite a part atmosphere, the atmosphere of an old house, a city street, a lonely marshland, plays in defining the mood of his stories. His eye is open. He sees. The opening of the novelist's inner eye, on the other hand, his eye for the intricate workings of the human soul, its queer mixture of noble and base motives, can be traced more strikingly in French novels, like those of Stendhal, or Benjamin Constant's cruel and incisive piece of introspection, *Adolphe*. *Adolphe* in form is a conventional eighteenth-century tale. There is no more description, or real evocation of scene, than in *Tom Jones*; but the human heart is laid bare in a way that is new and frightening. Finally, in the massive novels of the later part of the nineteenth century, in Tolstoy's *War and Peace* or in George Eliot's *Middlemarch*, we begin to feel that the structure of the novel is as solid, and its texture as supple and various, as that of life itself. It seems able to include, within its capacious but still tidy limits, everything. It is not enough to say that such works are merely 'modern.' They are among the great achievements of the human spirit at any time.

But if the novel, as an art-form, had perhaps reached its peak with George Eliot and the great Russians, the urge to experiment with it, to make it more elegant or more flexible, went on. With Henry James, the great interest is in refining the construction of the novel, so that there will be nothing superfluous, no phrase, paragraph, or sentence which will not contribute to the total effect. His masters were Flaubert and Turgeniev. If he wished to avoid the superfluous, he also wished to avoid the implausible. He disliked, as many readers dislike, the way a writer like Thackeray perpetually breaks down the illusion he is trying to create by addressing his readers in his own person and confessing that it is all a story. He introduced the technique of telling the story from the point of view of some observer who is not necessarily a main participant in the story; but this observer's curiosity, and his success or failure in satisfying it, may nevertheless become the main theme. He introduced into the novel points of view so subtle, characters so reserved and refined, delicacies of motive so intangible, that probably no previous writer would have thought them solid enough for fiction. He makes all other English novelists, except Jane Austen possibly, look a little lumpish.

But James is not fantasticating; he is exploring a real world though a world sometimes, to the ordinary reader's sensibility, almost frighteningly airy and impalpable: a world in which through labyrinthine sentences we pursue a dangerous central precision. Such exhaustive analysis might, in itself, be too tiring for most readers. But it is carried along, on the whole, with light grace and charm. And James can evoke a scene when he wants to (like the New York of the first few pages of *An International Episode*) in a magical fashion, with a succession of light, delicate, almost ghostly touches that recall the nocturnes of his compatriot, Whistler. He is rather a special taste, but for those who acquire it (and it is often a taste acquired rather late) the taste of a lifetime.

The danger, however, of the novelist relying too much on the subtlety and delicacy of his impressions of mood, and scene, and situation, and on his careful unravelling of the strands that make up these impressions, is that he may lose the sense of architecture, of structure; as impressionist painting occasionally, when it dissolved into mere evocative blobs of colour, may be said to have done. James's basic care, however, was for structure, he planned out what he called the *charpente*, the solid skeleton, of his stories well in advance. But in writers like Dorothy Richardson, or Katherine Mansfield, or Virginia Woolf, who carry the impressionist technique further, who introduce into the novel so much of the traditional material of poetry – diluted, as Professor I. A. Richards has observed, or 'like gold to airy thinness beat' – there is the danger that the novel as a structure, as an architecture of character and action, will begin to float apart: Professor Richards also makes this criticism of James Joyce's *Ulysses*, but unjustly I think, for one knows of few novels more elaborately constructed, and few characters more solidly imagined than Stephen Daedalus and Leopold Bloom. It is true, however, that the *first* impression of *Ulysses* on a reader may be one of rich confusion, that it takes some time, and some effort, before the artistic, and above all the moral structure, of the story can be firmly grasped; and also that though the theme of *Ulysses* is in all conscience adequate and complex enough, the plot – one, not outwardly terribly eventful day, in two, not outwardly terribly significant Dublin lives – seems at a first reading rather thin to support the enormous, dense weight or atmosphere of observed detail. But a proper reading of *Ulysses* is more like *living* the events which the book describes than is the reading of any other novel; in no other narrative that I know is the pressure of life so thick, so dense, so that the reader has almost to cut his way through. Thus some modern critics have considered the book as the culmination of the possibilities latent in the novel as an art-form: the novel to end all novels. And certainly after Joyce, though one can point to many writers of wonderful talent, like Virginia Woolf, and even to one writer of genius, D. H. Lawrence – but with a genius, alas, impatient both of the disciplining of his intelligence and sensibility and of the shaping of his books as works of art – one cannot point, in the same way, to any major figure. And one notes a tendency to recapture a clear and obvious structure at all costs (in Graham Greene's symbolical melodramas, for instance, in Rex Warner's social allegories, in Christopher Isherwood's concise and economical fictional 'documentaries') even at the cost of losing the new and stunning *richness* which Joyce had given to the atmosphere of the novel.

We can see then that 'realism' is an elusive and complicated conception, and that new subtleties of psychological approach, or nuances of delicacy in description, which at first may appear to open out fascinating new country for the novelist may in the end so bewilder him with their vivid, disparate detail that he forgets what he was, in the first instance, mainly after – a morally significant fable.

One should mention, however, before leaving the subject, one other incidental innovation of Joyce's in *Ulysses* which can be also considered as in the direction of 'realism': a new frankness about sexual matters, which was an inevitable result of the acceptance of the 'stream-of-thought' technique. I do not know whether all the results of this emancipation from an old reserve have been wholly happy ones. In spite of the distinction which D. H. Lawrence, for instance, made between 'obscenity' (legitimate) and 'pornography' (illegitimate) in the novel, I think it is true that young readers, in particular, may often derive an improper and unhealthy excitement from the detailed description of sexual episodes. I have not read Lawrence's own *Lady Chatterley's Lover* but my impression of it from what my friends tell me is that it is an artistic failure. Possibly the dogged puritanism which was one side of Lawrence's nature, the tendency in him to make almost a kind of religion out of sex, may have lain behind the failure; for it must be observed that the working of the sexual appetite in the human creature is often (as, for instance, Wycherley and Congreve knew) rather comic.

One might mention here, with a certain diffidence, but they are worth mentioning, some volumes published by the American expatriate, Henry Miller, in Paris, and unprocurable in an unexpurgated form (for perfectly sound reasons, too) in either London or New York. *Tropic of Cancer* and *Tropic of Capricorn* are perhaps less novels than fantasticated exercises in autobiography, but they have a verve, a style, and they convey the rich and complex impact of experience in a way in which it seems to me that no novelist since Joyce has done. 'At last,' said Ezra Pound, when he read *Tropic of Cancer*, 'at last an unprintable book that is fit to read.' Miller's books *are*, I am afraid, unprintable in Anglo-Saxon societies. He is not in the least *like* Joyce. He is perhaps a little like Rabelais and a little like Petronius, with more than a touch of Herman Melville and Walt Whitman. He has that perpetual rediscovery of the Absolute on every second page which is one of the grand contributions to the tradition of English writing of classic American literature.

At the same time, he is something like a permanent adolescent. Sex in itself, the machinery of sex, is wonderfully exciting when one is an adolescent, but as one grows older one becomes more interested in the permanent human relationships, at a moral level, which sex, like other human appetites and passions, subserves. I don't think Miller would do any harm to the right reader, but it would be quite a job deciding who the right reader might be. Also, he is a quite remarkably *naïf* writer, who pours out his words in a happy, uninhibited stream, as one might, over a few drinks, with intimate friends. He often writes sheer and conscious nonsense. There are expurgated selections from him, and books written specially for an Anglo-Saxon public, available in Great Britain and the United States, but these have to be studied rather selectively, for when he is off his favourite topic he is often not at his best. One might mention as a similar exercise in sexual frankness a semi-autobiographical novel, *The Black Book*, also only available in Paris, by a disciple of Miller's, the well-known poet Lawrence Durrell. This is more of a 'made' book, less spontaneous, full of beautiful passages of mannered prose, which recall, perhaps a little too obviously, Landor or De Quincey. Again, for all its imperfections of action and character, it has a richness and vitality lacking in most contemporary English fiction. But I feel, on the whole, that this taking of an impulse out for a ride is not after all 'realism,' in the sense in which I have been attempting to define 'realism' in this section; it is rather another, no doubt an exciting, mode of escape.

So, in so far as we are thinking of 'realism' as the pursuit of reality, it is hard to define it by outward characteristics. We might say that it is the opposite of evasion. But a striking sexual frankness, as we have seen, may be a way of evading social problems, and, more fundamentally, of evading moral problems. An elaborate technique for catching the flavour of every passing moment may be a way of avoiding a structural grasp of theme. A temporary rejection of experimental advances, as by many recent British novelists, may be a return towards the hard ground of reality at a more modest level. And there is a reality of beauty, of visions, and of dreams. All one can say finally is that the good contemporary writer, the novelist particularly, will have a firm respect for reality; but that everyone has to discover reality for himself; and from his own perspective and communicating to the account of his discovery the flavour of his own personality.

Section 4: Complexity, Allusiveness, Irony, Obscurity in Modern Poetry

It is, perhaps, more about poetry than about other forms of modern literature that people have a really sharp sense of what the 'modern' is, and whether they like it or not. It is hard to suggest a single and simple touchstone for the note of 'modernity' in world poetry (and may I point out again that much poetry of even the remote past strikes us as eminently 'modern,' while some good poetry of our own period seems to us not really contemporary with us?), but perhaps the nearest we can get to it is the presence, in a poem, of a feeling of harsh, unresolved complexity. Catullus for instance is very 'modern' when he says (I think the version I am quoting is Mr Jack Lindsay's, but since I cannot check the quotation, the responsibility for it may be my own):

> I hate and love.
> You ask, how can that be?
> I do not know, but know it tortures me.

Robert Bridges, on the other hand, though he was alive, unlike Catullus, only a few years ago, does not strike one as at all 'modern,' when, in his beautiful ode on Purcell's bicentenary, he writes:

> Love to Love calleth,
> Love unto Love replieth –
> From the ends of the earth, drawn by invisible bands,
> Over the dawning and darkening lands
> Love cometh to Love.
> To the heart by courage and might
> Escaped from hell,
> From the torment of raging fire,
> From the sighs of the drowning main,
> From the shipwreck of fear and pain,
> From the terror of night.

The complexity of feeling between hate and love, harsh and tight in Catullus, has here been diluted and resolved. 'Love' in Bridges (an abstract personification, a poetical idea) is something very different from the personal '*I* love' of Catullus; Catullus's 'I hate' and 'I know it tortures me' are soothed away in retrospective images, a horror that has been *escaped* from,

> Escaped from hell,
> From the torment of raging fire,
> From the sighs of the drowning main . . .

The resolution is perfect. And the whole poem from which this passage comes is, if a trifle too long, exceedingly beautiful. But one sees the difference. Though Bridges disliked the poetry of the Augustan age, he was essentially, in his views of poetic propriety, a poet in the Augustan tradition; he shared with Dryden and Pope the cult of decorum. Catullus writes about human passion as, in his own immediate painful experience, he knows it really to be; Bridges personifies the mind's notion of what human love ideally *ought* to be. This is not to say that Catullus's way of writing is, by some absolute standard, 'better' than Bridges'. It is merely to say that it comes home more intimately to *us*. I would be giving a very mistaken impression, indeed, if I let it be thought that I considered the tone of 'modernity' in world literature equivalent to general literary value. The 'modern' tone is simply the tone that appeals to us in our situation. That situation will change, and so, therefore, will the associations of the idea of 'modernity' – that is an idea that can be defined to some extent for one's own period, but never defined in an absolute sense. In fifty years, if things settle down, we may see a revival of the cult of decorum, and it will be Bridges who will appear 'modern,' Catullus old-fashioned. Meanwhile for us, here and now, the 'modern' in world literature is simply that which appeals in a troubled time to our troubled hearts.

One reason why the best poetry of at least the last fifty years (and if we take in France, almost of the last hundred years) has been notably complex is that so, of course, has there been a growing complication in the organisation of our world. Society has ceased to be local and organic, many customs, habits, and traditions have decayed, and the poet has become a much more isolated person than he was even in the elegant and urban eighteenth century; he has lost the kind of *niche* and status that Pope had, and one might say that so far as the poet in the Victorian age remained a public figure – as Tennyson did, for instance – so his poetry suffered. Bridges, in that wonderful ode from which I have quoted already, seems to lament the inadequacy of poetry in his own day to the great public occasion,

> Lament, fair hearted queen, lament with me –
> For when thy seer died no song was sung,
> Nor for our heroes fal'n by land and sea
> Hath honour found a tongue,

but when he himself became Poet Laureate he steadfastly eschewed the poem on the public occasion, leaving honour to find a tongue for our heroes fallen by land and sea through the brassier Muse of Rudyard Kipling. Kipling's special kind of success and failure showed that it was becoming more and more difficult for the poet in our time to catch the common ear, without catching also a 'common' tone. What is remarkable about him is how the banjo-twanging, the drum-thumping, and the Cockney impersonations, so often fail, in the end, to prevent the result being true poetry; and the unobtrusive skill that could put across a difficult and tricky form like the sestina (Kipling must have been one of the first, after Swinburne, to revive it since Sir Philip Sidney's time) by doctoring and diluting the true poetry with the required dose of plebeian humour and sentiment:

> Speakin' in general, I 've tried 'em all –
> The happy roads that take you o'er the world.
> Speakin' in general, I 've found them good
> For such as cannot use one bed too long,
> But must get 'ence, the same as I 've done,
> An' go observin' matters till they die.

What do it matter where or 'ow we die,
So long as we've our 'ealth to watch it all –
The different ways that different things are done,
An' men and women lovin' in this world;
Takin' our chances as they come along,
An' when they ain't, pretendin' they are good?

That does not ring quite true. There is a very strange balance between a humoristic Cockneyism, and an old-fashioned poetic formalism, which Kipling perhaps felt he could not get away with in a 'straight poem': his Tramp Royal in real life would no more have said "ence' than he would have said 'hence,' and this confusion between two manners reaches its climax perhaps in the first line of the coda,

Gawd bless this world! Whatever she 'ath done . . .

where the 'Gawd' and the "ath" seem to cancel each other out. Perhaps the idea is that an uneducated man is aiming at a dignified literary diction. But the total effect is rather as if Kipling, too shy to express his own sentiments in his own person, had tripped on to the stage in the cloth cap and false moustache of a music-hall 'serio-comic.' So Kipling, too, is an example of a 'modern' writer which Bridges is not, his complexity taking the form of an artful *imitation* of simplicity. I think the time for a final evaluation of Kipling's work is not yet. He certainly did manage to bridge for a time the growing gap between poetry and public, paying rather a high price. And his special road was not one that other poets cared to follow.

Nevertheless, Kipling's equivocal success like the high public status of Browning and Tennyson earlier on was a sign that the estrangement between poet and public had never become so acute in England as, for some important kinds of poet at least, it had become in France. Perhaps the historian of 'modern poetry' – in the sense of difficult, complex, abstruse poetry, poetry whose statements or whose attitudes puzzle the ordinary reader – might date its rise in England somewhere between 1910 and 1920: he would be thinking of the early work of Eliot and Pound, the realistic war poetry of Read, Sassoon, and Owen, the growing maturity of Yeats as seen in such a poem as *Easter, 1916*. He might mention Gerard Manley Hopkins, a poet of the 1880s who died fairly young, a Jesuit father, but whose poems were not published till 1919, as a 'modern poet' before his time; he might also allude to the work of Hardy, often gnarled and clumsy as to form, but impressive for its thought; and he might speak of some of the poets of the 1890s as 'modernising' influences, especially through their use of French models. He would say something about the Imagist movement and about early experiments in free verse, neither of which, again, go much further back than 1910. But if the same critic were to trace the 'modern' movement in poetry back in France, he would have to go at least as far back as Baudelaire. What is less than forty years old in England is more than a hundred years old in France. And one reason for this earlier development of 'modernism' in France was, I have suggested, an earlier and more complete estrangement of some important French poets from the tone and attitudes of the public life around them: not of all French poets – Lamartine and Victor Hugo are examples of poets who were deeply and actively involved in that public life. But they have not the kind of complexity that interests us to-day; they are not, as Baudelaire is, 'modern.'

It seems at first surprising that the estrangement of the poet from public life should have been more absolute, and should have become noticeable earlier, in France than in England. For in France literature has been generally a part of public life, and the man of letters a public figure, in a way that in England has not always been the case; but in fact the traditional values of much French literature – values of clear, rapid, sometimes superficial reasoning, of incisive generalisation, of dignified rhetoric and pointed wit, while real virtues in themselves were, as Baudelaire for instance noted, anti-poetic virtues. The whole tendency of French thought, after Descartes, was to exalt abstract reason as against concrete intuition; the tendency of French poetry after Malherbe was to exalt propriety and decorum of language as against an original and personal note; and the eighteenth century, though a very great century in French history, had been notable above all for its prose. In spite of the great triumphs of French romanticism, something of that anti-poetic tone lingered on in Baudelaire's time, and lingers on to-day, in French literature. The poet may not be merely a poet; he must justify himself at the bar of current opinion, which, in France, assumes always the airs of something final and absolute. Thus many French writers are busy to-day 'committing' themselves to various implausible and over-simple political creeds which the mere passing of time, and the changes of history, will make out of date and irrelevant in five or ten years – as the political creed of Victor Hugo, for instance, who *was* certainly a 'committed' poet is out of date and irrelevant now: something which has merely an historical interest, and which we put up with for the sake of a constant rhetorical, and an occasional poetic, splendour. It might not be wholly unfair to say that the claims of public life on the French poet have, since the early seventeenth century, tended to turn his poetry into rhetoric; and that there is a 'romantic' rhetoric (of which we have examples, too, in an English romantic poet like Byron) which is quite as poetically false, and much more garish and strident, than any 'classical' rhetoric; it is the noisy pretence of being carried away by tremendously profound and frightening thoughts and strange, tempestuous feelings. But the thoughts and feelings seem, on a closer examination, rather 'worked up' for the sake of the rhetoric; and the coherence of the one, the sincerity of the others, does not bear much analysis.

The doctrinaire, in France, in fact, thinks either that he is the superior of the poet intrinsically or that, even if the poet is a strange and wonderful creature, still he needs sensible and well-informed men to teach him what to feel and think; let him take what *we* are thinking and make poetic eloquence out of it! Sartre, the latest fashionable French doctrinaire, has (which is at least honest of him) announced almost defiantly that his philosophy has no guidance or help to offer poets; there is no doubt however that he considers himself intrinsically the superior of the poet. Indeed, in his essays on the nature of literature, he has made it clear that the purely 'literary' values of literature (let alone the deeper poetic values) are the last thing he is interested in. No, the questions he would ask the writer, rapping his desk like a schoolmaster, are of another kind: 'What did you do in the last war? What will you do in the next? What political party do you work for? How do you stand in regard to the social revolution? What is your line about the existence of a God?' This type of French intellectual drill-sergeant has been satirised adequately, once and for all, by Flaubert in his portrait of Homais. But no satire can destroy the vitality and persistence of the type, and from Voltaire, through Taine, to Sartre, the brilliant polemical popularising rationalists who have dominated one side of the French mind in the last two hundred years have been the enemies, conscious or unconscious, of true poetry.

With Sartre, indeed, that enmity is conscious. He has lately published what he calls an 'existential psycho-analysis' – that is to say, a conjectural biography, insufficiently documented – of Baudelaire, with the intention of proving that Baudelaire (whose unhappy personal history, certainly, does demand all our forbearance and charity when we consider it) was in the deepest sense a moral coward and intellectually consciously insincere. Baudelaire's own works, surely, are the answer to that accusation. The truth of poetry is not something that can be faked: but it is the case, on the other hand, that if the poet is hemmed in too much by a hostile, probing intellectualism, he may retreat, in pure self-defence, to a greater and greater eccentricity of attitude, defiance of ordinary convention, and privacy of language. Faced with what struck him as a lack of understanding and a blank hostility, not only in the populace at large, but in intellectual circles, the French poet of the last century of Baudelaire's type adopted, with the militant chivalry of his race, an attitude of defiance. Baudelaire himself put on the mask of the dandy; it being his hope, as it were, to outstare the starers and by his own insolence to make the insolent drop their eyes. Gautier (determined that if the world was going to insist on the irrelevance of poetry, poets should insist on the irrelevance of the world) proclaimed the doctrine of art for the sake of art; an inadequate doctrine in itself but a useful shield, then and since, for poets who did not feel like becoming the tools of eager short-sighted reformers.

It was about this period, too, that there was invented (if I remember, in reference to Vigny) the famous phrase about the poet's 'ivory tower.' It might have been a more accurate metaphor to talk of the poet as the inhabitant of a besieged city: a city not strong enough to sally forth and destroy her enemies, but well provisioned, and with strong walls. But by the time of the later Symbolists, Mallarmé and his school, it might have been truer perhaps to speak of the city as that of the philistines with the poets moving about in it as spies, wearing a disguise, and communicating by a code, that made their presence unsuspected. Baudelaire still made enough direct impact on his age to have his masterpiece condemned for immorality. Yet Baudelaire is essentially a poet of Christian feeling; he shocked his contemporaries just because in the century of gas-light, of the railway, of the Great Exhibition of 1850, of an unheard-of expansion of manufactures, population, and trade, he insisted that the only true progress consisted in the diminution of the traces of original sin; and because he knew, all too intimately, what sin is, in what its attraction and its horror consist. His life, in which, as Sartre truly observes, he 'did' nothing (apart from creating his masterpieces), was as momentous and as morally significant as that other contemporary, apparently monotonous, empty, and idle, and dawdling life, the life of Kierkegaard. In a bustling noisy age both of these were capable of contemplation, capable of realising the vanity of the world.

Mallarmé, on the other hand, the spy in disguise in the enemy city, made no such direct impact on that city as Baudelaire had; merely unobtrusively gathering round him, from the ranks of the philistines, his small fifth column. Living the life of a poor schoolmaster, he seemed, to the large world around him, merely the leader of a set of faddists, the high priest of a precious cult that would pass. Yet Mallarmé it might be said, was more profoundly subversive than Baudelaire, if his work had been accessible to the common reader. He is even, at times, a more vividly and disturbingly sensuous poet than Baudelaire; I quote from Aldous Huxley's version of L'*Après-Midi d'un Faune*:

> I love that virginal fury – ah, the wild
> Thrill when a maiden body shrinks, defiled,
> Shuddering like arctic light, from lips that sear
> Its nakedness . . . the flesh in secret fear!

But we are not to take that literally, as we are to take, with a sad literalness, so much that is sordid or sinister in Baudelaire. Mallarmé is, as Baudelaire is not, consciously a symbolist.

Let me quote, on the general subject of symbolism, from one of our most acute young critics to-day in England, Mr Iain Fletcher: he is distinguishing between allegorical and symbolical poetry, and he says that if a poem is allegorical, 'it works out the details of something already given, something which has received prior justification as theology or political theory, an organisation of intuitions and judgments. Valuation of this will depend on the structure of the poem, on its music, its detail. With the poetry of symbol none of these things is of the first importance. A symbol has been defined as the expression of some otherwise inexpressible truth; and it is not on the verbal music, or on the incidental illustrations of the theme that judgment will depend, but on the insight which the poem accords into the life of the soul.'

What insight does Mallarmé accord into the life of the soul in these lines I have quoted? The faun and the two nymphs, seen remotely, as on a moving tapestry, have a meaning other than themselves: not, however, that allegorical meaning which can be tightly tied down, but the symbolical meaning that opens out in vague, endless suggestions, that conveys what could not be conveyed otherwise. Perhaps we think, when we read these lines, of the beautiful possible poem, with its ideal existence even before it has been written, that shudderingly resists the poet's hot desire to grasp and embody it. For if it is not an

35

essential limitation of the symbolist method, as Mr Fletcher defines it, it does seem to be a limitation of it as Mallarmé developed it, that it becomes more and more shut in on itself, the subject of the poet being ever more narrowly confined to the nature of the poetic experience itself: poems being about poetry.

And the nature of poetry is perhaps something inexpressible, or something that can be expressed only through the symbols of particular poems. Let me quote my own version of one of Mallarmé's most famous sonnets, which will illustrate this truth: the terribly 'shut-in' nature of symbolist poetry, for all its beauty.

> The virgin, bright, and beautiful to-day
> Dare it now shatter with a drunken wing
> This hard forgotten lake, this ice where cling
> These flights of mine that never flew away . . .?
> Once was a swan, remembers it is he,
> Magnificent but hopeless in his strife
> For never having sung the realms of life
> When winter shone in bleak sterility.
> His neck in a white agony is shaken,
> Shattering the space that mocks him for his pride
> But not the soil in which his plumes are taken.
> Phantom mere brightness to this scene has drawn,
> Immobile in the cold, where dreams deride,
> Clothed in the useless exile of the swan.

It is of the very nature of symbolist poetry, as I have suggested, that it cannot be tied down to any single and simple interpretation, but, however much of its intention one may think one has dredged up to the surface, retains a residue of mysterious suggestiveness; so that the interpretation of such poems is almost as tricky, and as full of traps, as the interpretation of dreams. But I think that in this case we are at least not going very far wrong in equating

> This hard forgotten lake, this ice where cling
> These flights of mine that never flew away . . .

with the beautiful but almost entirely self-enclosed world of the symbolist poem itself; the poet is lamenting that it is his fate to be the poet, that is, to be himself, *only* in the poem, that is, in something other than himself, and other than himself in the most complete and hostile fashion; for one's own life is not and cannot be the 'life' as we call it, the 'order' as we perhaps ought to call it, of words upon a page. The most wonderful flights of the symbolist imagination cannot take it away from its merely symbolic mode of asserting itself: cannot take into reality, into life itself. The poet suffers, he is trapped like the swan (and the swan, in verse, is one of the permanent symbols of the poet) as a punishment for

> never having sung the realms of life
> When winter shone in bleak sterility.

The sterile bleakness of winter, the icy crystalline order of pure art, of the poem as something utterly self-contained, trapped and held that 'poetic' quality in Mallarmé's nature which should have flowed warmly, and perishably, out into life. The 'space' in which the swan's neck 'in a white agony is shaken' as well as being the perceptual space of the poem's winter landscape is perhaps the physical space of the outer universe, a space empty and meaningless to Mallarmé, who did not share Baudelaire's Christian beliefs. There was no God there, not even Baudelaire's harsh God of Justice. And we may remember the tremendous, frightening sentence of Pascal, battling with his own fears of atheism: 'The eternal silence of these infinite spaces frightens me.' The frosty soil in which the bird's wings are caught and trapped is that of the poem itself. It is only within the poem that poetry is now possible, the world outside has become unpoetical; yet that world 'outside' includes, of course, the poet's everyday self, and drawing no life even from that, the poem is acquiring a glittering and killing frigidity, which in the end will drive even the poet, or the possible poet, away. As poetry acquires more and more of a self-subsistent crystalline order, it becomes more and more difficult and painful for the poet to write it. So we are told in the last three lines that even the swan (that is, the poet as apart from the poem) has become an illusion:

> Phantom mere brightness to this scene has drawn,
> Immobile in the cold, where dreams deride,
> Clothed in the useless exile of the swan.

The 'brightness' of the ideal possible poem has drawn the poet rather as the brightness of a lamp draws a moth: but his death is a different kind of death, in the end the symbolist dream has become something too freezing and inimical to life for the poet to live in, or to live anything but a hallucination of life in. The poet is *elsewhere*, but his only proper place, as a poet, is inside this heartless, glittering, sterile poetic 'world.' So his 'exile' is 'useless,' since it is only in this world of poetry, which in purifying it so drastically he has now rendered uninhabitable, that he could have had his proper life. Thus the symbolist poet (like Mallarmé's disciple, Valéry, for many years) can cease to be a spy in the philistine city and become, to all outward appearances at least, for many years, a dutiful ordinary citizen; feeling that it is the poetic experience which matters and that the actual writing of a poem is in a sense a death and a profanation, an arbitrary and brutal limitation of an infinite and ideal world, the world of poetic possibilities. In the end is any actual poem as beautiful, or as suggestive, as a pure white page?

I have dealt with this one poem at great length because it seems a very handy model, indeed, of what I have called not only the complexity, but the allusiveness and the irony, of the typical 'modern' poem. The complexity is pretty obvious: but, as for the allusiveness, I have shown, I hope, that a reader can make no deep sense of this poem – no sense other than that of the beauty of phrases, the wintry brilliance of images, and the ghostly evocation of a landscape – unless he is on the look out for a complex set of allusions to the whole place of Mallarmé and his school in French literary history. And perhaps one must be a poet oneself, and also deeply interested in the history of poetry, to grasp immediately and intuitively that this, to put it crudely, is what the poem is *about*. I cannot see what clues and hints Mallarmé has given the ordinary reader, other than the use of that facile and common symbol (so unlike the run of his symbols) of the swan for the poet. The irony of the poem lies in the contrast between what it is and what it says. It is a strikingly beautiful poem (the reader will have to take my word for that, whatever he thinks of my own version): in its harmony, its brilliance, and its condensation it seems to embody almost a certain ideal of poetic beauty; and yet what it says is that it is impossible for the poet to go on writing the sort of poem it is. The winter images stand at once for an incredible bright beauty and for an atmosphere in which no life can persist. The price of the poem's beauty is the poet's death. With Mallarmé, indeed, we can think of pure symbolism as reaching its culmination, and making it necessary for subsequent important poets to free their wings from the ice and to find their way back, at whatever cost, to the 'realms of life.'

Strangely enough, one of the first results of this attempt by post-symbolist poets to bring art and life together again was not a new simplicity and clarity but a new confusion. Mallarmé is a difficult poet but it is doubtful whether he can be properly called an obscure one;

the difficulty of working out the meaning of such a poem as that which we have just examined is like that of solving a complicated set of equations; the symbols of symbolist poetry, like those of mathematics, offer us a severely coherent pattern of thought, held at some distance from life.

With Rimbaud, on the other hand, who may be taken as one of the main precursors of post-symbolist poetry, obscurity is intrinsic; for Rimbaud, unlike Mallarmé, does not know, or want to know, quite what he is doing. He speaks in a trance like a sort of inspired drunkard. He plunges poetry into life, and life into poetry once more, but at the cost of introducing into both a new element of bewilderment and disorder. Mallarmé led a life of sedate respectability. Rimbaud's life, during his short, dazzling period of creative activity, was one of drunkenness and vice; drunkenness and vice accompanied, moreover, by a savage and brutal violence of manner, a coarseness of language, which estranged from the young Rimbaud all the older men of letters, except the infatuated Verlaine, who might otherwise have wanted to help him. Yet it would be wrong to think of Rimbaud as simply a genius who happened to be a moral imbecile. He was rather a young man of sturdy peasant physique, of excellent intelligence (the best classical scholar in his country school), and of strong will who deliberately set out to disintegrate the normal patterns of life, to dislocate them, as Mallarmé had dislocated the normal patterns of language. The 'magical' world of poetry was, for Mallarmé, something that offered an escape from the drab emptiness of actual existence; but why, Rimbaud asked himself, should not the 'magic' be projected back on to existence, why should only poems, and not life, be 'poetical'? Why should one compromise ever with the prose world?

Rimbaud's excesses then were pursued not so much for their own sake, or for the sake of some delusive abstraction like 'pleasure,' as for the sake of an attempt at transformation and possession – an attempt to transform the matter of life into something magical, and to possess at every moment the feeling of tense, bewildering exaltation which belongs to a poet when he has completed a successful poem. Rimbaud would make no compromise with the outer world at all; in his writing, he did not start off from perceptions, but from self-induced hallucinations, from something like the state of delirium in which everything heard or seen is misinterpreted according to a momentary obsession. Through wallowing in excess and flirting with madness, he hoped to make himself a visionary, to reach a certain primal and primitive innocence of poetic awareness; even at the cost of moral suicide, for if we try to make life more intense by steadily increasing the doses of some stimulant, we either kill ourselves, or, if we are too strong for that, end in apathy. Rimbaud was too strong and he ended in apathy. He could not turn the real world permanently and successfully into the world of poetry after all. So he deserted poetry – that, perhaps, is more true than to say that poetry deserted him – became a merchant and an explorer in the Sudan and Ethiopia, wore himself out with his exertions, and died finally, back in France, in great pain, reconciled, perhaps, on his death-bed to the Catholic Church.

Rimbaud is the very type of the poet as rebel; not only against political orders and social conditions but against the very nature of human life, of reality, itself. He helped to inspire the French Surrealist movement, which, as its name suggests, refuses to reconcile itself to everyday reality; on the other hand he has very much influenced a great Catholic poet like Paul Claudel, who called him 'a mystic in the wild state.' The Surrealists on the one hand and Claudel on the other would be insulted by the suggestion that they have anything in common, but perhaps they have this, that they both seek to use words not merely to *record* existence but to key it up, for themselves and their readers, to a new pitch; they seek not merely to engage the reader's attention but to alter his life. By the power and richness of their language they hope to bewilder and overpower the reader, to drag him into their nets; it is a doctrine and a way of life and a means of persuasion that matter to them, not, as with Mallarmé and Valéry, the poem as detached from the poet, complete and perfect and crystalline in itself. Thus, it is almost hopeless to ask, as we have been asking with Mallarmé, what Rimbaud *means* by his poems. If to understand Mallarmé, we have to know the literary theories of his school, to understand Rimbaud we have to know every detail of his personal history; and the whole bulk of his poems can be taken as a single design, a sort of fantasticated autobiography, except that it is the fantastication, not the autobiography, that matters. Facts, what we call facts, are for this kind of poet nothing in themselves; they are merely a point of departure for imaginative transformations. Similarly, critics often discuss whether Surrealist texts of automatic writing, for instance, are 'meaningless'; and it can be pointed out that they have at least a clinical meaning, that they would give a psychiatrist many clues to the writer's obsessions, convictions, and general state of mind, but that clinical meaning is not what interests the Surrealists themselves –

rather what interests them is the delirium, the richness, the confusion, and the terror, of the sort of experience which the writing and reading of such texts (if one does not find them merely tedious) can evoke.

Such 'mad' poets would not exactly deny that they were mad, but would say that their 'madness' was a more alert and sensitive state, a state that gives a deeper insight into and a wider grasp of reality, than the state generally called 'sanity.' In England, and in the United States, poets are less likely to go all the way with a theory than in France; but a poet like Hart Crane with his dizzying use of language, in which the strict meaning of the sentences is irrelevant and everything depends upon the emotional associations of words and phrases; a poet like Dylan Thomas with his musical welter of dream images; a poet like W.S. Graham with his impenetrable personal syntax and his recurrent obsession with the sea,

> Very end then of land. What vast is here?
> The drowning saving while, the threshold sea
> Always is here. You may not move away,

are all in Rimbaud's tradition. The image of the sea which tends to play a major part in all poetry in this tradition has many possible associations and interpretations; but the most important for our purposes here, I think, is that the land is the surface on which we walk, as we think, safely – it is the waking conscious mind; the sea with its greater depth and density, in which we can drown under huge pressures and suffering unimaginable terrors, is the mind of sleep and the sub-conscious, as full of disturbing images as the sea is full of strange fish. We 'may not move away' from that in the sense that we must go to sleep every night and descend into this primitive part of ourselves. It is perhaps the larger and more important part, just as the real sea covers so much a greater portion of the globe's surface than the emergent patches of land. It is a part of which we feel a terror (the idea of losing consciousness, of being lost in the world of sleep for ever, is like the fear of hell); it is also a part for which we feel a certain nostalgia, a homing desire, for it was from the sea after all that all life first came – and just so, modern psychologists sometimes tell us, from the submerged, subconscious parts of ourselves come all the desires and impulses that move us in the waking world. Poets like Rimbaud should be thought of as the first explorers of this fatal ocean, its first explorers, at least, in terms of poetic art. We should not judge their lives, which so often seem, by the standards of the waking world, disastrous lives, too strictly. They are the first colonisers of a new realm, who may plant a flag or send home a report, but few of them indeed will ever return alive, to our ordinary world of surface consciousness, to tell in person, and from the perspective of final safety, their strange stories.

The most notable cause of obscurity in modern poetry is likely then to be this submergence of the poet in a sea in which he can no more account for his actions, or for his presence there, than any drowning or dreaming man. Yet poetry at the conscious level – or poetry, on the other hand, of what Mr Eliot has called 'the high dream' as opposed to the 'low dream' – has its own difficulties, too. The poems of Eliot and his fellow countryman, who influenced him so much in technique, Ezra Pound, avoid that dichotomy of art and life which may seem to have led the Symbolists on the one hand and the various explorers in the wake of Rimbaud on the other into so many difficulties. The idea of the work of pure art in abstraction from life is, as we have seen, and as Mallarmé saw, a finally sterile one; so is the idea of the utmost possible impurity, of vitality at all costs, for if many modern Surrealist verse texts are 'vital documents' in some sense or other – vital as witnessing the incoherence of our time – few of them are in any genuine or legitimate sense, and indeed few would really claim to be, 'poems.' Once the idea of a continual transformation of life into art, and of art into life, has been accepted from Rimbaud (as the Surrealists on the whole accepted it) as a mechanical formula, the quality of both art and life suffer; art deliberately assumes the untidy edges, the lack of beginning and end, the failure to fall into perspective, of life at its most tepid and insignificant, while life on the other hand assumes an element of unreal 'artistic' pose.

Eliot and Pound, however, like many Americans, were interested in the larger reconciling idea of 'culture'; for it is, after all, within the framework of the 'culture' of a human society that both life and art impact upon each other, and unless the 'culture' is of a fairly high quality, both life and art will be at a low ebb, while on the other hand we think of periods of 'high culture' as producing noble lives as well as noble art. For Americans, Europe as a whole is the ancestor of their culture, and they are therefore able to see the European scene in a broader perspective than the actual European, with his sharp sense of national differences, often can. The obscurity of Pound and Eliot comes not from any use of the subconscious dream material I have been talking about (they are both pre-Freudian poets) but from the bewildering wide range of their cultural allusions, assuming in the reader a knowledge of language and literature which he often does not possess.

In Eliot's later poetry the embedding of fragments from other writers whole into his work has become less obtrusive, but in Pound's later *Cantos* it has become more so: Chinese characters alternate with passages from Greek, Latin and the Romance languages. This display of erudition is sometimes irritating (more so in Pound than in Eliot) but it should not be dismissed as mere ostentation. It enables the poet to achieve most subtle effects of irony: thus when Eliot writes in *The Waste Land*,

> But at my back from time to time I hear
> The sound of horns and motors, which shall bring
> Sweeney to Mrs Porter in the spring.
> O the moon shone bright on Mrs Porter
> And on her daughter
> They wash their feet in soda water,

we are to think both of Marvell's famous

> But at my back I always hear
> Time's wingèd chariot hurrying near,
> And yonder all before us lie
> Deserts of vast Eternity,

and of the less known poem which Mr Eliot cites in the notes, Day's *Parliament of Bees*:

> When of the sudden, listening, you shall hear,
> A noise of horns and hunting, which shall bring
> Actaeon to Diana in the spring,
> Where all shall see her naked skin . . .

and so we are to contrast Marvell's grave seducer, for whom the thought of death and judgment gives a finer edge to passion, and on the other hand the simple lyricism of the Day passage (and yet Actaeon will be torn to pieces by the hounds for his presumption) with the slack immunity with which Sweeney, the modern unheroic equivalent of Marvell and Actaeon, pursues his sordid 'love-life': Sweeney lacks both the sense of sin and the sense of nemesis, and therefore he has no bright awareness of beauty . . . the lines from an Australian popular song,

> O the moon shone bright on Mrs Porter
> And on her daughter
> They wash their feet in soda water,

43

mock his banal idea of 'glamour.' So there is not a line in this passage which has not been either borrowed by Mr Eliot, or suggested to him by another poet's line and adapted; and yet the passage is very distinctively in his own manner. And this use of allusion and concealed quotation enables him to set the present and the past in perspective, and to exhibit ironically the decay of past standards in present-day life.

We have run over, then, some of the main qualities which poetry, written in whatever age, that strikes us as having a specifically 'modern' ring, is likely to possess; and we have seen that when we know something about the poet's relation to his age, and the particular contemporary problems that happened to obsess him, we become less bewildered by 'modern' poetry. I think much modern poetry *is* very difficult, and that it does not always repay the labour involved in working it out. There are times when we all fall back for refreshment on poetry that is *not* modern. For the qualities of simplicity and clearness are permanently valuable qualities in literature, as perennially refreshing as pure running water is. Complexity, however, has its proper place in literature; human life is a complex phenomenon, and in the last hundred years or so its complexity has been more and more heavily borne in on all of us; and a false, or affected, simplicity is a detestable thing.

Section 5: 'Modernity' in the Drama

This can be a very much shorter section than the ones which precede it. For one thing, there is a sense in which absolutely *all* great drama (Sophocles, Shakespeare, Racine, or Ibsen) strikes us as modern in spirit; and for another thing, in an age which has been notable for innovations in form by novelists and poets, dramatists, the better dramatists particularly, have been remarkably conservative about form. Thus Tchehov's best plays of fifty or sixty years ago, like Ibsen's of seventy or eighty years ago, do not seem to us, when we see them performed, the least old-fashioned.

It is true that neither Ibsen nor Tchehov any longer appears to us, as they may have done to their contemporaries, strictly 'naturalistic.' I have seen a performance of *The Cherry Orchard*, in fact, by Oxford undergraduates, in which an excessive emphasis on some of the technical mannerisms of Tchehov, combined no doubt with an immature response to his deeper themes, turned that melancholy, complex, and profound comedy into something like farce. Tchehov's technical device, by which his characters do not directly answer each other but

44

carry on vague soliloquies which they allow others to interrupt, is just as much of an 'artificial' convention as, for instance, the excessive logic and coherence of the interchanges in French classical tragedy; it is intended to underline the isolation of individuals, just as the opposite convention is intended to underline their interrelation; it is very typical, in fact, of the way in which self-absorbed and absent-minded people do talk; but Tchehov's characters can become, in the hands of all but very skilful actors, mere 'humours.' Ibsen's middle-class Scandinavian backgrounds have for us – and had even for his non-Scandinavian contemporaries – an irrelevant appeal of grotesque local colour; and his use of physical properties, like the wild duck in the attic, as symbolic centres for his plays is faintly disturbing just because such a profoundly poetic way of thinking underlies such a deliberately drab and gritty prosaic surface. There is a sense, though it is a shallow one, in which both these great dramatists may be said to lead us into fantasy worlds; the surface reality is rather superficial, fantasy lies close underneath it, and the fundamental reality of the human grasp has to be sought deeper still. In this, they might be compared to a writer like Dostoevsky who likes to give his narration and his conversations a surface air of the humdrum and the matter-of-fact; just under that surface, there is wild melodrama; under the wild melodrama, once more, there is tragic wisdom. It might be said, in fact, that one great achievement of 'naturalism' both in the nineteenth-century novel and the nineteenth-century drama was to make the tragic impact, the deep poetic perception, possible again, by rescuing it from the faded graces of an outworn literary style. But the non-literary approach can now itself be recognised as just another, though more cunning and inclusive, literary convention.

Tchehov and Ibsen were brilliant innovators, certainly; but their successors – even though these successors include men of genius, like George Bernard Shaw – have simply taken over their inventions, without adding to them, and without perhaps even making the fullest possible use of them. Shaw certainly differs from both of them in making a much wider use of the drama to air his views on current topics: so much so that Robert Graves considers him as not a dramatist in the proper sense, but rather a writer of satirical dialogues like Lucian, a 'philosopher turned demagogue'; and there is something in this, for the beautiful scene, for instance, between Don Juan and the Devil in *Man and Superman* is almost never acted in performances of that play, though for the reader it is the most exciting part of it. It is not acted, because it contributes nothing to the action; and it is the *action* after all of a play (and not any incidental ornaments of that action, like stray felicities of diction or fine set speeches) which is properly dramatic. On the other hand, if what Shaw adds to Ibsen and Tchehov is not properly dramatic, something that he fails to take over from them is. He took over from Ibsen the idea that real and serious themes of contemporary life could be handled on the stage; and in *Heartbreak House* he took advantage of Tchehov's technical invention of making characters in a play no more attend fully to each other than they do in real life, nor directly answer each other, but instead mirror in their dialogue their own continuing preoccupations. (And this, after all, was not a completely new invention, for it is basically the same idea as that of Ben Jonson's 'comedy of humours.') What Shaw failed to take over from Tchehov and Ibsen was their ability by the use of some piece of symbolism – the shot sea-gull, the cherry orchard that has to be sold, the wild duck in the attic – to give their plays, behind the flat prose surface, the third dimension of poetry. These symbols stand for some aspect of a situation that cannot be made fully explicit at a conceptual level, but Shaw always thinks that every situation can be made explicit, and therefore poetry escapes him; and the history of English prose drama in the last fifty years is that partly of the gradual exhaustion of the original inspiration Shaw provided – it *was* exhaustible, simply because of that lack of poetic depth in it – and of attempts to tap the roots of poetry elsewhere: in Irish peasant life by Synge, in Dublin slum life by O'Casey, and lately, in writers like Mr T.S. Eliot, in efforts to resuscitate and make contemporary a tradition of English poetic drama that has been moribund since the Restoration.

Shaw's successors in his own or a broadly similar vein – one might mention Galsworthy, Granville Barker, J.B.Priestley, James Bridie – have sometimes a closer feeling for everyday atmospheres, and a more warm and instinctive sympathy with the 'ordinary man,' than Shaw himself, but they are lesser men: and they also lack poetic vision. I would say that Sean O'Casey in his early plays of Dublin life was perhaps the only dramatist, domiciled in the British Isles, and writing in English, of this century who had gone afresh to Ibsen and Tchehov to learn their lesson of 'poetic realism': but since he has jettisoned the realism in his later plays in a German expressionistic style, and become more consciously 'poetical,' his poetry has gone bad on him. I would say the only hope for the English drama at the moment is a genuine revival of the verse drama tradition: but apart from Mr Eliot, and perhaps Mr Christopher Fry, one can only point there to a crowd of promising young writers, mostly true poets certainly, but mostly also with everything still to learn about the theatre.

The novelist and the poet can, of course, experiment as they please, if they can find some publisher to print them. But the dramatist requires a theatre, and somebody willing to risk paying the rent of that theatre and the salaries of the actors and the general cost of the production. So he cannot, as the poet and the novelist can, give the public twenty or thirty years to catch up with him: he must, however original his views, be ready to compromise with the conservative tastes of the 'big theatre' audience and the even more conservative standards of 'big theatre' actors and producers. That is why the history of the drama is so oddly different, in England certainly, but also I think in other European countries, from the history of any other kind of literature. Periods of high excellence in the drama tend to be short and to peter out towards the end, and then it takes a tremendous effort to get the drama started again. One reason for this is that, once a dramatic period *is* established, new dramatists tend to imitate not so much the life around them as the work of established elder dramatists. The plays of Beaumont and Fletcher, for instance, are full of this sort of literary imitation, and mark the decadence of Jacobean drama. One cannot say that Congreve actually marks the decadence of Restoration drama but, like all his contemporaries, he goes on writing in terms of the wits and rakes of good King Charles's golden days in a much more refined and respectable period; for he is the contemporary, after all, not of the wild Lord Rochester but of the smooth and pious Joseph Addison.

What seems 'natural' and 'realistic' dialogue, in fact, to actors, is not dialogue which catches the tones of contemporary speech, but dialogue which reminds them of what they are used to hearing and speaking on the stage. This applies not only to dialogue but to atmosphere and properties. The sort of typical bland comedy, for suburban middle-class consumption, which still makes a periodical mild success in the London West End, shows a spacious living-room with French windows, a comic servant dusting, and pleasant, leisurely people who most of them do not seem to have to work for a living. The middle-class audience in England to-day, which still enjoys these plays, is suffering from a housing shortage; finds servants both very difficult to get and beyond the ordinary person's means; and has, as a legal duty, to be doing useful work of some sort, even if it were feasible for it to live on its dividends. The audience on the whole would rather have an idealisation of a kind of life it once lived, or hoped to live, than a sharp and disturbing picture of the kind of life it is living now.

Thus the drama, because of this imitativeness of actors, and this tendency in audiences to acquiesce in what they are used to, again and again in English history simply runs to a dead stop. Then it has to be started again on almost completely fresh lines. The intervals between the starting and stopping can be very long; after the petering out of the Restoration impulse, around 1700, there are no English plays which have at once literary and theatrical value (with the two exceptions of Goldsmith's and Sheridan's comedies) till the 1890s. The Victorian age, one of the great periods in English life and literature, contributed nothing at all to the drama till it was almost at an end. And for the last fifty years we have been living on a double impulse, a brisk push, given by Shaw and Wilde – the one to the comedy of ideas, the other to the comedy of pure entertainment – but the balls they started rolling have come to a standstill. Perhaps Mr Eliot will give a new ball a new push; but certainly it does seem to me that in spite of the contributions of three Irish dramatists of genius – Shaw, Synge, and O'Casey – the history of the drama in the last fifty years makes a rather thin show compared to the history of poetry or the novel. There have been plenty of clever and successful playwrights like Mr Somerset Maugham and Mr Noel Coward; but even their plays in the last twenty or thirty years have begun to 'date' rather badly, and to look like what they are: extremely skilful contributions, but without a deep inner life of their own, and lying somewhere just on the other side of literature.

There has been experiment, of course, in what we call in England the 'little theatre' as opposed to the 'big theatre,' but it is doubtful whether these experiments mark a genuine progress. The techniques of German expressionism, for instance, which have been used in differing ways both by Sean O'Casey and by Auden and Isherwood, seem to me retrogressive in relation to the drama; instead of characters you get types; instead of situations in depth you get flat simplifications of topical issues: the direction is away back to the morality play and when you have the rare gift, which O'Casey has, of putting flesh and blood people and actual situations on the stage, and letting the poetry of reality speak for itself, it seems a pity to start writing in terms of the propaganda cartoon. With Auden and Isherwood, flippancy and cleverness, a gift for charade and pantomime, enable them to dodge the sweat of grappling with real drama; they are edifying and amusing, and they produce pieces of genuine entertainment like *The Dog*

Beneath the Skin or sincere uplift, like *The Ascent of F6*, but they never at any time give one the illusion of reality. And the illusion of reality matters; it is what makes a play. Many other so-called 'innovations' or 'experiments' in the theatre in our time similarly seem to be essentially retrogressive. Mr Eugene O'Neill has a device by which you not only hear what his characters say, you hear what they think; but if they were adequately conceived you should be able to guess their thoughts from the tone of their conversation; and this is really a reintroduction of that hammiest of all devices in 'realistic' drama, which writers otherwise of little moment like Pinero are praised for getting rid of, the 'aside' or the soliloquy spoken aloud in naturalistic prose, which the actor delivering it has to get off his chest without looking as if he had gone mad, while the other actors have an equally embarrassing time pretending they do not hear him. And one should remember this when one criticises dramatists of our time for their failure to experiment radically; so many of their experiments have been failures, and have made one see the real merits of the conventional thing, even of ideas which we all learned to jeer at when we were schoolboys, like the unity of time, place, and action. Mr Shaw writes *Back to Methuselah* which takes one several nights to see and has much more talk than action in it: and one begins to see the point of insisting that a play ideally should present a unified action within a certain limited space of time. Whatever pleasure *Back to Methuselah* gives us, it is not essentially a *dramatic* pleasure. Similarly, in a recent American play which has been a great success in London, *Death of a Salesman*, we get an application to the drama of the loose, flexible construction of the novel or the film, there are flashbacks, soliloquies, narrative commentaries, changes of scene made possible by having several sets ready on the stage at once and lighting up one or the other as it is needed. It is very ingenious. But is it really what we want from the drama? Is our idea of dramatic pleasure not really rather the idea of the rich implications that can be drawn out of a tight and strict construction?

To sum up then, let us repeat that all really *great* drama strikes us as essentially modern; but that our own period, in England, has not been so notable for the production of striking plays as for that of striking poetry and fiction. In reading nearly all contemporary plays in English (with the exception of perhaps half a dozen of Shaw's, which would include *Heartbreak House* and *John Bull's Other Island*, two or three of Synge's, which would include *The Playboy of the Western World*, but probably not the unfinished *Deirdre*, perhaps one or two of the later short plays of Yeats, particularly *Purgatory*, O'Casey's early Dublin tenement tragedies, perhaps Mr Eliot's *The Cocktail Party*, perhaps Joyce's *Exiles*, perhaps Stephen Spender's *The Trial of a Judge*) we are too obtrusively aware of the rapidly dating 'period' quality in the play: aware of its diction, sentiment, and character as belonging to a particular time and place, and unreal from the point of view of our own time and place. When we have this 'period' feeling about a play, we can be sure that it is not a great play. Thus when we read Beaumont and Fletcher, however much we have enjoyed a facile grace of style and a fertility in the invention of episode, we are never for a moment in doubt that this is something rather cold-bloodedly and very skilfully confected to hit the taste of a particular audience; and we do not have that feeling about Shakespeare. We have that feeling, again, of something specially trimmed to the audience in the comedies of Mr Somerset Maugham and Mr Noel Coward; not in Wilde's *The Importance of Being Earnest* or in Congreve's *The Way of the World* where we feel that a fine artist is incidentally delighting us in the course of delighting himself. The meretricious, or commercial, or essentially imitative product can be detected, in fact, quite easily, by the lack of that note of inner delight in it – and by an inescapable touch of the jaded or the shoddy in its use of language.

On the other hand, when we read Shakespeare, or some of the few genuinely great plays by his contemporaries – say, to take some of Mr T. S. Eliot's choices, *Volpone*, *The Revenger's Tragedy*, *The Changeling* – we forget about the element of 'local colour': about how much the moral attitudes, the manners, and the ways of speech of men in the early sixteenth century differed from our own: we are caught up in an intense illusion of reality. In fact, this illusion is more intense even in the mere reading of a great play (let alone the seeing of it adequately performed) than in the reading of a great novel. We take up *War and Peace* and lay it down again; the illusion is again and again broken. We read *Macbeth* or *The Wild Duck* at a sitting. Again, when we read a novel, we are in a sense passive: the novelist with his descriptions and analyses does much of our work for us; we have not to co-operate with him, merely to watch and listen. But we co-operate with the dramatist even in reading a play to ourselves in solitude. We become the characters; we recite their speeches to ourselves; we feel our muscles tensing with their emotions. Thus the drama at its rare heights – which always, as I say, seem to precede and usher in long periods of decadence – does seem to me (with the possible exception of some kinds of long narrative poem, *The Iliad* or *The Divine Comedy*) the great literary achievement of the human race (and for our own period the long narrative poem, anything in verse on the heroic scale, seems an impossibility).* For if one compares the great dramas even with the greatest novels, there is a sense in which the latter look like loose and extended scenarios for a possible drama (Henry James felt this very strongly). There is a sense also in which we could consider many lyrical or meditative poems as having their place ideally, and explaining themselves perfectly, in some drama of the poet's life of which only these eloquent fragments have been written. And the drama is our model in all kinds of writing when we want to cut out these passages, perhaps vividly and charmingly written in themselves, which contribute nothing to the total effect; it gives us our idea of *construction* in literature. And the best advice one can give, often, to a young writer who is not a dramatist (who writes stories, or poems, or even essays on general themes) is: 'Dramatise, dramatise!' That is to say: 'Do not be loose, and dawdling, and wavering, and expansive. Concentrate, eliminate. Space out, and weigh, and measure your important effects, so that you may be able to bring them home with the most obvious brutal strength.'

But the high ages of drama are few and far between, and it does not seem to me that our own is one of them. It is an age of good plays rather than great plays. There is too much drift and too much anxiety for the finest drama; there is not that easy inner confidence, that feeling of possessing an assured style of life, that belongs to such different places and times as the England of King James, the France of Louis XIV, classical Athens and early seventeenth-century Spain; and which in a completely independent civilisation belonged to the Japan that produced the Kabuki and the Noh plays. Since this book is so largely concerned with the qualities and achievements of 'modern' writing, it is well to emphasise that the typically 'modern' attitude seems incapable of producing really great drama. That will keep us humble. We shall avoid the mistake of thinking that literature 'progresses' just as science progresses; we shall realise that there are some basic inadequacies in our 'modern' attitude, and we shall look back with reverence to our ancestors, our inferiors no doubt in technical knowledge and range of information, but able to excel us

---

* But see my remarks later on Ezra Pound's *Cantos*, whose ultimate significance is perhaps that of a tremendous *failure* to write an 'heroic poem' in an unheroic age.

in some things: the writing of plays among them. We shall realise too that the 'modern' attitude, with its emphasis on harsh, unresolved complexities, is essentially a transitional attitude: and that some future society, more settled in its ways, and more happy about its assumptions than our own, may be able to produce a serene, objective art of a kind which we cannot possibly produce, ourselves, now; but can only long for and wistfully imagine.

CHAPTER TWO

THE NOVEL

Section 1: Two Ancestors

We can trace, I think, the immediate ancestry of the modern English novel back at least as far as the 1890s, to the work of two novelists who were at opposite poles in their conception of the novel, its form and its function, but who nevertheless felt a half-reluctant admiration for each other. These two friends were Henry James, then in the full maturity of his powers, and H. G. Wells, then making a brilliant beginning. I have said something already about James's high idea of the novel as an art-form; it is doubtful whether Wells ever regarded it primarily as an art-form or as anything but a vehicle for popularising his ideas. In his fascinating *Experiment in Autobiography*, Wells describes a conversation in which James reproached him for his lack of artistic conscience, in relation to a novel of his called *Marriage*. In this novel, a 'novel of ideas,' more important from Wells's point of view for the ideas discussed in it than for the story or characters, the hero and heroine at one point disappear into a country lane and emerge three hours later engaged. Wells gives no hint of what they were saying or doing during this long period, and Henry James hinted to him that this was because he simply did not *know*; and this for James, with his strict view of the rules of the game of novel writing, was just cheating. Wells, who had a very lively social conscience, but hardly any artistic conscience at all, could not see what the fuss was about. 'The Novel,' he writes, 'was not necessarily ... this real through and through absolutely true treatment of people more living than life. *It might be more and less than that and still be a novel.*' It would be 'more,' in many cases with Wells, in that it would include long discussions of, and digressions about, current social topics that struck Wells as urgently important; it would be 'less' in that these discussions would often not specially help the story along, and that the 'treatment' was often not 'through and through absolutely true' nor the 'people more living than' (nor, even, often, as living as) 'life.' Wells as a novelist simply hurried carelessly over what did not immediately excite him. Yet all that Wells writes has a certain vitality, and that came, as James noted, from the odd and perhaps irrelevant way in which he conveys, through a perhaps ill-constructed and implausible story, his own genuine excitement. 'The ground of the drama,' James wrote, 'is somehow most of all the adventure for *you*. . . .'

All life was a genuine adventure for Wells and what gives his vast uneven production in fiction and so many other fields a genuine if intermittent vitality even to-day is the fashion in which he does convey his oddly engaging personality; a personality bubbling over with hope, eagerness, and impatience; warm and irritable; given to the grandiose gesture but given also to humorously puncturing its own self-importance. Wells is a genuine artist in his early scientific fantasies and in such realistic studies of his own early environment as *Kipps*. He was also, in the field of ideas, a genuine liberating influence, especially for his own class – for the great new reading public, literate rather than educated, which was coming to the surface in the 1890s as a result of the growth of the population and the gradual spread of compulsory education during the Victorian age. Wells grew up at a time when Darwin and Huxley were turning the brighter young men of his class away from traditional religious beliefs and when their own ambitions were making them rebel against traditional social standards. They looked to science to transform the world – it was the time of the first telephones, gramophones, automobiles, even the homely bicycle seemed a revolutionary invention, and men were dreaming of the possibilities of heavier-than-air flying machines; science was going to transform the world, and literature, in comparison to science, was something of minor importance. That explains Wells's odd, humorous patronising air in his autobiography to friends and acquaintances of his, James, Conrad, Hueffer, Gissing, who took the art of the novel at all seriously. The novel for him was nothing in itself, it was a vehicle for more important matter; a sugaring of the pill of scientific and social instruction for a large new eager audience that could not yet be expected to read a serious book unless there was 'a story in it.' Wells felt that he was speaking for those who had been kept in their 'places' by their 'betters' long enough, and who must now have their own say; thus he was instinctively hostile to convention, formality, restraint, of any kind, which had helped to keep these underdogs in their 'places,' and that helps to explain his odd indifference (an indifference so strangely combined with a genuinely creative imagination) to the idea of 'art' as such; for art is based on convention, formality, restraint. Wells's god was science; his wish as a writer was not to produce masterpieces that might last for ever but to be an increasingly effective populariser of scientific ideas, especially in their relation to social change.

And Wells did achieve his ambition. From the point of view of pure literary criticism, he might be thought to have squandered his gifts. An early fantasy of his like *The Time Machine* is a real work of art; a later 'serious' and 'thoughtful' novel, like *The World of William Clissold*, is so much dead bulk. But Wells was, what he wanted to be, a liberator. It is easy to say now that one of the effects of the various emancipations for which he worked all his life has merely been to release untidy emotions from a traditional discipline; to make many people discontented with a necessary subordination in society and a necessary routine; and, in relaxing old codes, to destroy a sense of style. What we do with our new liberties is not the liberator's fault, and we should always honour liberators. Let us admit that Wells was an artist who often scamped his work and a thinker who let his emotions lead him astray. What is important is that he sought truth to the best of his abilities and that he loved his fellow-men; and in his hopes and fears, his enthusiasms and errors, he was more genuinely one of them than any other writer of his time. He might have said with one of his heroes, President Theodore Roosevelt: 'I am only an average man, but, by George, I work harder *at* it than the average man.' And if the modern novelist looks to James rather than to Wells for a model of scrupulosity in his art, he is none the worse for having a touch of Wells's eager, aspiring spirit.

The intellectual nourishment which Wells wished the novel to carry in panniers on its back, for James would have to be fully digested into its supple body. James writes novels on momentous themes; but he does not allow his characters to discuss these themes in an abstract way and still less does he interrupt his story to discuss them himself. He is one of the most 'intellectual' of novelists, but not, in Wells's sense, a 'novelist of ideas.' 'Ideas' in abstraction, by themselves, mean nothing to him; what interests him is how out of the proper handling and grasping of a 'story' there rises, in both writer and reader, an awareness of the 'grand theme,' of the informing design, 'the pattern in the carpet.' But the 'theme' is never wholly separable from the 'story'; it has its concrete weight and relevance in relation to the story, just as the story has its dignity, is raised above the status of mere anecdote, in relation to its emergent theme. Thus James *shows*, rather than *says*, what his novels are about; it is in an indirect and symbolical way (James's use of material properties in his stories to embody human attitudes has something in common with the symbolism of Ibsen and Tchehov) that he exposes and resolves the tensions and predicaments of civilised human life. His thinking is not (as too often in Wells's case) a kind of stucco plastered on the surface of his novels, but is built into their stone. That is why no novelist more quickly exasperates lazy readers; and even the most alert and attentive readers are likely to be kept upon the stretch.

The task, on the whole, of the novelist in our century has been to recognise that the foundations of the world he walks on are dangerously shifting, that we are living in a time of rapid and disturbing change, so that we can neither say with any precision *when* some new pattern of relative stability will emerge, nor *what* sort of pattern it will be; and yet, since the human heart hungers after permanence, to project into his own work some image of that aspiration: to give his novels a coherence, that is, either moral or aesthetic, that will hold together against the shocks of time. To attempt merely to 'keep up with things,' with every passing fashion in expression or thought, is fatal to the novelist; 'he that runs against Time,' as Dr Johnson said, 'has an antagonist not subject to casualties.'

It may be, in fact, that the conditions which make the writing of really great novels a possibility include the existence of that relatively stable background, to which we only to-day aspire; and it may be that the most suitable literary narrative form for the present and the immediate future is something other than the novel. Behind the great novels of the past, it might be said, there was the novelist's awareness of an established order which he might judge to be in the main a good or in the main an evil order, but which was in either case reliably *there*; and human acceptance of the order, or rebellion against it, had a constant significance. There is nothing of that sort to-day, it might be said, for us either to accept or rebel against. All arrangements have a very provisional air, and the marks of the time are uncertainty and anxiety. The individual to-day is exposed not only to petty humiliations and frustrations, as Wells's early hero Kipps was, but to mortal dangers – from wars, from revolutions, from slumps; he may have the luck to escape all these dangers, and if he does escape them, he may find a wider range of social opportunities open to him than Kipps did.

But Kipps felt that within limits he controlled his own life, and that is what it is becoming harder for the individual to feel to-day. Unless he is a person of very strong character, he is likely, therefore, to drift through life without any very passionate purpose or any very definite belief.

One of the greatest of modern novels in English, James Joyce's *Ulysses*, is concerned largely, as we shall see later, with just this sense of drift. Other novelists refuse to accept drift as something ultimate and desperately seek in their novels to find some belief or some purpose by which men can give meaning to their lives. The novelist like Joyce who appears merely to give a detached portrayal of drift is in the tradition of Henry James; he has a moral theme, but he allows that theme to emerge naturally from his story, he does not seek to abstract it from the story, and to draw the reader's attention to it as something separate. In this, he is aesthetically in the right; one is often asked, for instance, by people unfamiliar with modern poetry to tell them the 'real meaning' of some difficult poem, and they are disappointed when one says to them that the 'real meaning' is not something separable from the poem itself. For instance, one may be asked if the 'real meaning' of *The Waste Land* is that contemporary civilisation is in a state of crisis and decay; but that is only a drastic simplification of the 'real meaning.' Other 'real meanings' are that civilisation is always and everywhere in a state of crisis and decay and yet that the time is always redeemable. There is a true message of hope and a true message of despair in the poem; and the point of the frequent comparisons between the past and present in the poem is not necessarily merely that the past was noble, that the present is sordid, but probably also that, stripped of the illusions of the past, we are perhaps to-day more nakedly in touch with a timeless human predicament. The true waste land is not so much our culture, mechanical and meretricious as that is, as the proud and barren human heart that needs to obey a super-natural command and to be touched with a supernatural charity; and from that other side, from eternity's side, one time is much like another. All are unredeemed, and all redeemable . . . Even when one has said all this, one has not given the 'real meaning' of the poem; one has merely provided the reader with a slightly fuller set of rough clues. Similarly with a book like *Ulysses*: such great works of art without an obvious 'moral' in one sense, are far more 'moral' in another sense, than books with an immediate purpose of practical persuasion. Their morality is in their structure.

Artists of the type of Joyce, James, and Eliot, who can build their thinking *into* their work, are, however, at all times rare. The novelist like D. H. Lawrence, or Aldous Huxley, who uses the novel to propound, to advocate, to discuss some 'philosophy of life' is in the tradition of H. G. Wells; however strongly he may disagree with all, or some, or most of Wells's own extraordinarily varied and inconsistent set of philosophies. He may not rank so high as Joyce or James from the point of view of pure art; but he shows a commendably urgent concern with the immediate problems of his fellow men. If he never succeeds in arriving at a complete aesthetic coherence, the moral coherence of his work may nevertheless for a long time resist the dissolvents of social change.

Section 2: Indian Summer

In the years following the death of Queen Victoria, the sense of effortless moral and practical superiority which had been one of the marks of English history in her reign was replaced by a new uneasiness and doubt; there was doubt about the rights and wrongs of the Boer War, about the validity of the doctrine of free trade as an immutable economic truth. The growth of German industrial competition popularised the doctrine of Protectionism, while Germany's increasing military and naval power pointed the way to conscription, which was against all Victorian liberal traditions. There was uneasiness too about the problem of Irish Home Rule which had been shelved but not solved and about Mr Lloyd George's budgets and his National Insurance schemes, which meant the beginnings of State interference with the individual for the individual's own good.

There seemed to be also, in these years immediately following the death of Queen Victoria, a perceptible diminution in national grandeur and vitality. The politicians had still the same dignity but seemed to be on a smaller scale (Asquith compared with Gladstone, Balfour compared with Salisbury) and to lack the old fire of the Victorian giants. There was less, too, of that invigorating Victorian atmosphere of perpetual debate between Evolutionists and Bishops, between Protestants and Catholics, between Biblical Critics and Fundamentalists, between Hegelian and Utilitarian philosophers; there seemed to be no longer any broad and important intellectual issues which deeply divided the public and even the burning political topics of that day, tariffs or free trade, and national insurance, look from our present (certainly not intrinsically more enviable) point of view comfortably parochial. Even the early Fabians were becoming rather a *clique*, from which the livelier and more exploring mind of H. G. Wells would presently detach itself.

Nevertheless, if the Edwardian age was a time of plain thinking, it was also, for those reasonably comfortably situated, a time of high living. If the Victorian sun had set, it still left an afterglow; a fading splendour and a dying warmth still gilded the scene. The Edwardian decade and the years of the reign of King George V up to 1914 must have been for the larger part of the British people their last glimpse of 'normality,' of what they expected easy, ordinary everyday life to be. It was comfortable and jolly, after all, for so many people to be agreed, on a vague basis of sentiment, about so many things. Social barriers were gradually being lowered. The country houses of the aristocracy of birth which, in the latter part of the Victorian age, had been gradually opened to the new aristocracy of wealth were opened now to the still newer aristocracy of talent. H. G. Wells, the son of the lady's maid, the fervent radical, found himself chatting at dinner to Arthur Balfour or exchanging ideas and finding he had a good deal in common with a progressive Imperialist like Lord Milner. In fact the greatest of the new Imperialists, Joseph Chamberlain, had started off life as a radical, like Wells, and retained a great deal of the radical to the end; the new Unionist Party which had been formed when the anti-Home Rule Liberals left Gladstone was a much more capacious and tolerant body than the old Conservative Party had been, if also, perhaps, a body without such clear and definite principles. And the gradual rise of the Labour Party was pushing the Liberal Party, on the other hand, farther to the right. The leading politicians on the Liberal or Unionist side, whichever happened to be in power, kept up the old custom of 'dining with the Opposition'; and indeed perhaps the weakness of both Balfour and Asquith as leaders, from the point of view of their more eager followers, was that they lacked partisan zeal.

Thus in essence (in spite of furious rows occasionally in the House of Commons usually centring round Home Rule, Mr Lloyd George's still genuine and combatant radicalism, or Liberal threats to force their measures through the House of Lords by creating new Peers) the two great traditional parties were growing closer to each other. Nor was the working man being slighted or ignored. While the Fabians were happily busy at their ant-like labours of compiling exhaustive statistics about everything, a new small Labour Party, which had little connection with the Fabians, but represented rather the power of the Trade

Unions and the long traditions of English Noncomformist radicalism among the working classes, was feeling its way and getting its feet in the House of Commons. Apart from that, the working man had his new popular newspapers and Mr Kipling paid him the compliment of writing many of his poems in what he assumed to be the working man's spoken tongue. It was to him, too, or at least to the lower-middle-class layer of clerks, shop assistants, typists, who felt themselves just a little higher in the social scale, that Wells's novels of ideas made their great appeal. The common people were, at least, being 'kept in the picture'; and in spite of a number of serious strikes shortly before the outbreak of the Great War, Marxian Socialism among the workers was not, except in Glasgow and parts of Wales, a force yet seriously to be reckoned with.

On the whole, however, we shall not go far wrong if we think of the years from 1901 to 1914 as the great age, in English cultural and political history, of the middle classes. The working classes were not yet a major force in British life; the old aristocracy of birth were ceasing to be so (in the last decade of Queen Victoria's reign, two Prime Ministers, Salisbury and Rosebery, were peers, but in the present century all our Prime Ministers have been commoners). Thus, the most typical novelists of the Edwardian age were John Galsworthy and Arnold Bennett, and their novels epitomise this middle-class predominance. The picture of life which they give us, in fact, is a narrower picture than that of the great Victorian novelists; for it is a mark of the middle classes in nearly all societies that they 'know their place' in regard both to their superiors and inferiors, and tend to 'keep themselves to themselves.' What Galsworthy and Bennett give us, therefore, is not a complex picture of the Edwardian world as a whole, but rather a close view of a single very important section of society.

Galsworthy's world was that of the commercial upper middle classes, of large overfurnished houses in the suburbs, offices in the City of London, family ramifications, solemn dinner parties, the patient accumulation of wealth and the steady honouring of a code. Religion, philosophy, art, scholarship, even politics in any expert sense, lie outside the boundaries of this world. It is 'respectable,' that is enough, it does not want to be 'clever' or 'smart.' Galsworthy's most famous series of novels, *The Forsyte Saga*, is a study, at first with harsh satirical undertones, but latterly more and more warm and tolerant, and finally almost sentimental, of this world. In the first novel of the series, *The*

Man of Property, Galsworthy's chief male character, Soames Forsyte, has a sense of property which extends to his wife as well as to his house so that he breaks into her bedroom when she locks the door against him. Irene, who for Galsworthy symbolises the disruptive effect of beauty on the ordinary routines of life, then runs away with another man, and, once Soames is deserted by her, Galsworthy's attitude towards him, which has been very harsh at first, gradually softens. Starting off as something like the villain, he becomes in the end something like the hero of the long tale. He is a dry, rigid, limited person, but he is consistent, and he has his own code, and in the general dissolving of standards after the Great War Galsworthy came to feel that any code, even a stupid and limited one, was better than no code at all. So Soames becomes for him a symbol of sturdy and inarticulate English virtue, with a dignity and pathos of its own – it being part of the pathos, no doubt, that Beauty, as symbolised by Irene, instinctively flees from it.

The Forsyte Saga and its successor, *A Modern Comedy*, do therefore reflect a real change over the years in the temper of Galsworthy's mind; he begins by attacking those who cling too hard to tangible things but becomes in the end relieved that there *are* things, both tangible and intangible, to cling to. For the great quality of Galsworthy's mind was a sort of human piety, a respect in particular for the virtues of loyalty and self-restraint. The defect of his mind was a lack of curiosity or anxiety about ultimate things. His code was inherited and fundamentally unquestioned, for his questions, even when he appears to be a satirist, are not about the validity of the gentleman's code in itself but only about how honestly it is being applied. He had the nonsense knocked out of him at school and had never been to a university to have, in Max Beerbohm's phrase, the nonsense put gently back again. He was incapable of mental playfulness, scepticism, irony. So he fails in humour and falls short, in his more intense passages, of a truly tragic note: achieving in the stead of that a kind of muffled sentimentality. It was thus inevitable, in spite of his early leanings towards Socialism, that he should have become the favourite reading of middle-class ladies in suburban and provincial circulating libraries. His attitude to life was fundamentally the same as that of these ladies: a quiet, decent, well-mannered conventionality mitigated by an earnest but rather impracticable humanitarianism. His world is a solid but a rather grey one; we rarely glimpse the blue heavens above and hardly ever at all pierce down to the 'accepted hells beneath.'

Arnold Bennett had nothing of the high moral dignity, the vague but real distress about the injustice and unkindness of the world, which make Galsworthy such a very attractive figure in spite of his limitations. He was, however, more naturally and completely a creative artist, but an artist crippled, at least in the latter part of his career, by accepting the standards of vulgar success. There are critics who consider Bennett's *The Old Wives' Tale* the greatest English novel of this century. It is a novel in the French tradition, the tradition of Flaubertian realism. The life he describes in this book, the life of the English provincial lower middle classes in the pottery towns of the Midlands, Bennett knew intimately and all his best novels and collections of stories, such as *The Card* or *The Matador of the Five Towns*, have the Midlands as their background and their theme. If he had been a conscientious artist he would have continued to write about this gritty, humorous, provincial scene he knew so well, but he discovered that the sense of construction and depth he had learned from his French masters did not arouse any more applause, or make any more money, than his hastily written popular farces and romantic novels. He could produce works of ephemeral entertainment more rapidly and more profitably than works of art. He became famous and wealthy; he began to lead an expensive and gay life and to acquire a taste for the outward trappings of wealth, his yacht, his cigars, his wine, the deference of head-waiters. But the cost of becoming a popular figure in London society – and writers so different as Sir Osbert Sitwell and H.G.Wells have borne witness to Bennett's poise, and charm, and gaiety as a social lion – was a loss of touch with his dour provincial roots and the squandering of his gifts on literary journalism in the popular papers and on a steady production of potboilers.

It was Bennett's misfortune to have all the gifts of an honest artist, and to achieve his first successes in that Edwardian decade in which (in reaction against the 'art for art's sake' doctrine of the 1890s) almost nobody was judging, praising, or discussing literature from a purely aesthetic point of view: the literary journalism of Wells, and Shaw, and Chesterton was all about 'ideas.' Like many fine natural storytellers, Bennett had no 'ideas' to speak of; so there was thus nothing at all in his surrounding atmosphere to sustain him against the temptations of facile success. He wrote a really good novel or two, to show he could do it, and then settled down to enjoy himself. It was, in a sense, the lack of a philosophy that ruined him, but he also lacked a sense that any philosophy is necessary. Thus, even in his best books, one is wearied after a time by a lack of any deep curiosity on Bennett's part about the inner workings of people. He depicted minutely and exactly the hard surface detail of life, the appearance, behaviour, and speech of his Midlanders, the streets they walked in, the rooms they lived in, without suspecting that any mysteries might lie under that surface. Yet with all its limitations the world of his best books is solid and true and living and, all in all, one of the most accurate descriptions of English provincial life that has ever been made.

Of the other novelists of the Edwardian decade who have a moral or artistic interest, one of the most important is Joseph Conrad, a Pole, who, after an exciting career as a sea captain in the English Merchant Marine, settled down in England and wrote novels in the English language. Dr Leavis of Cambridge has recently stated in his book, *The Great Tradition*, that he considers Conrad one of the major English novelists. This is an interesting judgment, but it has to be questioned how far Conrad really belongs to the English tradition at all. He was a Pole by birth and a Pole in all his fundamental habits and loyalties; that is to say, an extravagant, brave, chivalrous man with a very sensitive 'sense of honour.' There is a story, for instance, that he once felt himself insulted by Shaw and wanted to challenge him to a duel. As a merchant skipper, the Englishman he knew best was the sort of man whom he met in distant ports, in outposts of the Empire, with a lingering touch of the Elizabethan adventurer about him. The qualities he loved in the English character were its courage, its capacity for self-sacrifice and for staunch silent endurance, and for a high, noble vision never articulately expressed. He was out for the heroic, wherever he could get it; he was one of the genuine 'last romantics' because he had lived romanticism as well as dreamt about it.

Thus many of his novels and short stories have a poetic quality, and they have been favourite reading among English poets of this century. Mr T. S. Eliot's *The Hollow Men* has an epigraph from Conrad's wonderful long-short story, *Heart of Darkness*: 'Mistah Kurtz – he dead.' This story is remarkable both for its evocation of the African jungle and for its parallel glimpse – of which the jungle, in a sense, is the symbolic prelude – of the possible depths of corruption in the human soul. Mr Kurtz is the agent of a trading company in a lonely African outpost and, carried away by drink, by loneliness, by a growing megalomania, he has made himself a tyrant over the natives around him more cruel and bloodthirsty than their own savage chiefs. They regard him with superstitious awe. In the story, we see him dying of fever and oppressed by hallucinations and bad dreams. It is his own diseased mind that is taking its revenge on him, not his victims. Eliot's very title, *The Hollow Men*, is probably suggested by Conrad's story since the narrator suggests that it was some inner emptiness, or hollowness, in Mr Kurtz, that allowed his lusts and fantasies to take possession of him. *Heart of Darkness* is a vision of evil, of evil in the heart of nature that has run riot without human discipline, and of evil in the unchastened heart of man; and perhaps the suggestion of the title *is* that the heart of darkness, the very core of Satan's kingdom, is not anything solid, but exactly a hollowness, an emptiness, a great gap around which everything living has rotted away. Thus Conrad at his best thinks, as a poet does, in grand symbols. He is by no means always at his best. Sometimes he writes what is not much more than a boy's adventure story, but dresses it up in an English too florid for his purpose. His style, indeed, never has an English ease, has always a foreign tang, sometimes beguiling, sometimes estranging; it reads often like a beautiful but not wholly idiomatic translation from some wonderful French original; and to the end of his life Conrad *spoke* French more easily than English.

One might mention, along with Conrad, Rudyard Kipling, whose view of life and whose range of subjects were not wholly dissimilar. Like Conrad, he very much admired strong, brave, silent men but, unlike Conrad's, his is the slightly wistful (and therefore slightly sentimentalised, slightly false) admiration of the intellectual, who has wanted very much to be a man of action, and never succeeded in becoming one. It might be said of Kipling, even more than of Galsworthy, that his attitude to life was never that of the adult, fully educated man but always that of the very clever and very plucky schoolboy; not, in Kipling's case as in Galsworthy's, the decent, worried, tolerant prefect, but rather the bookish boy who is shortsighted, dirty, and awkward but who very much admires dash and courage among his companions, the Stalkies and M'Turks, even if that is accompanied by ruthlessness. There was some streak in Kipling's character that made him respond sympathetically to ruthlessness, when accompanied by gusto and style; but it is far too easy to exaggerate that side of him, as also to exaggerate the touch of morbid obsession with horror (which made Andrew Lang say, when he read Kipling's terrifying early story, *The Mark of the Beast*, that the author of it would die mad before thirty). Kipling has written certain stories, like *Mary Postgate*, and certain poems, like the war-time one with the lines

> When Time shall count from the date
> That the English began to hate,

which, intended to shower hate and shame on England's enemies, are themselves hateful and shaming. But on the whole, apart from these occasional distressing lapses into a venom quite untypical of the English character, he was a genuine and honest patriot, and not necessarily of a diehard sort. He was, on the whole, for his time, up to date in his view of the responsibility of Empire, and his heroes, men like Rhodes, and Chamberlain, and Milner, were men who looked forward, not men who looked back. He could be chivalrous, as he was, on the whole, in his poems about the Boer War: compare his tribute to General Joubert,

> With those that bred, with those that loosed the strife,
> He had no part whose hands were clear of gain;
> But subtle, strong, and stubborn, gave his life
> To a lost cause, and knew the gift was vain,

with the appalling pomposity, frigidity, and falseness of Robert Bridges in one of his fortunately infrequent attempts at patriotic verse,

> Full thirty moons since unwilling enmity,
> Since daily suspense for hideous peril
> Of brethren unrescued, beleaguer'd,
> Plague-stricken in cities unprovided,
> Had quencht accustom'd gaiety from the day
> When first the Dutchman's implacable folly,
> The country of Shakespeare defying,
> Thought with a curse to appal the nation . . .

Kipling knew and understood the multifarious peoples of India with a deep and instinctive sympathy, which comes out in his one successful long narrative (one can hardly be certain whether it ought to be called a novel or not), *Kim*, and in many of his best short stories. But he had no sympathy for Indian, any more than for Irish, aspirations after independence. He saw the British as being, like the ancient Hebrews, a chosen people. Those whom they were called to rule, as well as their rivals in Europe, were 'the lesser breeds without the Law.' Nevertheless with all these limitations, it must be said that Kipling is (with the possible exception of D. H. Lawrence, in a quite different style, but not, I think, in his heat and suddenness, with a wholly dissimilar temperament) the best short-story writer in English of this century; and if he

3

could never manage a 'proper' novel, *Kim*, whatever it should be called, does call up the strange atmosphere of India to the senses and the imagination as does no other book in English about that great subcontinent.

Kipling is one of our great masters of prose, as he is one of our great masters of verse. His gift of style, his extraordinary mastery of language somehow sanctifies and excuses his lapses of taste, his stridencies of sentiment, even his moments of hysterical cruelty. If he can in every sort of way on occasion jar on our nerves, there is also in some of his stories a vision of the inner hearts of men, of trouble, of suffering, and of the possible supernatural consequences of earthly error, which astonishes one by its air of authority; especially when one contrasts it with what is crude, blatant, of too cheap and brassy an effectiveness, in other stories. Kipling in fact is a writer who must be rediscovered from time to time and who, when the quarrels in which he so furiously engaged himself are forgotten, will be remembered for a passionate exactness of language and for disturbing moments of deep vision that every now and again break, with the most startling effect, through the compact and jaunty surfaces of his verse and prose.

On the whole, however, it is probably not to Kipling or to Conrad that the more sensitive Edwardians turned for a lucid insight into the everyday problems of their own lives. The novelist who has best crystallised that age for us, and who has exposed its predicaments with the most delicate insight and sympathy, is Mr E. M. Forster: a novelist still living, still writing (though in the last thirty years he has written no more novels), still generally read, esteemed, and imitated. Mr Forster, unlike all the other novelists I have been dealing with in this section, enjoyed the advantage of having received that combined stimulation of the intellect and broadening of the emotional perspective which is the great gift to a favoured few in our country (not to all those who go up to Oxford and Cambridge but to those who make the most of their time there) of our ancient universities. Mr Forster had studied at Cambridge (he is now an Honorary Fellow of King's College, Cambridge) and had come under the influence of wise and humane thinkers of the type of Lowes Dickinson and G. E. Moore. Dickinson had given him an interest in the classical background of Western culture, in that amenity, suavity, tense but graceful balance between competing ideas and passions, which is the achievement at their highest of the ancient Greeks; Moore may have taught him that the assumptions of common sense are not so simple as they seem and that the most ordinary personal preferences and decisions may conceal all sorts of intellectual confusions, and will become clearer to us in their implications if we train ourselves to analyse them out.

In Forster's novels, therefore, we feel as we do not feel in Galsworthy's or Bennett's, or in Kipling's and Conrad's either, that a philosophical mind is at work. Forster is interested in human behaviour in so far as it presents us with moral problems; not with problems which can be solved in an obvious and heroic way, by embracing a cause, or joining an army, or going to some distant country as a missionary, but with the problems of everyday life, such problems as whether we have been kind and understanding enough to our neighbours, whether we are judging them by the same standards as we judge ourselves, and also on the other hand whether, in our wish to keep in with our neighbours, we are perhaps being unfair to our own ambitions and desires.

Mr Forster wrote very few novels – five in all. The first, *Where Angels Fear to Tread*, appeared in 1905, the last, *A Passage to India*, in 1924. In 1924 Mr Forster was still a comparatively young man (he is a gay and active figure even to-day) but he realised, I imagine, that the curtain had risen on a new scene, that the world after the war was not the world he had grown up in, and that he could not write with his old mastery about a shifting society of which he was no longer intimately a member; so in the last thirty years, though he has written some charming books of criticism, essays, and memories, he has produced no fiction.

Even in his productive period he was, in comparison with Galsworthy, Bennett, Conrad, or Kipling, or even with a perfectionist like Henry James, a remarkably sparse and cautious writer. In the nineteen years of that productive period he averaged just one novel every four years. Some of these novels, moreover, are short and perhaps none of them is, on the surface, what looks like a 'great' novel. They deal with pleasant, ordinary English middle-class people, just, usually, but no more than just on the 'upper' side of the great divide between 'upper' and 'lower' middle class. They are written in a smooth, tidy, sometimes just slightly precious style which has a touch of Cambridge preciseness about it and just a touch, also, of maiden-lady delicacy. Mr Forster, in fact, writes about 'nice' people in a 'nice' manner, but what makes him an important and disturbing writer is that his great interest is a critical examination of whatever it is in the atmosphere of English life that so often makes 'nice' people behave nastily. He is a critic, one might say, of that English passion for respectability and for correct behaviour at all costs, which makes so many English people afraid of passion, but, even more than of passion, of the sudden critical disloyalties of thought. Mr Forster's characters will go to quite unscrupulous lengths sometimes to prevent any unsettlement of their code, but to Mr Forster this tends to prove that there was something sadly inadequate, something smug and self-protective to say the least, about the code in the first place.

Thus, in Mr Forster's third novel, *A Room With a View*, the question at issue is an apparently trivial one, whether a nice, pretty, good-natured, rather ordinary girl should or should not marry a very nice young man who is genuinely in love with her but who is 'not quite of her class.' It is not a matter of 'class-warfare,' as we understand it to-day – or of any real broad or to the outside observer terribly perceptible gulf to be bridged; it is a matter of almost invisible distinctions of manner and behaviour between two of the almost innumerable segments of the English middle class. English people have a very strong sense of the exact social group they belong to, of its customs, its taboos. This is not an articulate sense; one would rather say that when two English strangers meet each other they sniff at each other like dogs, and see if the smell is a familiar one. If these imperceptible barriers are absurd, they are none the less real, and to break them down even on a small front, in the name of individual responsibility and initiative, has something mildly heroic about it.

This theme of the individual, the individual's own response, his own sense of responsibility, his own sense of reaction towards and trust in a 'stranger,' for which he must sacrifice 'tradition,' is really Mr Forster's main theme. In an early novel, *A Room With a View*, he treats the theme in a vein of genteel, almost ladylike comedy, but in his last novel, *A Passage to India*, it has become tragic. Now it is no longer a matter of gaps, barriers, misunderstandings between different sections of the English middle classes; it is a matter of gaps, barriers, and misunderstandings between the British in India and the native educated Indians. The story is that of a friendship between a native Indian doctor and an English official which has to stand the test of a false accusation against this doctor by an English girl that he has made indecent advances to her. The girl is not consciously insincere; she has been in a nervous state, the climate is telling on her, and while the Indian doctor is showing her round some local caves she has a kind of hallucination. Her accusation, however, has a very bad effect on both local communities, British and Indian, a terrible atmosphere of tension and hysteria is worked up. The girl is a lumpy, ordinary sort of girl but she has real intrinsic decency (Mr Forster does not go out of his way to make his 'good' characters necessarily glamorous ones) and before the Indian doctor is brought to trial she has plenty of time to think things over. At the trial, she confesses that she has been suffering from an hysterical delusion. The British community drop her, her young man breaks off their engagement, while on the other hand the Indian community show no gratitude for her courage and magnanimity but indulge in rather mean and vindictive demonstrations of triumph. She has ceased to be a 'person' in the views of both communities and has become a mere symbol of the tensions and the bad feelings that hold them apart.

The Indian doctor, of course, is let out of gaol, and his English friend has stood loyally by him throughout this crisis, but they have both felt the pressure of group opinion on them, and, now that the crisis is over, they begin to drift apart. The mere habits of their lives, different circles, different routines, separate them; yet they meet once again much later and, in spite of the fact that the Englishman has now married and is therefore tied very much more to his own community, and in spite of the other fact that the Indian is now much more bitterly nationalist than he used to be, they have a frank, friendly conversation as in the old days. Both sense that it will be for the last time. The moral of the story is that individual sincerity and loyalty are possible, but that the pressure of group life, and of accepted social conventions, works very hard against them.

Though Forster is a great master of social comedy there is in all his novels this tone of sadness which comes from realising how every individual, even the most liberal and tolerant individual, is weighed down by even the stupidest conventions of the particular group he belongs to. One might say that Forster is the best modern English novelist of the liberal tradition, the tradition which says it is up to every man to choose his own friends, his own job, to arrive at his own convictions. Forster realises the almost tragic inner struggle that is involved in living up to this ideal. Apart from that, however, he has a strong sense of how many of these virtues of the liberal tradition are inherent in the British character at its best. They are inherent especially in the upper middle classes, in British administrators and professional men and scholars, whose very mode of education is traditionally called a 'liberal education': that is an education (as opposed to a 'mechanical education') that will enlarge and humanise the mind and not merely prepare a man to earn his living at some particular trade. But on the other hand Forster knows how the mere code of manners of these classes, who are the custodians of the liberal tradition, tends to fence them off from other classes in the community. Foreigners, if they find Englishmen shy and awkward, might learn from Forster's novels what an honest struggle lies behind the British effort to be fair. It is not for the British a matter of having a given tradition of warm friendliness between all classes and communities. There is rather a tendency (partly due to shyness) to erect these barriers which Forster writes about. But there is also a strong puritan conscience at work in the British professional and administrative classes which makes them feel that any principle, which they apply to their own group, ought ideally to be applied to all groups, that discrimination is unfair; and it is from this basis, from the uneasy conscientiousness, the high principles, and the refined sensibilities of our traditional ruling classes in Great Britain that our present democratic order or system has partly evolved; there has also, of course, been pressure from below. But British democracy is not a democracy which has been achieved by violence or revolution; it has evolved rather through the fact that various social groups, deprived of advantages belonging to more privileged groups, have demanded a reasonable share in these advantages; and the more privileged classes, because of their honesty and conscientiousness, have had to recognise the justice of the demand. Forster then is a novelist not only of isolated individualism but of a tradition of moral independence in the individual which has helped in the past to secure for Great Britain social justice and peace.

Section 3: The Time of Transition (1910–1920)

The decade of the First World War happened to coincide with a very important period of creative experiment in English literature. The War was not in itself the cause of the new movements, which were mostly well under way before its outbreak; and some of the most notable innovators, like T. S. Eliot and Joyce – the one an American citizen domiciled in Great Britain, the other an Irishman exiled in Trieste – did not serve in the war; nor did another American domiciled in England, Ezra Pound, important both as an organiser of new movements and as a publicist for them. Joyce had been working on his great novel *Ulysses* and on his earlier *Dubliners* and *Portrait of the Artist as a Young Man* for years before the outbreak of the war; so, in France, had Marcel Proust been working for years at his immensely long novel,

A la Recherche du Temps Perdu, and the appearance of the first volume merely happened to coincide with the outbreak of hostilities. Percy Wyndham Lewis, the painter and polemicist, the founder of the magazine *Blast* and the soul of the Vorticist movement, did serve in the War, but never wrote about it at any great length. His influential first novel, *Tarr*, written in three weeks, was about bohemian life in Paris. New techniques of vivid imagery, and 'free verse' were used effectively by a war poet, like Herbert Read; but they came from Imagist movements, encouraged by Pound, and Richard Aldington, and Ford Madox Hueffer, which antedated the war by several years. What was happening, in fact, was a general and rather violent break-away by young writers from the contented attitudes, and the slovenly techniques of writing, that had been, as we have seen, so typical of the Edwardian age. The new novelists looked perhaps to James and Conrad, not exactly as models to be imitated, but as examples of artistic integrity. The new poets violently rejected what they regarded as the insipid decadence of contemporary British verse, and the smugness of the Victorian poet, and the soaring vagueness of the Romantics, and looked for models in other countries (in nineteenth-century France), in other ages (mediaeval Italy and Provence), even in other cultures (ancient China and Japan). There was a desperate desire to freshen up an atmosphere that seemed to have grown mawkish and stale.

The experimentalism of this decade can be compared, then, to the revolt of the Pre-Raphaelites, and even to the revolt of the 1890s, against the complacencies of Victorian Liberalism; but history itself, as the Great War showed, was *also* revolting against these complacencies, and therefore Eliot, and Pound, and Joyce, and Wyndham Lewis, and T. E. Hulme were not simply making a gesture but announcing, prophetically, the advent of a newer and harsher age. The reading public did not take to them at once; but in ten or in twenty years they were to seem to a new generation of young readers tremendously topical and in thirty or forty years, now in the middle of the century, they have almost the status of modern classics. The war unsettled society as their sharp, disturbing insights had earlier unsettled them.

The war unsettled society in two ways. It had, on the one hand, what a novelist like H. G. Wells, who clung all through it to his expansive optimism about the future of human society, would have called a 'liberating' effect. It hastened on that emancipation of women, political and social and sexual, which had in any case been making great strides since the beginning of the century. If women could serve as nurses or in the auxiliary armed forces, were they not also capable of exercising the vote? As women engaged in war work, and mixed more freely with men, their manners also became less lady-like and formal, more slangy and direct, more free and easy. The war also did something to promote that merging of social classes which had been already under way at the beginning of the century. Many young men from humble social backgrounds did well in the Army, became officers, came home with new ambitions and a new sense of dignity. Young officers from the upper classes, on the other hand, like Siegfried Sassoon or Robert Graves came home with a new questioning attitude towards their inherited code.

But this 'liberation' was also an undermining. The First World War destroyed a deep subconscious social confidence (based on the fact that since 1815 the existence of the British Empire had not really been at stake, nor the effort of the whole nation engaged, in any major conflict, and based also on a century of more or less peaceful expansion of wealth and population and imperial strength) that, whatever disasters might happen in the outer world, life, for the British, a 'business people,' would go on 'as usual.' Great Britain, it was felt up to 1914, was a 'going concern,' immune both from revolution and decay. The war, accelerating many social changes, good and bad, disrupting old habits of life, destroyed also that old, easy confidence.

When the war first broke out, indeed, it was greeted by many older writers, and also by young poets like Rupert Brooke, with eagerness. Perhaps Great Britain had been too long at peace, become slack and fat, and the war, for her young men, would be a heroic invigorating experience. What nobody foresaw was the squalor and monotony of trench warfare, its terrible costliness in life and, more profoundly, in the unhappiness of survivors. Soon the poets were ceasing to write the war up in romantic terms, but were instead, like Sassoon, Owen, Graves, and Read, giving vivid and terrible pictures of what actual war was like; and in the prose accounts of their experiences which many of these writers published after the war – often five or six years after – we can see the whole experience exploding in their imaginations, rending their nerves once more, like a bomb with a delayed-action fuse. Behind and beyond the actual fighting also, great social upheavals were taking place; of which the most important, the Russian revolution, gave a provisional and tentative appearance to all the rearrangements of Versailles. After the Armistice, the founding of the

League of Nations did arouse some idealistic hopes in persistently optimistic writers like H. G. Wells. For younger men, the years of the war, and the years immediately after it, were years of doubt, uncertainty, confusion. The young poets who had entered the Army in a mood of eagerness came out of it in a mood of disenchantment; and the old, easy, comfortable, thoughtless hopefulness of the Edwardian decade never really came back again as a main factor in English life or literature. Instead, both about human hopes and about human actions, there was a 'new realism' – a tendency to look facts, however unpleasant, in the face and to think, as T. E. Hulme thought, of man no longer as a giant figure striding to perfection but as a limited creature, who could know perfection, but who was necessarily imperfect; yet who with a harsh discipline of himself might achieve a certain decency.

A very famous novel of this decade, James Joyce's *Ulysses*, is symptomatic both of the new experimentalism and the new sad, realistic attitudes towards human society. *Ulysses* deals with the events of a single day in the life of its two heroes, in Dublin, at the beginning of this century. The two heroes are Leopold Bloom, a Jewish advertising agent, who stands for Ulysses in the Homeric epic; and Stephen Daedalus, a young poet, who stands for Telemachus. All the incidents of Homer's poem are elaborately paralleled, or parodied, in Joyce's novel; but the ordinary reader's enjoyment of the novel is not much enhanced by having these parallels pointed out to him; they were useful rather to Joyce himself, in forcing him to impose a complex outer structure on what might otherwise have become a mere flux of inner monologue. It is for the same reason, to give himself an outer framework, that he works out the itinerary of the story so elaborately; mentioning so many Dublin shops, offices, public-houses, back streets, low quarters, that his novel is almost at moments like a guide-book to the city, though not to its beauty spots. For most of his action does go on either inside the mind of Bloom or inside that of Stephen (though there are glimpses of the 'inner workings' of minor characters too, and at the very end of the book there is the torrential monologue of Mrs Bloom, who seems to stand for a kind of eternal feminine principle, passive but tenacious, a principle of eternal renewal and acceptance). Mrs Bloom's monologue at the end, uninterrupted by outer action, does show to what a shapeless fluidity this 'stream-of-thought' technique might lead; and therefore Joyce perpetually interrupts and deflects Bloom's inner monologues or Stephen's with impingements from the outer world; and he has one passage (that in which he parodies in succession all the most notable historical styles in English narrative prose) in which he steps outside the characters and discourses *about* them in the old style.

Thus Joyce's great achievement in *Ulysses* is not simply his use of a subjective method, but his success in building this up into an objective framework. We get inside the minds of Stephen and Bloom but we do not simply *identify* ourselves with them. Joyce enables us to put them into a wider perspective than they put themselves.

So much is this the case, in fact, that these two characters, individualised though they are in more elaborate detail than any other two characters in fiction, nevertheless have a large and general symbolic value, too. Bloom, a vulgarian in his attitude to the arts, blankly indifferent to religion, a timid but persistent sensualist, obsessed by sordid worries about his wife's faithfulness, is nevertheless generous, warmhearted, full of inquisitive alertness about science and politics; hoping that the world will be transformed by technical improvements and by the substitution of a new internationalism for the old, narrowminded nationalism. In a sense, in his general attitude to life, Bloom is like a typical Wells hero (or almost like Wells himself) seen from another point of view. To Stephen Daedalus, who represents the despair of the poet in a cultureless, commercial world, all Bloom's ideas are nonsense. But Bloom is not ridiculous to Stephen in himself, nor, indeed, to Joyce; and the spirit Bloom stands for is not ridiculous. Again and again (as in the episode, modelled on that of the Cyclops' Cave in Homer, where Bloom just escapes from being beaten up by a bigoted Irish nationalist) we see that Bloom stands in Joyce's mind for a human, a civilised, a rational attitude in contrast to native barbarism; for Joyce, if he was not a naive liberal progressive either, was far from being an Irish nationalist himself. Bloom is the sort of well-meaning Jew who, because of his liberal attitudes and his imperfect assimilation to a local culture, is the predestined victim of Fascism. He is a pathetic and comic figure in many ways, a compendium of many common human weaknesses, and with a touch, indeed, as Mr Percy Wyndham Lewis has noted, of the comic Jew of the music halls. But he is, as Mr Wyndham Lewis has also noted, a distinctly amiable figure, and even, perhaps, in many ways his middle-aged creator in disguise (as Stephen Daedalus, a frank piece of autobiography, is his youthful creator *without* disguise). Bloom, with all his faults, is the largest and most sympathetic *human* figure in *Ulysses*.

James Joyce himself said, emphatically, that he intended Bloom to be 'a good man.'

Bloom then is partly the symbol of that social optimism, based on a firm belief in science, which was so influential a creed in Joyce's own youth. It was partly the creed of one of Joyce's own masters, Ibsen. Stephen Daedalus, on the other hand, represents the cult, not exactly of pure art, but of art as 'the eternal affirmation of the spirit of man.' The acceptance of that cult is a common result of losing one's religious faith and of not finding in any merely practical social purpose an adequate substitute for it. It is not so much that Stephen despairs of society as that he cannot make a religion of society. Like T. E. Hulme, he sees the hopeless imperfection, and imperfectibility, of men in most of their practical relations; yet he knows too that man hungers for perfection, and can at once express that hunger, and perhaps on rare occasions satisfy it, through poetry and music and art. This is a very isolating position, and where Bloom on the whole is a morally strong character, Stephen is an extremely weak one. He has to pursue his dream of beauty hampered by hunger, and bad teeth, and family claims upon him, and his own uncontrollable adolescent lusts. He has always to be resisting appeals to his sympathy that strike him as irrelevant to his vocation, and that makes him seem conceited and peevish. One particular grief gnaws often at his heart, which is that, when his mother is dying, he refused to pray for her, because he thought that, after the loss of his faith, prayer would be hypocritical; and also because he was afraid that praying might revive his faith. Essentially, Stephen is a young man in search of a father – of a father to guide and help him (his own father, a drunkard going steadily downhill since his wife's death, is no use); and Bloom is a middle-aged man with no son (his only son died in infancy) who needs a son to give him confidence in his manhood; for, though gregarious, Bloom is lonely, his life is a shabby failure, none of his dreams has come true or is likely to, and he knows that his handsome, musical, sex-obsessed wife, Marion, is perpetually betraying him.

Though the theme of *Ulysses* is so momentous, the construction of the book so intricate, its atmosphere so dense, there is, nevertheless, in the working out of the plot, in the old-fashioned sense very little 'story.' Bloom, going about Dublin on his day's work, pausing now and again to attend a funeral, to stare at a girl, or to eat a meal, worrying about his money, his wife, his sexual needs and his digestion, but with an alert, inquisitive ear cocked, nevertheless, for what is going on

around him, runs into Stephen (wandering pointlessly and later
drunkenly around) once or twice, observes him with fatherly care,
and late in the evening is able to rescue Stephen from a drunken brawl
outside a brothel which they have both been visiting; to sober Stephen
up; and to persuade Stephen to come home with him. For both
Stephen and Bloom, the meeting is something momentous, though
both would find it hard to explain why. Each perhaps has a sense,
through the chance meeting, of having achieved human recognition,
and so of having enhanced his dignity. What is sad and ironical is that
these two people, who so much need each other's trust and affection,
have no common language. (And here we might have a kind of allegory
of the need in our time for, and the difficulties that lie in the way of,
a marriage of science and art.) It is impossible, in fact, for Bloom and
Stephen really to communicate with each other, but they can convey
good-will. Stephen is strengthened in his sense of vocation, and Bloom
draws enough courage from the encounter to assert himself mildly
with his wife. So much for the main shape of the book: what of its
conclusion, which might seem irrelevant to that shape, the long
interior monologue, in a state between dream and waking, of Marion
Bloom? That is to be taken, as I have already suggested, as a symbol
of a total, uncritical acceptance of life which lies beyond the scope of
both Stephen and Bloom, and perhaps beyond the scope of the
masculine human animal as such. Both Stephen and Bloom are
idealists; Stephen lives for perfection, and Bloom for improvement.
But Mrs Bloom stands for an impulse which has more to do with
keeping the race going than any ideal – for the blind and greedy, but
eternally creative, principle of life itself. It is only superficially that her
monologue seems a sordid record of a vulgar woman's erotic fantasies;
it is really a speech by an earth-goddess. Men discriminate and complain, they are always after something better; it is because women
discriminate less, and complain less, because they will always be
satisfied in the end with what they can get, that life goes on.

The atmosphere of *Ulysses* has the thickness, the almost stifling
density, of our sensuous and emotional experience of the 'real world.'
To many readers, when first published, the book, because of the
frankness that was inherent in its use of the naturalistic interior monologue, appeared unbearably depressing; to-day we are more likely to
be struck by Joyce's wisdom and compassion, by his deep understanding of and pity for human nature at all levels, by his sense of the
goodness that underlies Bloom's vulgarity, the poetic vision that

underlies Stephen's weak and peevish self-conceit, the affirmation of life that underlies Marion Bloom's gross fantasies, than by any undue emphasis on the sordid side of life. Rather we feel that Joyce 'sees life steadily and sees it whole' and that his attitude towards all his characters is one of comprehension and forgiveness. In one sense, the book *is* a tragic one, for it depicts a society in which the 'best men' – and both Bloom and Stephen represent the 'best men' – have lost the faiths and habits that make life in a society real and noble. It is because the reality of Dublin falls so far short of what it should be that Bloom and Stephen are both such uncompromising idealists. But if the picture of Dublin life is depressing at least we do see in Bloom and Stephen a kind of essential human nobility asserting itself, with however little practical effect, against discouraging circumstances. And Joyce himself, of course, accepts Dublin far more completely than they do; he is like Mrs Bloom in that respect Shabbiness and failure and genteel pretence and undergraduate brutality and the smells, and the smoke, and the clanging trams, and the crowded bars of a great city have all their own poetry for him. He conveys that poetry through the ear rather than the eye. He was a very shortsighted man, who saw the world around him through a blur or haze; he was also a singer, with a wonderful ear for music, and before he turned to prose had written some very slight but exquisitely singable lyrical poems. He uses his sentences, with their elaborate musical cadences, to call up impressions which are often all the more emotionally concrete for not being visually hard and precise. We are immersed *in* his world, not seeing it from a perspective. He had a wonderful 'ear' in another sense; just as he could mimic or parody any style in English prose literature, so he could catch in writing the pitch and rhythm and idiom of anybody's speaking voice. We do not always see his characters very clearly, but we can always hear *their* voices (and not, as so often in novels, some version of the author's *own* voice) while they are talking.

A friend and contemporary of James Joyce was Percy Wyndham Lewis, whom I have already mentioned. If Joyce was above all a musical writer, a writer whose appeal is to the 'auditory imagination,' Lewis, his primary genius that of a draughtsman, is a writer whose first appeal is to the eye. Towards the end of the decade we are considering, Lewis published a striking first novel, *Tarr*. All the important characters in *Ulysses* are seen, to a great extent, from the inside (though as I have suggested, by his care for 'grand structure,' Joyce also establishes an 'objective' view of them). In *Tarr*, and in Mr Lewis's subsequent novels, everything is seen from the outside. Lewis is not interested in the feelings and sensibilities of his characters; he is interested in their appearance and their behaviour, as that might strike a brilliantly acute outside observer, lacking in sympathy with the people he is describing, but not quite 'clinically' detached, since he has a bent towards satirical humour. For Lewis, the human animal in general is something rather pretentious and absurd, about whom it would be ridiculous to have strong feelings, one way or another; but one may permit oneself to laugh. The scene of *Tarr* is Paris, and the characters are a set of down-at-heel Bohemians, would-be writers, would-be artists, social pretenders. None of the characters is very likeable, but where Joyce would have found the side of them that was human and touching, for Lewis they are like a set of silly and clumsy automatons. The book, too, is full of episodes of violence: but Lewis refuses to exploit melodramatic possibilities. The main character is a neurotic German called Kreisler, who rapes the hero's mistress, kills an enemy with whom he is having a duel after the duel is officially over, finally kills himself. Kreisler is in his essence rather like a Dostoevsky character, 'wild' and 'tortured,' but for Lewis he is simply a silly, violent creature who destroys himself (like most human creatures, from Lewis's point of view) and therefore as 'good for a laugh,' or for a cold, satirical sneer, as anything else. This was a novel view of satire – satire directed not against some particular social class, some opinion or belief, some current folly, but against human existence in general. Lewis either lacked that natural sympathy with our fellow creatures which most of us feel, or was able, for the sake of a special artistic effect, to freeze that sympathy at its source. His book was admired, but, given this attitude to life of his, could never be widely popular. Some later satirical novels – particularly *The Apes of God*, a satire on many of his literary and artistic contemporaries – have made him more unpopular still, with the result that a brilliantly original philosophical fantasy of his, *The Childermass*, and many interesting general books on a variety of topics, have not had the success they deserved.

In these later books of his, however, Mr Lewis was to perfect his peculiar style. Just as every sentence in Joyce's prose has a musical cadence, a hint of the hidden lyric, so every sentence of Lewis's calls up some harsh, definite, frightening or absurd picture to the eye. This is not to say that his prose is *displeasing* to the ear; it has an explosive emphasis and a jogging mechanical force. Nevertheless, Lewis, in his works of fiction at least (his philosophical or critical works are another matter) is a hard writer to read. The reader feels like a punch-ball receiving thud after thud; he is never allowed to rest. One might say, perhaps, as a general criticism of Mr Lewis that he specialises too much in the exploitation of negative emotions. He shows up every kind of human activity as mechanical, or false, or meaningless, or hateful; the reader begins to wish that he were offered something to love and admire. Sometimes he is offered something; it is the notion of the lonely and persecuted 'great artist' or 'great man' among a ridiculous crowd of gibbering submen. Unfortunately this noble figure, free at last from all the frailties which so disgust and amuse Mr Lewis in the generality of the race, looks far too much like, in most cases, a projection of Mr Lewis himself. And 'the standpoint of genius,' from which Mr Lewis sometimes claims to write, is not the standpoint of genius in general; it is the standpoint of *a* genius (Mr Lewis is undoubtedly that) who has never been able to regard *himself* in a critical light, who gives as much weight to his passing furies as to his permanent insights, and who has never thought fit to fetter himself by any sort of schematic consistency. In the sour dignity with which Mr Lewis faces a world which has certainly never quite given his genius its due there is just a touch of Shakespeare's Malvolio; and one might hazard a guess that, like Malvolio, he is 'sick with self-love.' Joyce was a greater, not a smaller, writer for loving his fellow-men.

These two writers I have mentioned in this third section because they were both of them innovators of genius in a way in which at least two of the writers I am to deal with in the next section – Aldous Huxley and Virginia Woolf – were not; though Huxley was a writer of comprehensive intelligence and Mrs Woolf of the most exquisitely charming individual talent. D.H.Lawrence, the third of the writers I am to deal with in the next section, was a man of genius, but he was also an exasperatingly uneven writer who sacrificed, too often, his conscience as an artist to his mission as a prophet. The very originality of a man of genius often prevents him from having the immediate influence on the public of a writer who does not so much originate, as adapt originality for public consumption. One may find in Mrs Woolf a certain dilution of Joyce's inventions and in Aldous Huxley a certain softening and civilising of the satirical impact of Wyndham Lewis. And this would not be a matter of imitation but simply of new literary possibilities of a given period which the writer of genius carries, from the point of view of the general reading public, too far, and the writer of talent just far enough. Certainly Aldous Huxley,

Mrs Woolf, and D.H. Lawrence influenced the mood, and formed the taste, of the intelligent reading public in the 1920s to a far greater degree than Joyce or Wyndham Lewis. Lewis, in fact, had so much the sense of being pushed into a corner, of being deliberately chosen for the role of 'odd man out,' that in defiance he assumed the role of 'The Enemy': which for literature was not immediately a loss, since he has a great gift for satirical attack, but which may well have been a loss, from a longer perspective, in that it hindered the maturing of his personality and the deepening of his sympathies. There has been a natural tendency because of the undeserved neglect of him, for young writers to 'rediscover' him periodically and perhaps to pitch his standing too high. I am a very great admirer of his gifts myself, but I have tried to indicate here what I feel to be a human lack in him.

Another writer, not English, who should be mentioned here for his influence on English fiction in the 1920s is Marcel Proust. Proust's great theme is what the French call 'recueillement,' which means more than the English 'recollection'; it is the regathering of all the threads of one's life. Life is always flowing, yet it is easy enough for a man to go over in his mind the main incidents of his life. It is more difficult for him to relive them, to recapture the sense of what past time was like before it flowed away. It is more difficult still to get that recaptured and revived awareness of the past into perspective with the present. And finally to shape all this fluid material into a kind of crystalline unity of contemplation is very difficult indeed. Yet these are Proust's achievements. He is neither a novelist of the ear, of the musical cadence and the living echo, like Joyce, nor a novelist of the eye, of the bitter and incisive visual cartoon, like Wyndham Lewis. His long sentences certainly call up image after image and move generally with a graceful and undulating – if sometimes with a cumbrous and confused – motion, but what they are after is neither picture nor music for its own sake but the translation of experience into thought. Proust had at once the temperament of a woman and the mind of a philosopher. As we read him, we seem to be sinking into a glaucous and submarine, yet flutter-ing and excited landscape, in which the morning sun bleeding through the shutters of a hotel bedroom, the faces of pretty girls passing like figures on a frieze along a beach, the powdered hair of a flunkey on the stairway of a great mansion, the monocled mask and booming voice of some dandy at a party, the possibility of being smiled at, at the theatre, by a duchess, a small boy's hopeless need for his mother before he can sleep, and a young man's half romantic and half perverse craving for the nearness of a cold-hearted flirt, these, and more sinister images, make up a confused and flowing tapestry of personal impressions. We are not sure that we want to be so completely submerged in the warm and viscous depths of somebody else's life; we become oppressed at having to surrender, again and again, to all the temptations and vices that beset a young man of weak and yielding sensibility, but then we find this sensibility controlled by a persistent will and a powerful analysing intellect. The material, however questionable in itself, is being shaped towards some generalisation about love, about selfishness and insincerity, about possessiveness, about man's experience of time, which will have the validity of mathematics. So out of the material of erotic elegy, material which by its very nature tempts the writer to sentiment, to falsification, to a flattery both of himself and of those whom he loves, Proust gradually and patiently erects a structure of pitiless objective truth.

Thus Proust, like so many great French writers of the past, like Rochefoucauld, La Bruyère, or Vauvenargues, was essentially a 'moralist': a 'moralist' in the French sense of one who seeks out the laws of human conduct, rather than in the English sense of one who lays them down. It was just because he was a moralist in this sense that he dealt so often with what, to English tastes, are 'doubtful' subjects; for men's secret vices and follies do, in fact, afford us more subtle clues, often, to the springs of their conduct than the respectable fronts which they put up to the world. There is much that is perverse in the feelings Proust analyses, and much that is trivial and vulgar in the world of high society he describes; nor is he at all sparing to the weakness of his own character. The noble values, heroism, chastity, loyalty, might seem, apart from a few attractive figures like the narrator's grandmother and his friend Robert de St Loup, to have almost no place in Proust's world. But then Proust's devotion to his art and his eagerness to arrive at the truth within the limits of his own experience of society (an 'exclusive' and interesting, but not wholly typical experience), these are heroic and chaste and loyal.

Proust's novel was translated into magnificent English prose (it is said that the English version is a finer piece of writing than the French original) by the Scottish poet and scholar and soldier, Charles Scott-Moncrieff. This translation is certainly one of the most wonderful pieces of English prose produced over the last thirty years; it might be said that no original piece of English writing, brought out during the same period, has such poetically moving and such exquisitely elaborate evocations of landscape. And here a debt is being paid back to England, for Proust learned how to describe architecture and scenery, and how to suffuse such descriptions with personal feeling, through reading and translating Ruskin. The style, the mood, the manner of Proust, as transmuted through Scott-Moncrieff's version, had a profound and far-reaching effect on English writing in the 1920s – on the prose of Virginia Woolf, for instance, which like Proust's often seems to be seeking to translate experience into thought, and, from the descriptive side more especially, the side of Proust's *bravura* accumulations of detail, on the styles of Mr Sacheverell and Sir Osbert Sitwell. It was asserted, however, by some critics, that the mood of Proust's novel, its feminine and yielding mood, had a debilitating effect on the morale of English writers during this period; that was a point, for instance, which Mr Wyndham Lewis frequently and bitterly made. Proust was certainly a great writer and a great man, but he was not exactly an influence on English literature that made for blunt directness or for manly briskness.

A novelist of much less importance than any of these, but one who also set a fashion, and who was attractive and individual as a man, was Norman Douglas. A descendant of Deeside lairds on his father's, of German noblemen on his mother's, side, educated largely in Germany, Douglas as a young man entered the British Foreign Service, served in Russia, and travelled in India. By birth and background he belonged to an international ruling class; and a good deal of the cast of his mind, his lifelong interest in such subjects as geology and botany, and his elaborate scholarship in topographical literature, was typically German rather than English. After he left the Foreign Service, his life became that of a wandering bohemian, with many friends in most European countries, but with no close conventional ties. He was sometimes in funds, but often, especially during the years of the First World War, beset both by shortage of money and by bad health. He remained, however, indomitably cheerful; his aristocratic background, combined with his mixed experience of life, made him feel as much at home drinking coffee in a Paris railway station with an urchin who had stolen his coat as dominating the conversation at a fashionable dinner party. He was well served by the strenuous and athletic constitution he had inherited from his ancestors; though his books sometimes seem to propound a rather dangerous gospel of pleasure, he found his own great pleasures in long walks, in sight seeing, in simple meals in remote Italian inns. He was never drawn into purely literary circles, and was neither a social nor an intellectual snob. He could enjoy wealth, but he could also endure poverty; an unconscious vein of stoicism in his nature corrected his epicurean philosophy, and kept him on the whole both healthy and happy during his long life. *South Wind*, his most famous novel – indeed his only 'straight' novel – set a pattern for Mr Aldous Huxley's *These Barren Leaves* and, with a more exact following, for Sir Compton Mackenzie's *Vestal Fires* and *Extraordinary Women*. The rather thin thread of the story has to do with the impact of relaxed Mediterranean morals on Anglo-Saxon respectability. But what is memorable about the novel, as about Douglas's travel books, is the gently mocking commentary on things in general, the fantastic historical digressions, and the vivid evocations of landscape. Douglas at his best wrote as good prose as any author of his time. He is not always at his best, but even at his most tiresome he has his own characteristic flavour. In his impatient individualism, his amusing old-fashioned anti-clericalism, his passionate interest in the details of 'natural philosophy,' his bluff, hearty, enjoying temperament, and his rather simple-minded belief in sensuality as the cure for most human ills, he belonged neither to our own age or the last, but to the French eighteenth century. His gift for mockery is based on a firm limitation of interests not typical of the complex, uneasy modern mind; and his gay rebelliousness on a social assurance equally, to-day, untypical. And the occasional touch of spleen or brutality in his writings recalls the eighteenth century, too. *South Wind*, which is by no means the best of his works, appeals sometimes to an appetite in immature readers for rather facile sophistication. Douglas was too much of an egoist to have the objective interest in character and situation a novelist needs; but his travel books, where he himself is frankly at the centre of the picture, are another matter, and are probably the best written in English during this century.

Section 4: The 'Gay' 1920s

One can think of the 1920s as a decade in which the English people as a whole were recovering from the shock of the First World War and hoping desperately that things would get back to 'normal': to the material comfort and moral security of the Edwardian age, to the old Victorian confidence in the steady march of human progress. For the fighting soldier, on the other hand, as we can see from the war memoirs of Siegfried Sassoon and Robert Graves, the war had left something like a permanent scar on the mind, and they would never be able to believe in the illusion of 'normality' again. And to clever and sensitive people, even if they had not been through the war, the 'contemporary situation' seemed a hopeless muddle, and they sought for diversion and satisfaction rather in the interests and pleasure of the private life. At a popular level this attitude often led to a cheap hedonism, a cheap cynicism, and an equally cheap sentimentalism. There was a good deal of cant in the 1920s; cant in particular about 'freedom' (meaning especially freedom in sexual behaviour), about 'youth,' and about the 'old men who led us into the war.' 'Youth' became so very much of a cult that even to-day reviewers in English papers generally refer to us as brilliant representatives of the younger generation until we reach the age of fifty when, if we are sufficiently distinguished, we may gradually mature into respected elder figures or even, if we are lucky, grand old men. This cult of youth was satirised, with his usual pungency, by Mr Wyndham Lewis in *The Apes of God* and *The Doom of Youth*: he saw behind it a cult of immaturity, which he felt was being encouraged by sinister interests for ends of their own. For apart from all the other and more romantic and attractive characteristics of 'youth,' two obvious ones are that it is credulous and docile; the violent movements of our time, as well as many of the merely silly ones, have gained half their adherents at least from the young, the emotionally and intellectually immature, and a good proportion of the other half from older people who jealously preserve their immaturity or 'refuse to grow old.' As for the new sexual freedom, it was sometimes seriously defended, but often treated as a natural result of the war. Mrs Viveash, in Aldous Huxley's *Antic Hay*, is excused for breaking many hearts because her own heart was broken when the man she 'really' loved was killed in the war; and the war is often also brought forward in the fiction of the 1920s as an excuse for unmannerly or neurotic behaviour by young men. It was too convenient an excuse altogether for all kinds of personal weakness, and the more popular types of 'advanced' writing of that decade are vitiated by a soft streak of silliness and self-pity.

It would be wrong, however, to dismiss the whole decade as a period of rather brittle frivolity and of rather damp moral, or immoral, exhibitionism. The more vulgar and blatant symptoms of the age's unrest did, in fact, point to a general unease which was felt, at a deeper level, by wise and sensitive people. There was a lack of anything very stable outside the individual for him to hang on to. The social background was no longer a comforting, protective enclosure; the writer was flung back on his own sensibility – his anxieties, his curiosities, his pleasures and his dreams.

In the best novels of the 1920s, what we must look for therefore, is not a broad and comprehensive picture of society but rather an individual attempt at preserving personal coherence of attitude against a social background that is fragmentary and confused. The novelist of the 1920s, we might say, is not looking through a window at the world, he is seeing his own face and the faces of others in a mirror; the foreground is very clear to him, the background blurs away. Thus it could be said, even, that the three most distinguished novelists of the 1920s in England, Virginia Woolf, Aldous Huxley, and D.H. Lawrence, are none of them typically novelists: Huxley being essentially a philosopher, Mrs Woolf a poet of mood and sensation, D.H. Lawrence the prophet of a new and personal religion of dark emotional drive. Moreover, each of these novelists speaks not for the whole man but for a separate layer of the human structure; Huxley for the intellect, Mrs Woolf for the sensibilities, and Lawrence for the emotions. It is as if one could only think, the second only sensitively perceive, the third only express the most massive impulse of the moment. This is not to say that these are not good and improving writers. Aldous Huxley and Virginia Woolf have both very distinguished gifts, and Lawrence has genius; though we may doubt whether that genius ever found adequate formal expression.

Reading Mrs Woolf, we must not be chiefly interested in the active clash of character or the intricate working out of plot. What she does convey with almost unequalled delicacy is the complicated 'sensation of living,' of living from moment to moment, each moment having its own distinctive complexity of colour, texture, shape. Her characters do not engage other characters in overt dramatic conflict; rather, they wander through the park, looking at the play of light on leaves and grass, observe the dogs and nursemaids, the banana peel on the gravel path, the crinkled face of a bedraggled old man on a bench, while some tenuous but profound *inner* conflict plays itself out within their own selves in terms of this pattern of sensation. What bounds the human creature for Mrs Woolf is not the edge of his skin but the outer limits of his perceptions; and thus it is harder for her characters, each tightly if impalpably closed in an exquisite world of his own, to communicate or to come into any sort of collision than for characters more crudely conceived. For my view of the sunset does not communicate or collide with yours.

Perhaps the most solid and real of all Mrs Woolf's novels is *To the Lighthouse* where she used the experiences of her own childhood. She was the daughter of the great Victorian mountaineer, rationalist, critic, and scholar, Sir Leslie Stephen, and thus a member of one of these great families of the Victorian intellectual aristocracy – the Huxleys, the Stracheys, the Darwins, the Haldanes are others – which, generation after generation, have produced an extraordinarily large number of brilliant and public-spirited men and women. In the liberal atmosphere of Victorian England this kind of intellectual aristocracy had established itself almost as deeply in the country's life as the old aristocracy of blood and certainly more deeply than the new aristocracy of money. Thus, in everything she writes, Virginia Woolf is inescapably a scholar and a gentlewoman. Behind all her subtle and exact sensibility to shades of mood, there is, moreover, the background of her father's sturdy agnosticism and of the firm, if rather sad, rationalism of the Cambridge school of philosophy. She was one of a group of writers – Lord Keynes, Roger Fry, Clive Bell, were others – who were all influenced to a greater or lesser degree by the brilliant work of the Cambridge philosopher, G. E. Moore. Moore is a philosopher of great technical importance, whose work I have not the time, nor for that matter the competence, to analyse here, but his importance as an influence on these writers (the Bloomsbury group as they were often called, since many of them at one time or another had flats in that agreeable district of London) was that instead of emphasising some belief about God or some theory about history he tended to emphasise the importance of good and pleasant states of feeling in the individual human life. In all the writers who were influenced by him there is a passionate striving towards a clarity of good-will and understanding, and towards a perception of the passing but real beauty of the world. The good is to be found in individual experience and, though men and women are mortal, the good is not less real.

This refined and difficult but by no means sentimental philosophy gives the work of this Bloomsbury group its own dignity and pathos. They accepted the death of the individual as a final death and yet it was in the experience of the individual that they looked for what values there are in life; the values being *really* there, not merely a projection of individual feelings; this gave them a rigorous and stringent attitude towards all kinds of stupidity, unnecessary failure, and general sloppiness in human living. It robbed them perhaps of that charity which accepts failure as part of the essence of the human condition. There is not exactly a lack of warmth in their writing, but there is sometimes a rather frightening assumption that most human living is mere muddle and waste, and that only a few successful lives, those of intellectuals and artists, of truly 'civilised' people in short, really 'count': though of course at the same time the lives of 'outsiders' may, *for* the civilised people, have a value of pathos or comedy. At the same time, most of these writers, perhaps all of them, were humanitarian in their social attitudes. Their humanitarianism did not spring, however, from any self-identification with the struggling and suffering masses of the people, but rather from an impatience with what seemed to them irrational and untidy and destructive in ordinary life. Their pity was real but it was a little cold.

In Mrs Woolf's *To the Lighthouse* there is, as I have said, more warmth and body than in any of her other novels, because it is based on strong and deep memories of the sense of community in the family; and a sense of community of that sort, great as her gift for friendship was, was not something that she was ever really to find in any later setting in which she moved. In other novels of hers, one is too much aware of her condition as a brilliant solitary, guessing rather than grasping at the reality of other human lives. Thus in her brilliant experimental novel, *The Waves*, the characters present themselves not through conversation or action but through a series of soliloquies intended to give the essence of their histories and the key to their natures. But all the characters have too much the voice, too much the attitude, of Mrs Woolf herself; one feels that the book is a long monologue and that it would have been better as a straight piece of poetic introspection.

In spite of all their beauty and charm, the atmosphere of Mrs Woolf's novels is often rather a sad one. What she is most deeply aware of is what a contemporary poet, Mr Louis MacNeice, calls 'the loneliness,' the 'incommunicableness' of life. The moods and feelings which so obsess her characters are never, for reasons that I have already tried to explain, adequately communicated to the other characters; each lives in a lovely but almost completely self-enclosed world. She made one attempt, however, at a straightforward fictitious narrative in the traditional sense, the novel *Orlando*. This is a kind of affectionate parody of the historical biographies of her friend, Lytton Strachey. One might take the book at first for a straight historical biography until one realises, with a start, that the hero, an adolescent at the beginning of the book, has still hardly grown any older though we have covered the reigns of Queen Elizabeth, King James, and King Charles I. This scheme enables Mrs Woolf to give a brilliant picture of English social and literary life through three centuries and to indulge her peculiar, pungent sense of gaiety and fun – a side of her which does not get sufficient scope in most of her 'straight' novels. Perhaps indeed her essential gifts were not so much those of a novelist as those of a poet, a meditative and yet alertly observant poet, for whom mood and scene are one, and those of a literary critic with a wonderful power of bringing the past to life again. She was one of the fine stylists of her period, a wonderfully delicate and exact mistress of a just slightly mannered English prose. A sense of the changing and coloured flow of life was given form in that prose, by a wry, sad irony and a gift for implying, without expressing, passion; regret and longing were always held beautifully in check by an English gentlewoman's sense of decorum. Yet though Mrs Woolf will be read eagerly in years to come, she will not be read exactly for the picture she gives of ordinary English life, but rather for the revelation of her own rare and very beautiful personality. One feels that she writes fiction because, in her own period, the sort of poetry that she would have wanted to write was no longer a real possibility; she expresses a personal vision, and she expresses it in a poetical way.

Aldous Huxley is a much more uneven writer than Virginia Woolf, sometimes a rather flat, tiresome, didactic writer. Possibly his earliest novels, *Crome Yellow*, *Antic Hay*, *These Barren Leaves*, are his most charming. They are full of wit and sadness and a zest for caricature and an extravagantly youthful display of learning. The world they depict is in one sense a narrow one, the world partly of English country houses, and partly of London's literary Bohemia. Nearly all the characters are people with large unearned incomes, or artists, or writers; nobody appears to have a routine job to do, and thus everybody has leisure for endless discussions that make many pages of these novels read less like ordinary fiction than fragments from a philosophical debate. These early novels at least of Mr Huxley's are not, however, by any means so arid and abstract as such a description might suggest. They have the interest of satire. What Mr Huxley likes to show is how people's ideas and principles somehow fail to square with the actual lives they lead. He displays very amusingly various types of intellectual pretension and looks sharply about him for insincerity and falsehood. Some of his novels, particularly *Point Counter-Point*, have a considerable historical interest in that they offer us hardly disguised portraits of contemporaries such as D.H. Lawrence and John Middleton Murry. In his handling of tragic or violent incidents (of which he becomes much fonder in his later novels), Mr Huxley tends to be melodramatic and not nearly so convincing as when describing bright chatter at literary parties. He is the sort of man who understands people through their ideas but who is rather at a loss when he has to deal with the more direct and simple feelings and emotions and the tense situations that can arise from them.

The theme of many of these novels of his, perhaps the one essential theme of all of them, is the search for a workable faith in the bewildering world we live in to-day. In some of his novels, for instance, in *Point Counter-Point*, he seems to be trying to believe in a creed rather like that of D.H. Lawrence – the creed of what he calls a 'life-worshipper.' But Rampion, who stands for Lawrence in *Point Counter-Point*, is on the whole an unconvincing figure (Lawrence thought so himself), and more naturally and sincerely Huxley seeks salvation in a mystical attitude, one involving the renunciation of ordinary human appetites and passions and especially involving the renunciation of ordinary human egoism. The self is the great enemy and a state of non-attachment is the thing to be aimed at. That is Mr Huxley's present position.

It has been arrived at, however, after a long and difficult journey. Mr Huxley's novels express his own personal dilemma, as a man with a destructive sense of irony, and an extremely sceptical and critical intellect, who nevertheless feels very deeply the need for something to ground his life upon. Because he is so pre-eminently an intellectual, whatever faith he finally accepts must be one justifiable by logical argument; not merely by appeals to feeling or tradition. Mr Huxley in fact is so exclusively an intellectual that he has a certain squeamish horror of whatever lies below the level of the intellect, of the body with its needs and appetites, of the feelings and emotions in their raw state. This horror reflects itself in his picture of a scientifically planned society of the future, at once hygienic and inhuman (a Wellsian Utopia seen from another point of view), *Brave New World*. Because of this horror of the flesh, even the more or less settled religious attitude to life which Mr Huxley has now arrived at seems a somewhat joyless and pallid thing. One feels sometimes that he finds it easy to love God just because he finds it difficult to love men.

From a purely literary point of view, it might be contended that Mr Huxley has written too much – too many novels, essays, discursive travel books – so that he has not conserved his talents as he ought to have, and that in his later writing especially one is too obtrusively aware of repetitive stylistic mannerisms; there is a touch in a good deal of what he writes of the schoolmaster wagging a finger and pointing at the blackboard and making at regular intervals little propitiatory jokes – not always terribly good ones. Yet at its best Mr Huxley's writing expresses the temper of an urbane, civilised, and honourably serious mind. And in his earlier writing particularly he is often a genuine wit.

It is much more difficult to give a contemporary judgment on D.H. Lawrence than on either Mrs Woolf or Mr Huxley. There is power in his writing, undoubtedly, but power put to disturbing uses. Let me quote a passage from a short story:

> At a certain moment the men who are really living will come beseeching to put their lives into the hands of the greater men among them, beseeching the greater men to take the sacred responsibility of power . . . At last the masses will come to such men and say, 'You are greater than we. Be our lords. Take our life and our death in your hands, and dispose of us according to your will. Because we see a light in your face, and a burning on your mouth . . .' Ah, but my chosen aristocrat would say to those who chose him: 'If you choose me, you give up forever your right to judge me. If you have truly chosen to follow me, you have thereby rejected all your right to criticize me. You can no longer either approve or disapprove of me. You have performed the sacred act of choice. Henceforth you can only obey.'

That shows Lawrence's prophetic power (he is not speaking through his own mouth, however, but through that of a character in one of his stories); he is prophesying what the *morale* of a movement like National Socialism in Germany will be; and the passage is beautifully written, with power and simplicity – almost too beautifully, in fact, for Lawrence fails to realise not only that what he is prophesying will prove hateful but that there is something hateful in the motives of his hero, the German aristocrat Count Psanek, who prophesies it. He recognises a strong and sincere emotion, yields to it, and refuses to make judgments about good or evil, right or wrong. Or rather it is only the strong and sincere emotion (and an emotion, so very often in his stories, involving either the will to hurt or the will to dominate) that is 'good' to him. Thus from any more complex or more balancing point of view he is objectively 'wrong' in all his practical attitudes.

Lawrence's social background was very different from that of Mrs Woolf or Mr Huxley; where they came from the English mandarin class, Lawrence was the son of a miner, his mother being of a slightly higher social class than his father, who resented her 'refinement'; so that he was brought up in an atmosphere of struggle for dominance between man and wife, with his sympathies tugged sometimes towards his father's rowdiness and sometimes towards his mother's hymn-singing. His mother's Noncomformist piety gave him that serious Puritan streak which remained with him all his life, his father's humiliations and brutalities made him return again and again to the theme of the man of little education, of few words, who dominates a more subtle and complex woman by the dumb force of his masculinity. More generally, it can be said that the English lower classes have much less of that reticence and reserve which we think of as typically English than the middle classes; they are more direct and passionate in their expressions of love and hate, less likely to be argued out of a prejudice, and that directness and that obstinacy come out in everything Lawrence wrote. He felt a coldness and lack of true contact in English middle-class life, particularly but not exclusively where sexual relations were concerned. *Lady Chatterley's Lover*, the frankest of his novels from this point of view, is by no means his best one. Indeed, it is perhaps his worst. But it was by no means a pornographic book in Lawrence's own intention, but rather a passionate plea for honesty and frankness in the relations between men and women and for the recognition of the body's dignity and its needs. For Lawrence, the most important thing in life was something in people far deeper, less conscious, and less controllable than their outward attitudes and personalities; in a letter to Aldous Huxley, he once explained how he was interested in human beings at the elemental level – at the level, so to say, of the basic carbon that can be formed by different kinds of pressure into coal or diamonds, not at the level of the final complex product itself. Not, 'What have you made of yourself?' but, 'Of what sort of fundamental stuff are you made?' is the question he would ask about people. Surface personality or 'attitude' he thought of as being largely pose or a matter of social convention; what he looked for were the deep drives, and therefore he instinctively disliked invalids and cripples, in whom he felt that these drives have gone sick, and perhaps rather romanticised gamekeepers, miners, all kinds of healthy inarticulate men, in whom the expression of their emotional and physical need is direct.

He wanted, that is, people to be more 'primitively' themselves than they can be, really, in a civilised community; and he spent much of his life looking for the sort of simple life he wanted, in places like Sardinia, and Sicily, and Mexico, but probably never quite finding it. The wisdom he was looking for was no wisdom of the mind but what he would have called a 'wisdom of the blood,' and because of that deep sensibility of his to what is instinctive and natural no English writer of our time has been able to describe animals, or children, or natural scenes, or the basic drives of love or hate between persons, with so much power. But, though he is undeniably a writer of genius, he is also a strikingly uneven writer. In a tedious way he shovels into many of his novels conversations, scenes, personalities, taken from his private experience, with little regard for the shape of the book as a whole. He rants at the reader, he harangues him. The special vocabulary in which he expresses his deepest convictions, the vocabulary of the wisdom in the blood and the impulses in the solar plexus and the ganglia, is, to a reader of my own generation at least, at once philosophically absurd and poetically unconvincing. For all that, Lawrence's ideas are not to be dismissed in a hurry any more than his art is. He has perhaps only one novel which is completely satisfactory from the point of view of structure as well as texture, *Sons and Lovers*, but the short story was less of a strain on his powers of construction, and many of his short stories are masterpieces; so are his travel books *Sea and Sardinia* and *Etruscan Places* and his one critical book, *Classic American Literature*, very oddly indeed as it is written by the conventional standards of literary criticism, is enduringly vital and suggestive. His poems, from a formal point of view, are rough and unfinished, like, as Mr. T. S. Eliot has suggested, pages from the rough working note-book of a great poet; but his genius shines through them. As for his philosophy, in spite of the stridency of his manner and the claptrap of his vocabulary, there is something to be said, after all, for his belief that if the deepest natural impulses are habitually thwarted the whole superstructure of civilisation that has been built on them will gradually go wrong. His weakness as a thinker was in not allowing enough place in his scheme of things for the intellect; which, after all, *is* part of the human complex; and in supposing that in our world to-day we can really get on without it. The power of human reason has often been perverted to wrong ends, but for all that man is a rational as well as an appetitive, a passionate, and an imaginative being. The kind of animal harmony of which Lawrence dreamt is not something ultimately compatible with the dignity of the human condition. We must restrain our appetites and passions, we must cultivate self-control, and seek self-knowledge. Lawrence is full of energy; he has perhaps more energy than any other writer of his generation, but it is too often a blind energy. Sometimes it leads him to a wonderfully acute and tender perceptiveness, sometimes it makes him bang his head angrily against a stone wall. Nevertheless, in his own exasperating, untidy way he is perhaps the greatest and most significant prose writer of these troubled ten years.

Three other minor but still very significant writers of the 1920s should not be passed over in silence. One of them represents the extreme development of that dandified and disconcerting frivolity which was one aspect, for instance, of the early work of Aldous Huxley; the other two, in their different ways, represent firm reactions against that cult of the 'amusing.' The first of these three, Ronald Firbank, was the grandson of a railway magnate who had sprung from the working classes, and the son of a typically conventional middle-class Tory M.P.; in three generations, Firbank himself had somehow managed to acquire the appearance and attitudes of a decadent aristocrat. He had a lean, bony, exaggerated face, out of which still started the same masterful nose that had looked out from between the broad cushiony cheeks of his grandfather and that had given some dignity to his father's air of vapid complacency. Firbank's face, with its slightly Red Indian look, has been preserved by Augustus John and Wyndham Lewis, and his high thin voice, his hysterical giggle, his pathological shyness, his wriggling walk, and the mixture of brilliance and inconsequence in his conversation have been evoked by acquaintances like Lord Berners and Sir Osbert Sitwell. For a limited circle, those who frequented the Eiffel Tower and the Café Royal – London's wealthier Bohemia, in fact – he became something like a public figure, a mascot of the decade, without apparently ever making an intimate friend. Younger writers like the Sitwell brothers found him extraordinarily amusing, but only for the first ten minutes; his incoherence, his inability to conduct conversations except at a series of tangents, then became tiresome. Most of the descriptions of him suggest a high-grade mental defective with a streak of genius. He was a profoundly solitary person. He seems to have thought at one time that the Roman Catholic Church held the answer to his problems, but nobody in that Church seems to have worked for his conversion or watched over his morals; just as, though apparently he was an alcoholic who hardly ever ate, none of his acquaintances seems to have thought it worth while to bully him into going into a nursing home. He died at last in solitude in an Italian hotel, using what was left of his money to ward himself off from these human contacts which at once frightened and fascinated him.

Firbank's life was one of self-absorption and unhappy vanity; the saving elements in it seem to have been his deep affection for his mother and his genuine and fantastic sense of the absurd. The limited range of his experience helps to explain the peculiar quality of his novels. He retained his precarious balance by concentrating with an almost religious earnestness on the 'amusing'; in his world, to be obvious and to be serious were equal solecisms. His characters are seen neither in action, in profile, nor in depth, but in teasing fragments, through a haze of cocktail chatter. His pages are full of the oddest snatches of conversation, impossible clues never to be followed up. The smart dresses, the overheated rooms, the expensive bric-à-brac are on the same plane as the people, contribute as much to the total atmosphere, and show the same magpie-like collector's instinct as the scraps of fashionable recorded slang. The tales are fantasies but they spring from a deep feeling for what is really brittle and trivial in life. The heroes and heroines of the tales are, like Firbank himself, victims of a Narcissus complex, projecting fantasies, and automatically rejecting the fantasies of others. Everybody talks 'brilliantly,' nobody listens; beneath the high, thin giggling, there is the pathos of profound isolation. In spite of a life which seemed calculated to destroy him physically and morally, in spite of a perverse and cold schoolboyish fondness for equivocal subject matter, Firbank retained to the last an odd innocence of vision; his stories really belong on the same shelf with *Peter Rabbit* and *Through the Looking Glass* rather than in the case-book of some pathologist of literature like Professor Mario Praz. Like the books Alice liked, they are 'full of conversations' and the narrator wanders through them with an open-eyed Alician alertness. But for the more philistine reader, Firbank's puritan concentration on the 'amusing' soon becomes a strain; the writing, like the talk, is wonderful for about ten minutes at a time. Then life begins to leak away; one becomes tired as when, at a very bright and noisy party, one realises one is not going to get to know anybody any better.

The novels of L.H.Myers provide a kind of indirect commentary on Firbank's world. The best known of them, those collected under the title *The Root and the Flower*, are set in the India of the Moguls. They are not historical novels in the strict sense, though based on profound historical knowledge. Their theme is the spiritual life and how far, if at all, it can be adequately embodied in social institutions.

Myers's very unpleasant portrait of the great Mogul's degenerate son, Daniyal, and his court of buffoons and flatterers, 'the Camp,' devoted to art, gossip, trivial sensuality, mild malice, and amateur theatricals, is a criticism of the kind of aesthetic 'civilisation' for which Firbank lived and died. The frivolity of this mode of life, which refuses to make a choice between good and evil, seems to Myers more corrupting than the sincere choice of evil itself. There are, he feels, worse things than brutality. But serious power politicians are also treated harshly, and it seems to have been Myers's feeling that spiritual insight is denatured or deformed when embodied in institutions, and the representative of spiritual wisdom in his book, the Guru, is the enemy of institutional religion. The Guru's belief is also in original goodness rather than in original sin. It is interesting to learn, from an excellent article by Mr Walter Allen, that Myers had both a certain sympathy for Communism, a movement through which he felt a fresh wind of the spirit might be blowing, and an intense dislike of the Anglo-Catholicism of Mr T. S. Eliot. It is with spiritual rather than ordinary social problems that Myers is concerned. His characters are princes or courtiers, free from ordinary immediate frustrations, and the central problem for him is what, for the man who has the opportunity of a full and rich experience, is the good life. It seems, for Myers, to involve renunciation, but a renunciation that may be very long delayed. More generally, he is more impressed with the fertility of the basic human impulses than with the instability, which he is also aware of, of human institutions; his historical philosophy might be described as a kind of optimistic fatalism, and does in fact seem to apply better to Indian history than to the modern industrialised West. He is a writer who gives a general impression of wisdom, but whose wisdom may seem rather to lack particular relevance to our own affairs.

T. F. Powys resembles Myers, at least the Myers of *The Root and the Flower*, in that his books are essentially tracts or allegories; they have been described by Mr Empson as Buddhist death-plays with Christian imagery. Their setting is always rural, and the texture of the prose rather consciously recalls both Jane Austen, a little superficially, and more profoundly Bunyan. The characters tend to have Bunyanesque names, like Lord Titball, and to embody like Bunyan's a single personified human drive, often an unpleasant one, such as lust, stupidity, cruelty, or greed. The good characters, who are sometimes clergymen, are usually hated because of their goodness and come to a bad end. If one took these novels as realistic descriptions of country life in our day, one would feel profoundly relieved that one lived in town, but the unpleasant subject-matter is balanced by a gentleness of attitude, a tenderness for the rural scene, and a sincere if melancholy mysticism. Thus in *Mr Weston's Good Wine*, the wine is death, and we drink it to escape from this vale of troubles. Mr Powys is an excellent but minor artist. He has not Miss Austen's actuality; and the religious attitude which he expresses allegorically is not, like Bunyan's, that of the social group he realises for us but that of himself as an isolated and untypical observer. His mild insistence, moreover, on the brutality of rural life, pungent at first, becomes a mannerism, and lends itself to parodies, like that of *Cold Comfort Farm*. Yet he has created a world of his own; and, at his own level, he is one of the most genuine artists whom the history of the English novel can boast of in this century. It is not his fault that his art springs from his sensitivity to the life of a rural England, no longer proud and self-confident as in Bunyan's time or Miss Austen's, no longer central to the general life of the country, but in moral decay.

Section 5: The 'Serious' 1930s

If the 1920s were a decade when a writer tended to turn away from the everyday problems of social living and political choice, the circumstances of the 1930s forced his attention back in that direction. In 1929, there was the great Wall Street slump with its disastrous repercussions everywhere in Europe. Unemployment and distress, as well as militant nationalism, helped Hitler to power in Germany in 1933. His policy of rearmament put the Germans back to work but threatened the peace and the liberties of Europe. Later in the decade, the Spanish Civil War and the Italian invasion of Ethiopia forced writers and intellectuals to take definite political sides, divided their sympathies, aroused their passions, as no comparable set of political events in the 1920s had done. On top of all this, there was, as these ten years progressed, a gradually growing and intensifying and, alas, only too well justified fear that the Spanish episode, the Ethiopian adventure, the fighting in Manchuria, were perhaps mere preludes to a Second and more disastrous World War. Thus the typical and important literature of the 1930s is a literature of topical urgency, reflecting a feeling of tension and an awareness of crisis.

Since 1917, Russia had been very much isolated from the Western World. Her very isolation, the little that was known in any exact or reliable detail about the working of her new system of government was likely, on the principle of *omne ignotum pro magnifico*, to engage and tantalise the imagination particularly of the young. A young man growing up in Great Britain in the 1930s, with no certain prospect of a job in front of him, and an all too possible prospect of being caught up in another great war, with many instances of social distress brought sharply home to him by such incidents as the Hunger Marches, was likely to have his confidence in the British gift for 'muddling through,' in the virtues of compromise and improvisation, generally, rather badly dented. He would find himself thinking with interest and curiosity of this large country, Russia, in which, in however ruthless a fashion, the problems of preserving full employment and keeping production swinging upwards did seem to have been solved. Very few English writers in the 1930s actually became members of the Communist Party and those who did remained, usually, members for only a short time. But it could at least be said that just as the Roman Catholic Church in the 1890s provided a kind of focus of attraction for writers who in the end may have never taken the final step towards conversion, so, in the 1930s, did various versions of Marxist doctrine provide this kind of focus for many English intellectuals.

A well-known London publisher, Victor Gollancz, founded the Left Book Club, which besides publishing a magazine for its members sold them every month a book on some aspect of Socialist, or at least militant anti-Fascist, politics. If many young men of middle-class, or even upper-middle-class or actually aristocratic upbringing, were driven towards the extreme Left in these years, the same unsettlement and discontentment was driving others to the extreme Right. Sir Oswald Mosley's British Union of Fascists copied the Black Shirts of the Italian Fascisti but propagated, following a rising tide, the ideas rather of German National Socialism. A wider reaction than any of these was, as a natural reaction against the Fascist and Nazi glorification of war, a passionate but rather sentimental pacifism. This could be seen in the growth of the Peace Pledge Union, whose members were committed to taking up, in any future war, the position of conscientious objectors, but the same people who joined the Peace Pledge Union were often, misled by the amiable confusion of their enthusiasms, those who called most loudly for the carrying out of a policy of Collective Security and the imposition on Italy, in connection with the Ethiopian episode, of 'sanctions' (given the limiting condition, naturally ineffective sanctions) 'short of war.' Political meetings in these ten years in Great Britain had a more violent and dramatic flavour than is common in

British politics. Brawls between Fascists and Communists, and the beating up of interrupters at Fascist meetings, were common. The outbreak of the war itself, which pulled the British people together into one team again, as perhaps nothing else would have done, showed to what an extent all these domestic episodes were mere froth on the surface. But the young man who clung (as I, for instance, remember clinging myself during these years) to the old middle-of-the-road attitude, to the faith that Great Britain would in the long run solve her own problems in her own way, and did not need to borrow any foreign cheapjack remedies, still felt the emotional tug of these more melodramatic, more vividly coloured, and fundamentally of course infinitely less sane and humane policies of the extreme Right and Left. It seemed, in a sense, weak and old-fashioned of the intellectual to refuse to adopt bitter and drastic attitudes.

It might be said that two English poets, Roy Campbell and John Cornford, who fought in Spain in these years on opposite sides (Campbell as a Carlist, Cornford as a Communist) represented in their different ways the *same* response to the troubles and anxieties of the period – the response of a fierce radicalism, whether of the Left or Right, that wanted to be rid for good and all of what seemed old-fashioned, inefficient temporising. And of these two, it should be noted, Campbell, who had worked all his life with his hands, as cowboy, fisherman, farmer, was much more genuinely the 'man of the people' and Cornford, the son of a famous Greek scholar, much less so. For theoretical Marxism did, on the whole, tend to make its appeal rather to intellectuals themselves. Theoretical Marxism appealed to a sense of guilt in these upper middle classes: that sense of guilt sprang from a feeling, among young men like Cornford, that they ought not to be able to lead comfortable and satisfying lives while so many of their fellow-countrymen were condemned to poverty and insecurity. Thus those who, in the 1930s, accepted the myth of the revolution were not those who would have made the revolution, had there been one. The English Labour movement, in so far as it is a genuine working class movement (which it basically and centrally is) has always been moderate, slow-moving, sure-footed, and cautious.

Thus, we can say that the best English novels of the 1930s reflect a state of social tension. They can be divided, perhaps, into four main categories:

1) There is firstly what one may call the symbolic melodrama, or literary thriller. Novels of this sort use the mechanism of the old-

fashioned tale of crime and adventure to bring across to the reader a vivid sense of the insecure, frightening, dangerous state of the contemporary world.

2) Secondly, there were what one might call 'documentary' novels, novels in which the writer made use of his own personal experience and observation of various social situations to underline, usually in a rather quieter way, that same lesson of the world's insecurity and the need for some positive and constructive political faith.

3) Thirdly, there were what one might call novels of social allegory, novels in which a simple, sometimes fantastic tale was used to state and illustrate some troublesome contemporary problem, such as, for instance, that of the correct relation between the idea of tradition and the other idea of making society completely over anew, starting from scratch, or, if not exactly from scratch, on the basis of some doctrinaire notion either of how social change ought to take place or of what a truly 'rational' society would be.

4) Fourthly, there were novels written superficially in terms of comedy or even of farce, but with an underlying very disturbing note of bitterness which emphasised the ruthlessness, the nerviness, the unhappiness, the lack of purpose and the lack of love, in much contemporary British life.

Let us take these four types of novels in order.

The great master of the novel of symbolic melodrama was undoubtedly Mr Graham Greene. Greene divides his novels into what he calls 'serious' performances and 'entertainments,' but both kinds have a similar basic pattern. Both kinds are exercises in the very old narrative theme of the hunting down of a man: but the story is not seen, as in the ordinary detective novel, from the point of view of the hunters, but from that of the hunted man. Greene's 'entertainments,' like *Stamboul Train*, *A Gun for Sale*, or *The Ministry of Fear* are, as far as the plots go, plain, old-fashioned thrillers, full of spies, and secret documents, and chases in the dark, and murders. His mastery of the thriller form, and his ability to give it a wide significance, can be seen in his excellent scenario for that fast, gripping British film, *The Third Man*. On the other hand, in a fairly recent 'serious' novel, *The Heart of the Matter*, there is no violence but merely a study of the chain of events which leads a devout and good man, out of an excessive regard for others, first to commit what he regards as mortal sin (he commits adultery partly out of compassion for a lonely woman, and then takes communion without going to confession, so that his wife will not be upset by suspecting his adultery) and secondly, as a way out of what seems to him an utterly hopeless situation, to commit suicide thus cutting himself off completely, according to Catholic doctrine, from the possibility of a final act of contrition. The poor man is driven down to hell in fact by his excessive desire to do always 'the decent' – that is, the obliging, the unobtrusive, the self-surrendering – 'thing': though Greene, of course, points out that the mercy of God is infinitely mysterious and that we do not know whether it may not be stretched to cover even this odd case. But if it were possible for a man to decide to damn himself by rule and method, Greene's hero has almost done so. Yet he is an intrinsically 'nicer' person probably than most of those who read about him.

For Greene, in fact, who is a convert to Roman Catholicism, the ideas of 'good' and 'evil' (understood in some absolute, final, almost mystical sense), are much more important than the ideas of 'niceness' and 'decency' or even of 'right' and 'wrong.' Right and wrong for Greene are matters of social decorum, or of some traditional code accepted without thinking, but the choice of good and evil is a terrible, significant, and final choice presented to the individual soul. Good and evil, moreover, have nothing to do with respectability or success. Thus, in one of Greene's best novels, *England Made Me*, the powers of goodness, or rather the difficult final choice of the good, are represented by two weak and ineffective characters, Anthony, the hero, and his friend Minty.

Anthony is the sort of typical black sheep of a shabby-genteel English family, whose great preoccupation throughout his boyhood has been 'keeping up appearances.' Tragically, that has become Anthony's preoccupation, too. He has drifted about the world, from one job to another, and he has lost job after job through petty dishonesty (so that he can have money for drinks and cards, and take his place in the local community), or for boasting or lying (pretending to have gone to an important public school that he has not gone to, or to know people he doesn't know, or to have seen military service that he hasn't seen). He is handsome and quite attractive but essentially rather ordinary and his whole life has been an attempt to compensate for his ordinariness by trying to appear more socially important, more of a 'gentleman,' more of a 'man of the world' than he really is. He is a pathetic product, in fact, of English snobbery which will not allow him to be honestly, decently, rather drably himself. He has an essentially weak will and few assets other than a good appearance, a rather feeble cunning, and an undoubted sex-appeal.

Minty is not even a real black sheep. He comes from an excellent family, he has been to a good school: but he is a misfit and an eccentric, insignificant in appearance and slovenly in dress, the sort of person who just does not fit into the social pattern, who cannot 'do' anything effectively, and who is a constant source of embarrassment to his family and friends. He is physically a weakling, incapable of earning a living; with a mixture of prudence and heartlessness his family have provided him with a small pension so long as he lives in a Scandinavian city and does not come home to bother them. He is the typical 'remittance man,' but with none of the remittance man's traditional vices. He is not a man of scandalous life, he is merely irritating and futile. Naturally he is very lonely, mildly resentful of his social ostracism (he rather maliciously keeps up contacts with the British Ambassador in this Scandinavian city who, as an old schoolfellow, and in any case the representative of the interests of the British community there, can never quite finally 'drop' him). He is also pathetically eager to make friends and opens his heart at once to Anthony. The great consolation of Minty's life is, however, not his earthly friendships but his religious faith. Even his devoutness, however, expresses itself to the outward eye in a finicky old-maidish fashion and nobody takes it very seriously. Minty, nevertheless, is, we discover as the plot develops, an almost wholly good man; without self-will, without any deep in-grained malice, a man almost totally devoted, in spite of his weakness and insignificance, to a genuine vision of goodness, and at the same time a man with a terribly acute and painful intuition of evil. He is a kind of crippled saint – a man whose real goodness can never find adequate outward expression, because of the terrible sense of inferiority which crushes his spirit and makes him miserable.*

Anthony, in the story, when we first meet him, has not yet made his final choice between good and evil. He has come to the Scandinavian city where Minty lives because his sister, who has always dominated him, is living there, too. A very rich, powerful, wicked, and un-scrupulous financial magnate is in love with her and wants to marry her. She does not care greatly for him (she is a cold, capable, self-centred woman, her one great love being for Anthony) but she is willing to

* Few modern 'serious' novelists tell a story in a more straightforward way than Mr Greene, but one's interpretation of the story will be affected by one's point of view. I once heard a British Council lecturer describe the character of Minty as a terrible study of degeneracy and evil – and he is, of course, the sort of Englishman abroad whom official circles find embarrassing. But neurosis, though it may be even more of a nuisance, is not wickedness.

accept his advances, if, in this way, she can help her 'little brother.' The magnate gives Anthony a job as a kind of secretary and is friendly and nice to him for a time, and Anthony for the first time in his life enjoys that sense of wealth and social importance which he has always hankered after. But he has not reckoned with his own conscience. Some of the jobs that the magnate asks him to do strike him as rather dirty jobs, and finally when he is asked to behave very brutally to some poor man whom the magnate has ruined, and who is demanding an interview, he protests. It is not, he says in his weak but definite way, the decent thing to do. The magnate is angry, though he conceals his anger. He is deeply in love with Anthony's sister and he is in any case jealous of her affection for Anthony and the time she devotes to him; but especially he is not the sort of man who can put up with somebody always around him whose mere presence implies a perpetual moral reproach. So the magnate has a henchman of his push Anthony into a river on a foggy night. Minty guesses that a murder has been committed, and lets the murderer know that he guesses, but can do nothing about it. The marriage of Anthony's sister and the magnate goes ahead. Thus, in this story we see evil triumphant in the world, and yet the story is not wholly a story of mere loss, because good in the end has been triumphant in Anthony's soul – he has taken his stand for righteousness – and that is more important to Mr Greene, who thinks in terms of eternity, than the mere passing successes of the wicked in this life.

Mr Greene does not heavily underline the moral implications of his stories, as I have been doing here. His novels are written in a brisk, unpretentious, sharply visualised style (so that one remembers many scenes, but perhaps no sentences): and there is quick cutting from one episode to another as in the cinema, there are no long, dull, ruminative or padded passages. This technique, which assures that the reader is never bored, has nevertheless perhaps something a little mechanical about it. The words are almost too transparent and I am not sure that one really loses much by seeing one of Mr Greene's stories as a film instead of reading it, always supposing that, like *The Third Man*, the film is adequately made. One tends to think of Mr Greene, in fact, along with the great directors of cinema thrillers, like Alfred Hitchcock, rather than along with other novelists. He has Hitchcock's wonderful sense of atmosphere – of the atmosphere, in particular, of what he calls 'seediness,' an almost untranslatable English word which conjures up a composite feeling of the shabby, the homely, and the sinister. Greene loves, in fact, to set his most melodramatic episodes in the most homely surroundings, the cheap restaurant, the shabby newspaper office, the furnished room where the tasteless furniture fills one with a sense of spiritual emptiness, or the great railway station with its atmosphere of nervous waiting, tightness at the pit of the stomach, and uneasy departures towards unnamed dangers. He has a lively sense of that feeling of *deprivation* – the lack of style, or flavour, or roots, or manners – which is so typical of megalopolitan civilisation, but to the stripped, deprived, peeling backcloths of his urban scenes he manages to give a positive and exciting tang. He will describe in his first few pages some commonplace scene, introduce some dimly ordinary character; but we know that we are in a world that we too often ourselves live in, a world that is full of pockets of moral evil, just as, down its dark alleys, it is full of musty smells; and it is an exciting world, because it is a world in which we feel from the start that 'anything' (meaning probably something violent and unpleasant), 'anything at all can happen.'

So much for the symbolic melodrama. The documentary novel, on the other hand, our second kind, tends less to emphasise the melodramatic aspects of life than the quiet and homely and ordinary episodes which always make up most of the texture of the individual human life even in times of the utmost tension and crisis. For tension and crisis are the headlines in the morning paper, and the lingering nasty feeling in the mouth and the diaphragm, but they cannot fill up every minute of the work and the leisure of one's day. We have to 'go on living' even in a conquered city or after an earthquake or a devastating bombing raid, or after what seems some final blow to all our political hopes, and to some minds this wonderful obstinacy and staunchness of the individual in perpetually picking up the splintered fragments of his life will always seem more interesting than the grand catastrophe itself. Thus, one has heard that during the war refugees and exiles were happier if they could carry with them an old battered kettle or a patchwork quilt, some trivial object, however shabby, which symbolised to them 'the old home,' and if the pathos of this is almost unbearable from one point of view, from another point of view one is encouraged when one thinks of the strength of the human impulse for continuity. Shaken, battered, deprived of all that seems to make life worth living, human beings still refuse to drop the threads.

Thus, Christopher Isherwood's two books about Berlin before the rise to power of Hitler, *Good-bye to Berlin*, and *Mr Norris Changes*

Trains (published in the United States as *The Last of Mr Norris*) are very largely concerned with the small everyday adventures of the narrator, whose experiences and attitudes are very largely those of Mr Isherwood himself, as a young man teaching English in Berlin to private pupils, living in cheap boarding houses, casually making friends at many social levels, and talking with his friends. *Good-bye to Berlin*, in particular, could be taken as a mere series of pleasant, rather slight sketches of a random sample of the Berlin populace. But the deep theme of both books is the decay of a civilisation, the decay of tradition, and its tragic, or stultifying, or sometimes absurd and ridiculous, effects on individual human lives. We are not given a lot of abstract argument about how Hitler rose to power or about the moral implications of Nazism. We are merely shown, sitting in the kitchen, drinking tea with their friends, visiting flashy night-clubs, enjoying their holidays, a wide range of persons who have not only lost most of their traditional faiths but who, having failed to get any solid intellectual grip on the deteriorating world around them, are in the end easy meat for (or, in the case of the romantic young Socialists and the sophisticated middle-class Jewish or half-Jewish liberals, predestined victims of) the unscrupulous demagogue. There is, however, in all this demonstration, no tone of moral superiority. Isherwood nowhere suggests that, in the place of his Berlin friends, he, or anybody else, would have behaved more effectively. They are trapped, the poor among them by hunger and insecurity and the need for something positive and exciting to believe, to live for; the rich by their almost over-civilised isolation, by the gentle rhythm of their lives that makes it hard for them to imagine, and impossible for them to cope with, violence. Instead of any patronising tone, there is instead in these books of Isherwood's a great charity and a detached and penetrating good-will, so that even where Isherwood depicts a real scoundrel, like his Mr Norris, he manages (while conveying his own disapproval very clearly) both to make us laugh at him and feel rather sorry for him, too.

The actual writing in Isherwood's novels is much more interesting and distinctive than that in Greene's. Greene's clipped, vivid sentences make us see what he wants us to see, but they do not convey the deeper resonances of judgment or personality. Isherwood, on the other hand, has style; any competent writer could get hold of Greene's techniques (and, in fact, many have) but the special and inimitable note of Isherwood's writing springs from his personality. The style is the man. It looks easy and simple, it is exactly like somebody talking to us, and Isherwood never seems to be taking any special pains with his writing, but at the same time there is no waste; the deceptively casual-looking sentences create the impression, convey the idea, hit the exact tone, that Isherwood is aiming at. This complete lack of wastage gives Isherwood's books, which are all rather short – a rapid reader like myself can get through any one of them in an hour – and all smooth, easy reading, a density which they do not at first appear to have. One knows many longer and more ambitious-looking books that are far less packed with genuine *matter* (that is to say, with what has genuinely been felt, observed, correlated) than these two short books about Berlin. The air of easy, careless, modest charm in the writing disguises a tense economy of structure. Isherwood's earlier novels, *All the Conspirators* and *The Memorial*, have the same grace of style and give one a similarly tight, exact picture, this time of the troubles and anxieties of English middle-class life in the 1920s. Since the outbreak of the late war, like his friend the poet W. H. Auden, Mr Isherwood has been in the United States, chiefly in California, where he writes film-scripts. Like so many of the leading writers of the 1930s, he has to-day moved away from his old tendency to interpret life chiefly in political terms, and has taken up a more or less religious attitude. He has published nothing in fiction since the war apart from a rather slight *nouvelle* – not up to his best standard – about the film industry in England in the 1930s. He has however written a lively and amusing, if sometimes rather superficial, travel book about South America called *The Condor and the Cows*. His style is as lively as ever, if sometimes (what is natural, perhaps, in a travel diary) more relaxed. It will be a great pity if he never writes any more novels though the atmosphere of Hollywood, where he spends so much of his time, is perhaps likely to baffle the talent of a novelist whose great gift is not the notation of garishness but the conveying of fine, and gentle, and subtle differences of shade and tone.

Let us turn now to our third type of novel, which I have called the 'social allegory.' The most important writer of this kind of novel (if novel, in the strict sense, it should be properly considered) in the 1930s was Rex Warner. Warner was a classical scholar, who in that decade was a master in a public school, teaching Greek and Latin, and who is now an official of the British Council. He was head of the Council in Athens for some time. He was a friend of Auden and Isherwood, and their group, and is also known as a translator, a critic, and a poet. His two best-known allegorical novels are *The Aerodrome*

4*

and *The Professor*. Both deal, though from slightly different perspectives, with essentially the same theme.

The setting of *The Aerodrome* is a small, sleepy, rather backward and out of the way village in the south of England, on the outskirts of which the Air Ministry decide to erect a large new aerodrome for experimental purposes. In charge of the aerodrome is an Air Vice-Marshal who is a man of great intelligence and driving ambition. It soon becomes obvious to the reader that the village is not an ordinary village, and the aerodrome not an ordinary aerodrome. The Air Vice-Marshal takes charge of village life and starts to dominate and organise the local inhabitants in a way which would be inconceivable in real life, and if we take the story as a true story, we are likely to find it thin, implausible, and fantastic. But the allegorical meaning is not difficult to grasp. The Air Vice-Marshal represents the radical planning, organising mind, the mind that wants to build society anew from its foundations and that is more interested in social efficiency than in individual happiness. Indeed, according to theories like the Air Vice-Marshal's it is not good for society that the individual should be too happy, too comfortable, too much at his ease. He will become lazy then and will resist necessary change. He must be kept 'on his toes.' It is a theory of military discipline applied to civil society. If the Air Vice-Marshal represents such radical anti-traditional movements as Communism, Nazism, or Fascism, the village, on the other hand, stands for habit and tradition, for man's accustomed ways of doing things, which may not be ideally either the best or the most effective ways, but are the ways he is used to and feels warm about. The village, in fact, stands for whatever forces those are in human life that make men, rightly or wrongly, resist change. The Air Vice-Marshal is clever and strong, the villagers, taken individually, are mostly either weak or stupid, but, in spite of the Air Vice-Marshal's dazzling and ruthless tactics, it is the village that triumphs in the end. The Air Vice-Marshal is defeated and killed and his plans for taking over and re-organising not only the village but the country come to nothing.

It is the great weakness of the Air Vice-Marshal (who, though in one sense he is the 'villain' of the novel, is a man with certain heroic and attractive qualities) that he does not make enough allowance in his grand schemes for the dignity of the individual human personality and particularly for the ties of local loyalty and of family love and affection. Yet we are not left feeling that there is nothing *at all* to be said for his point of view. The village itself is not idealised. It is a backward place.

Many of the villagers' cottages are insanitary, many of their pleasures are brutal, many of their traditional habits are crude and unpleasant. They are used to the life they lead, and they have an inner warmth that the Air Vice-Marshal lacks, but the life they lead is often a muddled and thwarted one, by no means corresponding to one's highest notions of what human life might be. What Mr Warner is perhaps driving at is that we cannot live either wholly by habit and custom, on the one hand, or wholly by abstract reason on the other, that we must find some working compromise between the two, and some compromise too between a fanatical and ruthless devotion to some abstract ideal, like the Air Vice-Marshal's, and a mere complacent jogging along in our old ruts, accompanied by a bland indifference to all larger issues. Mr Warner seems to suggest that the way for us to find this working compromise between reason and tradition – and there is a tradition of reasonableness in human affairs, after all, and also a reason for there being traditions – is by having respect and affection for each other and therefore a receptive and tolerant attitude towards each other's points of view.

The Professor is a rather sadder story, in which in an imaginary country a professor, who is a great scholar and a great believer in liberal ideas, is invited to form a government at a time when tension between the extreme Right and the extreme Left – say, between the Fascists and the Communists – is threatening to plunge the country into civil war. He hopes to found a government of liberty and order which will rally to its side, on a patriotic basis, men of goodwill in all classes and in all parties, and bring a new idealistic spirit into public life. In point of fact, he is used as a tool by extremists – extremists of the Right in the story, though recent history suggests that it might as easily have been by extremists of the Left – and in the end swept from power, put in prison, and put to death. He dies in great moral loneliness, for if the Right sweep him ruthlessly aside, for the Left he is the foolish dupe who has betrayed them to their enemies and destroyed all their hopes. The professor does represent the spirit of rationality, modified by goodwill towards his fellow men and by a respect for tradition, which Mr Warner seemed to be advocating in *The Aerodrome*, but in this case that high spirit of love and reason seems much less strong than the crude passions of class-hatred. On the other hand, the Professor, even though he completely fails, does manage to retain a moral dignity which the more forceful and successful characters in the book lack. There is something very fine in his refusal to countenance cruelty and hate, whatever the refusal may cost him, and in the dignity with which he meets his death. One thinks almost of the death of Socrates and one feels that the spirit of reason will, in this as in that case, long survive the momentary triumph of the crude passions that destroy its representative.

But there is more to be said than that. The tone of the book implies not only Mr Warner's sense of the tragic dignity of the Professor's predicament, but a certain ironical criticism of the practical inadequacy of the Professor's attitude. The Professor is a noble, heroic figure, but it cannot be denied that in his view of life and politics he is a little unreal and bookish. He has thought all his life too much in terms of abstract ideas and has not grappled enough with the complex world of men. The Professor's mistress, whom he loves very deeply, is secretly the lover of an exiled Fascist leader, and there is a suggestion that this man, morally so far below the Professor, has a certain coarse vitality and strength about him, a 'manliness' in the crudest sense, which the Professor lacks, and is the less effective for lacking. So the lesson of *The Professor* may be that though political leaders certainly should have high purposes and should not betray those purposes, still they should have, too, a realism about human nature, and that they should have enough of the earthy and the common in them to be able to arouse a response in – to guide, and to check the earthy, common material they are dealing with – average human nature, with all its prejudices, interests, and passions. With a little more hardness and a little more scepticism in his nature, the Professor, not pitching his immediate hopes so high, might have at once ridden his storm and postponed the immediate defeat, as well, perhaps, as preparing for the ultimate victory, of his own high ideals. Mr Warner may have been thinking of such a figure as President Wilson, who, by insisting too narrowly at Versailles on his own ideals, in abstraction both from the reality of the situation in Europe and that of the situation in the United States, in a sense betrayed these ideals by his very eagerness to impose them; by yielding more, by a greater resilience, he would probably in the end have gained more of what he was actually after. And again, as in the Air Vice-Marshal's case, it is never *one* man who imposes his ideals on history, but history is shaped rather by the concurrence of many factors of sentiment, opinion, and interest, and by the co-operation, and competition, of many diverse minds. The Professor had great strength (as President Wilson had before he came to Versailles) as a symbolic figure; but nothing is more fragile and transitory than this symbolic strength, which comes from accidentally embodying many vague and perhaps contradictory aspirations, and no politician should rely on it when he steps down off his pedestal into the dust and heat of the arena.

Whatever puzzles of interpretation there may be about the details of these two books, one can, however, say with confidence that they deal with a debate between innovation and custom, as also between an idealistic and a realistic view of politics, which was going on in many intelligent people's minds in the 1930s, and is indeed still going on now. One may say that the Air Vice-Marshal betrays his ideals, and even formulates them wrongly in the first place, by being too ruthlessly 'realistic' about his way of achieving them; the Professor betrays them by not being realistic enough. The Air Vice-Marshal is so obsessed with the efficiency of power, that he forgets that power is of the order of means, that it must subserve justice; the Professor is so obsessed with the beauty of justice that he forgets that justice, such imperfect justice as is achievable in this world, if it is to have a firm base at all, must be based upon power.

The fourth type of novel that I mentioned was the farcical comedy with bitter undertones. The most successful writer of this kind of novel, in the 1930s, was Evelyn Waugh. The pattern of Evelyn Waugh's novels will recall to many readers that of the earlier novels – say *Antic Hay* or *These Barren Leaves* – of Mr Aldous Huxley. There are the same parties, the same casual love affairs, the same sense of a glimpse at an inner circle, the same endless buzz of witty or amusingly fatuous conversation. But Mr Waugh's characters belong less to the intellectual world than Mr Huxley's and much more exclusively to the world of high fashion. They are the young men and women whose handsome or horse-like faces, flushed a little sometimes with surprise or indignation that the flashlight photographer should direct his lens at them, we may trace week by week through old numbers of *The Sporting and Dramatic* or *The Tatler*. The clothes of the women, and the furniture of their rooms, have a quiet and tasteful expensiveness that comes from a thorough study of *Vogue*. Mr Waugh's characters, in fact, are what journalists of his period called 'the bright young people.' They go in one's mind with horses, and long rakish cars, and spats and bowler hats, and Mayfair and St James's Street. Moreover, Mr Waugh's attitude to this fashionable world is much more ambivalent than Mr Huxley's. In one sense, yes, he is mocking it for its lack of any sense of direction, of any intellectual ballast; in another sense he cannot help being rather impressed by its sheer brave foolhardiness, its dash and tone. Thus characters who in his earlier novels, like *Decline and Fall* or *Vile Bodies*, exist chiefly as butts of his malicious drollery can be packed into uniform and die bravely for their country (as, indeed, their originals did, too) in a wartime novel like *Put Out More Flags*. If Mr Waugh's early novels are chiefly concerned with 'taking off' fashionable society, his retrospective view of it, in his later work, grows more indulgent, and perhaps almost sentimental. In his wholly serious novel, *Brideshead Revisited*, the aristocracy are shown as, for all their waywardness, the last custodians in England of honour and faith – and this is a tenable position in itself, but hard to square with such portraits in the earlier, purely farcical or satirical novels as that of Miles Malpractice.

This difference in tone can no doubt be explained by a growing moral commitment. Mr Waugh's earliest novels, written before he became a Roman Catholic convert, set out to depict, from its comic or absurd aspect, a world from which all serious and permanent values have been evacuated, a world intent mainly on the getting of money, so that money may be spent on a 'good time.' The disasters in which such a world is likely to abound are presented in a flat, non-committal way, with an effect of shocking humour, of a joke in the worst of taste which is nevertheless genuinely funny, and with no effect at all of pathos except in so far as Mr Waugh's very indifference to the misfortunes of his characters may sometimes rouse a protesting feeling on their behalf in the reader's breast. The white slave traffic, sexual inversion, drug taking, a horrid murder in a prison cell, the lingering death of a schoolboy who has been accidentally shot in the heel by the starter of a race, the death of a gay young woman in hospital while her friends hold a cocktail party in her private ward, the sinister coincidence by which the dish presented to a young Englishman by African tribesmen turns out to be the girl he is engaged to – all these events, in the earlier novels, at least, are 'good for a laugh' or, in the case of the last one, good at least for a wry ironic shudder. It is not at all surprising that older critics like G. K. Chesterton protested that they could find nothing funny in such a novel as *Decline and Fall* at all, but on the contrary found it extremely shocking and distressing. It is a kind of humour, of course, on the verge of hysteria, but I think nobody of my generation, at least, can deny that it is irresistibly funny. Violence, I suppose, is in the air, and we are all to some extent obsessed by violence. Mr Waugh's way of turning this obsession of ours into absurd farce – for, of course, he needs our co-operation, and cannot be accused of teaching us a perverse taste all of his own – is at least more cathartic, I think, than the glum plugging away at episodes of violence, with a direct appeal to sinister impulses in the reader, by 'novelists of action' like Hemingway, Malraux, or Koestler.* Mr Waugh does not ask us to connive at anything but, in his best satirical vein, presents us rather with the picture of a society so disintegrated that death has become almost as meaningless as life. To preserve that attitude of satirical detachment, even for his first few novels, must have involved an enormous moral strain. Not only are no valid beliefs or principles represented as operative among the characters, but neither is it suggested – as in Mr Huxley's novels, for instance, it is always suggested – that at least the author and his readers know better. All foundations are deftly whipped away and we have the dizzying exhilarating sensation of walking briskly with nothing, but absolutely nothing, beneath the floor.

It could not last. Mr Waugh, like the rest of us, needed something beneath the floor, and he discovered his foundations in an acceptance of Roman Catholic dogma and in the gradual adoptance of a more and more protective and proprietary air towards that society of 'bright young people' which had formerly provided him with his most amusing and pungent illustrations of the meaninglessness of life. Thus, in his later novels, up to *Brideshead Revisited*, there is an odd mixture of tones. The bright young people may behave in a caddish or absurd way but there is often a tone of affection, or almost of admiration, in the way he writes about them and his really sharp satire is now directed more against 'outsiders.'

Finally, in *Brideshead Revisited*, the characters cease altogether to be puppets and begin to exist for Mr Waugh as people in the round. The disintegration which had aroused such hysterical laughter in the earlier novels is seen in sad perspective as part of the disintegration of belief, of standards, in our time, and Mr Waugh sees that as partly reflecting the break-down of an aristocratic society. It is only in his remarks on the sample 'common man,' in this novel, Lieutenant Hooper, that his old cruel and unscrupulous satirical humour gets full swing; though he was later to give that sinister but creative impulse a short outing in *The Loved One* in which the hero ends by cremating the heroine in a dog's cemetery. But *The Loved One* is not really innocently funny in

---

* I don't mean that these aren't important writers, but merely that there is an element of *unconscious* 'viciousness' in all of them.

the same way as *Decline and Fall* is. And *Brideshead Revisited* is, perhaps, as a serious novel, sometimes a little too innocent.

There is a characteristic in Mr Waugh which one can only call snobbishness; and it is not a snobbishness on quite the same subtle and excusable level, say, as that of Proust or Henry James, for it is the attitude not so much of one who wants to understand as one who wants to belong. The son of a respectable but outmoded literary critic, and the younger brother of a prolific popular novelist, Mr Waugh belongs by achievement rather than by birth to that aristocratic world of country houses, and that smart London world of Mayfair flats, towards which his attitude of wistfulness and reverence, as he grows older, seems gradually to intensify. And in his admiration for the expensiveness, smartness, and dash of that world there is an excessive innocence, just as in his very sour attitude towards the lower classes (Hooper, and the evacuees in *Put Out More Flags*) he does reveal, too clearly and probably quite unconsciously, a middle-class rather than an aristocratic habit of mind; for *noblesse*, one is always told, *oblige* and doesn't need to be always reassuring itself about its status by jeering at the awful vulgarity and inadequacy of the lower orders. It is only the well-born and the rich and gay and handsome who really engage Mr Waugh's sympathies, and this is a weakness, even from the point of view of his own religious beliefs; for we are not told that it is easier for a camel to pass through a needle's eye than for a poor man to enter the kingdom of heaven.

It can be seen, I think, from the earlier paragraphs of this section that Mr Waugh's 'world' is not a wholly representative world, and that his strictures on the decay of English society are not wholly justified. People outside his group, like Isherwood and Warner, had in the 1930s a strong and serious, if inevitably slightly confused, sense of moral purpose. So far was it from being true that the alleged decay of the aristocracy was bringing with it a general decay of English morale, for lack of leadership, that Mr Waugh himself might be considered (I do not know whether he would find this flattering) as an instance of the continuing energy and vitality of the English middle classes. It must be said that the impression Mr Waugh's own personality, as apart from his objective art, leaves on his readers is often (and perhaps notably and particularly in his later works) a distinctly unpleasant one. His attitude towards most of his fellow countrymen is one of sulky superiority, a superiority, moreover, based not on pride of intellect or the consciousness of possessing great gifts but rather on the accidents, adoptive rather than inherited, of his social position. Nevertheless, Mr Waugh is a sufficiently objective writer to keep the intrusions of his own personality into his novels down to a minimum; it is rather in his travel books, like those on Mexico and Ethiopia, that he lets his prejudices rip – particularly prejudice in favour of keeping the underdog, Ethiopian tribesman or Mexican peon, wherever he finds him, down. And these books tend to leave a nasty taste in the mouth, however much justice there may be in Mr Waugh's criticisms of the discomfort of life, for a person of his tastes, in backward countries and of the confusion of social arrangements in Mexico and Ethiopia.

His moral fault, here as in his novels, is a failure to respond to people outside his own class, colour, cultural background, as persons: a tendency to nag at them for not being Englishmen of the upper middle class, which, after all, they have had no opportunity of being: in a word, a lack of imagination, outside the narrow circle he is at home in, and a lack of charity. I think that possibly Mr Waugh has more of the real gifts of the novelist, more of the potentialities of a major novelist, than any other of the writers I have mentioned in this section, except possibly Mr Isherwood. But all these others have something that he lacks, a coherent attitude towards, if not a coherent philosophy of, life. He is not in any sense, himself, coherent. He is rather the bellicose and irate person who thinks it enough in life to stand by his friends and stick up for his beliefs, while keeping up a stiff and suspicious attitude towards all outsiders. This is quite adequate, no doubt, as a practical personal attitude, but it is inadequate as the attitude of a novelist; for a novelist ought to have a quite general sympathy with, and a quite general understanding of, human nature. Probably, however, Mr Waugh writes novels as well as they can be written on a basis of fierce, unreasoned admiration and equally fierce, unreasoned dislike.

A writer who had a great deal in common with Mr Waugh, in a drier and more bilious vein, was Mr Anthony Powell. At his most satirical, Mr Waugh has always some characters with whom we are invited more or less to identify ourselves; and others, like Captain Grimes, who may be both ludicrous and deplorable, but with whom we feel a sneaking sympathy. In his earlier work at least Mr Waugh cannot help conveying the feeling that life, in spite of everything, is great fun. Mr Powell covers a similar scene and castigates similar follies; but his characters tend to be uniformly unpleasant. In a novel like *Agents and Patients*, he harks back to the Jonsonian comedy of humours, the agents are rogues and the patients fools, and he makes us abhor both of them alike. At the most, he will sometimes make one of his characters pitiable, like the poor old gentleman in *From A View to a Death* who has the perverse but innocent eccentricity of dressing himself, in his wife's absence, in her clothes; its discovery leads to what, in another context, would be called tragedy. The skilled economy of style, the sour accuracy of observation, and the ingenious farcical inventiveness displayed in these early novels makes them good reading; but they do express a peculiarly negative attitude. Since the end of the war, Mr Powell has published two instalments of a longer novel in a rather different vein, a broader study of English social life. The first of these, *A Question of Upbringing*, is notable for the skill with which it handles two subjects that lend themselves easily to lush romanticism or to easy farce, public school and university life. The broader theme, however, is that of social demarcation. The three schoolboys, in whose study the story begins, represent three broad divisions of the English middle classes. The narrator represents, in a sense, the norm, the type of the English professional classes. A wealthier but flashier young friend, who does not go to a university, represents the commercial classes. And another friend, superficially charming but growingly ruthless, who goes to a university but does not find it necessary to take a degree, represents power and wealth. The three boys, who in the beginning seemed very like each other, by the end have each found their own quite separate places. And a comic school misfit is struggling to find his. I have heard Mr Powell's technique, in this new work, described as that of a 'dehydrated Proust.' The phrase pays proper tribute to his skill in working out large general implications from small incidents; and also to a dryness of sympathy and a power of compression which are not typically Proustian at all. His gift remains primarily that of a satirist, and his comic vision still depends chiefly on intelligent dislike. But there is perhaps implied, at least, in this later novel a more firm criticism of hardness of heart than was obvious in the earlier ones. The portraits of misfits, of the awkward or the self-assertive, are as finely balanced as ever, but if the scales were to tip it would perhaps now be on the side of pity rather than on that of contempt.

Section 6: The Last Ten Years

So far, taking the history of the English novel in periods of roughly ten years from the beginning of the century, we have been able to trace out a fairly clear and consistent pattern of development. It is not so easy to do this for the last ten years. Everything is too near us, it is hard to get the decade into perspective, and to see what names really stand out. These ten years also have been years of hurry and confusion for the writer as for other people. There were five years of war in which Great Britain was fighting, not only for the liberties of Europe and the traditional decencies of civilised life, but, at the beginning at least, for her very existence. The writer, like everybody else, was caught up in the struggle. Young writers were fighting in the ranks: older ones often had official jobs of one sort or another that prevented them from concentrating on creative work even if, in a time of national crisis, they had wished to do so. The end of the war, moreover, did not really bring with it that period of relaxation and relief which the end of the First World War had brought, at least for the intellectual. The English writer, the young writer, particularly, with his way to make, faced the same drab practical problems that confronted his fellow subjects. There was a housing shortage. That 'room of one's own,' which Virginia Woolf saw as essential to the protection of the writer's creative sensibility, was something almost impossible to obtain. The young writer just out of the army either would have to share a flat with his family or with some group of wartime friends, with whom he would club together to pay the rent. The publishers to whom he looked to encourage him were friendly but themselves handicapped by shortage of paper and shortage of staff. A book might be accepted in 1945 but not published, through one technical hitch after another, till 1947 or 1948. And if there were difficulties, there were also distractions: the new and fascinating world of literary London to be explored, 'contacts' to be made that might at some remote time prove useful but more immediately proved to be seductive time-wasters. There was the sense of freedom from army discipline to be enjoyed, and the old acquaintances to renew, the drinks, the parties. Life on this wide sociable basis can become a routine. Years may pass before the young writer realises that he is not so young as he was, that chances are slipping past him: and that on the long book which he imagined writing in the war years he has done no fundamental work at all.

Perhaps a larger obstacle, however, to the new young writers getting on with their work, was the continuing state of international tension. The young writer was often emotionally and physically exhausted by his years of war service. He wanted to look forward to long years of peace, in which he could concentrate on refining his talent and deepening his insight; but the dark and ominous clouds which overhung the European sky warned him that perhaps he was being granted only an interval, only an extended furlough, of pleasure and repose. Thus it might seem to a superficial observer that many promising young talents in England, that announced themselves in the war years, have in the last few years of peace gradually dissipated themselves over too wide a social surface. But that judgment would, indeed, be superficial. As Mr Ernest Hemingway says in the preface to his collected short stories, the writer cannot be spending all his time sharpening his tools: he must take a holiday from the problems of writing sometimes to receive the impact of life. The writer ought not to expect 'experience' to be immediately and crudely usable: but it would be a mistake to think that, in the writer who, whatever the discouragements, refuses to desert his vocation, experience is ever wasted. It sums itself up, at some time or another, in a significant shape.

How then is it likely that the experience of the younger generation of English writers in the last ten years will ultimately sum itself up? During the first five years of the past decade they have to adapt themselves to the ways of service life in strange countries: during the second five years to London literary life. They have cultivated the arts of friendship, but sometimes at the expense of solitude and awareness of perspective. They have not found it easy, in the French sense, to 'commit' themselves to some single view of life that would enable them to sift and co-ordinate multifarious impressions. Most of them cannot any longer accept the simple Marxist thesis which satisfied, for a short time, their predecessors in the 1930s. They have acquired a perhaps at first reluctant but now very genuine respect for the idea of tradition: more particularly, having seen the opposites of these in the outer world during their war years, for the traditional British emphasis on the value of tolerance, of good will, of social diversity and contrast, of rooted local habit and custom. Nevertheless, at the same time these young writers feel a growing need for some universal faith which will unite a divided and agonised world. For most of them, it is impossible to turn, as some of their elders have turned, to a simple orthodox religious faith and to the type of Toryism, based on the profound speculations of Edmund Burke, which sees in existing institutions and actually operative traditions a wisdom far deeper than that of the critical, self-conscious, rational individual: the wisdom of society itself.

For, in spite of all the fascination of Burke's thought, modern great societies cannot be thought of as developing themselves through unconscious instinct, as a great tree grows and puts out, year after year, its leaves. They seem to resemble, far more, sleep-walkers lurching disastrously through the dark. At the same time, where some genuine organic tradition still persists, it is something to be cherished: but for the over-individualised life of great cities, for what Dr Alex Comfort calls the 'telephone exchange society,' it does seem that we can no longer rely on wisdom springing from popular roots and from imitation of popular heroes, and that if we want to improve this society, to put new life into it, we must to some extent at least plan this improvement on the basis of considerations of abstract reason; yet what has been planned has never the natural, the rich and leafy, life of what has grown.

Thus it is the fate of the young writer to-day to cling to what elements of style, of tradition, of formed and stable manners that he can find in the bewilderingly fragmented world around while at the same time feeling that one of his duties is to offer what advice, what leadership he can to that much larger section of society which, at a first glance at least, seems to be almost totally lacking in manners, tradition, and style. Thus the young writer may tend to be exclusive and selective in his personal life, though in his theory of what a writer should be he probably stands for an all-embracing sympathy; similarly he may live chiefly on the culture of the past, while believing chiefly in the popular education of the future. But though he clings to this 'forward-looking' attitude which is something inherited by everyone brought up in the liberal tradition, more fundamentally, if less consciously, the recurrent disasters of history in this century may have implanted in him a profound but not openly admitted scepticism about the possibility of improving, in any permanent way, the basis and the constitution of human society. He may feel that in reality all one can do is to spread what happiness one can among the immediate circles of one's friends; to avoid adopting any attitudes or policies which are likely to be publicly harmful; and to purify one's own will and discipline one's appetites and desires. Our typical young writer of the last ten years is thus being driven in many cases from a secular to a religious view of life, and yet his whole intellectual training, which has probably been entirely secular, tends to make it impossible for him to formulate these religious intuitions of his in a coherent or rational way, or to make any outward act of faith and acceptance.

Our young writer, therefore, in his typical case, is a humanitarian agnostic, who wishes to acknowledge the element of goodness and truth, or at the very least the element of vitality, in all existing religions, philosophies, and attitudes. This general sympathy with the human predicament, and its contrasting modes of expressing itself, though a noble and admirable thing in itself, makes it difficult, on the other hand, for him to formulate his own distinctive point of view. Thus we can consider the past ten years, as they have affected him, as a period of adaptation and improvisation, a period arousing in him a deep inner uneasiness, which is nevertheless in its way an expression of goodwill. In theological terms, our young writer has to walk on a tight-rope between the gulfs of presumption and despair. He finds it hard to see any clear and happy way out of the tangles and nets in which our world to-day has trapped itself: yet he must refuse merely to throw up his hands, must refuse merely to say that evil has come and worse must happen, and the worst remains behind. A stoical indifference is no answer to our problems; there must be an active willingness to help; but on the other hand it is presumptuous to suppose that our efforts to help will have any very large or tangible result, or that we may not often be mistaken in our choice of what we think a good cause to support. One of the arguments, in fact, against the fashionable French doctrine of the writer's 'commitment' is that it is presumptuous in this sense, it assumes for the writer a kind of pontifical infallibility. But it is possible for a man to be imprudent in his moral and political choices, and mistaken in his view of the ultimate nature of the universe, and yet to be a good man and act virtuously, within the limits of human nature; for we judge morality by intentions, not by results.

The very imprecision of language which marks much verse and prose by young writers in the last ten years, if one compares it with the sharp and definite and sometimes no doubt rather jejune notions of the 1930s, reflects this new comprehensiveness and charity in the young writer's approach but at the same time this diffident, veering uncertainty of attitude. Perhaps no generation of writers has had to reconcile in the inner self a greater number of contradictory stresses, of tugs in opposite directions, than our own. In the end, if the contradictory stresses have not torn him apart, the young writer probably to-day has arrived at the position of rejecting any idea of wholesale revolution, and of accepting the link with the past, accepting the validity of tradition: but the idea of tradition, accepted after these refined agonies and these deep soul-searchings, is something quite different from tradition accepted as an unquestioned and unexamined code. Thus an air of uneasiness and hesitation seems to me to hang over much of the best writing of the last ten years: and the unity of tone in that writing seems not to depend upon any clearly formulated schemes of what must be done, and what must not be done, in the world to-day, but rather on an anxious goodwill.

Thus if much of the best writing of the 1930s was based on a clear scheme of notions; and much of the best writing of the 1920s on the proud self-assertion of the individual sensibility; some of the best novels and stories of the last ten years, on the other hand, are not based on either of these things, but rather on a clinging to what seems in human life, in a shifting and dangerous world, centrally and lastingly important.

This idea is expressed with wonderful elegance, and illustrated with striking skill, in a long short story by Miss Rosamund Lehmann, which appeared in print in the early years of the war, called *The Red-Haired Miss Daintreys*. The first few paragraphs of this story are a disquisition on the novel in general, in which Miss Lehmann says that she is very distrustful of novelists who desire to illustrate a general theme and who therefore plan out the development of their novels, in too abstract a fashion, in advance. She would have more confidence in the novelist who did not quite know what he was setting out to do but merely said, 'I want to write about some people.' Our centrally and lastingly important experiences, she feels, are experiences of intimate and affectionate response to other people, and more than that, of imaginative response: it is from such experiences that truly creative writing springs. The experiences, and the feelings that have gathered round them, are what engage the writer's conscious attention: the abstract theme, on the other hand, emerges without the writer being at first consciously aware of it.

Miss Lehmann's own novels illustrate this conception. One feels that they are based not on abstract ideas but on a varied and sensitive personal experience, which has given Miss Lehmann a deep under-standing of English life. One of the best novels of the last ten years is her *The Ballad and the Source*, based on the contrast between a young girl's impression, a very favourable and romantic impression, of an older woman, and the rather grim truth about this older woman's life. The child's impression is as it were the 'ballad,' like some beautiful Scottish Border ballad based on an incident that may have been cruel and sinister enough in actual fact, but which has been made beautiful by the passing of time, the dimming of memory, and the charity of the folk imagination: and the actual facts about the older woman's life are the 'source,' like the raid or the killing, hateful in itself, which in later years the balladist is going to turn into an heroic tale. What Miss Lehmann very rightly insists on is that not only the 'source' but also the 'ballad' has its own kind of validity; and that the kind of literary 'realism' which leaves out entirely the noble fantasies we weave round other people, and the unreasonably high expectations that we form about their characters, impoverishes the experience of actual life. In all Miss Lehmann's novels, she is vividly aware of the 'glamour' of life, of the personal charm and delightfulness of people who, from a strict moral point of view, may not be very soundly based. For there is a point up to which pretences, if they are carried off with enough style, are valid. The charm and the glamour have their own reality, the superficial brilliant impression that people make on us has its own reality: if not, very often, the reality of what we take to go with it. When people's manners are more engaging than their characters, we are not to dismiss the manners as mere hypocrisy; but to think of them often as representing a genuine ideal, at which people do aim, though in general they tragically fail to achieve it. Miss Lehmann presents this sort of situation, usually, through the fresh and expectant sensibility of some young woman, her heroine; and if this heroine is to be continually disappointed, because her vitality and her imagination always pitch her expectations too high, nevertheless the vitality is perennial, and when we meet her as an older and more experienced woman – as in *The Weather in the Streets*, a beautiful novel about love – she will not have dried up and gone dead but will still be riding the waves with careless zest and risking the final shock, which never comes, against the harsh rocks of the shore.

Miss Lehmann thus carries on to some extent the tradition of Virginia Woolf, in her receptiveness to the poetry of what is transitory and pungent. Though she writes very well, she has not Mrs Woolf's distinction of style; but, on the other hand, just because we do not notice the sentences and paragraphs so much, perhaps we find it easier to get lost in the story: and the story does not tend to break itself up, as it does so often in Mrs Woolf, into a series of sharp, separate impressions. Miss Lehmann in fact can tell a story, in the ordinary crude sense of 'story,' in a more gripping and exciting way than Mrs Woolf could or probably wanted to. She has something of the roominess, the readiness to gather everything in and find a place for it, of the Victorian novelists: I do not know whether one could claim that she is a major figure, but she is certainly one of the contemporary English novelists from whom I myself in recent years have derived most pleasure.

Miss Elizabeth Bowen is a novelist who has something in common with Miss Lehmann. The world that they are both at home in is a world with traditions of space and privilege – perhaps, if one is making fine distinctions, 'upper class' in Miss Bowen's case, 'upper middle class' in Miss Lehmann's – and they both have a story to tell, and tell it on the whole in what strikes the ordinary reader as a 'sound, old-fashioned way': the interest in experiment showing itself rather in the shaping of paragraphs and sentences, the freshening up of the novelist's language, than in the structure of the book as a whole. Miss Bowen's most recent novel, her first in ten years, published a year or two ago, is called *The Heat of the Day*. It is a study of London life during the war, in the days of the great German air raids, and it evokes the tense, exalted atmosphere of that period better than any other book I know. Its story is what might seem an almost melodramatic one, of a woman (a gentlewoman, a 'lady' in the old sense) who discovers that her lover is a traitor and who is blackmailed by a government secret agent, who offers to spare the lover, if, as a reward, the lady will 'yield herself' to him. But on this harsh and what might seem this rather flashy framework, Miss Bowen has erected a living structure of words which allows us to grasp, not only a particular scene at a particular time, but a general pattern running through English life. No character in the novel (and this helps Miss Bowen to avoid real melodrama) is made wholly hateful. We are shown enough of the unhappy family background of Robert, the traitor, to realise that what has led him into a terrible and fatal course of action is no real evil will but rather a disgust at what he conceives (wrongly, but given his awful family, excusably) to be the purely commercial, purely materialistic, purely sordid and empty atmosphere of English life. Even for the government secret agent, who appears both to be neglecting his duty and to be making a most caddish use of his power, we feel sorry. He is the kind of man who has efficiency without personality, usefulness without joy. Nobody will ever love him, he will never be happy in any personal relationship; even as a menace to the heroine's happiness, he is queerly without colour or impact. Robert, the unfortunate hero (in spite of his treachery he is in a sense the hero) of the book saves the situation by committing suicide. Out of a kind of pity, the heroine is still willing to let the secret agent spend the night with her; but love was what he wanted, and love, he now realises, he will never get, so he retreats back into the drab everyday danger and routine of his life. The heroine herself is one of the most attractive characters in recent English fiction, a person whose traditional kindness and decency is bewildered by the queer inner twistedness of the two men she has to deal with but who, nevertheless, has enough magnanimity and charity to reach out towards them and try to understand them. And there is one untwisted male in the book. The portrait of the heroine's son (for she is not a young flighty creature, but a mature woman in her forties, with a son in the army) is a wonderfully vivid and attractive portrait, not in the least romanticised or sentimentalised, of the best type of young Englishman; he embodies, in a rather sad and troubled story, the spirit of hope.

While we are dealing with female novelists, one, in particular, should not be overlooked. Miss I. Compton Burnett has been writing for a long time, but though her sinister and compelling imagination has always fascinated a small group of admirers it is perhaps only in the last ten years that she has drawn the wider public into her circle. It is hard, however, to think of her as typical of any specific decade. The setting of her stories is more often than not a large country house in a period that suggests, but very vaguely, the later Victorian age; and the characters are usually members of a large and painfully ingrown family. But the outer world does not really impinge; however unbearably tense the family situation may become none of Miss Compton Burnett's characters ever really considers the obvious solution of leaving home and earning a living. The younger members of the family depend upon and resent their elders. Either the father or the mother is usually a tyrant and the parent who is not a tyrant is usually something of a weakling and a fool. The motive most profoundly at work in all members of the group is a lust for power. They exist to torment, to dominate each other, or at the very least to undermine each other with witty criticisms; but this aggressive instinct, their main drive, is civilised by a convention, recalling that of French classical tragedy, which forces them always to express themselves with extreme artificial politeness. It is in this polished dialogue that the stories are mainly told. The tension usually leads to some central episode of crime: the poisoning of a mother by her son, the exposure of an invalid to the night air so that she dies, at the least the breaking of a heart and the destruction of a will. But the criminals do not suffer the direct consequences of their acts, and even the infrequent revelation of their crimes does not disturb the formal politeness of the dialogue. The son announces at table that he has poisoned his mother, the remark is civilly ignored as evidence of hysteria, and conversation goes on as usual. In other stories, the criminal even more fully gets what he or she wants. Miss Compton Burnett appeals, in fact, to two separate tastes at the same time; that for melodrama, and that for high comedy; she may also appeal, and that is why I have described her power as sinister, to something in us that enjoys seeing wickedness triumph. The simplest way of describing her stories is as Victorian thrillers, such as might have been invented by Miss Braddon, conceived and presented in terms of comic artifice, such as might have appealed to George Meredith. Her more fervent admirers are mistaken, however, I feel, when they compare her to Jane Austen. Miss Austen's world was fundamentally wholesome. Miss Compton Burnett's is not. Apart from her children, who have a spoiled precocious charm, those of her characters who are not actively evil tend to be passively selfish and indolent; nobody is positively good. All her characters are engaged in an incessant competition of petty self-assertion, none has any general interests or principles, few any useful occupation. Their motives, too, seem fundamentally disproportionate to the narrow circle in which they have to act: Miss Compton Burnett makes her people fascinating while one is reading, but in real life their equivalents would seem self-important bores. The emotional ingrowing of large families, with its resultant horrors, is no doubt a perfectly legitimate theme; but because they are not set against a wider world, Miss Compton Burnett's people seem to lack the stature for tragedy. Their intensity and violence seem overloaded; such prizes as are open to them are not worth all that dust and heat. Their minds are subtle, but the matter the minds have to play with crude. And the artificiality of the dialogue, which does become wearing in the end (it is impossible to read two of Miss Compton Burnett's novels in succession, just as one cannot eat pigeon on two successive days), suggests that not only they but their creator is fighting a losing battle with fundamental tedium. The stories grip, at reasonably intermittent readings; they do not enrich our sense of positive life; and as a commentary on what frustrates life they are archaic. They have, also, that faint smell of evil about them. They nevertheless remain distinguished minor works of art – evoking a perhaps fortunately vanished past with elegance, nostalgia, and hatred.

One can say that both Miss Lehmann and Miss Bowen mark a certain return, in English fiction, to traditionalism. For ten, or twenty, or thirty years, some of the best novelists had been consciously rejecting tradition. In a period of stress like our own, these two brilliant women, with a woman's intuition, realise that if tradition is not something to be blindly accepted, it is not to be blindly rejected either; it is something of which the best elements must be grasped at and preserved – or it is a kind of continuing life in the community, that must be kept healthy and alert. There is a great strain of sadness in the novels of both of them, but nevertheless there is a definite note of hopefulness. Both realise that human creatures, weak and veering as they are, are capable of happiness, of loyalty, of at once showing sympathy with those who have strayed from the path of honour and strictly preserving honour themselves. Thus questions of principle, which a male novelist like Aldous Huxley would argue about, blunt-fingeredly, in an abstract fashion, they feel immediately through a kind of fineness of moral sensibility.

One often does feel that something like this is a basic difference between the temperaments of male and female writers. The male writer tends to stand back from life, to abstract from experience, to consider the business of living as a series of discrete 'problems,' each to be solved, as it crops up, by intellectual means. He looks on life rather as the administrator of an office does, the various tasks he has to deal with neatly separated in different files. Woman, on the other hand, even to-day remains a more natural and organic creature. The running of a household cannot be so tidy and abstract a thing as the running of an office, it is not a matter of solving separate and unconnected 'problems,' it is a matter of embracing and enjoying the branching continuities of life; a meal has to be cooked, a room to be made tidy, a letter to be written, a telephone call to be made, a visitor has dropped in who must be talked to, there are flowers to arrange in a bowl, and while the woman is arranging them she looks out of the window and wonders where her neighbour, Mrs Smith, is going to, walking so briskly on a rainy afternoon. Thus where the life of the male in our day tends to be compartmented off, work, home, pleasure, not one of these compartments really impacting on another, for the woman work and home and pleasure are a single organic complex. She does not separate herself tidily out from herself; she reaches out to life rather at several levels, or in several directions at once. Thus writing by women in our days often tends to have a warmth and richness, a particular charm of its own, which writing by men lacks.

The male attitude as contrasted with the female attitude in our times can be seen very well exemplified in the very popular novels of Nigel Balchin. These have sold very well, and films have been made out of some of them, but the attitude of literary critics towards them has been, I think, a trifle cagy. They have that rather charmless efficiency which is so typical, as I have been saying, of the life to-day of the administrative male. They tend to be studies of a man who is doing a job, and doing it well, but whose life lacks the richness that comes from having settled roots and satisfying habits that he can fall back upon; they are studies, one might say, in a kind of uncushioned integrity. The two best known of Mr Balchin's novels are *The Small Back Room* and *Mine Own Executioner*. *The Small Back Room* is a story about scientists during the late war, engaged in experimental war work – hence the title, for these research experts used to be slangily described as 'the back-room boys.' It is also a story of the personal rivalries, the jockeyings for positions, the pullings of wires that seem unfortunately (side by side, of course, with much hard work and much selfless devotion) to be inseparable from the patterns of war-time temporary administration, and perhaps inseparable from the patterns of administration in general. Mr Balchin himself has been a high administrator and is a distinguished scientist, so he knows the world he is talking about inside out. At the same time, it is a criticism of his work that he tends rather to romanticise that world, and finds it hard to imagine any other one. The theme of many of his novels tends to be the old one, 'himself he could not save.' His heroes are men who inspire affection and respect in others, who get necessary and sometimes dangerous jobs efficiently done, but who suffer from a gnawing sense of inner emptiness that puts personal happiness, or even self-esteem, for ever out of their reach.

The hero of *The Small Back Room* is a research expert with a crippled foot. This causes him great pain; he can soothe the pain by drinking whisky, but whisky makes him quarrelsome. He wants simply to get ahead with his job, and he is impatient of the pattern of intrigue and wire-pulling going on around him. His ideas, which are sound and good ideas, about how his particular department should be run, are continually thwarted because he has not the art of self-advertisement, of putting himself over. At the end of the story, he has an opportunity to regain his self-respect by doing a very dangerous job – taking to pieces an unexploded bomb of a new pattern which, if he makes any mistake, will blow up and kill him. He shows the greatest courage and skill in carrying out this task, but, handicapped by his crippled foot and the pain it is causing him, needs some help at the very last stage. So, though everybody praises him, he is still left with the inner feeling of failure.

Mine Own Executioner is a story about a very similar type of man, this time a psychiatrist, who is able to give real help to others, but not to solve the emotional problems of his own life – problems which lead him to nag at his devoted wife, and to indulge in silly flirtations. Partly because the psychiatrist is too much preoccupied with his own personal problems, a patient of his – an ex-R.A.F. man whose psychosis has been immediately induced by terrible war experiences but has its deeper roots in his childhood – commits a murder and then commits suicide. Again, as in *The Small Back Room*, the hero shows great bravery towards the end of the story: by clinging on a roof, alone and unarmed, to reason with the murderer, who has a pistol. At the inquest on the murderer, the coroner wants to put the blame on the psychiatrist (who is not a qualified medical man), but his friends defend him, and he is exonerated; nevertheless he does feel in his heart that with more care and devotion on his part the tragedy might have been averted. He has a deep sense of inner failure, but he still has a job to do, and he gets on with it. The moral, in a sense, of both these novels is that to-day it is very difficult for an intelligent man to be happy or settled in himself but that he can do useful, practical work in the world.

This is an admirable moral, in so far as it goes, a moral in tune with the best traditions of English puritanism: at the same time this very puritanism, this failure or unwillingness to imagine conditions of stable happiness, this lack of any feeling for the everyday poetry of life, gives Mr Balchin's novels a notable thinness of texture if one compares them to Miss Lehmann's or Miss Bowen's. He is a typical example of the male administrative mind that I have been talking about, that sees life as just one problem after another. He does not raise the question of what it is in life that makes it worth our while to go on solving these problems, or of at what moment the kind of strained, noble conscientiousness he describes would merely crack up. None of Mr Balchin's heroes actually *has* a nervous break-down, but they all seem to me (like certain admirable administrative types that one knows in real life) to be at least headed that way. Or the alternative to the breakdown might be a certain inner slackening off, a relapsing into routine – one also knows examples of that in real life. Thus there seems to me to be a slight element of sentimentality in both these stories in that they tend to treat as a possible permanent and stable poise something which one knows not to be so; it is rather as if, in a cruder kind of story, the hero were permanently 'keeping a stiff upper lip.' The sentimentality invades the style. Mr Balchin's novels tend to be written in the first person, and the heroes, as I say, are conceived as diffident and self-torturing men, unaware of their own exceptional worth: but this conception of them as exceptional, as well as the superficial diffidence, tends to invade the writing, so one feels in the note of the heroes' descriptions of their own doings an unconscious touch of self-admiration, and in the frequent patches of 'noble' self-pity something just a little mawkish. The reader tends to project himself into, and identify himself with, Mr Balchin's heroes at a level somewhere below that of critical observation. . . . Nevertheless, as crisp, readable narratives, as giving a detailed and accurate picture of one side, at least, of modern life, Mr Balchin's books are well worth reading.

One novelist of the 1940s deserves special attention as carrying on, more definitely than any of his contemporaries, the tradition of the novel as a comic or satirical criticism of manners. Mr Angus Wilson is an official in the Reading Room of the British Museum, a point of vantage which must present him with a fascinating view of the eccentricities of scholars; more broadly, it must offer him a useful cross-section of the more literate English public generally. Few people with intellectual interests in Great Britain have not used the reading room at one time or another, and within its more coherent limits it resembles a little one of these great London railway stations where, if you wait long enough, you will see everybody you know. Acquaintance with the melancholy of those to whom reading is an addiction, the indifference to time of enthusiasts, the burrowing persistence of cranks, has probably sharpened Mr Wilson's sense of the individual as a type. He is one of the few contemporary novelists who, without forgetting their social roots, tends to see people as 'characters' almost in the Dickensian sense. He has a firm grasp also of what at a first glance appear to be totally disparate social scenes: the smugness of a Scottish university, the dignity and decay of an English country house, the sodden bonhomie of a flashy London night-club, the stiff self-righteousness of progressive opinions in the suburbs, the wanton extravagance of a wealthy hostess in Mayfair, all seem equally familiar to him. He isolates the essence of such atmospheres, again in a rather Dickensian way, by bold flat caricature and by concentration on the self-betraying trick of speech; and with this there sometimes goes an extravagant Dickensian fantasy, and a touch of Dickensian sentiment, particularly about the decent and inarticulate young. Mr Wilson has also something of what Bagehot, too contemptuously, dismissed as Dickens's 'sentimental radicalism'; he sees cold and narrow, or arrogantly selfish, social sympathies as symptoms of some basic inadequacy in personal generosity; but he can also sketch in, with sardonic objectiveness, the dry and doctrinaire fanaticism of the Left.

Mr Wilson is perhaps at his best in his two volumes of short stories, *The Wrong Set* and *These Darling Dodos*. His one novel, *Hemlock and After*, shows both the qualities and limitations of a writer, whose gift is for the vivid isolated episode, in working out a coherent sustained narrative. Page for page, chapter for chapter, *Hemlock and After* is immensely more lively than the ordinary novel; the critical question is about its total effect. Yet it has a very important general theme. In the character of his hero, Mr Wilson tackles the problem, centrally significant for our day, of the liberal humanist (probably all that is nicest in us is a hangover from the liberalism of the last century) who is suddenly and reluctantly confronted both with the sense of the transcendent, or the absolute, and the fact of evil. The hero, a distinguished writer, who, though a married man with children now adult, has allowed play to his homosexual impulses for the sake of 'the full life' suddenly finds that far more sinister urges than he imagined, including an urge towards cruelty, underlie his mainly sentimental fondness for the company of handsome and clever young men; and while he is recovering from this shock about his own nature, he discovers also that his tolerance has abrupt limitations when it comes to the abnormality of others. He finds himself morally impelled to expose, and thus to drive to suicide, an acquaintance who has been corrupting immature girls. The hero's state can be regarded from different points of view as one of disintegration or of self-discovery. Is his new road to self-completion mainly, after all, just the old road to hell? Yet after his death – a death rather imposed on the book, for the sake of a tidy ending – there is a suggestion that his painful and sometimes apparently cruel honesty may bear good fruit in the lives of others. The 'moral' of the book may be not that he was 'wrong from the start' but that no attitudes are absolutely right and that his, dangerous, and difficult to sustain though they were, represented a higher though therefore more painful and unstable level of integration than most people's. If he has always been an unsettling influence is that not because, like Socrates of whom the title reminds us, he has been a dangerously honest man – refusing to accept the Platonic 'noble lie,' the middle-class English decent pretence, or the revived myths of fashionable religion and politics?

Mr Wilson's characters in this novel, other than the hero, are of a rich variety of type and treatment: the cosy, vulgar, wicked procuress who seems to have stepped out of some unwritten, because unprintable, Victorian masterpiece: the sensitive, neurotic, saintly lady who belongs to the world of Virginia Woolf: the good adolescent boy who might have stepped out of a franker Talbot Baines Read story about the dangers of London life, and the bad one who belongs to the most mocking and scabrous tradition of picaresque romance, almost to the tradition of Petronius. The shifts of view are a danger. We jump about. The story as a whole exists at several levels that seem incongruous with each other, of perception in depth and cartoon in profile, of subtle comedy and pain explored gently juxtaposed with violent melodrama and bawdy farce. These successive projections are never quite brought into common focus. Partly, of course, this disparity of moral levels *is* an objective feature of our society. Mr Wilson knows that every household is, makes, and projects its own world, and that worlds which seem utterly separate can have odd and sinister meeting-places; *what* we are is partly *where* we are. Yet one feels that about certain fundamentals Mr Wilson has not made up his mind. His attitude to life has something in common with that of the early Aldous Huxley though the hero of *Hemlock and After* more resembles, if such a thing were possible, an English Gide. It will be interesting to see whether Mr Wilson's future development is, like Gide's, towards a scrupulous and sensitive avoidance of at least dogmatic transcendental commitments, towards what might be called a rejection of faith for religious reasons; or, like that of Mr Huxley, towards a rationalised mysticism.

Another very masculine writer, and one very much concerned (but more profoundly concerned) with the public side of life, who has produced notable books since the war is the late George Orwell. Orwell had already made a reputation before the war for novels based on personal experience, like *Burmese Days* and *Down and Out in Paris and London* and for books on social problems, like *The Road to Wigan Pier*. He belongs to a wider history than that of the novel. His fierce satirical passion allies him to Jonathan Swift: his blunt, harsh honesty and passionate defence of the underdog, to William Cobbett. Orwell is a writer in a well-known tradition in England, that of the gentleman-radical. Educated at Eton, he was not a man of the people by birth: he had knocked about the world in various jobs, as a police officer in Burma among other things, and had known much of the grimness of the life of the poor and also of the humour and sturdiness of it. Unlike so many radical critics of social arrangements in the years between the wars, he had remained a passionate lover of England, of the English people even in their earthiness and limitations, of everything that struck him as true and vital in the English tradition. The poet Roy Campbell, who fought for General Franco in the Spanish Civil War, where Orwell fought on the other side, nevertheless cherished a warm admiration for him and has described him in a recent article as a 'valiant, generous heart.' Orwell died in 1949 when only in his early forties: the general hardship of his life, and the injuries he had suffered in Spain, had worn down a sturdy constitution. He died of tuberculosis; and he wrote his last novel, the terrifying *1984*, on a remote island to the west of Scotland, when, if he had obeyed his doctors, he should have been taking life easy in a Swiss sanatorium. He never spared himself, took life hard, was always a fighter; and if he had not an immediate social or political cause to fight for, he would fight his own bodily weakness.

Orwell's passionate love for the English common people is shown, outside his novels, in books like *The Road to Wigan Pier*, published before the last war, and *The Lion and the Unicorn*, published during it. What is remarkable about these books is their lack both of sentimentality and snobbery. He writes about the actual culture of the working classes – the culture that reflects itself in boys' twopenny magazines and in vulgar comic postcards, in fish and chip shops, in eel bars and whelk stalls, in miners' choirs, in street corner oratory – without trying to make it out more grand and important than it is, but without any patronising tone. If the English masses are philistine, so, to some extent, is Orwell philistine himself. He thinks there are more important things in the world than taste and refinement; loyalty, courage, humour, generosity being among these. He knows how drab and constricting working-class life in large industrial cities often is, and he does not grudge the working classes the garish or pathetic pleasures that sweeten it, though he wants them, too, to take a more responsible attitude towards life. His radicalism was based on a firm belief that, if they are let alone, and not deliberately misled, you can trust the instincts of the people. Though he was a firm supporter of the Labour Party, as the popular party, himself, he hated the type of long-haired, short-sighted 'progressive' who wears odd clothes, eats a vegetarian diet, combines his Socialism with all sorts of eccentric notions about art, religion, or sex, and expresses himself in a kind of bleating and superior verbiage. He distrusted doctrinaires of whatever kind: distrusted all evasion of plain fact and straight feeling, all abstract and wordy and pretentious thinking about politics. He was even something of a jingo, distrusting foreign influences, from the Left and not only from the Right, on British life. Thus he perhaps comes near to making articulate the instinctive prejudices and unformulated principles, of the ordinary English man in the street, or man in the pub, than any other contemporary writer.

His temperament was much more like that of a radical of similar temperament, on the opposite side, Roy Campbell, than like that of the Leftist poets and novelists of Auden's generation; Auden himself Orwell once described incisively and contemptuously as a 'gutless Kipling' – a coiner of slogans for which he would not be willing, when it came to the push, to make a personal stand. Thus the angry, impatient tone of Orwell's writing, though so radical in its intention, was one that might sometimes be approved by old-fashioned Tories and disliked by the more squeamish or the more sensitive of his own 'progressive' friends. He was swinging a great flail round his head, and it was as likely to knock out the supporters cheering behind him as the opponents cowering in front. This fearlessness of Orwell's, his contempt for official party-lines, made him a formidable figure: and in a wider sense it is this uncomfortable, passionate, tactless honesty of his that, as a writer, makes him significant.

The two works of fiction produced by Orwell in the years since the war were social allegories. *Animal Farm* is not only an allegory but a fable. In this story, some farm animals get tired of their servitude to men, and start a revolution to run the farm in their own way, but are betrayed by the more cunning and self-seeking of their leaders into a worse servitude. Orwell had in mind the Russian revolution of 1917 which seemed to him, after having started off with high ideals and noble hopes, to have degenerated into a hypocritical tyranny. Though *Animal Farm* is a pungent, it is a slight book, and perhaps the symbolism of the fable is unfortunate; it might be taken to mean, what was not really Orwell's intention, that just as it would be foolish for animals to rebel against human control, so, such is the innate difference between them, is it impossible for oppressed masses to rebel against ruling classes.

One cannot accept quite seriously (as one can accept, say, the big men and the little men in *Gulliver's Travels*) the idea of the rebellious animals. They are obviously, like many animals in fables, men in disguise; but on the other hand, the illusion is spoilt when real men, and not only animals, figure in the fable. In other words, *Animal Farm* does not quite hold together as an allegory: *Gulliver's Travels* can be read merely as a story, but in *Animal Farm* we have to be constantly thinking of the *meaning* of the story, in contemporary terms, to avoid noting the inconsistencies of the story as a shape in itself.

Orwell's last novel, *1984*, is on a much vaster scale, a terrible study of what the totalitarian state may, in our century, develop into, if it is given its head. Orwell describes a society in which the driving motives are hatred, fear, the lust for cruelty, and in which the ordinary citizen lives in a continual state of degradation, of terror, or of both. The society he describes has deliberately rejected all genuine and objective standards of behaviour: in particular the standards of charity, joy, truth. It is perhaps a criticism of Orwell's general conception that it is hard to see how the kind of society he describes, a society rejecting the very notion of objectivity, could persist for long. It would collapse fairly soon, deceived by its own lies, rendered stupid by its own propaganda, and robbed of nerve by its own terrorism, into some kind of barbaric decay: yet the barbaric decay, which might have the seeds of new life in it, would at least be better than the kind of perversion of civilisation that Orwell describes. Nevertheless, we have evidence enough at present to show that societies such as Orwell describes can at least establish themselves; can hold power for a considerable period; are infinitely more aggressive, during that period, than traditional civilised societies, and therefore in a position to do almost incalculable damage to traditional decencies of behaviour.

Orwell's terrible picture of the deliberate evil of which man is capable owes, perhaps, something to the famous, sinister, and very important writer of the French Revolutionary period, the Marquis de Sade. Sade had imagined the possibility of a society based, not, as most human societies so far have been based, on an imperfect good will, but on a positive lust for power for its own sake, and a positive lust for cruelty. Sade was, however, though a man of brilliant intellectual gifts, a madman: he took pleasure in imagining a society of this kind. Orwell, who is one of the bravest defenders of human decency in our age, feels, as he imagines this society, the profoundest horror. But his vision is definitely, like Sade's, a vision of evil, and in *1984* (written,

we must remember, by a dying man) that vision seems almost unredeemed by hope: Orwell sees in *1984* almost too clearly, almost
unbearably clearly, how the noblest ideas and the highest purposes
can be perverted, by the active, intelligent wickedness of a few, and
the passive stupidity of the many, to the most perverse and horrible
purposes.

When we read this terrible book we should not, however, yield
ourselves completely to despair. That would never be Orwell's intention, to crush our last hopes. We should realise rather what a very evil
thing we have to fight in our time (to fight in our own hearts, as well
as in the outer world) and we should strengthen our wills for a long
and implacable struggle. Orwell did not intend *1984*, as some critics
have thought, as an attack or a satire upon the very idea of Socialism.
He was all his life a staunch supporter of the British Labour Party; but
he differed from most political writers to-day, whether of the Left or
Right, in that he tested his political principles by his traditional feelings
for honour and decency, and not his traditional feelings for honour
and decency by his political principles. He wrote not out of any
abstract doctrine swallowed whole, and lying like lead upon his
stomach, but out of a wide, and deep, and thoroughly if painfully
digested experience of life. He loved the British common people
because he had shared their hardships in the lean years between the
wars, and knew them, with all their qualities and all their limitations
and shortcomings and positive faults. He loved personal liberty because
all his life he had fought to preserve his own intellectual and moral
independence, at whatever cost in estrangement from admirers and
friends. He loved that honest and direct comradeship of man to man
which can transcend, in the happy few who are capable of it, barriers
of nationality, colour, opinion, class. He loved courage and he loved
ordinary happiness (though he rather hated the cold and selfish pursuit
of pleasure), and he hated anything that tended to intimidate people
or make them unnecessarily miserable. So in the end he became a
fighter not for any party, or any slogan, or any theory, but for justice
and truth themselves, so constantly threatened, so persistently sapped
at, in our world. Perhaps no writer of his own generation (of the men
born, that is, in the first decade of this century) has been such a morally
impressive figure as Orwell; built on so gaunt, so haggard, and so
heroic a scale.

Younger British novelists of to-day, set against the background
of Orwell's achievement, often seem to be evading total problems:

treating selected aspects of life, rather than life as a whole. Thus the books of William Sansom or of Denton Welch, to mention only two of the younger novelists who have been very highly praised, do seem taken up with expressions of the personal view, the special sensibility, life not so much as it is, or might be, in itself, but as it looks from a particular personal perspective, seen through one pair of eyes. Denton Welch began to make his name in his 'teens with a brilliant travel book about China and went on publishing occasional stories and novels, obviously in most cases grounded in personal experience, after an accident had made him a chronic invalid. He died a year or two ago, after enduring much pain, and many periods in hospital, still a very young man. The adolescent and the invalid are in everything he writes, the adolescent's innocent and passionate simplicity of vision, the invalid's acute, painful sensibility and his hunger for distraction. Mr William Sansom, a more robust person, happily still with us, has imitated the allegorical manner of Kafka and has also written vivid sketches, impressions, 'stories' in a certain sense (but one thinks how the 'story' to-day can fade into the meditative essay or the descriptive article) based on his experience in the war in the National Fire Service and later travelling about Europe. I still remember very vividly a story of his about the National Fire Service called *The Wall*: describing how the wall of a bombed and burning house collapses while a fireman is climbing up it. It was a memorable and disturbing recreation of what, fortunately, is not a common experience. But it was a notation of that experience: not a 'story' in the sense of having a plot, or involving a clash of characters, or a development of character. Similarly, on his travels, Mr Sansom has a sharp eye for the oddly picturesque personality and an exceedingly vivid, if sometimes rather arbitrarily selective, perceptiveness about the visual surface of life. But one is often more aware of scenes and characters than of an 'action,' even of the anecdotal sort. Both Welch and Mr Sansom write beautiful sentences and paragraphs: both create little scenes and episodes that come painfully and vividly alive. But it is rather like flipping through somebody's snapshot album: one feels the lack of a strong, continuing moral theme (or a theme accessible to the reader, at least, for, as with the snapshot album, a theme may be latent for the writer) that would bind the bright and beautiful fragments into some coherent whole.

One feels also in Welch and Sansom (and in certain others, less known and gifted, who may be considered as of their 'type' or their 'school') something like a fundamental lack of curiosity about the inner workings of other people. People are described as trees or flowers or other details in a landscape might be described, with a scrupulous care about their value as isolated strange objects, that are also elements in a pattern: but without a fundamental informing sympathy. What one feels lacking, in fact, in this kind of writing, as an evocation of life, is some strong habitual context of ideas or feelings; characters are seen, like fish in an aquarium, lucidly but estrangingly, through glass; the writer has no deep *rapport* with his characters; his point of view is too much that of the spectator, too little that of the participant.

This air of rather excessive 'objective detachment' (not truly objective, since the writer should be in, and aware of, the same kind of general predicaments as his characters) and this 'fragmentariness' that goes with it are, perhaps, too common in contemporary English fiction by younger writers. The unsettling circumstances of the time (let me revert here to my themes at the beginning of this section) have left many young writers not only without a 'faith' in the ambitious sense of the word, but without any very fixed and stable set of 'working principles': without even the feeling of having inherited a conventional code of behaviour which, whether or not it is 'right' by the highest standards, is at least 'moral.' It is not very good for the novelist or for any imaginative writer to have to think out too many of his basic ideas for himself (the artist and the philosopher are two opposite types of human creature) and perhaps one of the reasons for the many failures to develop of promising young writers in our age is that they cannot merely concentrate on their proper creative tasks: they have to think out and justify their own philosophies of life, their own codes of behaviour. Writers like Welch and Sansom in preserving a deliberate blankness of aspect about general values, and fundamental problems, are at least attempting to concentrate strictly on the creative writer's proper task: but then, if he is not a philosopher, he at least needs to be nourished by some philosophy, or by some complex of stable social values. The writer who because of his strict artistic conscience deliberately ignores, or for the time being sets aside, these larger problems of belief and conduct which beset us all to-day is rather like the man who, in ordinary conversation, talks in a very witty and vivid fashion but who contributes nothing to the topic which everybody else, until he came in, had been passionately discussing. This is not to say that writers should be ideologues: but it is to say that it is disturbing when one feels that they are, as it were, bouncing energetically up and down in a kind of moral vacuum.

What applies to young writers of some fame like Welch and Sansom is even more true of the more obscure and struggling young writers of my own immediate generation, writers who went through the war, who have been endeavouring in the last five years to settle down in London, carry on with their work, and at the same time earn some sort of reasonable living, and who are faced to-day with the unsettlement of a new threat of war. These grew up in childhood in a time of tension with war looming over them, spent their young manhood in far countries, have been adjusting themselves ever since to new situations and to a continuously overhanging cloudily ominous sky. This kind of tension, if prolonged over too long a period, ceases to be fruitful for creative writing. One retains one's good-will and one's persistent hope that what is wise and tender in human nature will in the long run conquer what is stupid and angry, but the nervous anxiety of our time does certainly inhibit concentration on the creation of any considerable literary work, any work on the grand scale, and it makes it hard to arrive at that working habit of life which every good writer needs.

A writer should be conscious about his writing, he should have the most intense and supple consciousness about that, but much of the rest of his life should pass as in a kind of pleasant trance or dream. He should drift about from scene to scene, from friend to friend, from conversation to conversation, simply taking things in in a quiet and calm way. All this, if he is lucky, if he is alert, if he is really a writer, will build itself up in his mind as sentences, paragraphs, pages, chapters of convincing prose. But the too rapid and too mechanically conscious and sometimes too jarringly painful changes and adjustments of our own world tend to blur and confuse all such impressions. The poet perhaps is in a different case from the novelist, and in a luckier one, he can condense and refine his impression of a place, a group, a situation into perhaps a dozen lines, but the novelist is more closely tied down to documented plausibility. He must describe how institutions work, how people look, how they talk, and if he is shifted too rapidly from scene to scene (and from hope to hope, and from assumption to assumption), his impressions are likely to lose their sharp accurate edge, and, more profoundly, it becomes difficult for him to 'connect' – to relate the moral atmosphere of one scene to the moral atmosphere of another, perhaps apparently completely discrepant. This is a great age for journalists, who can visit a country for a few weeks and skim off the cream of it in vivid and garish prose, but not such a good age for the novelist who must sink, very deep indeed, into the mind and habit of a community. Possibly, for that very reason, the novel as an art-form may be coming to an end, and what we need, perhaps, in our odd, violent, unintegrated age, is rather the exact and sensitive record of personal experience: the diary, the autobiography, the travel book, some flying joy of perception caught on the wing. It is possible to make a clear shape of the merely personal life and to reach out to other persons of similar temperament. But it looks less and less true, to-day, that the more we let our social experience mature, the clearer the shape it will take: our angles may merely become more obtuse, our perspectives muddled.

Perhaps some of the best writing of the last ten years is the hastiest writing, impressions scribbled by soldiers in army camps, on coarse paper, with blunt pencils, by the light of a candle in their tents. It is very hard to make a solid and lasting pattern of the strange confusion of our time. Nevertheless, there are in London, I think, perhaps two, or three, or four young men, among those one knows, of course (there may be very many unknowns), who have it in them some time to write the novel which will catch, without false abstraction or tendentiousness, the strange rhythm of our time, with its continual overhanging tension, its storms, and its calm, fatalistic drift. The question is this, however: when and how will they get the odd six months of almost complete isolation and security, of frigid and exact perspective, that will enable them to write it? There is too much hurry: what Matthew Arnold called the 'strange disease of modern life' has now become the customary disease, everybody's disease, the disease regarded as a normal state of health. But if we have less to show in work from the younger men in the last ten years than in previous decades of English literary history in this century, I myself do not believe that this is due to some failure of talent, or dying away of genius, in our generation. I rather think that the pressures are too hard, and yet I have a deep faith that the passion of the writer (one of the very deepest and most persistent of all human passions) will resist somehow and surmount the pressures.

5*

CHAPTER THREE

THE DRAMA

Section 1: The Weakness of the Victorian Age in Dramatic Literature

The nineteenth century, a century so strong and so rich in other kinds of literature, was peculiarly weak in the drama. It might be almost true to say that between Sheridan's *The School for Scandal*, written towards the end of the eighteenth century, and the early comedies of Oscar Wilde and George Bernard Shaw, there was no English working playwright who could produce acting plays that had any literary interest; and, on the other hand, there was no Englishman of letters, whether novelist or poet, who could produce plays that would have held the attention of an audience on a stage. Even as reading matter, indeed, the verse dramas of the great Romantic and Victorian poets tend to be quite the weakest part of their performance. Byron's poetic dramas, for instance, show all the worst sides of his poetic character – the hasty, careless writing, the taste for garish melodrama, the tendency to strike poses. They have nothing of the wit, the flippancy, the gay mastery of light verse which makes *Don Juan* still the only English poem of its length which can be read right through merely for entertainment and pleasure. The plays of Keats are deplorably weak imitations of the surface mannerisms of Elizabethan drama, with none of the Elizabethan drama's bite or grip. There are some plays of the Romantic period which have more intrinsic interest than those I have mentioned, for instance, Wordsworth's *The Borderers*, and Shelley's *The Cenci*. But the interest of these two plays is rather as curious, not quite edifying revelation of the poet's psychology, than as living constructions presenting real plots and life-like characters. Wordsworth's play, in fact, was a stiff study in the kind of morbid state of mind which he imagined might really result from the complete acceptance of the rationalistic and egoistic philosophy of Godwin. He wanted to show that if we do not trust our feelings, our habits and our instinctive reactions as a moral guide, we might be led by sophistical reasoning into acts of desperate wickedness.

Shelley's *The Cenci*, a finer play, was taken from an actual historical episode, too horrible and too powerful *in itself* to be artificially transmuted into anything but *superfluous* poetry. Shelley's intentions are high, but the fascination of the story of *The Cenci* is for him obviously a rather sinister and unhealthy one; and the language of his play lacks originality, it is made up of scraps of imitation from Elizabethan drama, and in imitating he has weakened and vitiated his originals. Shelley's *Prometheus Unbound*, on the other hand, is in its way a real masterpiece of original lyrical inspiration, but one cannot imagine it really being acted; it lacks the body of a real drama.

In the later poets of the nineteenth century, the poets of the Victorian Age, Browning, Tennyson, Swinburne, Matthew Arnold, even the original psychological impulse which gives some life to *The Borderers* and *The Cenci* has vanished away. The plays of all these writers are excessively, in a bad sense, 'literary.' There are imitations of Greek classical drama, like Swinburne's *Atalanta in Calydon* or Matthew Arnold's *Merope*. There are imitations of Elizabethan drama, like Swinburne's plays on Mary Stuart, or Tennyson's on Archbishop Becket, or like Browning's plays on an even wider variety of historical themes. Of all these plays it may be said that here and there they contain pages of fine writing and even of genuinely poetic imagination, but that one cannot imagine them being acted, and that their writers show, and perhaps would wish to show, no real and intimate feeling for the stage. This is even truer of the one Victorian poet, Thomas Lovell Beddoes, who in a strange and fantastic fashion did manage to create, in the Victorian age, some genuine echo of the word-magic of Elizabethan times. If you were to read an isolated page from Beddoes' plays, you would probably say this is a dramatist with the same sort of genius as Webster or Ford, or Cyril Tourneur; but when you attempt to read the whole play you find a complete lack of consistency and purpose in working out a plot, and an interest in death, in ghosts, and the romantic supernatural, which robs Beddoes of any power of imagining living characters in a possible situation.

One might say that the whole immense, deplorable Victorian 'literary' drama springs from the romantic heresy expressed in the famous essay of Charles Lamb's, that it is much better to read the plays of Shakespeare than to see them acted on the stage. The imagination of the sensitive reader – this is what lies behind Lamb's theory – can embody *Hamlet*, for instance, in a more satisfactory fashion than any actor, on any stage. But unless a dramatist writes for the stage he loses touch with the limitations of reality. It is only the awareness of an audience that keeps him, for instance, from writing speeches which are far too long, from substituting the rhetoric of ornament for that of action, and from diversifying his work with whimsies and humours which may amuse himself in his study, but which would make any audience, in any theatre, yawn its head off. Shakespeare, in fact, was misunderstood by critics like Lamb; there are many passages in his plays of what look like bad or hasty writing that do justify themselves in performance; he was an excellent and, in fact, often an unscrupulous craftsman of the theatre. His plays are not shaped on the classical model, but they have nevertheless a living shape of their own, and the danger of the romantic approach to him was that poets tended to think that dramas could be constructed out of fragmentary poetic conceits, noble isolated speeches, Elizabethan mannerisms, without having been felt in advance as wholes.

What is true of the failure of great poets in the drama is also true of the failure of such a great novelist as Henry James. James, who had been a dramatic critic, had a 'sense of theatre' and an uneasy awareness that the literary playwright would have to come to terms with the demands and the standards of the commercial theatre. But the successful commercial plays of James's own time, with which he was best acquainted, were the so-called 'well-made' melodramas of the contemporary French theatre in which actresses like Sarah Bernhardt starred. The psychology of such plays was as crude as could be; the dialogue has no literary quality; the themes had no moral validity; all one could say about them was that these plays were skilfully constructed, and gave great actors and actresses an opportunity to thrill an audience.

James's own refined and delicate talent was at the opposite extreme from this sort of crude and cynical commercialism and he observed bitterly, after the rejection of one of his own plays by a manager, that 'you cannot make a sow's ear out of a silk purse.' Perhaps if he had not attempted to flatten, to simplify and to vulgarise his own astonishing talents to suit the demands of the theatre, he might have made more of a success on the stage. So at least the critic William Archer thought. But James had never the courage to write his plays with the same contempt for the more obtuse part of his audience as he displayed in his stories and novels. A writer like Dickens, again, had a genuine dramatic imagination, but in his amateur acting, and his public readings this imagination revealed itself as that crude sense of melodrama which provides us with so many of the weakest, and coarsest, or least edifying passages in his novels.

Thus, just as the Victorian poets failed to produce a great tragic dramatist, so the Victorian novelists failed to produce the kind of high comedy which, in Congreve or in Sheridan, gives us a genuine criticism of society. To sum up we might say that, so far as prose comedy goes, a certain conventionality, prudishness, or smugness made it impossible for Victorian writers to produce comedy which would be a really vital criticism of current manners and ideas. One centrally important subject to the comic dramatist, the relations of the sexes, was more or less taboo in the Victorian age. In the novels of the time, the young women tend to be extremely innocent and marriage for most of them is regarded as the end of their emotional lives. Anything outside marriage is regarded as 'vice,' an occasion for regretful moralisings, or as 'scandal' which may bring about the ruin of family life and these subjects are treated by Victorian novelists melodramatically. More serious contemporary subjects, like the vexed question of women's independence, are not treated at all.

This explains the extraordinary and hysterical rage with which the dramas of the great Scandinavian, Henrik Ibsen, were received when they were first presented on the London stage. No dramatist could be more profoundly moral than Ibsen is, but it shocked the London critics very much that, for instance, in *A Doll's House* Nora, the heroine, leaves her husband, a dull domineering husband, who seeks to crush her personality and keep her permanently in a childlike, irresponsible state, and that Ibsen obviously approves of the step Nora is taking.

One might say that the drama began to revive again when dramatists claimed the right, as Ibsen claimed the right, to discuss serious social and moral problems in a calm, sensible way. That was one important factor in its revival. The other was the rather *blasé*, cynical, *fin de siècle* atmosphere of the 1890s, which allowed men like Oscar Wilde, without perhaps seriously questioning the moral assumptions of the great Victorian Age, to treat them with a certain frivolity, make polite fun of them. The element of mockery had come back to the stage rather earlier than Wilde with the comic operas of Gilbert and Sullivan. Rather hard-hitting satire was accepted in these comic operas because it was disguised as burlesque or fantasy, because these two men of genius appealed to the insatiable Victorian appetite for nonsense –

for the sort of comic dream-literature provided also by Lewis Carroll or by Edward Lear. Wilde's own very best comedy, *The Importance of Being Earnest*, which is, as far as its construction goes, a typical late-Victorian farce, is deliberately nonsensical in its characterisation and motivation, like *Charley's Aunt* or *The Private Secretary*. Wilde uses this farcical form, which has no literary value in itself, to express his flippant, detached, and dandified attitude towards life. The sparkle of his wit keeps the absurd thing alive, and it is still revived very frequently and with great success, on the London West End stage.

As always, when the dramatist is in a weak position, the *actor* tended to dominate the Victorian stage. It would be wrong to say that though the drama was in decay in the Victorian Age, the theatre was necessarily in decay. Out of plays with no literary value, an actor like Sir Henry Irving could construct spectacles which genuinely enthralled and terrified his audiences. The English stage under Irving had something in common in fact with the kabuki stage in Japan, in which the fine settings, the wonderful acting, and the audience's interest in, and knowledge of the stories, make up for a lack of separable literary value in the acted texts. The text was almost nothing to Irving when he acted Shakespeare; it would be drastically cut, except for his own part. It *had* to be drastically cut, for Sir Henry's manner for instance of delivering one of Hamlet's soliloquies might make it last for minutes with many pauses instead of the short time in which an Elizabethan actor, in the 'two hour traffic of his stage,' would reel it off. Sir Henry's manner of delivery quite destroyed the effect of Shakespeare's words as verse, while his manner of production distorted and truncated the plays, but his own strange, original, personal genius left the audience with an undeniable memorable experience. But he was no more memorable in Shakespeare than in trashy current plays like Bulwer Lytton's *The Lady of Lyons*, or in a worthless melodrama translated from the German, *The Bells*, in which according to all contemporary accounts he gave his most impressive performance.

Another great Victorian actor, Sir Herbert Beerbohm Tree lacked Irving's powerful stage personality, but attracted attention by the lavish scenery of his productions of Shakespeare. The time which such scenery took to mount again led to a drastic cutting of the text, but people were pleased by the feeling that no expense had been spared in honour of 'the Bard.' Thus when in the 1890s an actor like Forbes Robertson started restoring some of the scenes in *Hamlet* which had always been cut – for instance, the last scene in which Fortinbras says,

'Go bid the soldiers shoot,' and a salute is fired over the dead Hamlet's body – this seemed to critics of the time, like Bernard Shaw, and in fact was, a startling innovation. Unfortunately, perhaps, in their reaction from the reign of the actor-manager, new dramatists like Shaw went too far in the other direction, became too anxious that the dialogue by itself should make all the theatrical effect, and ignored the poetic and dramatic value of spectacle.

Thus the 1890s saw the rebirth of English prose comedy, and this was to have a prosperous fifty years in front of it. Shakespeare also began to be produced with some regard for the value of his own text, for the conditions of the Elizabethan theatre for which, after all, he had written his plays, and for the conclusions of modern Shakespearean scholarship. But the reaction against the shoddy and showy side of the Victorian theatre – a theatre which nevertheless had, as I have been trying to show, its own element of bizarre poetry – postponed the revival of a living and contemporary poetic drama in England almost till our own day.

Section 2: The Revival of the Drama in the 1890s

It is an interesting fact that the two men who brought back vitality to the English drama in the 1890s were both Irishmen. Since the eighteenth century Ireland has contributed a very high proportion of great writers, great orators, great dramatists and great poets to the English tradition. The Irish are remarkable among the peoples of the British Isles for their fluency of speech, their ready wit, and their taste for rhetoric. Shaw and Wilde, besides being famous dramatists, were famous talkers, famous social figures. They were, however, men of very different character.

Both came from that Protestant Irish Ascendancy which has on the whole contributed more men of genius to English life and literature than the Roman Catholic tradition of the Irish peasantry and working classes. Shaw however represented the Puritan side of the Anglo-Irish tradition, where Wilde was more built on the model of the swaggering and amusing Irish adventurer of old novels and plays. Wilde was a man of the world, a man of pleasure, who needed a life of ostentation and luxury and whose vanity and appetites finally landed him in disaster. He was not a deep or thorough or passionate thinker as Shaw was; his attitude to ideas was essentially a playful one. He is full of witty paradoxes, but if one attempts to arrive at his fundamental philosophy of life it seems to consist of selective borrowings from more creative thinkers, from Walter Pater, from Ruskin, from William Morris and from the famous painter Whistler. Whistler, who was as great a wit in ordinary conversation as Wilde was, accused him of 'peddling in the provinces' the ideas which he had stolen from his betters. He thought of Wilde as a kind of populariser, vulgariser, or middle-man of ideas. There is the famous story of Wilde remarking on some witticism of Whistler's, 'I wish I had said that, Jimmy,' and of Whistler replying, 'You will, Oscar, you will.'

Wilde's originality then was not so much in his thinking as in his personality, in a certain grace and impudence which enabled him to deploy his second-hand material with the most striking social effect; Yeats, another contemporary of his, and another Irishman of the same social class and religious background, said of him that he should not have been a writer, but a man of action, and certainly he aimed, not as the writer does, at the greatest depth and finish, but rather as the man of action does at the most striking immediate effect. His success both as a writer and a man was the success of the social entertainer, and it is as 'entertainment' that his plays have survived. Three of his plays, *Lady Windermere's Fan*, *An Ideal Husband*, and *A Woman of No Importance*, are built on the model of the conventional social melodramas of the time. They are given sparkle and literary interest by the flashing, if sometimes flashy, wit of the dialogue. *The Importance of Being Earnest*, on the other hand, is built on the model of the popular farce of the time. Wilde in fact took up the ordinary commercial type of play of his day, dressed it up with a new smartness and elegance so that clever people could enjoy its trite situations or its mechanical absurdities and not lose their self-respect. He is not necessarily to be blamed or reproved for this, for much great drama of the past, the early plays of Shakespeare, for example, or the plays of Congreve or Sheridan, can be considered as a rehandling and a raising to a higher level by a man of genius of the average product of the time. Except, however, in *The Importance of Being Earnest*, we are too conscious in Wilde's plays of the contrast between their 'serious' element, which is merely melodramatic or merely sentimental, and the passages of epigrammatic wit which are not really adapted to the plot of the play or to the characters of those who pronounce the epigrams. What Wilde did unscrupulously and remarkably well has been done with sometimes more scrupulosity, but hardly ever with such sparkling wit, by the long series of British dramatists who have taken over his role of the social entertainer in the last fifty years.

From Wilde descend more or less directly the Somerset Maugham of such plays as *Our Betters* and the Noel Coward of such plays as *Hay Fever*, while at a lower literary level the comedies of such a writer as Frederick Lonsdale and to-day the lighter work of somebody like Terence Rattigan are very much in his tradition. In fact it might be said that Wilde is the father of the comedy of pure entertainment in our time just as Shaw is the father of the comedy of ideas. This kind of comedy of polished wit and gaiety, which skims the deeper issue of life, has in our own day become temporarily exhausted. It was remarkable how even the plays of a really brilliant craftsman of the theatre like Noel Coward have 'dated' so that a play like Coward's *Fallen Angels*, which struck the audience of the 1920s when it was first produced as rather daring and shocking, could be revived recently in London by two famous comediennes, Hermione Gingold and Hermione Baddeley, in terms of pure burlesque.

Social manners change so rapidly in our own time, that the comedy of manners dates more rapidly than any other type of drama. Such comedies are not so much true to life itself, as to the current falsifications of life; and with the lapse of even ten years we become jarringly aware of this. The modes of speech, the attitudes to life which ten years ago seemed smart and emancipated and up-to-date, to-day seem as odd and tasteless as the fashions of dress in old snapshots. If Wilde's plays of almost sixty years ago seem still more lively and contemporary than Coward's plays of only twenty or thirty years ago, it is because Wilde's wit acts as a preservative element. Coward has not so much 'wit' in the real sense, as smartness and flippancy, and smartness and flippancy do not stay fresh. Somerset Maugham's comedies show certainly a more solid construction than Wilde's and the plotting of a play like Maugham's *The Circle* is certainly wonderfully ingenious. But Maugham's wit is too obviously rather mechanically modelled on Wilde's, and while his grasp of human nature, or of some aspect of human nature, is remarkably shrewd, he lacks that affection for his characters which helps to give theatrical inventions permanent life.

So we can say that the artificial comedy of the last fifty years in England does not really compare with the artificial comedy of the Restoration, of the period that begins with Wycherley and ends belatedly with Sheridan. Artificial comedy *should* of course be conventional, but the conventions invented by Wilde and developed and exploited by his successors were not sufficiently penetrating and elegant. They did not permit a sufficiently deep and subtle criticism of social life. They were too much bound up with two different kinds of coarseness, that of melodrama and that of farce. One can see this very clearly if one looks at one of Somerset Maugham's most successful plays, *Our Betters*, which I have mentioned already, and compares it with the novels and short stories of Henry James. On a similar theme, the effect of English social life on rich American women who marry into the European aristocracy, Maugham's assumptions, if one compares them with those of James, are altogether too crude and simple. His Americans are either of an impossible nobility and innocence, or too completely bowled over by the alleged corrupt glamour of European high life. His English aristocrats are altogether too parasitical and too eager to acquire money. There are none of the fine shades and hesitating delicacy on both sides that make James's stories so fascinating. The play is an effective moralistic melodrama, diversified with some good broad comedy verging on farce. It is like a piece of network strongly and capably constructed but with the meshes so large that most of what matters in life escapes through it.

In Noel Coward's plays, on the other hand, the more slangy and careless dialogue, and the more informal manners presented, do occasionally give us much more of the illusion of actual life, but when Coward's characters are faced with a serious or subtle situation they, too, have no way out but the way of sentimentality or of angry hysteria.

One might say that the failure of artificial comedy in our own century is partly the failure of society itself to establish and to recognise a code. High comedy gets its point from the recognition and the exposure of current infractions of some high and genuine code of behaviour which most people find it too hard to live up to. When there is an ultimate confusion and scepticism about what such a code might be, comedy loses its perspective and the comic writer loses his most important instrument. Not one of the plays that I have mentioned as representative of artificial comedy in this century can compare, for instance, in subtlety and depth with such a novel as George Meredith's *The Egoist*. Meredith had a clear idea of what human behaviour should be and a clear perception of how people fall short of what it should be, and of how they deceive themselves about their falling short. He wrote in a style too strained and pretentious to make it possible for him to succeed in the theatre, or to think of succeeding there. But he had a more exact and adequate conception of the nature of artificial comedy than any of the writers whom I have mentioned.

With social comedy, or the comedy of ideas, it might on the other hand appear that we have a more cheerful story to tell, but in its essence it is the same story. George Bernard Shaw, the father of the comedy of ideas in our time, was a man of intellectual genius, not merely of personal genius, on a much more impressive scale than Oscar Wilde. If Wilde represented the ebullience and the frivolity of the Irish character, Shaw represented its stern Puritan seriousness. That came out in his life, a life so very different from that of Wilde, the vegetarian meals instead of banquets at Claridge's, the cups of black coffee instead of magnums of champagne, and the life of poverty, of industry, and of comparative failure, which was his until well after his fortieth year. He had failed as a novelist, though he had made a certain reputation for himself, both as a dramatic critic and as a critic of music, long before he had his first theatrical successes. As a dramatic critic, in fact, he helped to create the taste by which he himself later was to be appreciated. His book, *The Quintessence of Ibsenism*, put across his own interpretation of the great Norwegian dramatist – an interpretation which perhaps did not do full justice to the element of deep and painful poetry in Ibsen, to that slight degree of confusion and hesitation in Ibsen's own moral judgments on his characters which gives his plays even to-day their peculiar, uncomfortable tang of reality, or to the extent to which this great 'dramatist of ideas' was full of inner doubts about all ideas, including his own.

Shaw was very much more a conscious partisan of his favourite ideas than Ibsen was and he was less deeply interested than Ibsen was in individual human character. The difference in the depth of genius in the two men can be stated simply: Shaw has never written a play which, under the surface of prosaic realism, has all the elements of poetic tragedy, like Ibsen's *The Wild Duck*. He has not Ibsen's profound sense of the 'pity of things.' What he does have is a greater mastery of dramatic dialogue than any other English dramatist since Congreve, combined with a gift for lucid and graceful exposition of new ideas which might remind one of another great Irishman, the eighteenth-century philosopher, George Berkeley, the Bishop of Cloyne. His plays are not only a series of lively and entrancing performances, but a kind of running commentary on the burning topics and leading ideas of the age. Because his approach to these ideas is a dialectical one, not like that of his rival and contemporary, H. G. Wells, a sentimental one, we can read his passages of abstract discussion with the liveliest pleasure even when the topics are no longer burning and the leading ideas no longer give anyone a lead.

His plays on the whole are of two main kinds. There are those like *Mrs Warren's Profession* or *Widowers' Houses* or *The Philanderer* which tackle some urgent contemporary problem, and depict a contemporary social scene rather in Ibsen's manner. There are those like *Man and Superman* or *Back to Methuselah* which allow themselves much more fantasy and freedom in their development and are mainly concerned with the exposition of Shaw's own philosophy of life. Thus in *Man and Superman* the most exciting passage, purely from the reader's point of view, the dialogue between Don Juan and the Devil in Hell, contributes nothing to the action of the play and is generally omitted in performance. *Back to Methuselah*, again, has, properly speaking, hardly any dramatic development at all, but is rather a panoramic series of scenes to illustrate Shaw's view of the significance of human history and its probable future development. There are other plays like *Getting Married* in which Shaw seems to fall between the two stools of the particular situation grasped and the general exposition of the idea, and presents rather a large but inconclusive discussion within the framework of a somewhat untidy plot. He sometimes, in fact, uses the drama, as Wells used the novel, as a kind of 'hold-all' for all the ideas that are at the moment engaging his mind, whether these ideas have any intrinsic relation to each other, or to the fable which he has invented to illustrate them, or not; he is sure that his unending spontaneity in creating amusing diversions in his dialogue will carry him through. How very well and solidly he can construct, however, is shown in such a play as *John Bull's Other Island* or in *Saint Joan*. *Saint Joan* might appear an exception to my statement that, for all his great gifts, he is incapable of creating a tragedy. Nevertheless, to me at least, this play does appear to have the values of an inspiring and ennobling pageant rather than those of tragedy in the proper sense.

There is a lack that one feels in Shaw, something brittle and heartless about his optimism, and his assumption that some immanent spirit – what he calls 'the life-force' – is somehow or other, through all the disasters of history, always working towards greater good. This belief in an immanent spirit working through history, a belief which has something in common with the philosophy of Thomas Carlyle, makes him strangely indifferent to the values of the liberal tradition, the values of tolerance and respect for hard facts, and too ready to welcome all the 'men of power,' from Lenin to Hitler, who have appeared in such uncomfortable profusion on the European stage in our century. He is far too ready to excuse the excesses and inhumanities of these institutions in human history, from the Inquisition to the Ogpu, which have at various times attempted to impose an orthodox point of view upon the mass of men not by argument but by terror. His belief in the 'life-force' makes him suppose that wherever there is might there must be some mystical right, even though from an ordinary point of view of human decency there is nothing but bloodthirsty despotism. Yeats, who had a far deeper and more tragic sense of the age of calamity which we are now living through, once described a dream he had about Shaw in which he saw the great dramatist as a sewing machine, clicking out words mechanically, but all the time grinning, grinning, grinning. . . .

What this great man does lack is a sense of poetry. That can be seen when, in one of his most charming comedies, *Candida*, he brings an alleged poet on the stage and makes him talk in the bastardised watered-down lingo of a fifth-rate advertising hack. It can also be seen in his attempts at blank verse and in his irreverent criticisms of Shakespeare, the grand coherence of whose mind Shaw is quite unable to grasp; and thus there are few modern writers whose greatness one more readily recognises, and yet about whose fundamental attitudes of life one has more reserves, than George Bernard Shaw.

If the history of artificial comedy after Wilde is on the whole a history of degeneration, so is the history of the comedy of ideas after Shaw. None is a complete success in this genre; neither Galsworthy nor James Bridie nor J.B. Priestley has Shaw's stature or Shaw's wonderful gift of creating subtle, muscular, and living dialogue. Galsworthy's plays are carefully constructed and very well-meaning, but one is too much aware all the time, when reading them or watching them, of the author's intention to present an example and state a case. As in the mediaeval morality play the fact that the characters must represent certain points of view means that they are not able to develop and that there can be in the working out of the plot no real reversal of situation, no real poignancy or surprise. Galsworthy's dialogue, again, though sober and careful and fairly sensitive, lacks Shaw's pungency and wit. It has the same subdued realism, vitiated by a certain sentimentality, as has the dialogue of Galsworthy's novels.

Mr Bridie on the other hand had something of Shaw's wit, fertility of invention and gift of giving the reader or the audience a sharp jog when a jog is needed, but he never really learned how to construct a play. His three-act plays generally resemble three different very brilliant first-acts of some ideal play which he has never had the patience to construct along a single line of development and argument.

Mr Priestley, again, is certainly not at his best in such plays, as *An Inspector Calls*, which, in their allegorical exposition of some simple thesis, very much recall Galsworthy's, though perhaps Mr Priestley's general philosophy of life is more like Shaw's. He is at his best in such pieces as his amusing farce of local colour, *When We Were Married*, or in such sensitive studies of the atmosphere of middle-class life as *Eden End*, or in such a play as *The Linden Tree*, in which he mirrors very exactly some of the confusions and the disillusionments of contemporary post-war life in Great Britain. His quality as a playwright in fact is a certain solid sensitivity to the atmosphere of ordinary living, and though one must praise his tireless readiness to experiment with new forms, as in *Johnson Over Jordan*, or with new technical devices, as in his various plays on themes connected with the problem of time, it is as a recorder, perhaps, rather than as an intellectual interpreter, of the contemporary atmosphere that Mr Priestley has dramatic importance. One may feel that he would have achieved more in an age in which it was sufficient for the dramatist to record and that his intellectual preoccupations have to some extent inhibited the development of his very real sensibility to background and character. He might have achieved very much in that tradition of the realistic presentation of the problems of provincial life which in Manchester in the 1910s did seem to be producing a new, a strong, and a local tradition.

It is a pity that the centring of the English theatrical world in London and the demand for plays of intellectual topicality has tended to prevent playwrights on the whole from exploring the more solid and settled, and therefore richer and more rewarding, atmospheres of English provincial life. It is a lack in the broadest sense of 'atmosphere,' a lack of the quality of 'felt life' that one must complain about in the more serious English drama of the last fifty years. For all Shaw's undeniable greatness, there is equally undeniably sometimes a certain airy thinness about his texture, and it is notable that the one play of his, *John Bull's Other Island*, in which he goes back to the world of his ancestry and his childhood to Ireland, has more of this brooding and atmospheric quality, more of this quality of 'felt life' than any other of his performances. A certain rootlessness in fact in the personal lives of English dramatists in the last fifty years has reflected itself in this lack of richness and body and poetic depths in their work. They have worked too much with the surface of the mind, with the conscious mind, and their deeper and more obscure feelings about life have never found a wholly adequate expression. It is a sense of this inadequacy in the prose drama of this century, striking and admirable as it is in many ways, that has led in recent years to the attempt by writers like Mr T. S. Eliot, Mr Stephen Spender, Mr W. H. Auden, Mr Christopher Isherwood, Mr Christopher Fry, and Mr Ronald Duncan to revive the poetic drama. It is too early to say whether this attempt will be wholly successful but it is certainly a step in the right direction.

Section 3: Suburban Domestic Drama

Neither the drama of ideas fathered by Shaw, nor the comedy of pure entertainment fathered by Wilde, made a direct appeal to the typical English suburban audience. About Shaw, the remark might be, 'Very clever, no doubt, but a bit above my head, and I do get sick of all that talking for talking's sake'; about Noel Coward in his riskier moods, 'Very amusing, no doubt, if you're broadminded, but frankly I'm old-fashioned about that sort of thing, and it's not the sort of show I'd like the children to see.' One can imagine this sort of conversation taking place over bridge and tea in one of these dormitory suburbs about an hour by train from London, which offend the architectural purist by the frantic individualism of their houses, but nevertheless are very charming in their way with their trees, their pure air, the riot of flowers in the gardens, and the odd contrasts of the various building styles.

The suburb is neither the country nor the town. The Industrial Revolution pushed more and more people into the towns in Great Britain but the desire to get away from the 'shop,' the crowdedness and inconvenience of London flats if one is bringing up children, the expense of a house with a garden in London, the wish of busy office workers to get into touch with nature, if only at week-ends, all these pushed the new middle classes out to the edges of London again; and the same kind of process was taking place in all the larger industrial and commercial towns. There was thus brought into being a way of life which, if it lacked urban sophistication, lacked also the deep, slow, natural rhythms of genuine country life. The social centre of the English village is still the parish church. In the suburb, that centre is often rather the local tennis club or golf club. Parasitical, in a sense, both on the country and the town, with no function other than a residential one – or, more deeply, a function of escape – the suburbs are strangely insulated from the pressures of the life about them. Suburbanites belong to the middle classes. They would not claim to be 'upper' middle class, but would be properly offended if you suggested they were 'lower.' If they come in little direct contact with the lower orders, except as shop-keepers or servants, they are also incurious about the upper classes (and particularly about what one might call the intellectual upper classes, about literary and artistic circles). They would not claim to be 'fashionable' or 'advanced,' but they would insist, and rightly, that they are not 'common.'

They are neither poor nor rich. The fathers, who go up to the city every day by train, have probably sound, subordinate jobs in some old-established commercial firm. They will save up to send their sons to a good minor public school, but in very few cases think of putting them through a university. At eighteen, the boys may become bank clerks, or may become articled to a solicitor, or a modest opening may be found for them in the firm in which their father works. It is hoped that the girls will marry, but perhaps they are given a course at a business college, or train in domestic science, or become nurses. Because of its isolation in its suburban fastnesses, and that insulation, of which I have spoken, from disturbing currents of feeling and thought, this section of the middle classes (and one might describe it as the dead centre of middle-class life in Great Britain) represents one of the most stable factors in our national life. Its young men, in any great war like the last two, provide a high proportion of the new officers. It is a very intelligent, staunch, and capable class but not in the least an intellectual class. It has probably few books in its pleasant, sunny houses and these accumulated rather at random over the years. When it wants something new to read, it goes to the circulating library at the local chemist's. Father chooses a detective story, mother a slightly sentimental novel of family life. To read much, and to read books other than novels, is thought slightly odd. It is odd, too, to discuss general topics too intensely. Bridges can be crossed when we come to them. For the outsider, the atmosphere of suburban life is likely to seem a little complacent and smug, but the other side of the smugness is the staunchness which this section of English society always shows in times of crisis. England, after all, owes a great deal to her philistines. A too lively imagination, a too vivid and ominous pre-monition of change, too widely diffused among the people, is not always a source of national strength. And the sort of suburban English men and women whose traits I am trying to sketch in, in this summary fashion, would not be in the least offended, I am sure, at one's assertion that imagination is not one of their notable characteristics.

Out of this kind of negative virtue, however, with its wariness of involving itself in intellectual complications or getting out of its emotional depths, no very profound drama or literature can be expected to emerge. In the 1920s and 1930s, people of this class, when they ran up to London or the nearest large town to see a play, looked for a kind of drama which would reflect the comfort and the safe boundaries of their own lives. And since a demand, on a free market, always creates a supply, they were given the kind of drama they wanted.

One can almost give a generic description of it. In retrospect, one play of this sort does not sort itself sharply out in one's mind from another. The setting is the living room of a suburban villa, with French windows opening out on to the garden, and through these French windows young people in white flannels wander in and out with tennis rackets under their arms. The play perhaps begins with a comic servant dusting the furniture and describing to a curious visitor the various endearing characteristics of the family. The young people are probably minor characters. The heroine is as likely as not a sweet, fluttering, managing mother (in her forties, but still very attractive) in whom every suburban matron in the audience can see herself. The young people's complications are put in to show her powers of management, but the main plot is perhaps the wistful revival and the gracious laying to rest of some romance in her own past life – perhaps the return of some old admirer, bronzed and still handsome, from the Far East. Nothing will come of his return except that it arouses her husband, who is such a nice man, but who perhaps has been taking her too much for granted, to a new attentiveness. Or perhaps the admirer can be shunted off on a daughter. The dialogue of the play does not aim at wit or incisiveness, but at an effect of pleasant natural chatter.

The author? At various times in the past twenty or thirty years it might have been (though it is invidious to mention names where so many playwrights have made a success in this genre), A. A. Milne, or Dodie Smith, or Esther McCracken, or John Van Druten, or Merton Hodge, or Daphne du Maurier. But however often one sees it, and whoever the author is, and however the local colour may be altered or the emphasis shifted from time to time, it is always 'a very nice play.' The plot is sometimes a little thin, perhaps; but the very cushioning of the action by the conventions of middle-class decorum allows one to sit back in one's stall with a reassuring sense of safety.

In dealing with the work of writers who would not claim to be more than honest entertainers, and who have given so many people so much harmless pleasure, one should avoid, I know, being heavy-handed. Yet if we look back, I think, at the play which seems to me to be the original ancestor of all suburban domestic dramas, Goldsmith's *She Stoops to Conquer*, it is impossible, I think, to avoid the conclusion that they represent a certain decadence. Like the plays I have been talking about, *She Stoops to Conquer* is notable for the amiable, almost too amiable, golden mellowness of its mood – one thinks of Yeats's phrase about Goldsmith 'sipping from the honeypot of his mind.' Yet we do see, nevertheless, that the rural society which Goldsmith describes is at once more fully integrated and more vital than the suburban society of the plays of A. A. Milne and Dodie Smith. Tony Lumpkin is alive in a way in which the young man with the tennis racket under his arm is not; Mrs Hardcastle, compared to the attractive mother in her forties of the latest West End success, is, for Goldsmith, almost an *unkind* portrait: and yet she is permanently alive in a way in which that mother, and her successors, and her predecessors, all weaving together in a ghostly unity in one's mind, are not. Lastly, the dialogue of *She Stoops to Conquer* is, for the eighteenth century, almost naturalistic; it has none of the polished artificial point and antithesis of Congreve or Sheridan. Yet it is alive on the page as well as on the boards; the play is a contribution to literature; the modern suburban comedies I have been describing are not.

The suburban domestic drama is a special instance of a phenomenon of the inter-war years which is worth touching on – the phenomenon of what Virginia Woolf called 'middlebrow literature.' By this she meant the abundance of books and plays which are reasonably well constructed, which have had some pains taken with them, but which are not intended to make any real disturbance, any sharp impact, to unsettle in any way anybody's feelings or convictions. The popularity of middlebrow literature had something to do with the limitations of suburban existence as a training-ground for discrimination in the arts. Great drama or literature is generally aristocratic in its regard for finish and form, but has its roots, on the other hand, deep in a popular culture. I have described already the insulation of suburban life both from any kind of aristocracy, whether of birth, intellect, or manners, and from the life of the people at large. That insulation leads in many cases to a feeling of emptiness, which is not, of course, reflected in the suburban domestic dramas I have been talking about. Or at least not consciously reflected; for the more critical spectator of such plays is conscious of a certain airlessness, he misses room for his mind to move in, he wonders what life can be like in such circumstances when no great issues are ever mentioned, where all moral problems are taken as solved, where all the talk is an endless going over and over of family gossip.* It is what everybody takes as charming, soothing, and reassuring and a few days of it would drive the more critical spectator mad. . . . But there is a sense at least, I think, in which suburban women particularly (for the men after all have their work to take up their time and to diversify their lives) turned to this kind of play, as they turned to a similar kind of novel, to dissipate a sense of inner emptiness and fatigue. It gave them a flattering picture of what their lives were not but what they might have day-dreams of them as being. And we may observe, rather severely, that it is *never* the business of the writer to encourage day-dreams; *never* his business to flatter.

Thus our reasons for rejecting the achievements of the middlebrow in drama and fiction are not reasons of intellectual self-conceit. They have to do rather with deep and sincere doubts about the wholesomeness of the product, even for those most addicted to it, for those whose great consolation it has become. One can, out of an effort of good will, attempt to surrender oneself to the impact of the sort of play and story I have been talking of, but, if one has cultivated one's sense of discrimination at all, one will be overcome in the end by an oppressive feeling of listlessness. There is often quite a high finish on products of this sort, but there is never any real inner 'go.' In the genuinely vulgar, the genuinely lowbrow product, on the other hand, there is this 'go.' When Marie Lloyd, the great vulgar music-hall singer died, Mr T. S. Eliot pointed out that she and her like represented something which the lower orders in England had and which the middle classes appeared to be losing – a deep and genuine recognition, and enjoyment, of the pattern of their own lives. Marie Lloyd's song, 'I'm One of the Ruins that Cromwell Knocked Abaht a Bit' caught up, echoed, diversified and fantasticated, and flung back to a delighted audience a part of their own lives – with no holds barred, with no genteel reserves of decorum – in a way in which no West End drawing-room comedy does. Marie Lloyd's song, one may say, had life in it, but the West End comedy has machinery that keeps it in motion.

* The most recent equivalent of the suburban domestic drama, for even wider consumption, is probably the very popular – and unending – radio series, *Mrs Dale's Diary*.

One can think of similar contrasts outside the strict realm of litera-ture. One thinks of the London pub, vulgar and ornate, with its frosted glass, its gilding, its barley sugar wooden pillars, its signed photographs of Georges Carpentier and Vesta Tilley; and then one thinks of the genteel, jazz-modernistic lounge of some road house twenty or thirty miles from London, built a few years before the war to cater for passing motorists. The pub has been there three parts of a century, gay, elaborate, ugly, all the time accreting more life and character. The roadhouse was perhaps built fifteen or twenty years ago. Already, in that time, its thin, rootless smartness has acquired an almost ghostly air. A lack of density, of thickness, of the pressure of 'lived life,' is what we have to complain about in all suburban pleasures and especially in suburban art and literature. The insulation of one class from another, of one way of life from another, however peaceful and tolerant an insulation, in the years between the wars in England, was not wholly a wholesome thing.

Perhaps things are changing now. The suburban middle classes are having a harder time since the end of the war. They cannot get servants as they used to; they have probably, because of the petrol rationing which has only recently come to an end, laid up their cars; even if only because they are so surprised and shocked not to find a Conservative government in power,* they are tending to take a new interest in social and political questions; their young people have been unsettled, from one point of view, or had their horizons broadened, from another, by the war. The suburbanites retain, of course, all their old moderation and cheerfulness and staunchness. Are they likely also to acquire a new imaginative grasp of the significance of their own kind of life, and its relation to the life of the rest of the nation? All I can say is that some of the most promising younger poets I know in London come from this suburban background and have begun to write about it in an imaginative way.† For the rest, we shall see.

Section 4: The Irish Dramatic Revival

Some of the criticisms that I have been making of the new realistic drama in England are made with great vigour by the Irish dramatist, John Millington Synge.

* Written before the last General Election.
† See Iain Fletcher's *Orisons, Picaresque and Metaphysical* (Editions Poetry London), par-ticularly the long, queer, and moving poem called *The Agony of Dying Houses*. The setting is Bromley, Kent.

In his preface to his most famous play – which has elements in it at once of farce and tragedy – *The Playboy of the Western World*, Synge pointed out what an advantage the Irish dramatist had over the contemporary English dramatist in being able to draw upon a rich and racy peasant speech.

'When I was writing *The Shadow of the Glen* some years ago,' he wrote, 'I got more than any learning could have given me from a chink in the floor of the old Wicklow house where I was staying, which let me hear what was being said by the servant girls in the kitchen. . . . In countries where the imagination of the people, and the language they use, is rich and living, it is possible for a writer to be rich and copious in his words, and at the same time to give the reality, which is the root of all poetry, in a comprehensive and natural form. In the modern literature of towns, however, richness is found only in sonnets, or prose poems, or in one or two elaborate books which are far away from the profound and common interests of life. One has on the one side Mallarmé and Huysmans producing this literature, and on the other Ibsen and Zola dealing with the realities of life in joyless and pallid words. On the stage one must have reality, and one must have joy; and that is why the intellectual modern drama has failed, and people have grown sick of the false joy of musical comedy, that has been given them in place of the rich joy found only in what is superb and wild in reality. In a good play every speech should be as fully flavoured as a nut or apple and such speeches cannot be written by anyone who works among people who have shut their lips on poetry. In Ireland for a few years more, we have a popular imagination that is fiery, and magnificent, and tender; so that those of us who wish to write, start with a chance that is not given to writers in places where the springtime of the local life has been forgotten, and the harvest is a memory only, and the straws have been turned into bricks.'

Synge died when still a comparatively young man, having written only a few plays, but for their combination of what he called reality and joy, of profound human insight and richness of language, these plays are rare among the dramas of this century. It might be questioned, however, whether they genuinely belong to the English tradition, or even whether the beautiful language they are written in with its many Celtic tricks of syntax and word order, and its abundant local idioms, is really 'English' in a strict sense. Certainly, they do not provide a model for a young man setting out to write plays in Birmingham or Manchester, and it is clear that Synge's tricks of language might in a lesser dramatist become mere mannerisms, as they do to some extent in his last unfinished tragedy, *Deirdre*. Synge is on the whole saved from mannerism by his heartiness and earthiness but in the dialect comedies of Lady Gregory, for instance, one feels that the local colour is being laid thickly on a substratum of ideas that has almost something in common with the world of suburban cosiness that we were considering in our last section.

Again, admitting that *The Playboy of the Western World* is a dramatic masterpiece, we might still ask whether it is a masterpiece of 'contemporary' drama or rather more essentially a piece, in the wide sense, of 'pastoral' writing: of writing, that is, which evades the current issues of life in a complex society by inventing, or at least depicting with a certain added glow of poetic tenderness, a world of simpler characters and simpler problems than those of the actual world.* James Joyce, at least, who was as great a master of language as Synge, did not dismiss the intellectual drama of Ibsen as a failure and did not see the solution of the Irish writer's problem as involving a retreat from urban complexities and an exploitation of the richness of peasant culture. One of Joyce's earliest writings was a tribute to Ibsen and his one play, *Exiles* deals, in Ibsen's manner, with contemporary problems. Its characters are subtle and evolved, its statement of its issues an intellectual one, its background urban.

One may say, perhaps, that, great man though Synge was, his 'programme' involved an undue degree of artificial simplification and that it is the task of the dramatist to-day, not merely to look for the raw poetry of rustic speech and life where it still survives, but to make a poetic and dramatic shape out of the outwardly intractable and even outwardly anti-poetic material of the life that he and his friends lead. The weakness of Synge's programme can be seen not only in the rather too couthy 'kitchen comedies' of Lady Gregory, but in the plays of W. B. Yeats, where the most absolute mastery of language, and a deep and real feeling for the folk roots of Irish tradition, somehow fail, on the whole, to compensate for a lack of dramatic 'body,' a lack of that gritty complexity and harsh solidity, which we ask from the plot and the characters of a 'real play.' In some of Yeats's very last plays, like *Purgatory*, he seemed to be developing towards a harsher and more effective sense of dramatic reality, but on the whole the impression that most of his plays leave upon us is a pleasant, but faint,

---

* For this notion of 'the pastoral mode,' see William Empson's brilliant book, *Some Versions of Pastoral* (Chatto and Windus).

one, like that of a tapestry scene, rippling and moving through water. They are very beautiful but very remote and far less genuinely dramatic in force of language or concentration of character than Yeats's purely lyrical and meditative poems of his personal life.

The most promising Irish dramatist, after Synge, was Sean O'Casey, who does seem to have realised, at least in his earlier plays, the dramatic inadequacy of the pastoral attitude – the dramatic inadequacy, that is, of setting one's characters in a setting that is not one's own, assuming the existence in them of a simplicity and directness which is not in oneself, and thus shelving, for the time being, the proper statement of one's own problems. O'Casey grew up in the Dublin slums, and he writes about them; and if his attitude towards them is a warm and generous one, it is not in the least sentimental. His earliest and best plays, *Juno and the Paycock*, *The Shadow of a Gunman* (which is somewhat slighter than the first) and the splendid *The Plough and the Stars* (this was the flag of the Irish Republic for which the Irish patriots rose at Easter in 1916) are harshly realistic tragedies. They are shot through, nevertheless, with a broad and deep and effective humour – the vital humour of the Irish poor. The Irish 'troubles' give O'Casey a background which enables him to introduce plausibly the acts of violence which he needs to resolve, in a tragic sense, what might otherwise be the merely static pathos or humour of his scene; thus the atmosphere of these wonderful plays is sometimes like that of a music-hall crosstalk act (but of a kind that could only be invented by a genius) interrupted by a murder. No writer of our time has caught the whole atmosphere of working-class life more beautifully than O'Casey, or has been able to raise that atmosphere, as he has, to the pitch of tragic dignity. His plays are poetic in their total effect, but in detail they are sharply realistic. O'Casey listened to the language of the Dublin poor as Synge had listened to that of the Irish peasantry, but with a different purpose. He was not looking for cadences out of which he could artfully construct his own poetry but, like a reporter, looking for the effect of language which – whether or not it would be poetic or beautiful – would be unmistakably true to life. One does not ask, reading these early plays of O'Casey's, what his style is like; one simply believes that all his characters say exactly what he makes them say. This complete illusion of reality is a very rare thing in the theatre, indeed.

Thus, we might say that, though O'Casey is not a 'lord of language' in the sense of Synge or Yeats, he is more properly a dramatist of our own age than either of them; in that he does know exactly what a given range of characters, over a given range of situations, will say. Unfortunately, he knows this only in reference to a sharply defined milieu – the Dublin tenements of his boyhood and youth. His gift is one of specific sensitivity. When he enlarges his theme, he loses his touch. In his later plays, *The Silver Tassie, The Star Turns Red, Within the Gates, Red Roses for Me,* and *Oak Leaves and Lavender,* he deserts the poetic realism of his wonderful early Irish plays for a kind of symbolic expressionism, whose failure lies, precisely, in a lack of genuine poetry. His characters no longer talk in their own style, but in a style that O'Casey has invented for them; in a florid and rhetorical language which is always aiming at, and for ever falling short of, poetic eloquence. Moreover, they are no longer, except in snatches, real people – they are symbols of various social attitudes that O'Casey disapproves of or admires, like the characters in a mediaeval morality play. The melodrama is now obvious, the pathos overweighted, and the humour, when there is any humour, has lost its old music-hall earthiness and gaiety. We can no longer believe – as in the earlier plays we completely and unquestioningly believe – in the detail of what is happening at the 'realistic' level. And O'Casey has not the verbal art which could make us believe in it at any other level. In a country of poets, he was, in his beginnings, a great prose dramatist (though with the underlying poetic vision which the greatest prose dramatists, Ibsen, Tchehov, always have). It is his personal tragedy that he has attempted to transform himself, by a sheer effort of will, into the overtly poetic dramatist which he was not fitted to be.

He is trying to-day to give his characters and actions a symbolic reality. But the characters of Mr O'Casey's earliest plays, Juno and Jack Boyle, 'Joxer,' Nora, and Fluther, have not the reality of symbols, they have something more important and harder to achieve, the reality of flesh and blood; perhaps a more tangible and poignant reality than that of the characters of any other dramatist, in the English language, of this century. Possibly Mr O'Casey was right in feeling that he had exhausted that early vein of gold, and possibly he was right in leaving Ireland, in the fear that if he remained there his dramas might become provincial, but the fact remains that he is a dramatist of undeniable genius who seems, since he cut apart from his roots, to have lost his way.

Another Irish dramatist who, for reasons that it is harder to divine, has never quite fulfilled a splendid early promise is Mr Denis Johnston.

He is a younger man than Mr O'Casey and his second play, to which he mainly owes his reputation, *The Moon in the Yellow River*, had its first production, at the Abbey Theatre in Dublin, in 1931. In some of his interests and attitudes, as in some of his stage techniques, Mr Johnston has, in fact, perhaps less in common with the general tradition of the Irish theatrical revival than with such typical writers of the 1930s as Mr Auden and Mr Isherwood; a very fascinating non-realistic play of his, *A Bride for the Unicorn*, a poetic fantasy in prose with much incidental social satire and some verse choruses, very much resembles in flavour their *The Dog Beneath the Skin*. The hero, again, of Mr Johnston's *Storm Song*, a play about the making of a film in the Aran Islands, is very much a typical hero of the Auden generation. He sees his art as one of social documentation, he resents the commercial interests that strangle it, and at the end of the play he deserts the heroine (who is an emancipated representative of the old landed aristocracy) to go on studying the art of the film in Russia. 'Like many of his type,' Mr Johnston tells us, 'he would probably call himself an anarchist, while meaning that he was a communist, though in fact he is neither, being an artist – which is the last thing he would admit.' Mr Johnston's background is obviously a different one from Mr O'Casey's. He touches in lower-class humours and patches of Irish local colour, with a masterly hand, but he has not O'Casey's intimate feeling for the tragedies of Irish working-class life, and his best characters, like the disillusioned Catholic, Dobelle, the romantic rebel, Darrell Blake, and the German engineer, Tausch, in *The Moon in the Yellow River*, are extremely articulate people – almost as articulate sometimes as characters in Shaw – who belong to the 'ruling few.'

In this play, Tausch, the German engineer, is in charge of a power-house in a remote part of Ireland. The period is that of the early days of Irish independence, when the government in Dublin has still to deal with sporadic partisan activity by extreme Republicans who disapprove of the compromise treaty signed with England. Tausch has to confront a charming captain of partisans, Darrell Blake, who wants to blow his power-house up, but only superficially for political reasons. Fundamentally, Blake is defending a traditional way of life, the Ireland of the peasant and the craftsman, against the deadening order of managerial industrial society. Tausch, for his part, is defending not only his power-house, but his ideal of the rational ordering of the world through science. Both are completely honest men. Dobelle, in whose house most of the action takes place, is a more complex character. Both Tausch and Blake seem to him to be fighting for illusions. His attitude to life is ironically defeatist. Years before, in accordance with Catholic practice, he has let his wife die in childbirth, rather than save her by sacrificing the child. Unconsciously, he has revenged himself on his daughter by refusing to love her; more consciously he has revenged himself on the Church by 'returning God his ticket.' He has not lost his faith, but he has lost his hope and his charity. The eternal torments of the damned and the sufferings of the living are, for him, much too high a price to pay for the eternal bliss of the redeemed. Dobelle is too humane and fastidious to give himself deliberately over to evil, but all positive human enthusiasms now seem to him mistaken and futile; perhaps life itself seems to him a misfortune, and the creation of the world, from a rational human standpoint, God's great mistake. Dobelle is the most profoundly conceived character in the play, and though he takes no active part in the debate between Tausch and Blake, his more inclusive, even though temporarily negative, attitude suggests their limitations. In mere verbal combat, Tausch's heavy-handed German seriousness loses ground all along to Blake's poetic wit. But Tausch unconsciously breaks the sporting rules of this sort of situation by calling in a local police official, Commandant Lanigan, an old comrade of Blake's in the days of the troubles. For Lanigan, heavy, inarticulate, and sullen, there is one practical solution to the problem, and he takes it. The power-house may be saved now, but it will certainly be blown up some time if Blake survives. So he shoots Blake dead. Tausch is morally overwhelmed; he has called in the law to help him, and it has behaved illegally. And as a final irony his power-house (farcically incompetent attempts to destroy it have been going on all through the play) is in the end blown up after all. All that emerges positively from the action is that, as a result of this violence, Dobelle is shaken out of his negative attitude, realises that his daughter needs his love, and regains his hope and his charity. The play can be read as an extremely brilliant farcical melodrama, just skirting the verge of tragedy, but its fundamental significance, perhaps, is as a modern morality. Tausch, Blake, and Dobelle represent not so much three Shavian 'points of view' as three stages in the progress of the soul: the practical, the poetic, the religious. Dobelle represents the latency, the negative pole, of an attitude that could reconcile Tausch's blind science and Blake's irresponsible poetry; but to do so it needs to be awakened to life by a kind of 'shock treatment.'

Storm Song, an extremely interesting, but less successful play, deals perhaps with too many conflicts on too many levels, and resolves some of them rather perfunctorily. There are two main groups of characters, a set of young English people making a film in a group of islands off the west coast of Ireland, under a famous continental director, and a set of Irish aristocrats, robbed of their old power, and turning to culture, whisky, or bitter grumbling about the younger generation, as a diversion. The film director, Szilard, who dies at sea in a storm making the last shots of his great film, is less a character than a symbol; he represents for the play the heroic attitude rather as airmen, mountaineers, and explorers do for the poetry of the Auden group. Gordon King, the hero, who attracts the heroine, Jal Joyce, away from the defeated aristocrat, Martin Burke, hero-worships Szilard and his feelings for Jal can never be equally important to him; when he leaves her at the end of the play to go to Russia he is still following symbolically in the dead Szilard's footsteps. For him, as for many young heroes of the Auden generation, social activities have in the long run more glamour than the personal life, and he is more at ease in practical comradeship with men than in any emotional relationship with women. In his hopefulness, his courage, his impatience, and also in a certain unconscious callowness and callousness, he is very much a type of his decade. Thus in spite of its loose ends, *Storm Song* has a peculiar interest as a documentary record of typical attitudes of the 1930s. A very young reader would find it good background reading for the study of Auden's poems and Isherwood's novels.

A Bride for the Unicorn, a poetic play in prose, has prophetic rather than documentary importance. It anticipates the central part played by myth in the work of writers like Robert Graves, Edwin Muir, and Kathleen Raine in recent years, and its central theme is that dealt with by Mr Graves in *The White Goddess*. A young man, who has just left school, meets a beautiful masked woman who goes with him to a room in a hotel. In the hotel, he meets a number of old school friends, who chaff him, and when he goes back to the room the masked woman has vanished. All through the rest of the play, she haunts him, but he does not find her. He marries somebody else and settles down and, with various old school friends, who typify conventional attitudes, has adventures in the fields of commerce, war, and politics. His adventures are at once a satire on the general contemporary situation (particularly, perhaps, on the recent history of Ireland) and a gay but poetic parody of the exploits of various classical heroes. Without the presence of the masked woman, they can never attain to tragic seriousness; not only with the hero, but with all the other characters, lightly sketched in as they are, one has the feeling that the real life of the adult can never be *as* real as memories of schoolboy comradeship and of a first experience of romantic love or initiation into sexual maturity. (The old school, the original assembling of comrades, looms as large in the plot, though it is not given the same poetic underlining, as the elusive goddess.) In the end, the hero, John Foss, finds the masked woman again, but with her finds death. He embraces her cloaked figure and 'it collapses in his grasp into empty air, and he falls dead upon the ground, holding to his heart the folds of the garment.' (This is an aspect of the White Goddess on which Mr Graves has hardly touched, that perhaps her existence must be imaginary, perhaps no real woman can satisfactorily embody her.) John's companions mourn for him, as for Adonis. This is one of Mr Johnston's most original and fascinating plays, but I imagine Mr Graves, for instance, might find something sinister both in the fact that her status, as I have said, seems to be almost that of a subjective illusion, and in the other fact that Apollo, her male supplanter (the god, for Mr Graves, rather of rhetoric than of true poetry), plays such a prominent part in the choruses:

> Sing of your brother, Phoebus, of the golden hair
> Who rules Parnassus and the Delphic stream
> Flowing from the fair Castalian hill.

In the long run, in fact, the moral of the play might be that the main social use of the goddess has been as a spur of impossible hope to keep the hero going through a round of useful practical activities. Ambivalent as its theme is, and rather sketchy as its execution sometimes is (with a flavour of brilliant conversation, of charade), *A Bride for the Unicorn* has nevertheless gaiety, pathos, and charm. Mr Johnston has written no plays in recent years, but he is still a comparatively young man, and it is to be hoped that he has still something to offer us. Among dramatists of the 1930s, he stands almost alone for his flexible stagecraft, his grasp both of general social situations and particular types of character, and his mastery of witty yet natural dialogue.

Since the time of Mr O'Casey's early plays, Ireland has not produced any other dramatist of the first rank, and it may be that the peculiar social tensions, the atmospheres of exultation and crisis, which fostered the geniuses of Synge and Yeats and O'Casey, have now vanished from what is, at the present time, merely a rather sheltered and remote and, in intellectual matters, rather cautious and puritanical farmers' republic. It may be also that when Synge said that the peculiar raciness and vivacity of Irish speech and life had only a few more years to run, he was right, and that now that the study of the Irish language and of Celtic mythology have become, not the passion of rebellious enthusiasts, but a burdensome task for schoolboys, the sense of Irish destiny may have lost something of its old magic. At all events, there was a time when it did seem that Dublin rather than London was going to be the centre of everything new and interesting in the English-speaking theatre; but, in spite of splendid isolated achievements, that hope has not been fulfilled.

Section 5: The Revival of the Poetic Drama

We have seen that by the 1930s all the various types of prose drama which we have been considering might be said to have reached a dead end. In Shaw's later plays, for instance, such as *The Millionairess* or *The Simpleton of the Unexpected Isles*, we feel that fantasy is being substituted for plot, caricature for character, the reiteration of old, settled notions for fresh thinking. And the prefaces to these later plays, though written (as the plays themselves, to give them their due, often are) with as much sparkle as ever, show a certain loss of emotional touch with the moral issues of the age. A brisk and cheerful consideration of the uses of extermination as a political method, for instance, might have seemed an amusing paradox in the 1890s: in the 1930s, when Hitler was forming his plans for the general extirpation of the Jews in Europe, it was too topical to be funny. But for Shaw the violence and cruelty of Hitler, of Mussolini, of the Tcheka in the early days of the Russian revolution, were all simply means, though no doubt imperfect means, by which the 'life-force' in our time was achieving its purpose; a view possible to take only if, like Shaw himself, you are fortunate enough to live in a civilised country, a country sheltered from all these horrors, in which nobody would dream of lifting a hand to harm you however much pernicious nonsense you write. But for that humane and liberal society which had done so much to foster and protect his genius, Shaw had never a word of courtesy, even in these years when it was so soon to fight, against the new barbarisms, at once raw and decadent, for its life. His great countryman, Yeats, who was no more of a liberal, but had a high chivalry and in spite of his arrogance an innate gentleness of temperament, knew better. Thinking as Shaw thought that the rule of law, the society which respects liberty and protects the individual, were things gone in our time for good, he nevertheless saluted their memory:

> We too had many pretty toys when young;
> A law indifferent to blame or praise,
> To bribe or threat; habits that made old wrong
> Melt down, as it were wax in the sun's rays;
> Public opinion ripening for so long
> We thought it would outlive all future days.
> O what fine thought we had because we thought
> That the worst rogues and rascals had died out!

Yeats saw with a poet's eagle eye at once what should be obvious now, some thirty years after he wrote, that the attack of violent, passionate, ignorant men on the majestic, crumbling fabric of the nineteenth-century liberal idea was not 'progress':

> Now days are dragon-ridden, the nightmare
> Rides upon sleep: a drunken soldiery
> Can leave the mother, murdered at her door,
> To crawl in her own blood, and go scot-free;
> The night can sweat with terror as before
> We pieced our thoughts into philosophy,
> And planned to bring the world under a rule . . .

Yeats, in fact, recognised what is obviously the case that, as far as the high traditions of civilisation go, our time is a time of loss. Shaw, for all his dialectical gifts – 'the philosopher turned demagogue,' Robert Graves has called him – was reluctant to admit this. He had always relied on argument, lacking the poet's more profound and more immediate grasp of reality, the simple 'feel' of the age. He was dogmatic as well as dialectical; and one of the dogmas he had always accepted (trimming it up in the garments of his 'life-force' religion or philosophy) was the old Victorian Liberal one of automatic progress. Rejecting so much that was so much more true and important in Liberalism, he retained that. Progress is automatic, the result of an immanent spirit driving onwards through history; therefore the 'strong men' at any given moment, the Hitlers, Mussolinis, and so on, must be the instruments of progress. . . . But one must not suppose that Shaw had (as Carlyle had, for instance) a sneaking appetite for brutality in history, for exhibitions of the smashing mailed fist. His humanitarianism, however thin and abstract, however fundamentally unconcerned with individual suffering, was perfectly genuine. But he lacked imagination; he could not know – as the most ordinary man in the street would have tended to suspect – that the 'strong men' he praised would cling desperately to power even if it involved the total ruin of their countries and that if they killed and tortured many people, it was often less for any high-minded or even practical reason, than because they enjoyed doing so.

If the drama of ideas, in the hands of its greatest living master, was failing to grasp the realities of the age, the drama of entertainment and suburban domestic comedy were both in the 1930s (and the process has continued into our own decade) growing more pallid and insignificant. It was notable that Noel Coward in the 1930s tended to turn away from the comedy of entertainment, which may also be a comedy of social criticism, to plays of sheer patriotic and sentimental spectacle like *Cavalcade* (effective on the stage but unbearably dull to read) or romantic musical comedies like *Bitter Sweet*: these latter rather recalling the style of a successful confectioner of romantic spectacles, who does not, however, quite belong to a history of literature, the author-actor-producer, Ivor Novello. Younger playwrights, more or less in Coward's tradition, like Terence Rattigan, had even less genuine wit in their pieces than Coward had and aimed, on the whole, at some fetching combination of lively farce and sound sentiment. There were still in the 1930s, of course, as there are to-day, certain sober and honest craftsmen of the theatre such as Mr J.B.Priestley, with his solid feeling for the backgrounds and atmospheres of the more thoughtful and serious kind of English middle-class life, but even Mr Priestley's constant experimentation, either with technical devices involving some new conception of time or with various kinds of modern allegory or morality play, showed that he, like most people, felt that the tradition of realistic prose drama was needing, in the 1930s and the 1940s, an injection of fresh blood.

It was in these circumstances that various writers who had made their reputation and had their training not as dramatists but as poets were to make the attempt to revive that tradition of the poetic drama which had been dead, if not since Jacobean times, at least since the Restoration. Most people would agree that the Restoration dramatist Thomas Otway's tragedy *Venice Preserved* is the last English play in verse till our own times which can claim at once to be a work of literature and a piece of 'good theatre.' The revival of the poetic drama in the 1930s and the 1940s took various forms, and it was in a sense significant that the new attempts at poetic drama had a much closer connection with the deeper religious beliefs or social attitudes of their authors than had most of the prose drama of the time.

Thus Mr T.S. Eliot (who is certainly the most important name in this context) commenced his career as a practical dramatist by writing a pageant-play to encourage the collection of funds for the building of new London churches. The pageant-play was called *The Rock*. The outline of this play, and many of the details of it, were suggested to Mr Eliot by other persons, and it is scarcely either a 'play' in the proper sense or typical anywhere of Mr Eliot at his best, though it has some fine rhetorical choruses; but it undoubtedly gave Mr Eliot useful practice in stagecraft. Mr Eliot's second play, *Murder in the Cathedral*, written to be performed in Canterbury Cathedral at the yearly Canterbury Festival, commemorated the death of St Thomas à Becket, Canterbury's famous martyr, who had been murdered in the very Cathedral where Mr Eliot's play was first performed. So the impulse behind this play too was a religious rather than a properly theatrical one.

Nevertheless, *Murder in the Cathedral* is closer to being a drama in the real sense than *The Rock* is. It makes, again, a particularly effective use of the chorus; and perhaps the women of Canterbury, who make up the chorus, have a more impressive dramatic reality even than the dignified and impressive but rather thin, flat, sharply outlined character of the protagonist himself. If St Thomas strikes us, in the end, as failing to have reality in depth – as being rather a symbol than a person – the other characters in the play have even less independent significance, are personifications of various simple abstract attitudes, meaningful only in relation to St Thomas himself. The real 'action' of the play, in fact, lies not really in the violent killing of St Thomas at the end but rather in his confrontation with, and his triumphing over, various temptations, of which the most serious and dangerous is the temptation to accept his martyrdom, not out of Christian humility and obedience and the wish to bear witness to God's truth, but out of spiritual pride. The drama, in so far as there is a drama, is thus strictly 'interior,' and the outward value of the play is rather that of a spectacle and a commemorative ritual. Thus, in spite of marking an advance on *The Rock*, *Murder in the Cathedral* still belongs to the special religious occasion rather than the wider world of the theatre; and to get the most out of it, one must approach it in a religious frame of mind.

In Mr Eliot's third play, however, *The Family Reunion*, he is at last beginning to acquire a proper sense of the stage. This is no longer a religious work, with edification or commemoration as its primary aim. The setting is one of English aristocratic country-house life and the plot is concerned with the return of a young nobleman, Harry, Lord Monchensey, to his ancestral home, of which his widowed mother wishes him now to become the head, settling down happily to his traditional status of local grandee. It is soon obvious that Harry is tormented by anxieties and fears of his own and is both indifferent to, and in fact hardly consciously aware of, his mother's schemes for him. These anxieties and fears are personified, not only for Harry but for his chauffeur, and of course for the audience, as the Eumenides or Furies, who pursue Harry (who has murdered, or thinks he has murdered, his wife) as they pursued Orestes after he murdered his mother, Clytemnestra: and these archaic and frightening beings, with their glittering eyes, do in fact occasionally stare through the French windows of the manorial living-room. Mr Eliot was looking, as he has explained, for a symbol of remorse and guilt which would be more widely acceptable in a largely sceptical, agnostic, or pagan age like our own than any overtly Christian one. Gradually in conversation with a sympathetic aunt and cousin, Agatha and Mary, the story about Harry's wife (he asserts that he pushed her overboard off a passenger steamer on a dark night and has been 'on the run' from the Furies ever since) comes out. It is not made quite explicit but we do feel either that this belief of Harry's that he has killed his wife is a hallucination or else that what is haunting him is something more complex and more deeply rooted than a single violent act. In an attempt to help Harry to recover his spiritual balance and to get at the roots of his sense of trouble, his aunt Agatha reveals to him the tragic circumstances connected with his own birth. Harry's father, the late Lord, had not loved his wife Amy but had passionately loved her sister Agatha and had wished to murder his wife. Agatha, though she returned his love, had persuaded him not to commit this crime, partly because Amy at that time was about to have a child. The child of course, turned out to be Harry. Harry can thus feel that his own obsession that he has killed his wife is simply a kind of inherited, unconscious memory of his father's desire to kill his mother. Whatever Harry himself may be guilty of, it is something far deeper and wider than any guilt of his that he is expiating. Agatha also lets Harry know that she feels that she, rather than Amy, is spiritually his mother, for she had genuinely loved Harry's father, as Amy, who cared only about her place and her possessions, never had. Harry now realises that the Furies are not instruments of blind vindictiveness but rather of purification; and he is like Orestes too, in that when he has been driven finally to the place of his purification, the internal divisions that have rent his family and are now, as it were, personified in him, will at last be reconciled. But the place of his peace will certainly not be his ancestral home; so Harry sets out again on his travels, in his expensive car, accompanied by his chauffeur, and this shock, and the disappointment to all her hopes, kills his mother.

There are a few technical remarks to be made about *The Family Reunion.* The verse has perhaps fewer easily memorable or obviously eloquent passages than that of *Murder in the Cathedral,* but the reason is that Mr Eliot is now aiming at catching the tones, idioms, and rhythms of contemporary speech; so the 'poetry,' in the obvious sense, is muffled and subdued. Similarly, the 'formal' element is muffled and subdued; instead of the elaborate choruses of *The Rock* and *Murder in the Cathedral,* there are a number of minor characters – less important uncles and aunts of Harry's – who occasionally express their thoughts in unison, thus giving an ironical effect of a background of well-mannered, well-intentioned dimness and incomprehension, to which Harry's inner sufferings are disturbing from their very lack of everyday palpableness: if only it were something that an aspirin, a hot-water bottle, a day in bed, a drink after a tiring journey, an understanding talk with a fellow man of the world, or, at the very outside edge, a consultation with a nerve specialist could put right! Yet for all their pathetic kindness and inadequacy these faded gentlefolk have their own kind of sensitivity too, and feel uneasily that there is something in Harry's predicament beyond their intellectual and moral grasp. Here, in fact, we have an adaptation of the tragic Greek chorus to the purposes of a modern 'serious' play and also, occasionally, to those of ironic or comic relief. Contemporary reviewers of this play who complained that Mr Eliot had flattened out his poetry in it missed the point. The first requisite of any play is that, within its own convention, it should convey the illusion of reality; a richer use, however, of language would have destroyed the play's grey, tense, edgy contemporaneity of atmosphere. One might almost say, if the statement does not sound too paradoxical, that Mr Eliot was looking for the verse equivalent of what Synge called Ibsen's way of 'dealing with the realities of life in joyless and pallid words.' He needed a kind of dramatic verse which, whatever other virtues it had, would at least have those of prose; especially the prose virtue of convincingness.

Some critics had, indeed, even felt this grey quality in his non-dramatic poems. 'Eliot,' says Yeats, in every way temperamentally his opposite, 'has produced his great effect upon his generation because he has described men and women that get out of bed or into it from mere habit; in describing this life that has lost heart his own art seems grey, cold, dry. He is an Alexander Pope, working without apparent imagination, producing his effect by a rejection of all rhythms and metaphor used by the more popular romantics rather than by the discovery of his own, this rejection giving his work an unexaggerated plainness that has the effect of novelty.' One does not expect one great poet to be fair about another, and this seems to me very unfair; there is a grain of truth in it, however, and especially in his two plays of modern life, *The Family Reunion* and *The Cocktail Party*, it is the case, I think, that Eliot, seeking above all things to convince his audience of the reality of what they are listening to, has aimed especially at this 'unexaggerated plainness.' There are moments of high eloquence and there is a submerged rhythm making the speech more exciting than prose – but it is submerged, an underswell, it does not often break in foam on the surface.

Apart from the fact that the poetry is submerged in *The Family Reunion*, it might be said that the drama, in so far as one thinks of drama involving a violent or crucial *action* of some sort, is submerged too. Miss Helen Gardiner, in her very perceptive study, *The Art of T. S. Eliot*, makes the observation that what is novel in this play, and what leads perhaps to its lack of complete effectiveness on the stage, is that it sets out to dramatise not guilt but sin. Guilt springs from some specific thing we have done; the sense of sin from our general human condition; it is therefore hard to illustrate it in a dramatic way since there is no particular state of affairs to which it can be related rather than to any other – it is involved more or less in everything we think and do. On the other hand, some people are blind to it, as nobody is blind to a specific instance of guilt; and to those who are blind Harry is likely to appear a mere neurotic, badly in need of treatment, but of more expert treatment than Agatha can give him; and the Eumenides are likely to appear a tactless piece of archaic poeticising, which rather destroys the illusion. Certainly, though *The Family Reunion* is a far more ambitious and interesting play than *Murder in the Cathedral*, its effect on the stage is an oddly (and unsatisfactorily, because not I think consciously or intentionally) ambiguous one. The main characters, or at least the characters with whom Mr Eliot seems to be most in sympathy, Harry, Agatha, and Mary, are in a sense too transparent, too spiritual and introspective – there is something very 'materialistic' about the stage and we like a character to become an opaque and solid manifestation; something not so much that grasps itself, as that *we* grasp. But Harry, Agatha, and Mary are so nearly pure minds, so much presented in terms of consciousness and so little in terms of unconscious habits of speech, feeling, behaviour, that they elude us. We cannot imagine them *outside* the particular context of the action. We do not know what Harry was like before he turned up and he seems almost to vanish away from us completely when he finally steps outside the door. But Hamlet and Falstaff go on existing for us both when they are off stage and also after the play is over: and in *The Family Reunion* the character of Amy, the mother, with whom Mr Eliot is not so anxiously in sympathy, whose 'inner states' do not interest him much, by her very opacity acquires a solid theatrical power, which does not belong to the more 'spiritual' characters in the piece. Amy's death is perhaps the most moving thing in the play, at least when one sees it performed; much more moving than Harry's final departure. It is very wrong, of course, to think of Harry as a mere neurotic and weakling: but one might say that the heroic element in his character is not made manifest with sufficient crudity. The distinction between his being on the run at the beginning, with the Furies after him, and his departure at the end, not as a fugitive now but rather as the modern equivalent of a pilgrim or seeker, is a distinction which it is hard to make dramatically palpable. And the sympathy which Amy arouses, without, probably, Mr Eliot's intending to arouse it for her to that degree, makes Harry's general attitude of indifference or absent-mindedness towards her estranging: as if Mr Eliot were saying, 'We are all sinners, of course, but what happens to the more earthy and practical-minded sinner is, really, of little interest.' All this tends to dislocate the moral pattern of the play. Yet if on the whole we must judge it to be a failure, it is a failure more distinguished and more intrinsically interesting than the normal commercial, or even than the normal literary and dramatic, success. It has the touch of genius in it.

Mr Eliot's latest play, *The Cocktail Party*, is, on the other hand, a success at all levels, including that of accessibility and acceptability in the ordinary commercial theatre. It does seem to surmount that gap which lies between the poet's privacies of sensibility and that obvious, direct, and crude appeal which is necessary in a successful play; to surmount that more confidently than any of his previous dramas. It is a comedy, and in the light and gay texture of its witty conversations it beats, on his own ground, such a dramatist as Mr Noel Coward at his best. At the same time, *The Cocktail Party* has a profoundly serious underlying theme, that of the various kinds of self-deception in which even cultivated and pleasant and well-meaning people tend to indulge, as one might indulge in a drug, in our uneasy society; and of the way in which self-deception prevents people from living the life and doing the work they were meant to do, from following their true vocation.

The play begins with a cocktail party at which the host is exceedingly embarrassed because he does not know all the guests. They have been invited, and the party arranged by his wife – and shortly before the curtain goes up, he has discovered that his wife has left him, without notifying him where she has gone. He keeps up appearances as well as he can, pretends that his wife has had to pay a sudden visit to an aunt in the country, but an eccentric guest whose name he does not know stays behind after the others have left and shows both an uncanny penetration into the host's state of mind and an apparent knowledge of his secret. In the next act, it turns out that this guest is neither a brilliant madman nor a supernatural visitant, both of which he at a first glance might seem to be, but rather a famous Harley Street psychiatrist. And in a scene in which he confronts the distraught husband and the wife who has temporarily deserted him, it becomes clear what are the roots of the failure of the marriage. The husband is a capable and clever man, but a man dogged with a sense of his own inescapable mediocrity of spirit, and in particular possessed by a guilty feeling that he can never love anybody adequately. This has been made clear, in fact, already in the first act, where the husband, in an interview with a young woman, with whom he has been having a love affair, has refused to welcome the fact that, now his wife has left him, he is 'free.' It is not that his wife's leaving him has suddenly made him feel that it is, after all, his wife he loves. It is rather that he hates having his habits of life broken into, and that he thinks more of the social ridicule and awkwardness which may follow his wife's desertion of him than of his personal feelings, confused and dull feelings in any case, for either his wife or his mistress: and his coldness and timidity and irritable self-centredness have the effect of completely disillusioning the latter young woman, not only about the husband, but about human relations in general, so that she too comes to consult the psychiatrist. The wife, on the other hand, who has been having her own love affair – with a young man, a man much younger than herself, who is secretly, however, in love with the husband's mistress, whom he does not realise to be the husband's mistress – is not obsessed as her husband is with the feeling of being incapable of loving but rather of being intrinsically unlovable. She is the sort of successful, hard-working society hostess who takes a great deal of pains to be popular, but she never feels that people can take to her for her own sake. They are being kind or polite or find her socially useful, but it is not im-mediately to herself, her nature, her personality, that they respond; that, she feels, has for everybody something, not necessarily repellent, but flavourless, uninteresting about it. The psychiatrist points out to these two that their very sense of inadequacy on both sides – the husband's failure to rise properly to an emotional occasion, the wife's failure properly to provoke one – provides a moral basis for successful marriage; if they honestly realise their limitations, give up their romantic dreams, and accept an honourable 'second best,' they can help each other on life's way. They must accept the fact that they are rather ordinary people, but that there are very many much worse things in life than being decently ordinary.

It has become clear by this stage in the play that the psychiatrist is not a mere psychiatrist but rather one of a group of people – the other two are a gossipy old woman and a facetious man-about-town – who have either assumed, or in some mysterious fashion been given, the roles of spiritual guardians to the less enlightened people in their circle. They see it as their job, in a word, to help to save souls from damnation; also lives, useful in this world, from ruin and waste at the practical level. If the husband and wife are diverted by the guardians into the channels of a decent, ordinary marriage, the girl who has been the husband's mistress is a much more exceptional person, and the voca-tion which she is gradually led to accept is that of a missionary: a vocation which is to lead in a very short time to her martyrdom in a primitive country. The young man who has been in love with her, and who has simultaneously been the lover of the wife, has literary ambitions which have not exactly come to nothing, but which he has thought about with an exaggeratedly self-centred idea of his own importance and his own talent; he is sent off by the guardians to a more practical job, at which he is to do very well, getting rid at the same time of some of his egoism, in the film industry in Hollywood. But this young man, too, has high spiritual possibilities and when, in the last act, he learns of the martyrdom of the girl whom he has so long secretly loved, we see that this news brings about in him a kind of painful but healthy inner awakening. The last act, however, is very largely concerned with the husband and wife – the girl's terrible death, naturally, is merely reported, it is not part of the action on stage – and it shows how, having accepted the order and limitations of married life for people of their temperaments, they are able to make something happy and creative out of it. They are much more mature and likeable people now than they were in the earlier acts.

Thus Mr Eliot has managed to write a play which at once keeps us continually amused and expectant and yet deals seriously with typical problems of ordinary behaviour in our time. Critics have noted, as in the case of *The Family Reunion*, that he does so rather at the expense of an obvious poetic richness of language: it is even more true of this play than of the earlier one that the run of the dialogue, especially in the lighter passages, is often almost, though never quite, indistinguishable from the run of conversational prose. Mr Eliot is certainly sparing of flowers and purple patches: though there are several movingly eloquent passages, like this one, in which the psychiatrist describes the sort of 'ordinary' happy marriage to which he wishes the husband and wife to settle down:

> They may remember
> The vision they have had, but they cease to regret it,
> Maintain themselves by the common routine,
> Learn to avoid expectation,
> Become tolerant of themselves and others,
> Giving and taking, in the usual actions
> What there is to give and take. They do not repine;
> Are contented with the morning that separates
> And with the evening that brings together
> For casual talk before the fire
> Two people who know they do not understand each other,
> Breeding children whom they do not understand
> And who will never understand them.

That is surely genuine poetry: an austere and mature poetry, however, whose beauty is that of structure, not of ornament. One should look, in fact, not for sudden flaring rockets of language but for the sustained steady glow: not for 'bits' of poetry, toothsome verbal details, but for the poetic validity, which is surely there, of the conception as a whole, and for the effectiveness of the detail – even if, in isolation, it might sometimes seem prosaic detail – in its place.

A striking contrast, however, to the spareness of language in *The Cocktail Party* and *The Family Reunion* is to be found in the various verse comedies of Christopher Fry. I shall quote a speech from one of them, in which it can be seen that there is an abundant richness of fanciful detail, not to be found in that speech I have quoted from *The Cocktail Party*: but neither on the other hand is there the massive and compressed moral strength of that speech:

> For me
> The world is all with Charon, all, all
> Even the metal and plume of the rose garden,
> And the forest where the sea fumes overhead
> In vegetable tides, and particularly
> The entrance to the warm baths in Arcite Street
> Where we first met; – all! – the sun itself
> Trails an evening hand in the sultry river
> Far away down by Acheron. I am lonely,
> Virilius. Where is the punctual eye
> And where is the cautious voice which made
> Balance-sheets sound like Homer and Homer sound
> Like balance-sheets? The precision of limbs, the amiable
> Laugh, the exact festivity? Gone from the world . . .

There our essential feeling is one of playfulness; the lines very gently mock the woman who is mourning just a little more eloquently than her feelings justify for her dead husband, while at the same time allowing a lyrical quality to her grief: as in such lines as

> Trails an evening hand in the sultry river.

There is a great facility of phrases and images, and, in fact, if I were to quote the whole of this long speech from Mr Fry's comedy, *A Phoenix too Frequent*, I do not think the reader would have a sense so much of the development of idea and character as of a surprising fertility in the various ornamentation of a static theme. What is remarkable about Mr Fry's verse comedies, *A Phoenix too Frequent*, *The Lady's Not for Burning*, and *Venus Observed* is this playful and fantastic wealth of language, which at moments might almost recall the young Shakespeare, the Shakespeare drunk with words, of a play full of conceits and quibbles and speeches written not as dramatic speeches but as lovely youthful lyrics, such as *Love's Labour's Lost*. But Mr Fry's weakness is possibly that of those brilliant but meretricious dramatists of phrase and situation, not of theme, action, or character, Beaumont and Fletcher; he lacks a coherent conception of his play as a whole. His plays have often the air of wonderfully clever improvisations and though I left the only one which I have seen performed, *The Lady's*

Not for Burning, having enjoyed every moment of it, I would find it hard to compress the series of vivid and pleasant impressions with which the play left me into any very coherent account of the plot or the theme. Watching the play, too, I had the sense, about episodes as well as speeches, that Mr Fry, like somebody telling a story to children, was 'making it up as he went along.' This fecundity of episodic invention, like this 'fowth of language,' are both, of course, very exceptional qualities in our grey, inhibited, rationed time. One does not expect the age to foster the copious and florid talent, any more than one expects to have the fountains flowing with wine on state occasions or whole oxen roasted, in a hard winter, upon the frozen Thames. The agreeable anachronistic shock of Fry's careless abundance of episode and epithet may have indeed been one contributing factor to his remarkable popular success.

It is too early, I think, to pass any very definite literary judgment on Mr Fry's work but one may say that it fills a need in our time and may be the precursor of a more gay and gallant attitude to life, than our own is, in coming generations: but at the same time, it has something of the quality of a *soufflé* very light and very delicious, but liable to collapse into a flat pancaky mess if it is left too long to grow cold after it is taken out of the oven. One does not know how it will taste or how it will look in five or ten years. (Was there not a Mr Ashley Dukes, twenty years or so ago, who was going to restore to the prose rhythms of drama something of the sprightly elegance of Congreve? And where are his works now? One can never be sure how long a borrowed glow will last.)

One might mention in this connection the great success of the verse plays of Stephen Phillips in the 1890s and in the early part of our own century. These had an immediately captivating quality upon the stage, but after a certain lapse of time their spangles ceased to glitter and their rapid rhetorical speeches lost that look of vital convincingness. I would not say that this is likely to happen to Mr Fry, but I would say that if he is to develop his great quality as a dramatist, he needs to acquire a harder and perhaps a sadder sense of structure both in language and event. At present one cannot honestly say whether the language of his plays is really poetry or a skilful imitation, almost more stunning at a first glance, like artificial pearls of a large size and a beautiful rotundity, than the real thing.

These are the two names of poetic dramatists that one can mention as having stormed and held the West End stage. When one thinks, on the other hand, of the 'little theatre,' as it is called, and of the broadcast verse play, there are many other names to mention: too many for me to cover in any detail. I had better mention first the one play out of a very large set which does strike me as being completely a play, and a poetic play, in the true sense. This is Stephen Spender's *The Trial of a Judge*, which has not been revived, though it ought to be revived, since a few experimental performances in the late 1930s. This is a play on the same theme as Rex Warner's novel, *The Professor*. The Judge, the hero of the play, is the honest old Liberal caught between the two fires of Fascism and Communism. He is a man who, though he has no personal sympathy with Communism, and probably feels that the Fascists, though equally in error, are the more 'patriotic' party, is determined to administer the law without fear or favour. This gets him into trouble with the Fascists, who want judges to be mere instruments of their policy and so, for trying to hold the scales of the law even between Fascists and Communists, he is in the end treated as if he were a Communist himself: disgraced, imprisoned, killed, and even his fellow victims, being passionate Marxists, keep on assuring him that the ideal of 'impartial justice' for which he is dying is a *bourgeois* illusion. Fire must be fought with fire, they say, lies with lies, crime with crime, violence with violence: but for the judge it seems that rebellion, when its principles are stated in this fashion, becomes merely the other face of tyranny. Thus, as in Warner's novel, the man who in a time of crisis stands for abstract justice is weaker than the man carried away by passion: and yet he has greater dignity than the passionate man, he stands for permanent human values, that will still have their appeals and their demands to make when the storm has passed away.

The very qualities and defects of language which sometimes make Mr Spender seem a little thin as a poet of the personal life assist him as a dramatist. His personal poems are always fluent and sincere but lack sometimes the compression, complexity, irony, which we tend to demand to-day from personal poetry. What some of these poems, such as *I Think Continually of Those Who Were Truly Great*, convey is less the inward experience, noted and examined, than the tone of a public speech on some high occasion: an expression of noble sentiment, vibrant and sincere, but not directly related to any grasped experience. Quite generally, one might say, Mr Spender is 'rhetorical' in his poetry, in the sense in which T. E. Hulme defined 'rhetoric': that is to say, in expressing emotion sincerely and vigorously without relating that emotion to something firmly grasped in the outer world.

But all this, which sometimes weakens Mr Spender as a poet, strengthens him as a dramatist: for his way of writing is equivalent to the confused but dignified and moving way in which men, in tense and crucial circumstances, do actually speak under the stress of strong feeling. What makes for confusion in the personal poem makes for convincingness in the dramatic speech. It is a great pity that, since the publication of *The Trial of a Judge* in the late 1930s, Mr Spender has written no other dramas; for the contemporary critics who described this as the most effective piece of poetic theatre since Otway's *Venice Preserved*, were not, I think, wrong.

The plays in verse and prose written by Mr W. H. Auden and Mr Christopher Isherwood (Auden often concentrating on the verse choruses, Isherwood, with his training as a novelist behind him, on the crisp and neat prose dialogue), though they made a greater stir than Mr Spender's one play in the 1930s, do not seem to me to have quite such a lasting importance. They have, even more than Mr Christopher Fry's plays (which they do not resemble in any other important respect), an air of improvisation: even an air of what Mr Auden called 'charade.' The gay, knockabout, satirical and expressionistic farce of such a play as *The Dog Beneath the Skin* is, in a sense, engaging: rather as a kind of compound of a pageant play, a pantomime, and improvised school theatricals. But the techniques of German expressionism which are effective in an extravaganza of this sort tend in the more 'serious' Auden-Isherwood plays, *The Ascent of F6* and *Across the Frontier* to substitute for a solid exploration of the depths of reality an exploitation of its surface, through symbolic situations and simplified cartoon characters: and if edification of a sort perhaps, or political propaganda certainly, is feasible at that level, tragedy is not. Moreover, apart from the characters being types rather than persons, the symbolism is topical rather than permanent; what Auden and Isherwood gained in immediate impact by such an approach, they lost in lasting interest. Their plays tend to suggest, as certainly *The Trial of a Judge* does not suggest, that there is a definite and formulable, and essentially quite simple and quite easily worked out, 'answer' to our 'problems.' No attitude could seem more unreal, or in fact more jejune and irritating, in the 1950s: and to give them their due, it is no longer the attitude of Auden and Isherwood themselves.

There are some excellent eloquent and witty pieces of writing in these three plays of Auden and Isherwood, but taken as wholes they have neither the values of tragedy – that is, of the statement of human problems which are perhaps permanently insoluble at the merely human level – nor the values of comedy – that is, of the statement of human problems which are permanently soluble, but which the run of men, through their average shortcomings, as often as not quite fail to solve. The tone of these plays has a kind of bright, evangelical eagerness, an air of superior knowingness, and a hint of 'the good time around the corner': it was perhaps only through adopting some thin and abstract final optimism of this kind that young men, in the 1930s, could face with cheerfulness the actual distresses, dangers, and horrors of the time. These plays typically reflect, in fact, the confusions of a critical, transitional decade: and that gives them an historical interest, which may well keep curiosity alive about them in times to come, in spite of their lack of permanent satire and permanent pathos. But they were certainly bad models for the young poet in a more sober decade, a decade perhaps with a longer and sadder perspective, like our own.

The other names that one has to mention in this section are more or less, at least so far, minor names; and must be dealt with more rapidly. On the whole, if the tone of mind and the mode of expression among young poets in the 1930s was predominantly political, to-day it is predominantly religious: and it is, of course, those young poets whose religious attitude has, like Mr Eliot's, a traditional and orthodox bias, who find it easiest to dramatise this attitude. It is difficult to dramatise the more common attitudes of partial acceptance, of hesitation, and of doubt. Mr Norman Nicholson, Miss Anne Ridler, Mr Ronald Duncan, are three young dramatists whose plays cannot be said yet to have quite moved out of the shadow of the church porch; they are at the stage of *Murder in the Cathedral* or even of *The Rock*, rather than at the stage of *The Family Reunion* or *The Cocktail Party*. A too obvious wish to edify, to preach at the audience, weakens their plays as drama still, though not necessarily as poetry. Mr Duncan is probably the one of the three who has so far the largest grasp of the possibilities of the stage; and he reinforces his piety by a vein, lacking in the others, of often crude, surly, and schoolboyish, but often also rather effective satire: as well as by a vein of rich and sensuous lyricism, which reflects, as it were, a pagan substratum underlying his top layer of Christian belief. Many of Duncan's qualities are to be explained by the fact that he earns his living as a farmer: that therefore he has something of the countryman's natural distrust of the 'city slicker,' and, what is rare in English literature, the peasant's strong and passionate sense of concrete ownership and his distrust of government interference. On his remote

West of England farm, Duncan grows his own tobacco, bottles his
own wine, thus making himself as independent as possible of a government which taxes such luxuries; curses the government forms which
farmers have to fill in to-day; and vents his anger at government
interference, and his sturdy feelings about the farmer's independence
and the importance of local traditions, in a regular feature in the
Evening Standard, called 'Jan's Journal.' Before the war, he expressed
the same intransigent attitudes in a vivid and acrid little magazine
called *The Townsman*. He is thus a personification of what the conventionally 'progressive' person would call 'reaction': and without identi-
fying myself with that person, I do nevertheless feel that Duncan's
attitude to life, though no doubt in its way a gallant one, does not take
cognisance of a wide enough range of facts. Thus in the satirical anti-
masque to his religious masque, *This Way to the Tomb*, he reproaches
ostensibly from a Christian point of view the democratic creed for
being international, not based on blood and soil and the natural
rhythms of life. But so is Christianity international and so does it
transcend, and sometimes break down and transform, local traditions
and customs. It is not such an 'earthy' religion as Mr Duncan would
instinctively like it to be: and it is religion that inculcates a spirit of
charity, not always to be found in his own writings. The world which,
in the more satirical parts of his plays, Mr Duncan attacks with such
rough anger is after all the world, with all its faults, which we have to
live in: and the world which, from the Christian point of view, we
have to help to redeem. It is a weakness in a dramatist if certain kinds
of background, attitude, personality arouse in him not the desire to
understand but simply a wild unreasoning anger; and I feel that this
weakness is Mr Duncan's. His own anger arouses a responsive anger
in that townee intellectual audience (I dare say I myself am representative of it) which dislikes having its face slapped and its head buffeted
by a vociferous country cousin who often does not seem to know, in
any deep and intimate sense, the sense which might make his malice
fertile, the world that he is attacking. For all that, the ability to rouse
anger is a sign of vitality; and Mr Duncan's is a vital talent. And he
has other gifts too, gifts which when developed with a less hasty energy,
may make him an important dramatist.

Mr Nicholson and Mrs Ridler have, on the other hand, more to
learn about the craft of the theatre than Mr Duncan: and they have,
unlike him, a gentleness and sensitiveness of temperament, a spirit of
wide charity, in their plays, that is likely to make their work more

refreshing and less estranging to the respectful agnostic – who is, after all, I suppose the typical reader and witness to-day of religious plays – than Mr Duncan's. Mr Nicholson's plays are set against that background of the Cumberland dales which gives such a solid and real Wordsworthian quality to his poems; the same Wordsworthian quality sometimes makes his plays a little plodding and slow in their development, and it gives them a 'pastoral' quality – that is we feel they deal with people simpler than Mr Nicholson, and with motives less complex, his understandings less comprehensive, than their own. This weakens their impact in putting across a Christian message, for we feel, 'That argument is a simplification; true in the play's context, not necessarily true in ours.' Mrs Ridler, on the other hand, a poet of great charm, subtlety, and distinction, who deals in her personal pieces chiefly with domestic themes in a religious context, has in her plays, though so far on a slighter scale, something of Mr Eliot's gift in *The Cocktail Party* of taking what might look like prosaic modern situations and bringing out their deeper implications; I thought one particular play in her last volume, *The Missing Bridegroom*, showed a remarkable advance on any of her previous dramatic work in its poetic handling of the lives, and rendering of the conversation, of sophisticated and complex people. I would say that her dialogue in that play has a true contemporary ring in a way in which Mr Duncan's dialogue and Mr Nicholson's, in their different ways, have not; Mr Duncan being in a sense too personal, too much having his own voices and not the voices of his characters, Mr Nicholson being too much confined within a dignified but restricting convention. Mrs Ridler is nevertheless still too much concerned with the *overt* expression of the Christian theme, and to a certain extent with the overt inculcation of the Christian message: one looks forward to seeing her write some play in which the facts, with their intrinsic dramatic interrelation from any point of view, will be on top, and the values implicit.

CHAPTER FOUR

POETRY

Section 1: The 1890s to the First World War

The 1890s saw the emergence into the English poetic consciousness of that sense, which had been so long alive in France, of the great gulf fixed between the world of poetry and that of everyday life. The Pre-Raphaelites had also felt that gulf but, inspired by Ruskin's social enthusiasms, the more energetic of them, like William Morris, had hoped to transform the world of everyday life. The poets of the 1890s lacked that energy; like Baudelaire, one of their heroes, they took up towards the world around them the bored, indifferent attitude of the dandy; like Gautier, another of their heroes, they adopted the creed of 'art for art's sake.' It is not a very nourishing creed, and many of them, pursued by melancholy, by ill-health, by remorse for the excesses of their lives, ended by becoming Roman Catholics. Their approach to religion was through sadness and the sense of sin, through the weariness of life which Dowson so beautifully expresses,

> Labour and longing and despair the long day brings;
> Patient till evening men watch the sun go west;
> Deferred, expected night at last brings sleep and rest:
> *Sufficient for the day are the day's evil things,*

and through that sense of a personal struggle with the Adversary that is the theme of Lionel Johnson's most sustained and powerful poem:

> Dark Angel, with thine aching lust!
> Of two defeats, of two despairs:
> Less dread, a change to drifting dust,
> Than thine eternity of cares.
>
> Do what thou wilt, thou shalt not so,
> Dark Angel! triumph over me:
> *Lonely, unto the Lone I go:*
> *Divine, to the Divinity.*

The note that is heard with intensity in these two quotations is, at a more subdued and muted level, the common note of the most typical poetry of the 1890s; there is the burden of life and the fear of death, even when the poet seeks to distract himself by dissipation. To quote Dowson again,

> Wine and woman and song,
>   Three things garnish our way:
> *Yet is day over long.*

The originality of the poets of the 1890s was not then in choice of language and theme. Dowson, Johnson, A. E. Housman, and of course Yeats have their recognisable individual note, but even they have also very much the note of their time. And minor figures have almost nothing but the note of the time, though they catch that sometimes very exquisitely. Almost anybody with a feeling for period in literature could date the following quotations as belonging to the 1890s; it would require an expert on the decade, however, to identify their authors at a glance.

1) Who in this small urn reposes,
       Celt or Roman, man or woman,
   Steel of steel, or rose of roses?

2) For all the things I do, and not well:
   All the forced drawings of a mortal breath:
   Are as the hollow music of a bell
   That times the slow approach of perfect death.

3) Sidon and Tyre were such as ye,
   How bright they shone upon the tree!
   Since Time hath gathered, both are gone
   And no man sails to Babylon.

4) Love stays a summer night,
       Till lights of morning come;
   Then takes her wingèd flight
       Back to her starry home.

5) I cannot look upon thy grave
       Though there the rose is sweet:
   Better to hear the long wave wash
       These wastes about my feet.

6) But lo! these gifts, the heirlooms of past years,
   Are made sad things to grace thy coffin shell,
   Take them, all drenchèd with a brother's tears,
   And brother, for all time, hail and farewell!

7) Send not on your soul before
   To dive from that beguiling shore
   And let not yet the swimmer leave
   His clothes upon the sands of eve.

8) We who are old, old and gay,
   O so old!
   Thousands of years, thousands of years
   If all were told . . .

All these quotations, except the last, have a common theme, that of the mortality of things, and a common note, that of gloom: even the last quotation, where the Irish fairy folk are rejoicing in their immortality, has, to my ears at least, dolorous cadence. I think a reasonably well-read person ought to spot (2), (7) and perhaps (8), but that it will be a fluke if he spots any of the others. The authors in order are Victor Plarr, Lionel Johnson, Richard le Gallienne, Ernest Dowson, Stephen Phillips, Aubrey Beardsley, A. E. Housman, W. B. Yeats. The quotations between them cover a good part of the range of the typical poetry of the 1890s; what one has left out is the less sombre type of poem, more rich in detail, aiming at daintiness or quaintness, like Theo Marzials'

> The griffins grinned in the moonlight green,
>   The hound by the thin red embers slept;
> I scraped a chord on my mandoline,
> A chord, pardie, that might ruin a queen,

or John Gray's

> Beautiful ladies through the orchard pass;
> Bent under crutched-up branches, forked and low;
> Trailing their samet palls o'er dew-drenched grass.

And that quaintness could become grotesque and sinister, as in Wilde's

> Like wire-pulled automatons
> Slim-silhouetted skeletons
> Went sidling through the slow quadrille.
>
> They took each other by the hand,
> And danced a stately saraband;
> Their laughter echoed thin and shrill.

But the elegiac note is more typical and also, on the whole, achieves more lasting poetry; the stage properties of the other sort of thing, the griffins, the mandolines, the samet palls, the skeletons and the sarabands have become a little dusty. So we might almost say that the most typical poetry of the 1890s is remarkable for its monotony, its lack of range, a peculiar faded quality in its diction – its complete conventionality, in short. Why then, in spite of everything, do we find a charm in it and even a note that is distinctively 'modern'?

The charm is partly that of something which sets itself a limited aim and achieves it. Very much of Browning, Tennyson, Arnold, Swinburne, can only be described as failing on the grand scale; as not finally convincing in spite of the major energy and skill that has gone into it. It is with a conscious effort of sympathy and understanding that we plough through the voluminous collected works of the great Victorians; they are trying to do so much else besides merely write poetry, to be prophets, philosophers, psychologists, representative figures of their age or voices of a new dawn. But the slim collected volumes of Dowson, or of Lionel Johnson, or of A.E.Housman, demand no such effort from us; the poems in them are not great failures but small successes. Are the themes commonplace? So are the themes of many of Shakespeare's sonnets and of most Elizabethan lyrics; love and death and the sad transience of beauty. Such common-places have a permanent validity, poets return to them in every generation, and when a poet has not to worry about his matter he can take special care of his form. Let me quote a stanza from Dowson's most famous, though not necessarily his best, poem,

> I have forgot much, Cynara! gone with the wind,
> Flung roses, roses riotously with the throng,
> Dancing to put thy pale lost lilies out of mind;
> But I was desolate and sick of an old passion,
>   Yea, all the time, because the dance was long:
> I have been faithful to thee, Cynara! in my fashion.

It is easy enough to be brutal about that stanza. In one sense, it is all literary flummery. There is 'forgot' instead of 'forgotten,' 'wind' pronounced like 'wined': the roses and lilies are borrowed from Swinburne's deplorable 'lilies and languors of virtue' and 'roses and raptures of vice.' If one thinks the poet's biography relevant, Dowson when he 'cried for madder music and stronger wine' meant that he was going down Fleet Street to have a few whiskies with his literary friends; and perhaps he never really 'danced,' even in a ballroom, let alone as a dionysiac reveller. We can say that the images, the diction, the whole conception of the poem are faded, imitative, the poet's verse a *pastiche* and his life a pose. . . . But when we have said all that, the fact remains that the poem has form; that it is an intricate pattern of rhythms consciously designed and sensitively shaped; and that it is impossible to read it aloud to oneself – even after dwelling on all its limitations, as I have been doing – and not be moved.

By the very narrowness of the tasks they set themselves, in fact, these poets of the 1890s, minor figures as most of them were, did achieve, from the formal point of view, a quality of dignified impersonality which is rare in some far greater predecessors; they detached themselves from the poem as a completed object; one cannot have Browning's poems, as a general rule, without having Browning too, but here one is solely concerned with the statue of King Charles I and forgets about Lionel Johnson:

> Comely and calm, he rides
> Hard by his own Whitehall:
> Only the night wind glides:
> No crowds, nor rebels, brawl.
>
> Gone, too, his Court; and yet
> The stars his courtiers are:
> Stars in their stations set;
> And every wandering star.

Thus, the poets of the 1890s, though they are often called 'the last romantics,' might also be called the first neo-classics. The best of them, like Johnson himself, tended to have a passion for Latin poetry; that poem on the statue of King Charles has some of the qualities of an Horatian ode. Housman, of course, was a very great classical scholar and it is his classical quality that stiffens him against a natural tendency to sentimentality. ('*The Shropshire Lad*,' said Yeats, 'is worthy of its fame, but a mile further and all had been marsh.') He is at his best, for instance, in an actual translation of Horace:

> Thaw follows frost; hard on the heels of spring
>   Treads summer sure to die, for hard on hers
> Comes autumn with his apples scattering;
>   Then back to wintertide when nothing stirs.
>
> But, oh, whate'er the sky-led seasons mar,
>   Moon upon moon rebuilds it with her beams;
> Come *we* where Tullus and where Ancus are
>   And good Aeneas, we are dust and dreams.

This 'classical' quality in the best typical verse of the 1890s was not, of course, what contemporaries noted; they noted rather the irregular and sometimes scandalous lives, the early and sometimes tragic deaths, of a group of poets whom Yeats's father called 'a generation of Hamlets.' They noted that streak of deliberate perversity which can be seen in Wilde's life rather than his art, and in Beardsley's art rather than his life. So the whole ten years were stamped, rather unfairly, with the label 'decadent' and 'then in 1900,' says Yeats, 'everybody got down off his stilts; henceforth nobody drank absinthe with his black coffee; nobody went mad; nobody committed suicide; nobody joined the Catholic church; or if they did I have forgotten.'

In poetry, as in prose, what the Edwardian decade witnessed was a kind of temporary recrudescence, a false fitful afterglow, of the sturdy self-confidence of the Victorian age – but with the sweep and range of Victorian poetry adapted now (and to some extent inevitably cheapened and vulgarised in the process) to a much wider and less critical audience. It is the too alert awareness of that audience, the eagerness to get across to them at whatever cost, that is responsible, I think, for the vulgarities that jar upon us in Kipling. Here he is addressing, in imagination, a typical City man after the Boer War:

> Let us admit it fairly, as a business people should,
> We have had no end of a lesson; it will do us no end of good.

How annoying is that jaunty 'no end' – which Kipling, we may be sure, as a man of education and of taste in language, would never have used naturally in his own conversation. He is talking *down* to his audience here, just as certainly as in

> I went into a public-'ouse to get a pint o' beer,
> The publican 'e up an' sez, "We serve no red-coats here,"

if more subtly. To bring colloquial English and contemporary themes back into English verse was a great service of Kipling's; but it is his weakness that he seems not to have a voice of his own in poetry, that he is nearly always talking in what he assumes to be the language of his audience, and that, even for really solemn moments, the best he can do, often, is to fall back on the language of the hymn-book:

> The earth is full of anger,
>   The seas are dark with wrath,
> The Nations in their harness
>   Go up against our path . . .

Poetry, as such, he perhaps never worried about; he knew that he was a great master of verse, and that he had the ear of his audience; he used his verse as a serviceable instrument for the propagation of his beliefs, and what the superior critics thought was neither here nor there. Yet he was and remained a poet, he could never smother the flame, and moreover the poetry cannot be neatly separated from the verse. It breaks out through the jaunty rhythms, and the banjo twang,

> For the wind is in the palm-trees, and the temple-bells they say:
> 'Come you back, you British soldier; come you back to Mandalay!',

it breaks through the stage-cockney,

> For they're hangin' Danny Deever, you can hear the Dead March play,
> The regiment's in 'ollow square – they're 'angin' 'im to-day;
> They've taken of his buttons off an' cut his stripes away:
> An' they're hangin' Danny Deever in the mornin',

and it is to be heard through the vocabulary of the hymn-book:

> Far-called, our navies melt away:
>   On dune and headland sinks the fire:
> Lo, all our pomp of yesterday
>   Is one with Nineveh and Tyre!

Perhaps Kipling on the whole is at his best as a poet, or at his least uneven, when he has a story to tell, whether of an Afghan chieftain,

> Abdhur Rahman, the Durani Chief, of him is the story told.
> His mercy fills the Khyber hills—his grace is manifold . . .

or of an English Queen,

> The Queen was in her chamber, and she was middling old.
> Her petticoat was satin and her stomacher was gold.
> Backwards and forwards and sideways did she pass,
> Making up her mind to face the cruel looking-glass.
> The cruel looking-glass that will never show a lass
> As comely or as kindly as what she was!
> *Queen Bess was Harry's daughter. Now hand your partners all!*

Perhaps he is at his least good when he becomes too completely the vehicle of some wave of public sentiment.

He has something in common with other poets of the Edwardian Age, Belloc and Chesterton, who were on opposite sides to him in politics, but who had something of the same gift for what one may call, without meaning to be offensive, versified journalism. What one has to complain about in Chesterton especially, both in his prose and his verse, is a certain dilution or expansion, rather than concentration, of his material. Verses of the type of

> Before the Roman came to Rye or out to Severn strode,
> The rolling English drunkard made the rolling English road,
> A reeling road, a rolling road, that rambles round the shire,
> And after him the sexton ran, the parson, and the squire,

are sonorous, rollicking stuff, showing great skill, conveying no doubt a most delightful personality, and jolly to read aloud; but with all respect, it is my humble submission they are not what most of us mean by 'poetry.' As for *Lepanto*, I would admit it as poetry rather on the same terms as I admit Lord Macaulay's *Lays of Ancient Rome*. It 'stirs the blood,' as these do; it does not send a little authentic shiver up the spine as these lines I have quoted of Kipling's do,

> Backwards and forwards and sideways did she pass,
> Making up her mind to face the cruel looking-glass . . .

Belloc, on the other hand, had an astonishing mastery of the techniques of verse, and nobody who has ever read the poem is likely to forget the last portion of *Miranda*:

> Never more;
> Miranda,
> Never more.
> Only the high peaks hoar:
> And Aragon a torrent at the door.
> No sound
> In the walls of the Halls where falls
> The tread
> Of the feet of the dead to the ground.
> No sound:
> Only the boom
> Of the far Waterfall like Doom,

but, like the other writers of that generation, he was too easy with too many things, with journalism, controversy, politics, novels, essays, histories, travel books, ever to make the most, among all his gifts, of his best gift, the gift of poetry. In the rather slim bulk of his collected poems there is almost no criticism that one can make as to form; except that a certain affectation of robustness, or a false sturdiness, which is intrinsic to so much of the matter, seems often to affect the form, too. Belloc, like Chesterton or Kipling, is too conscious of his role; too much aware of himself striding over the Sussex Downs and quaffing great mugs of ale and feeling a simple religious awe and faith, and admiring the classics, and in fact being the very model of his own half-French notion of the traditional Englishman. Mr Belloc is eighty years old as I write and is being widely hailed (as he always has been by his co-religionists) as our 'greatest living poet.' Even though Yeats is dead, while Eliot and Graves and de la Mare and Campbell and Auden are living one can hardly pass this remark, except as a well-meant but injudicious compliment to a very fine old man.

The tendency of the Edwardian age to dilute and expand the substance of poetry can also be seen in the verse narratives of John Masefield, which have often a real interest as stories combined with a rather fluent and careless handling of the actual verse; and in the poetry, inferior to Masefield's in the interest of its matter, but sharing and surpassing its slacknesses of form, of Alfred Noyes. It is a sad reflection, in fact, on the general level of taste of the Edwardian age that a poet like Noyes could be accepted as almost a major figure on the strength of the sheer bulk of his production, rather than on that of any other qualities that one can assign to it. The same age took to its bosom one of the really bad popular poetesses of all time, Ella Wheeler Wilcox, whose little books, in squashy leather bindings, one can still find in old-fashioned English drawing-rooms. It was in a spirit, in fact, of savage revolt against what seemed to them the sheer hopeless ineptitude of current English taste that the younger poets of the next generation – Pound, Eliot, Read, Aldington, and others – were to make their fierce and deliberate break with the immediate past.

Other poets, for whom poetry in itself mattered, were, of course, continuing to write in the Edwardian decade, though not for the same large audience as Chesterton, Kipling, or Masefield. Robert Bridges, in whom a wonderful lyrical delicacy was always fighting against a pedantic frigidity of temperament, and perhaps towards the end of his life losing the battle, was typical of a number of poets – Sturge Moore, Lascelles Abercrombie, Laurence Binyon were others – who, disgusted by the brassiness of contemporary popular poetry, sought refreshment in history or in myth, or in technical experiment. Bridges was trying to accommodate classical metres to the English language, as in these lines from his version of the sixth book of the *Aeneid*:

> They were amid the shadows by night in loneliness obscure
> Walking forth i' the void and vasty dominyon of Ades;
> As by an uncertain moonray secretly illumin'd
> One goeth in the forest, when heaven is gloomily clouded,
> And black night hath robbed the colours and beauty from things . . .

One admires the skill of the experiment, and yet the necessary contortions and inversions – 'lōnĕlĭnĕ̆ss ōbscūre' – seems fatal to natural English.

The same scholarly delicacy can be seen in Sturge Moore's half-affectionate, half-mocking parodies of Rimbaud

> The cow eats grass;
> Alas, alas!
> Nothing to eat
> Surrounds my feet!

or of Ronsard,

> Time flits away, time flits away, lady;
> Alas, not time, but we
> Whose childish limbs once skipped so fairily,
> And still to dance are free,

and in Binyon's poem on Tristram, or Abercrombie's called *Mary and the Bramble*, which are both in Yeats's *Oxford Book of Modern Verse*. One feels a lack of vitality and 'body' in such poems, and perhaps Binyon's gifts receive their proper embodiment only in his splendid translation of Dante.

For the more sensitive poets of the time scholarship, myth, history were places of retreat from the vulgarity of life but they were in retreat also from the sources of their own vitality. Yeats describes himself as at one time a poet of the school of Sturge Moore and that of the younger 'Michael Field'; there is a vitality in his use of myth, however, which is not in that of the others:

> Do you not hear me calling, white deer with no horns!
> I have been changed to a hound with one red ear;
> I have been in the Path of Stones and the Wood of Thorns,
> For somebody hid hatred and hope and desire and fear
> Under my feet that they follow you night and day!
> A man with a hazel wand came without sound;
> He changed me suddenly; I was looking another way;

And now my calling is but the calling of a hound;
And Time and Birth and Change are hurrying by.
I would that the Boar without bristles had come from the West
And had rooted the sun and the moon and the stars out of the sky
And lay in the darkness, grunting, and turning to his rest.

More than any others of his contemporaries of the 1890s (whose appreciation of current French poetry tended to stop short at Verlaine, or even to hark all the way back to Baudelaire), Yeats had grasped what Mallarmé was after. But his own symbolism in such a poem as the one I have just quoted is not an intellectual thing. It has rather the quality of a primitive magical lyric; and Yeats's figures out of 'old mythologies,' out of the 'book of the people,' because they had a direct ancestral magic for him, strike far deeper into the imagination than Binyon's attempts to revive the Arthurian legend or Sturge Moore's or Lascelles Abercrombie's similar attempts with Biblical and Christian legend. Yeats himself in the end came to distrust the direct use of myths turning instead to themes from his own life and from contemporary Irish history:

> I made my song a coat
> Covered with embroideries
> Out of old mythologies
> From heel to throat;
> But the fools caught it,
> Wore it in the world's eye
> As though they'd wrought it.
> Song, let them take it,
> For there's more enterprise
> In walking naked,

and one should compare that with the words of Yeats's younger contemporary, John Millington Synge, in his preface to his collected poems: 'The poetry of exaltation will always be the highest; but when men lose their poetic feeling for ordinary life, and cannot write poetry of ordinary things, their exalted poetry is likely to lose its strength of exaltation, in the way men cease to build beautiful churches when they have lost happiness in building shops. Many of the older poets, such as Villon and Herrick and Burns, used the whole of their personal life as their material, and the verse written in this way was read by strong men, and thieves, and deacons, not by little cliques only. Then, in the town writing of the eighteenth century, ordinary life was put into verse that was not poetry, and when poetry came back with Coleridge and Shelley, it went into verse that was not always human. In these days, poetry is usually a flower of evil or good; but it is the timber of poetry that wears most surely, and there is no timber that has not strong roots among the clay and the worms. . . .'

That poem of Yeats's, published at the end of his volume significantly entitled *Responsibilities*, which came out in 1914, and that phrase of Synge's about the 'strong roots among the clay and the worms,' both announce the great change that was going to come over poetry between 1910 and 1920; but in England itself the only notable immediate reaction away from brassiness on the one hand and pedantry on the other, before the outbreak of the war, was the movement that is sometimes vaguely called the 'Georgian movement.' Pound, Aldington, and the Imagists were certainly at work already along more revolutionary lines, but the full importance of their experiments was not realised till much later, and it will be better to treat them in the next section.

'Georgian' poetry, on the other hand, as typified by Edward Thomas, by Harold Monro, by Ralph Hodgson, and later on by poets like Siegfried Sassoon (in his pieces about country life, not in his war pieces), by Rupert Brooke in poems like *The Old Vicarage, Grantchester*, by Edmund Blunden, and by very many other poets, struck at once a responsive chord in English readers. It was quiet, intimate, unambitious. It dealt with familiar sights and scenes of English country life; its tone was much nearer the natural tone of the speaking voice than the tone of Sturge Moore or Binyon or Bridges, on the one hand, or of Kipling and Chesterton on the other. It was neither precious nor strident. It may be that in the years before 1914 many young poets had a kind of unconscious premonition of the disaster that was going to overwhelm them, and wanted to record their feeling about the English countryside while they could still look on it with innocent, untroubled eyes.

For the best of these poets, however, for Graves, for Blunden, or for Sassoon, though the war was a searing experience, it was not an experience that destroyed their poetry. But in all their later work there would be a sense of trouble. One of Edmund Blunden's most beautiful and moving poems describes the new and disturbed attitude to natural beauty that the war brought in its train:

> I saw the sunlit vale, and the pastoral fairy-tale;
> The sweet and bitter scent of the may drifted by;
> And never have I seen such a bright bewildering green,
> But it looked like a lie,
> Like a kindly meant lie.

When gods are in dispute, one a Sidney, one a brute,
It would seem that human sense might not know, might not spy;
But though nature smile and feign where foul play has stabbed and slain,
    There's a witness, an eye,
    Nor will charms blind that eye.

Nymph of the upland song and the sparkling leafage young,
For your merciful desire with these charms to beguile,
For ever be adored; muses yield you rich reward;
    But you fail, though you smile –
    The other does not smile.

It is with a sharp sense in one's mind of what these young men were to endure that one should turn to their poems, being patient with what may seem childish or whimsical, as in Edward Thomas,

> If I should ever by chance grow rich
> I'll buy Codham, Cockridden, and Childerditch,
> Roses, Pyrgo, and Lapwater,
> And let them all to my eldest daughter,

or on the verge of sentimentality, as in Rupert Brooke,

> Just now the lilac is in bloom,
> All before my little room;
> And in my flower-beds, I think,
> Smile the carnation and the pink . . .

And there is very much that needs no such allowance made for it: Wilfred Owen's

> Leaves
>   Murmuring by myriads in the shimmering trees.
> Lives
>   Wakening with wonder in the Pyrenees.
> Birds
>   Cheerily chirping in the early day.
> Bards
>   Singing of summer scything thro' the hay . . .

or Harold Monro's

> The everlasting grass – how bright, how cool!
>   The day has gone too suddenly, too soon.
> There's something white and shiny in that pool –
>   Throw in a stone, and you will hit the moon.

197

What can be said in criticism of Georgian poetry has been said very succinctly by Mr T.S. Eliot, in his critical introduction to the poems of Harold Monro: 'But with Georgian poetry he had little in common. Of that poetry I speak with much diffidence. What I remember about it is a small number of poems by two or three men. I supposed, long ago, that Harold Monro's poetry belonged to that category – with the poetry of writers not unfairly representable in anthologies; and in those days I was interested only in the sort of thing I wanted to do myself, and took no interest in what diverged from my own direction. But his poetry differs from Georgian verse proper in important respects. The majority of those writers occupied themselves with subject matter which is – and not in the best sense – impersonal; which belongs to the sensibility of the ordinary sensitive person, not primarily only to that of the sensitive poet; it was not always easy to distinguish the work of one author from the work of another; the result was a considerable number of pleasing anthology pieces.'

But if Monro's work is distinguishable from this typical sort of Georgian poem, so it would seem to me is Blunden's, is Graves's, is Sassoon's, especially in its more mature development during and after the war. Edward Thomas's is perhaps completely typical of what we mean by Georgian verse, but to conform to type so quite completely is surely to be individual; for perhaps when we describe some poem as 'typically Georgian,' what we mean at the back of our minds is, 'It reminds one of Edward Thomas.' And even if much of the writing of this period did express, in pleasant verse, a rather ordinary sort of sensitivity, can we be sure – if Brooke, for instance, had survived – that he might not in the end have developed the same tough individuality of style as Mr Robert Graves has? We are to think of Georgian poetry, in fact, as something that began very promisingly, but that the war never allowed to develop as it might otherwise have.

One great, unfashionable figure inspired many of the Georgian poets: Thomas Hardy. He had always been aloof from fashions in verse, and cannot be fitted tidily into any 'movement' but what made him attractive was his love for the English countryside and English tradition, combined with the gnarled honesty of his mind and verse, and the spirit of high, anguished doubt about man's and the world's destiny in his heart. He is the most uneven of great poets, but with a special magic that comes from his very awkwardness and innocence. He was aware of the settled Victorian world he had grown up in decaying around him:

> The bower we shrined to Tennyson,
>   Gentlemen,
> Is roof-wrecked; damps there drip upon
> Sagged seats, the creeper-nails are rust,
> The spider is sole denizen;
> Even she who voiced those rhymes is dust,
>   Gentlemen.

Still, however, in the country, the outer world, the same countryside as Shakespeare's, remained. But for how long would it remain? He was old, and he was mortal, and the world was given over to change.

> When the Present has latched its postern behind my tremulous stay,
> And the May month flaps its glad green leaves like wings,
> Delicate-filmed as new-spun silk, will the neighbours say,
> 'He was a man who used to notice such things'?

So we can see Hardy as a kind of brooding, presiding spirit inspiring these Georgian poets; younger men, lesser men, but not less sincere or sensitive in their love of the English scene than he – we can see him, and them, even, as the last of the 'old English.' The war was to make many changes and in particular to make this sort of poetry of local mood and habit and brooding recollection impossible. The green landscape was henceforth to look

>   like a lie,
> Like a kindly meant lie,

and the poet was no longer to be able to escape, even like Harold Monro for a week-end, from his inner anxieties. And behind the new kind of poetry that was soon to come into being, and to alter the sensibilities of more than one generation, there was not to be an English genius, old or new, but the work of two Americans, T. S. Eliot and Ezra Pound, and an Irishman, W. B. Yeats.

None of these three fought in the war, and they were able during the years of the war to concentrate on maturing and perfecting their gifts; for English poets like Graves and Blunden and Sassoon, for those who, unlike Brooke or Owen or Julian Grenfell, survived the war was to be something with which their imaginations would wrestle – which they would have to recreate in imagination, in order to survive it in imagination – for all the rest of their lives. So the year 1914 marks, at least symbolically, a real and very important break in the history of

English poetry. It was going, in the next twenty or thirty years, to reach out far more widely than it had done for a very long time to the world; at the same time an old sense of homeliness and rootedness was to be almost permanently lost.

I have noted about Hardy a certain clumsiness. His poems, I think, are often close to what his own speech must have been like: that of an earnest, self-educated man, groping among ideas that he found portentous and difficult. Lytton Strachey, an unexpectedly sympathetic critic, noted how Hardy's work was 'full of ugly and cumbrous expressions, clumsy metres, and flat prosaic turns of speech. . . . In the second of the following lines, cacophony is incarnate:

> Dear ghost, in the past did you ever find
> Me one whom consequence influenced much,

while a line like,

> And the daytime talk of the Roman investigations,

trails along in the manner of an undistinguished phrase in prose. Hardy is incorrect; but then how unreal and artificial a thing is correctness. He fumbles; but it is that very fumbling that brings him so near to ourselves. In that "me one whom consequence influenced much" does one not seem to catch the very accent of hesitating and half-ironical affection? And in the drab rhythm of that "daytime talk of the Roman investigations" does not all the dreariness of long hours of boredom lie compressed?' Hardy then, as far as diction and metrics go, was, according to Strachey, a fumbler, whose fumbles suddenly click. So he could hardly create a tradition. The critic, like Strachey, who is able to point out this felicitous clumsiness, will be the last person, in his own verses, to imitate it. All we can imitate is skill: or rather the deliberate imitation of clumsiness or naivety becomes something quite different from its original, becomes a sort of clownishness. And Hardy is never clownish. But, as a self-taught master he could hardly, except in some degree in relation to his moods and his favourite topics, form a school: for the writers who might be thought of as his school (Edward Thomas, Blunden, Sassoon, Graves, the latter two not consistently, but at various stages) were not self-taught. And they admired, I am sure, this clumsiness of Hardy's not for itself, but for the touching and expressive use he made of it. For all that, Hardy was more important as an influence on the 'new poetry' than, say,

Kipling: Kipling's soldiers do not think or hesitate; and what poetry needed, in our confused time, was to recapture the thoughtful, hesitant note.

This was the great achievement of Pound and Eliot. Ezra Pound, a young American from the Middle West, had been in England since around 1907. He had published a number of slim volumes of verse, several of them with the title 'Personae': this Latin word he used as it is used in the phrase, *dramatis personae*, the parts (or more literally, the masks) in a play. Etymologically, *persona* is something *through* which ('per') *sound* is produced ('sona'), thus a mask, thus, through the fact that in the classical theatre every main character was masked, a role. It should not be confused in its general sense with the English word 'person.' Pound's point, in choosing the title, was that on the whole he preferred to appear in poetry *not*, as we say in English, *in person*, but behind a 'persona,' that is, in an assumed role, wearing a formal mask. Thus many of his best early poems are translations or adaptations from an extremely wide range of languages – Provençal, Old French, Italian, Latin, Greek, even (with the help of the notes of the famous scholar, Ernest Fenollosa) classical Chinese.

There is no poet of our time with a more magnificent historical imagination than Pound, no poet who has brought such a variety of past worlds to life again for us. It is not that he is an exact scholar. He can make blunders in translation that an intelligent schoolboy would be ashamed of. But he imaginatively grasps the poem in a strange tongue, wrestles with it, and finally brings over its emotional equivalent in English. There is the world of classical China, of enormous space scattered with tiny human elegiac landscapes, of open-air tables by country inns where scholarly friends, who have failed their examinations and are departing to dull and dangerous administrative jobs at remote barbarian frontiers, say good-bye to each other for the last time:

> Light rain is on the light dust.
> The willows of the inn-yard
> Will be growing greener and greener.
> But you, Sir, had better take wine ere your departure
> For you will have no friends about you
> When you come to the gates of Go.

There is the quite different world of Provence, where the tawny rock and the blue air, the sharp, bare shapes, the heat and the shimmer, putting a fine edge on life, led to the invention of romantic love. Let me quote a translation,

> Though thou well dost wish me ill,
>   Audiart, Audiart,
> Where thy bodice laces start
> As ivy fingers clutching through
> Its crevices,
>   Audiart, Audiart,
> Stately, tall and lovely tender
> Who shall render,
>   Audiart, Audiart,
> Praises meet unto thy fashion?
> Here a word kiss!
>   Pass I on . . .

and a dramatisation,

> She who could never live save through one person,
> She who could never speak save to one person,
> And all the rest of her a shifting change,
> A broken bundle of mirrors . . .

There is the world, terribly jaded and old compared with these two, of decaying Rome, where speech has the compressed and dense quality of fatigued, exacerbated passion:

> Here let thy clemency, Persephone, hold firm,
> Do thou, Pluto, bring here no greater harshness,
> So many thousand beauties are gone down to Avernus,
> Ye might let one remain above with us . . .

Pound's contemporary world appears, too, and he also of course appears from time to time in person as well as behind a *persona*. But his only long and elaborate 'personal' poem in *our* sense is *Hugh Selwyn Mauberley*, which some critics think his finest achievement: an account of his own bitter struggle with a commercial age,

> For three years, out of key with his time,
> He strove to resuscitate the dead art
> Of poetry; to maintain 'the sublime'
> In the old sense. Wrong from the start . . .

Pound there bids farewell to London, which he feels has let him down,

> Conduct, on the other hand, the soul
> 'Which the highest cultures have nourished'
> To Fleet Street where
> Dr Johnson flourished:
>
> Beside this thoroughfare
> The sale of half-hose has
> Long since superseded the cultivation
> Of Pierian roses.

He notes the waste and destruction of the Great War, in the death of the young and brave,

> Charm, smiling at the good mouth,
> Quick eyes gone under the earth's lid
> For two gross of broken statues,
> For a few thousand battered books.

Mauberley is one of the very saddest and most penetrating (though at the same time one of the wittiest) poems of our time: an account of the artist's defeat.

But the bitterness that was to overtake Pound, and that was to be even more notable in the early poems of his brilliant young fellow-countryman, T. S. Eliot, was not the practically important thing about the early poems of either of them. The practically important thing was the new and revolutionary use of language. Hardy, as we have seen, was a rustic poet, both in a good and a bad sense: one imagines him as speaking and thinking very slowly, groping even for simple thoughts: but the verse of Pound and Eliot, where it had the tone of common speech, suggested the quick, light, incisive talk of intellectuals in a capital. Pound's little poems of three or four lines probably struck contemporary readers as jokes. Many of them *are* jokes, and good ones:

> Phidon neither purged me, nor touched me,
> But I remembered the name of his fever medicine, and died.

Others are more than that. The wife or concubine of a Chinese Emperor, neglected by her lord, paints three lines of verse on a fan:

> O fan of white silk,
>   clear as frost on the grass-blade,
> you also are laid aside.

An Alexandrian poet meditates on women:

> Woman? Oh, woman is a consummate rage,
>   but dead, or asleep, she pleases.
> Take her. She has two excellent seasons.

Pound, in his own guise for once, considers the crowd in the Paris underground:

> The apparition of these faces in the crowd:
> Petals on a wet, black bough.

And here, in a London teashop, is a scene, a mood, almost an action:

> The girl in the tea-shop
> Is not so beautiful as she was,
> The August has worn against her,
> She does not get up the stairs so eagerly:
> Yes, she also will turn middle-aged,
> And the glow of youth that she spread about us
> As she brought us our muffins
> Will be spread about us no longer.
> She also will turn middle-aged.

When one first reads these little poems, one thinks how frail and slight they are. It is strange how many of them one finds one has by heart, it is strange how the language has hardly dated after a lapse of forty years. It has hardly dated, because Pound was an anticipator.

That Eliot learned much from Pound is common knowledge. He had, of course, special sources of his own, particularly the English metaphysical poets and Jacobean dramatists, for whom Pound hardly shared his admiration. And from the beginning it might have been guessed that he was going to be a dramatist in verse, Pound not. When we can compare them on a similar theme, Pound is much more static. Here is part of Pound's *Portrait d'une Femme*:

> Yes, you richly pay.
> You are a person of some interest, one comes to you
> And takes strange gain away:
>
> Trophies fished up: some curious suggestion;
> Facts that lead nowhere; and a tale or two,
> Pregnant with mandrakes, and with something else
> That might prove useful, and yet never proves,
> That never fits a corner or shows use,
> Or finds its hour upon the loom of days:

The tarnished, gaudy, wonderful old work,
Idols and ambergris and rare inlays,
These are your riches, your great store; and yet
For all this sea-hoard of deciduous things,
Strange woods half-sodden, and new brighter stuff:
In the strange float of differing light and deep,
No! there is nothing! In the whole and all,
Nothing that's quite your own.
                                    Yet this is you.

And here is a part of Eliot's *Portrait of a Lady*:

Now that lilacs are in bloom
She has a bowl of lilacs in her room
And twists one in her fingers while she talks.
'Ah, my friend, you do not know, you do not know
What life is, you should hold it in your hands';
(Slowly twisting the lilac stalks)
'You let it flow from you, you let it flow,
And youth is cruel and has no remorse
And smiles at situations which it cannot see.'
I smile, of course,
And go on drinking tea.
'Yet with these April sunsets, that somehow recall
My buried life, and Paris in the Spring,
I feel immeasurably at peace, and find the world
To be wonderful and youthful after all.'

Pound is describing and expatiating: Eliot dramatising and implying.
But both poets are making verse do the same sort of new thing. They
are making a tentative, exploring use of verse, using poetry to get
closer to the shape of a real situation: not starting off with a preconceived notion of what the situation is, nor with a simple, fixed attitude
towards it. What made contemporary readers puzzle over passages
like these quoted here – the *sense* of these passages is perfectly straightforward, surely – was that Eliot and Pound habitually presented in
verse situations which were quite as puzzling as those of real life. What
does Pound feel about the girl in the teashop, for instance? What does
Eliot feel about the talkative, romantic middle-aged lady twisting lilac
stalks? Well, what does the reader feel? In real life, we are not loving
or hating people with a simple concentrated intensity all the time. We
have mixed and uncertain feelings, and it is these which Pound and
Eliot are conveying. So this hesitant, tentative, apparently rather flat
use of language gave poetry a new psychological immediacy: it made,

for its admirers, the diction, attitudes, and situations of much Georgian poetry unreal. Eliot himself has admitted that he was never able to give a fair and detailed consideration to Georgian poetry because the special new thing he was after was so completely different. It was, in any case, this new disturbing and uncomfortable use of language, at a sensitive colloquial level, that younger poets like Auden and MacNeice, a generation later, were to take over from Pound and Eliot: the use of language, rather than the attitude and themes.

As far as themes and attitudes were concerned, many younger poets were to find Pound unsympathetic and Eliot not exactly unsympathetic but, in his conservative attitudes in politics and his religious orthodoxy, on the opposite side of the fence from them. They found a moral inspiration rather in Wilfred Owen's fragmentary preface to his war poems:

> Above all, I am not concerned with Poetry.

> My subject is War, and the pity of War.

> The Poetry is in the pity.

Yet these elegies are to this generation in no sense consolatory. They may be to the next. All a poet can do to-day is warn. That is why the true Poets must be truthful.

And Owen's own techniques, not at all like those of Eliot or Pound, but intense and hortatory, were to compete with Eliot and Pound for influence over younger poets like Stephen Spender:

> But cursed are dullards whom no cannon stuns,
> That they should be as stones;
> Wretched are they, and mean
> With paucity that never was simplicity.
> By choice they made themselves immune
> To pity and whatever moans in man
> Before the last sea and the hapless stars;
> Whatever mourns when many leave these shores;
> Whatever shares
> The eternal reciprocity of tears.

There is a grandeur and simplicity in that which is not to be found, and was not aimed at, in the subtle and ironic social commentaries of Pound and Eliot. And perhaps the stark sincerity of Owen might make one question even the tone of Yeats's wonderful *Easter, 1916*:

> Hearts with one purpose alone
> Through summer and winter seem
> Enchanted to a stone
> To trouble the living stream.
> The horse that comes from the road,
> The rider, the birds that range
> From cloud to tumbling cloud,
> Minute by minute they change;
> A shadow of cloud on the stream
> Changes minute by minute;
> A horse-hoof slides on the brim
> And a horse plashes within it;
> The long-legged moor-hens dive,
> And hens to moor-cocks call;
> Minute by minute they live:
> The stone's in the midst of all.

Is the beautiful, complex symbolism of that – the stream as the flow of daily life, the stone as the purpose of the Irish revolutionaries – too much 'concerned with Poetry,' in Owen's sense? Is Yeats, always so much concerned with myth and fantasy, one of those of whom he is thinking when he says 'the true Poets must be truthful'? Would he think of Pound and Eliot, working on translation and satire while men were dying in the trenches, as 'dullards whom no cannon stuns'? If he would, I think he is taking an intense but narrow view of things. It may be the chief *secondary* duty of a poet to-day to warn but his primary duty to-day, as at all times, to be a poet. And the poetry of life is not *only* in the pity, but in the irony, the humour, the heroism, in what Mr Eliot has called 'the boredom, the horror, and the glory,' in the whole grand complex. Owen is demanding, certainly for the noblest reasons, an oversimplification of the poet's task. Yet that preface, and that stanza, have both about them the stern and simple authority of the English puritan tradition; and they will be listened to, generation after generation, by earnest young men who have turned away in exasperation from more balanced and sophisticated but (for the moment, and to them) less inspiring masters.

Section 2: The 1920s

In the 1920s, and indeed in the 1930s and up to our own time, poets like Pound and Eliot whose early experimental work I have dealt with in the last section were, of course, continuing to develop their talents. Eliot's most widely known poem, indeed, *The Waste Land*, was published in the early 1920s and it expressed better than any other poem

207

of that decade the sense of hopeless drift which afflicted the post-war generation. Herbert Read with that simplicity and dignity, that perfect candour of tone, which are his great qualities as a writer, has explained in the preface to his autobiography, *Annals of Innocence and Experience*, the sort of background from which poems like *The Waste Land* arose: 'These pages will make sufficiently clear that I consider the no-man's-years between the wars as largely futile, spent unprofitably by me and all my kind. I do not pretend to know how we could have made them more positive: the forces against us were not human, but satanic – blind forces of economic drift, with the walls of faith and reason turning to air behind us.'

The Waste Land, however, did not merely express this negative sense of hopelessness; it differed from most poetry of its time in expressing, if not yet a positive faith (it is only with *Ash Wednesday* that Mr Eliot begins to express in his poems a positive Christian attitude), at least an anguished sense that some faith is necessary and that there is some source of spiritual authority that transcends the historic flux. This feeling of personal anguish was what led Mr Eliot into the fold of the Church of England, and his more important poems from *Ash Wednesday* onwards have been, not like his early poems strictly objective studies of social disintegration in our time, but rather records of personal spiritual experience.

In one of his essays, on the philosophy of the American 'humanists' like Irving Babbitt and Paul Elmer More, Mr. Eliot has explained that the intellectual acceptance of a religious faith must, for a man of his own temperament, precede the adjustment of the will, the emotions, and the sensibilities to that faith, and *Ash Wednesday*, a very beautiful but also a very difficult poem, can be considered at least partly as a record of that slow and painful purification of the inner self in Mr Eliot's own case. The *Four Quartets*, Mr Eliot's most recent series of long poems, are a sort of philosophical meditation on the relation of time to eternity, or of human history to the will of God, and again in these poems much of the material is that of personal reminiscence and of meditation over the meaning of the tense and high moments in an individual life.

The imagery in these later poems of Mr. Eliot's has fewer flashes of isolated vividness than that in his earlier poems, like *Prufrock* or *The Waste Land*, the transitions are less striking and abrupt, there is not the same disquieting use in a 'serious' context of flippant wit or heroic burlesque or sardonic anti-climax. And though these later poems are mature and profound in a way that the earlier poems are not, indeed just because they have this special maturity and profundity, they are not likely to have the same immediate influence as the earlier poems on the techniques and attitudes of younger writers. *Prufrock* and *The Waste Land* influenced young men partly because they were a young man's poems. *The Waste Land* had its enormous influence partly because it expressed so perfectly the disquiet and bitterness of a whole generation; partly because of the range of new technical inventions in it: the use of abrupt cinematic cutting from one scene or episode to another, the shifts of tone, the sharp and glaring contrasts, the juxta-position of sordid incidents and colloquial phrases from modern urban life with allusions and quotations that called up the style and splendour of the past. The poem has a dreamlike irrational vividness even before its underlying themes have been grasped, a vividness which resembles, perhaps, more than anything else in English literature, the first impact on the mind of that otherwise totally dissimilar poem, Coleridge's *The Ancient Mariner*. And just as, according to Professor Livingstone Lowes, *The Ancient Mariner* embodies all sorts of fragments from Coleridge's wide, multifarious, unsystematic reading, sent up from his subconscious mind at just the poetically appropriate moment, so the quotations and allusions and passages of rhetorical *pastiche* which make up so much of the complex fabric of *The Waste Land* are a record of Mr Eliot's much more orderly but just as adventurously ranging reading and taste.

It is possible, as I say, to enjoy *The Waste Land* and to feel almost its full poetic impact without grasping the underlying legendary, anthropological, religious theme of the barren land which can only be reclaimed to fertility by a ritual sacrifice. This primitive theme under-lies the legend of the Grail and it is behind the lovely myths of Adonis or Osiris, the young men slain in the springtime and mourned by the goddess; for originally those who mourned them would have also been those who slew them. The sacrificial victim was a sacred king and the representative of a god; the fertility of the land was magically involved in his own youth and strength, and so he had to be regularly sacrificed in case, with his own old age and decay, the land should wither, too. That is the significance of the sick king in the Grail legend; it is because he is sick that his lands are barren, and they can only become fertile when he is healed. The Christian interpretation of this traditional myth is the highest one: the sacrificed king is Christ, as God incarnate, and the barren land which has to be reclaimed to fertility is the human heart, full of selfishness and lust, choked with the tares of sin.

Though we can take the impact of *The Waste Land* without knowing all this, the poem certainly does become more coherent, less bewildering, when these underlying ideas are grasped. Moreover, the fact that a reader may regard these old fertility cults, and the legends associated with them, as mere relics of error and superstition, or even the fact that he may reject the claims to supernatural validity of the Christian religion itself, need not invalidate the poetic attractiveness or even the poetic 'truth' of *The Waste Land* for him. The need for sacrifice, for a coherent faith, and for some living bond of union in our modern mechanised society is felt by many people to-day who are consciously 'rationalistic,' who are not at all 'religious' in the old traditional sense; and in fact many of Mr Eliot's most ardent poetic disciples have been at one time or another in their careers either Communists or on the verge of accepting Communism. They too have felt the need for sacrifice, for a coherent faith, and for a living bond of union, though they have interpreted these ideas in a quite other sense than Mr Eliot's. This relevance at several levels belongs, I think, to all really great poetry and it makes irrelevant the approach of critics, whether Christian or Marxist, who take up a sectarian attitude to poetry and refuse to praise any writer who is not obviously on their side. For poetry is not primarily an instrument of propaganda or even of simple edification, but a way of exploring and unifying what can be called in the widest sense our 'moral' experiences; and confrontation with a great unified structure of this sort does not call upon the reader to take up the exact practical attitudes of the poet, but rather to perform a parallel or analogous act of exploration and unification at the level of his own deeper responses.

After *Hugh Selwyn Mauberley*, which critics like Dr Leavis consider his best poem and his culminating achievement, Ezra Pound set out on a much wider task of exploration even than that undertaken by Eliot in *The Waste Land*, but it is still an open critical question whether in the enormous bulk of the still uncompleted *Cantos*, one of the longest English poems of our time or any time, he has achieved a parallel task of unification. We have already seen that Pound had a curious reluctance to appear or speak in person in his poetry and that he was often at his happiest when speaking in an assumed role. Pound's poetic attention is always, or nearly always, directed to the outer world, not to his inner states; he has not that gift of scrupulous and alert introspectiveness which has made Mr Eliot in his later works such a profound and moving religious poet. Neither, for that matter,

though he had the same impatient sense as Mr Eliot of the disorder
and drift of contemporary society and of the lack of 'style' in that
society, did he have that profound sense of sin and that personal
humility which are at the root (on the human side, at least, for we
must allow for the mysterious interventions of divine grace) of Mr
Eliot's religious beliefs.

Even *Hugh Selwyn Mauberley*, which is as near as Pound gets in his
earlier and shorter poems to the statement of a complex personal
attitude, to a poetry of 'self-regard' either in a good or a bad sense, is
still less a poem of self-exploration than of self-dramatisation, or rather
of the dramatisation of one of Pound's roles in the world. Mauberley
is not quite Pound himself but rather what Pound might have been
with less toughness and determination. He is a poet who in the 1910s
carries on some of the traditions of the 1890s, who lives, to put it
crudely, for beauty and for art, and who is defeated by the vulgar,
grasping, commercial spirit of the age and by the decay of the grand
tradition; 'The Nineties tried your game,' the poet is told by a brassily
successful *arriviste*, 'and died, there's nothing in it,' and Mauberley's
end is to drift away and die on a South Sea island:

> I was
> And I no more exist;
> Here drifted
> An Hedonist.

But Mauberley's end was not to be Pound's end, and Pound's attitude
was less narrowly concentrated on art for art's sake, on the mere
aesthetic attitude, than Mauberley's. Instead of drifting away to a
South Sea island, Pound settled down in Rapallo in Italy to construct
the long poem, *The Cantos*, which is essentially an attempt to create
a kind of personal anthology of what Pound regards as the high and
noble moments in human culture.

The poem begins with a translation from a famous passage in the
Odyssey in which Odysseus visits the underworld and, sacrificing a
black ram, calls up the ghosts of the mighty dead. This, in the earlier
cantos of his poem, is what Pound himself is largely doing and we
switch in a rather bewilderingly zigzag fashion from Greek mythology
to the heroes and villains of the Italian High Renaissance and from these
again to the Founding Fathers of the American Revolution. The
structural pattern of these early cantos, as Mr R. P. Blackmur has noted,
is that of the interrupted anecdote; Pound starts telling a story about

someone, breaks it off in the middle, and starts telling another story about someone else, someone usually belonging to a contrasting place and time; the dropped threads may or may not be picked up again somewhere later in the story. In the later cantos, however, this method of kaleidoscopic juxtaposition is dropped and there are two fairly long and straightforward sets of narrative cantos, one about John Adams, the second president of the United States, the other about the history of China.

It has become clear by this stage that the multifarious and contrasting material of the earlier cantos has been assembled not just for its vividness and picturesqueness, not just as old bright bits, but as documentation for some thesis about society. The passages about Adams and about China make the thesis clearer, though certain earlier passages – about Andrew Jackson and Martin Van Buren and their struggle with great national banking interests in the United States in the name of cheap money and the small man – have already given a hint of its nature. Adams is the type of the good ruler; he stands for an American culture, in Pound's eyes, that will be based on the independent farmer and the wealth of the land, as against Alexander Hamilton's vision (the vision which was to come truer in the end) of concentrated financial power and growing industrialisation. Jefferson is the more usual symbol of the anti-Hamiltonian attitude, but probably Pound thought Jefferson a weaker man than Adams. China, again, is the symbol of a stable agrarian society, held together by its respect for a traditional code of wisdom, that of Confucius; we are meant to contrast its long history, on the whole such a remarkably peaceful history, with the short and violent history of the Western world since the Industrial Revolution: to contrast the serene wisdom of Confucius with our own hesitations and anxieties and uncertainties, our lack of firm standards. We are meant to see usury and other-worldliness – if Pound admires Confucianism, he hates Taoism – as the great evils that destroy society. We are to ask ourselves where in the end all our industrial 'progress' has got us to.

Pound's ideas, in fact, have a great deal in common with those of the English 'distributists,' Belloc and Chesterton, who also dreamt of a return to a society of small peasant proprietorship and respect for traditional wisdom. The practical weakness of all such philosophies is that, after all, our industrial world, and our industrial population, are here; they cannot simply be abolished with the wave of a wand. History can never go back to a simpler state of affairs when its present problems had not arisen; its present problems are what it has to solve – that is, it has to go forward. But in Italy, which is still largely an agrarian country, apart from its pockets of heavy industry in the north, these ideas no doubt seemed more plausible to Pound than they would have done in the grey labyrinth of London. He became an admirer of Mussolini, thinking mainly, to give him his due, not of Mussolini's role as a militant nationalist – Pound has always detested war and war-mongering – but of his big public works, like his draining of malarial marshes and settling of landless peasants on them. He also thought that he had managed to interest Mussolini, or might manage to interest him, in the economic notions of Major C.H. Douglas.

The essence of these notions is that booms and slumps and unemployment and the other disorders of a free enterprise society are fundamentally due to the fact that under the present banking and currency systems not enough money is issued to enable the public to buy the whole available supply of consumable goods; goods pile up in the shops, shopkeepers cease to order more goods, manufacturers stop manufacturing, manufacturers therefore have to dismiss workmen, the dismissed workmen have even less money on hand than usual to purchase the available supplies of consumable goods, so things get progressively worse and worse till the only way left to boost production and restore employment is by starting an armament programme which, in the long or even in the short run, will lead to war. Douglas's remedy for this state of affairs was the issue of a national dividend, paid to everybody, regardless of merit, that would close up the gap between supply and effective demand. I am not in any sense an expert on economics, and in any case discussion of the soundness or otherwise of these views would be irrelevant in my present context. It is obvious, I think, that they are ideas which make a special appeal to the man of letters looking for some alternative to Socialism, which will create a certain stability and order in society, without interfering with his personal freedom, as he fears Socialism might do.

Pound's general fondness for the atmosphere of Italy, where he had lived for seventeen years, and his belief that Mussolini had the root of the matter in him in economics, led him during the war to broadcast from Italy on behalf of the Axis, though he had never relinquished his American citizenship. Thus at the end of the war he was arrested by the American forces and would have stood his trial as a traitor to his country if a medical board had not certified him to be mentally unbalanced. He has now been confined for some years in a lunatic asylum, but nevertheless has been able to carry on with the writing of his long poem and the last instalment, *The Pisan Cantos*, won the Bollingen Prize as the best volume of poems published in the United States in 1949 – a fact which is a remarkable tribute to the liberality and tolerance of the best critical opinion in the United States. *The Pisan Cantos* are largely taken up with Pound's meditations in his prison camp in Italy, and they are the most personal in tone of the cantos so far, full of reminiscences of friends and allusions to past experience. They have the form of a rambling monologue, often hard to understand without some knowledge of Pound's history; but they are sincere and touching and they contain one sustained passage at least, which I have quoted in the first chapter of this book, which is quite obviously of the highest order of poetry.

It is very difficult at the present moment to make any very definite judgment either on Pound himself as a person or on this major work at which he has been labouring for the past thirty years. The main critical question, I suppose, is whether his ideas about society and its organisation (let us suppose them fundamentally sound or unsound, as we please) have the wide human relevance of for instance Mr Eliot's ideas about history and its possible redemption. Mr Eliot's ideas, Christian in their basis, have a relevance for readers who are not Christians as well as for readers who are. But Pound's economics, which are central to his thesis, have for uninstructed readers at least an air of crankiness about them. His economic ideas, whether or not they are accurate, are very technical; and it might be said than an obsession with the techniques rather than with the spirit of high human culture which is very notable in Pound's critical work also to some extent vitiates the thesis of *The Cantos*. When we look at the world around us, so full of unhappiness and aggressiveness, we find it hard to believe that everything can be set right by any manipulation of the currency, however ingenious. There seems to be a disproportion (not merely a rational disproportion, which would not matter so much, but an aesthetic one) between the complicated disease Pound diagnoses and the simple remedy he suggests. And he seems also, with a touch of American pragmatism, to reject a great deal in the Western tradition, including for instance Platonism and Christianity, without which the history of Europe might certainly have been more peaceful or at least more static, more like the history of China, but without which also the history of Europe would have been much less heroic and interesting.

Pound's notion of 'tradition,' in fact, is an exceedingly fragmentary and selective one, in spite of its wide and scattering geographical and historical range. One comes back perhaps in the end to the notion of a personal anthology, of one man's selective response to the whole of human history, and in that sense the *Cantos* are not only a kind of modern epic but also, in spite of Pound's hatred for the subjective approach, a kind of intellectual autobiography. Thus one's final judgment about them will be a judgment really about Pound – about the measure of truth, and the measure of illusion, in his grasp of the world; perhaps more deeply about the measure of sincerity, and the measure of self-deception, in his inner attitudes. All one can say at the moment, perhaps, is that the *Cantos* are a very ambitious, a very brilliant, a very confusing and sometimes intrinsically confused body of work; that they are a manual of useful techniques for younger poets; that they preserve in paraphrase, or translation, or condensed anecdote, many of the high moments of man's culture and history, and that they convey these with an authentic nobility of spirit; that their brilliance in detail is even now, at this late stage in their development, more obvious than their total moral or intellectual coherence; that they nevertheless are, as Mr Eliot has said, the only readable long poem of our time; and that, in short, they cannot be ignored.*

William Butler Yeats in his development in the 1920s was stimulated, influenced, and irritated by Pound. Eliot, on the other hand, Yeats admired but could get nothing from of use to himself: Eliot seemed to him a grey, controlled writer, a master of satire, like Pope. His irritation with Pound Yeats expressed when he described Pound in a letter to Lady Dorothy Wellesley as a sexless attitudinising American professor. His appreciation he expressed when he prefaced his famous book of occult philosophy, *A Vision*, with a section called 'A Packet for Ezra Pound.' Yeats is undoubtedly a very great poet and a poet whose work, partly because it is traditional and more obviously coherent in form, is likely to retain its popularity when Pound and Eliot have undergone a temporary lapse from favour (for the latter two are so urgently and topically of this age, that the next age – say the young men who start writing poetry around 1960 or 1970 – is almost bound to react against them). But it would be hard to explain in abstract

* To many readers it may seem that I have given Pound far too much space in this book. Orthodox progressives would dismiss him as (literally) 'a mad Fascist.' Academic scholars point out that as a translator he falls again and again into schoolboy howlers. For these very reasons, willingness to acknowledge his importance is a test of critical honesty.

terms to that typical modern reader whom one imagines as liberal, rationalistic, and scientific in his outlook, just in what Yeats's greatness consists. In politics, Yeats is even more definitely a 'reactionary' than Pound, though living as he did in a small agrarian country, Ireland, which still retained in its manners, or those of its gentry, something of the style of the eighteenth century, Yeats was able to relate his own obstinate resistance to change to a similar set of attitudes in his countrymen. He always had a background in a sense in which Pound, a wanderer and an exile from his native country for most of his life, never had one.

Yeats, moreover, unlike most of his younger contemporaries, rode rather loosely to the age. For them the urgent choice was between a religious and a scientific attitude; Yeats was neither orthodoxly religious in the sense of Eliot nor orthodoxly scientific in the sense of the young radical Marxist and Freudian poets of the 1930s. His attitude might be more properly described as a magical attitude: or one might say that Yeats had both a science of his own and a religion of his own, united, as primitive science and primitive religion are, at the level of magic. That science and religion are expounded in beautiful prose in A Vision. They are more than merely expounded, they are woven into something that must be called a philosophy. It is a philosophy in which pious or rational readers may pick many holes: but from the poet's point of view it has the great advantage, which most modern philosophies lack, of being at once inclusive and systematic. We feel that Yeats's experiences fit in an orderly way into a framework of notions and attitudes: we feel that this is a large and hospitable framework, and that no really important type of experience has to be left out. Should we then ask ourselves whether the framework is 'true' or whether we, or even Yeats, can 'believe' in it? (Yeats himself said that he thought the notion of believing, or not believing, was largely irrelevant to his speculations in A Vision.) The only meaning of 'true' that is relevant to our criticism of A Vision is not 'true' as 'corresponding, point by point, to known facts' but 'true' as 'fitting together into a broadly meaningful and aesthetically satisfying pattern.' A Vision is a coherent book. At his occult or magical level, Yeats does reconcile his own 'facts' and his own 'values,' even if to the ordinary reader the facts seem only dubiously factual and the values odd and arbitrary: but these questions will arise only after the book is closed, for Yeats, in prose or verse, carries the completest conviction while one is reading him. The obvious comparison here is with Blake. It is a mistake, I think, to regard Blake as an inspired religious teacher and to accept the Prophetic Books as a new gospel: but it is a worse mistake to dismiss them as ravings. It would be a mistake similarly to swallow *A Vision* whole: but a worse mistake to dismiss it as merely odd and eccentric, having no relation to the greatness of Yeats's poetry.

As I have said in the first chapter of this book, Yeats owed a great deal both to Vico and to Nietzsche, and a leading idea in many of his poems is that history is a fated and eternally recurrent pattern, in which like actors we must again and again play the particular parts assigned to us. The great thing is that, however painful our part may be, we should play it with style: 'Hamlet and Lear,' said Yeats, 'are gay.' There was a mixture, in fact, in Yeats's temperament of a passionate lust for life, the strong animal life of blood and bone, and another wish for the remote contemplative immortality of a pure withdrawn spirit: and it was his occult philosophy of history that enabled him to reconcile these two aspects of his character. He saw death first as the road to another kind of life, the life of pure contemplative wisdom, but ultimately as the road back, both through reincarnation and through the returning wheel, to our own life here. For that physical life of the body in the world, he had a deep lust, at any level – even at that of 'a blind man battering blind men.' On the other hand, his sense that our life here is a kind of play, that we wear a formal mask, and express merely the symbolical outward show of a hidden supernatural reality, saved him from being really battered down, as so many fine writers of our generation have been, by the spectacle of the misery, the squalor, and the injustice of the world.

Indeed, it is a common criticism of Yeats as a man and a poet, that he lacked pity and his dismissal of the poetry of the first world war as a poetry of 'passive suffering' is perhaps an indication of hardness. The kind of human experience that will not take a strong and stylish mould of form, Yeats tended temperamentally to neglect; and there is probably rather a large range of typical contemporary human experience, where his general advice to put a good face on things and to swagger seems silly and futile. And yet when that has been said, one still wonders whether the source of Yeats's greatness as a poet was really his ideas and not rather that temperament of his, harshly limited as it was. For if he lacked pity for those drab mass sufferings of our time, which so sadly do lack 'style' certainly, if he lacked, in a word, the humanitarian spirit, he certainly did not, in a broader sense, lack humanity. No poet of our time has loved and admired his friends more or incised their profiles for us in more firm and enduring verse.

And even in regard to what has been said about his lack of pity, one should make qualifications: it implied no lack of *pietas*. In the bitter and violent Ireland of his time, the Ireland of heroes, fanatics, and assassins, rebellion and civil war, Yeats was always, for all his grand romantic airs, a moderating influence, a humanising influence: it might almost be said a liberal influence. He hated barbaric waste and destruction, and this hatred is beautifully expressed in his series of poems about the Irish 'troubles' called *1919*:

> We had fed the heart on fantasies.
> The heart's grown brutal from the fare.
> More substance in our enmities
> Than in our love. O honey bees
> Come nest in the empty house of the stare.

The 'stare' is a starling, an Irish word for that bird, and one that had nested near Yeats's house had deserted its old home in these years. The honey-bees are symbols of sweetness and construction, just as the starling is the symbol of the lyric poet. The Irish people had fed too long on fantasies of national self-sufficiency, and Yeats himself had encouraged them by brooding on old mythologies. The result in the end was brutal civil war, whose brutality sent the bird and the poet away. The hatred behind the civil war was more real, more substantial, had more body to it, than the fantastic love, the love of Ireland as an imaginary old woman, Kathleen ni Houlihan, about which Yeats had written so many of his earlier poems. Well, let the starlings stop singing and the lyric poets be silent, since they only inspire the average men who listen to them to violence and brutality. Let men look at the bees instead, less romantic and solitary creatures than birds or poets, but who provide an example of useful and peaceful social co-operation. There are all these implications in these lines, and the tone of almost unbearable sadness comes from the fact that it is the poet, the lover of fantasies, the admirer of heroic violence, who is making this sharp criticism of himself, and so much that he has admired and inspired and stood for. It is this tone of sharp, penetrating self-criticism that prevents Yeats, however strange and out of step with the direction of the world his attitudes may seem to be, from ever becoming an unreal or stagy poet. He sees himself, and makes even more sharply than we do, the criticisms of his 'romantic' attitude that we might wish to make. He knows the price of his own kind of greatness, and pays it out to the last penny with a kind of arrogant generosity.

One might say that Yeats's own temperament was gentle and humane and moderate, if not given to abstract humanitarian enthusiasm or to progressive sentiment: but that he assumed in verse, as the aesthetic antithesis to his natural temperament, the heroic mask. One reads him certainly not merely for his 'ideas' or for what he himself called 'the half-read wisdom of daemonic images,' the ideas which he got from table-rapping or from automatic writing, or through his wife's mediumistic capacity, but which the spirits, he said, who communicated them to him, were not interested in his interpreting or understanding: merely wishing to provide him with material for verse. One reads him also, and perhaps one specially reads him, for the reflection in his verse of a traditional culture with a tragic dignity about it: a culture still unified, still vital, still rooted in the soil, which (or the English analogy to which, surviving still in rural areas) no English poet of comparable stature expresses with comparable eloquence. There is, of course, the work of Hardy: but what Hardy has to say he expresses, if we compare him with Yeats, in a clumsy and stammering way. And Hardy's regretful rejection of the Christian faith, and the if not exactly pessimistic yet glum and grey pantheism which takes the place of the lost faith in his mind, if they lend themselves sometimes to a peculiar, slow, fumbling sincerity – more 'honest,' perhaps, in one sense, than anything in Yeats, who from Hardy's point of view would perhaps seem a brilliant charlatan – do not provide him with the framework that Yeats's occult philosophy provides for Yeats. The mythological background of *The Dynasts*, with its Spirit Sinister and Spirit Ironic, its abundant use of awkward philosophical neologisms, has not at all the convincing quality of Yeats's use of Celtic legends, rooted in the folk mind.

One might say that Yeats, unlike almost all the other poets whom we have been considering in this chapter, had not had to digest the Industrial Revolution. The only great, shapeless, modern commercial town he had ever lived in for a long period was London, and his London, after all, had not been that of the City or the suburbs, or the Surrey side of the river, but the London of the Rhymers' Club, of gatherings of poets like Johnson and Dowson, Plarr and Davidson and Wratislaw, in the 'Cheshire Cheese' in Fleet Street. Moreover, he had been rescued from London, by the benevolence of Lady Gregory, just in time. And in Ireland he had a direct experience of that traditional, aristocratic culture, based on the land and on the loyalty of a peasantry, which her poets with the same romantic, 'reactionary' notions knew only as a remote ideal. In the small literary community of Dublin, moreover, he stood out as a giant and could be on intimate terms with all the most significant of his contemporaries; where in London the writer, however distinguished, tends to be lost in an anonymous mass, or in a bundle of competing talents, and gradually to have what is distinctive and individual in him rubbed away. Also Ireland escaped the direct, harsh impact of the First World War and its aftermath. The Easter Rebellion of 1916 and the subsequent Irish 'troubles,' harsh and painful as they were, were very different in quality from the trench warfare in which English poets like Edmund Blunden, Robert Graves, Siegfried Sassoon, or Richard Aldington stood up for years in the filthy mud to shoot at, and be shot at by, invisible enemies: and to come back home with war neuroses which it would take the rest of their lives to cure and to resolve into art.

Thus Yeats in a sense seems to have been, perhaps through a set of accidental circumstances, the most fortunately placed of all the great English poets of this century. One might add that he had a great gift for both feeling and inspiring romantic love and that in the Ireland of his time he found many beautiful women to break his heart over. He was the last of the great romantics; but because his life as a poet was so much longer than that of Keats or Shelley, and so much more complex and passionate and interesting than that of Wordsworth, it seems to me that there is a humanity, a solidity, a coherence, a constant awareness of the demands of decorum and style in his work, which one does not find in theirs. The body of his work is reasonably large and extends over something like fifty years of active continuous production, but I am not aware that in it one can put one's finger on more than half a dozen bad or false poems, of which *The Lake Isle of Innisfree*, ironically his most popular and his most widely known piece, is certainly one.* The same thing cannot be said of Wordsworth, of Coleridge, of Shelley, or of Keats: indeed what one wants to preserve of, or what one comes back to again and again in, these great romantic pioneers is rather a startlingly small proportion of their total work.

So, on the whole, I am ready to risk rashness, and to claim for Yeats the position of a major English poet, ranking with Donne, with Milton, and with Wordsworth in the great succession. I think he is very much *greater* than Browning or Tennyson or Arnold, and as I have said, that he has possibly more lasting qualities than poets like

---

* There are some comparatively *weak* poems (the long *Wanderings of Oisin*), some *mannered* and *minor* ones, but that is another matter.

Pound or Eliot, who have for us to-day, with our particular problems of a megalopolitan society, a more urgent topical appeal. One tests this sort of thing by personal experience: I bought Yeats's collected poems when I was in my teens, I carried them with me through my university days and through the war, I have them now; and I find that I turn to them again and again for a kind of reassurance, a stimulation, a general keying up of my responses, which I can get from no other contemporary source.

Though these three figures seem in retrospect to dominate the poetic achievement of the 1920s, they did not necessarily seem to do so to poets and critics of the time. In magazines like *The London Mercury*, edited by Sir John Squire, poetry in the Georgian tradition still flourished, though possibly in a rather decadent form. The poet Roy Campbell in a brisk and vigorous satirical piece called *Georgian Spring* wrote:

> But still the air is full of happy voices,
> All bloody: but no matter, let them sing!
> For who would frown when all the world rejoices,
> And who would contradict, when in the spring,
> The English Muse her annual theme rehearses
> To tell us birds are singing in the sky?
> Only the poet slams the door and curses
> And all the little sparrows wonder why!

But there were many interesting and individual poets in the 1920s who did not belong to the Georgian tradition and at the same time were not merely followers of Yeats, Pound, or Eliot. The Sitwell family formed a little group in themselves and gathered around them in the magazine *Wheels* young poets who shared some of their tastes and sympathies, like Aldous Huxley and Sherard Vines. The early work of all three Sitwells, Edith, Osbert, and Sacheverell, shows a strong family likeness, a common range of themes and attitudes, though Osbert had from the beginning more of a bent for satire than his brother and sister: and Sacheverell, in his verse as in his prose, showed a special fondness for the imaginative description of great works of architectural and pictorial art and for evoking, with a wealth of epithet, the visual impact of the past. Edith's special subject in her earlier poems was the memories and dreams of childhood, as transformed by fantasy. The style of all three writers, if we compare it with that of Eliot or Pound, or even with a traditionally romantic style like that of Yeats, is rather precious and elaborate: it seems to aim not so much at colloquial directness or at high eloquence as at a certain mocking elusiveness, a certain fashionable *chic*, an ornate, intricate decorative effect. It is, in these early poems, to use two favourite epithets of the 1920s, 'gay' and 'amusing.' Edith in particular was interested in exercises in pure technical virtuosity, as in the set of poems for which Sir William Walton wrote music, *Façade*. She, like her brothers, was also interested in the use of poetry of subtle associations of perception – a particular intense shade of green would be described, in terms of sound, as *shrill*: a particular effect of light, again in terms of sound but also partly in terms of muscular effort, as *creaking*: or rain falling stiffly at a certain angle might be described, partly in terms of sight but also partly in terms of imagined tactual sensation, as *wooden*. This idea of a correspondence between different kinds of sensation, and this gift of transforming, with the rapidity of hallucination, one complex of perceptions into another, owed something of course both to the theory and to the practice of Rimbaud. It led to vivid effects, but also sometimes to an air of affectation, and to what looked like purely arbitrary associations.*

Miss Sitwell was also, like all her family, especially interested in what she called the 'texture' of verse, the value of certain combinations of vowels and consonants in themselves, and as arranged in the line. Here, too, one has sometimes, when one reads her critical writings (for her practice is self-justifying), a certain sense of arbitrariness: for her vocabulary of 'light' and 'heavy' or of 'light' and 'dark' vowels, of 'gross' and 'thick' or 'thin' and 'shrill' syllables, of syllables that 'leap,' is, however sensitive, very subjective, and cannot be exactly squared with any ordinary system of metrics or phonetics. Moreover, the range of pronunciation of a line of verse – say in Southern English, in the English of Miss Sitwell's native Yorkshire, in that of Ireland, various regions of Scotland, various regions of the United States – can vary extremely without the line being robbed of poetic beauty. A poet like Roy Campbell, who seems when one reads him on the page to have a perfect ear, nevertheless reads his poems *aloud* in a South African twang that turns them into burlesque. Many lines of Chaucer or Dunbar do not need to be read in an absolutely correct Middle English pronunciation to convey their beauty: and modern scholars think that Shakespeare's plays were spoken contemporarily in what now sounds to us like a rather rustic Midland dialect. Wordsworth, who had a

---

* See a very amusing correspondence in the *Observer* of 1951 about the adjective Emily-coloured as applied to primulas and hands.

northern burr in his speech, said 'earth's diurnal course,' sounding all the r's.* In modern Southern English they are silent or only equivalent to a tiny slur or drag, and yet, for a Southern English reader, the poem from which the phrase comes retains its great beauty. This is not to say that sound effects in poetry can be ignored, but that the structure of a line of verse on the page corresponds to a whole range of phonetic possibilities, all or most of which may have an aesthetic validity; and that there is a danger of the poet attributing to combinations of sound, as to combinations of sensation, which have a special value to himself – perhaps through his own way of speaking and hearing, perhaps through peculiarities of his own mode of perception, perhaps also through arbitrary and irrelevant associations – an absolute value that they do not necessarily possess. Thus it is notable that Miss Sitwell's experiments in working out correspondences of sensation, and patterns of verbal texture, though they have obviously helped her own personal development, have had on the whole little direct influence on other poets.

Like all her family, Miss Sitwell was devoted to the Russian ballet, and from that devotion comes a certain tendency in her earlier work to describe landscapes or personages in terms of formal theatrical décor. That earlier work was perhaps more intrinsically interesting from such purely technical points of view than for its actual content, which, if we compare it with the content of Yeats, Pound, or Eliot, seems often a little repetitive and thin: a sophisticated child's story-book world or, more simply, the world of an enclosed dream. In her long poem, however, *Gold Coast Customs*, Miss Sitwell seemed to awaken sharply to a vision of the distress and evil in the outer world, and in her later poems, published during and since the war, she has become much more massive, simple, and direct in the kind of statements she makes and also in her verse techniques. These later poems of hers are a sustained protest in the name both of Christian belief and the natural rhythms of life that we associate with the high Pagan traditions against the mechanical and destructive forces at work in the world to-day. Miss Sitwell has been sharply taken to task by Mr Geoffrey Grigson, among others, for a lack of 'truth to nature' in the Wordsworthian sense and for a certain formal largeness or looseness in the structure of these later poems, which he has even described as 'gilded sprawlings': but the former criticism is irrelevant to Miss Sitwell's heraldic and mythical world, which does not pretend, in these later poems, to be the world

* I owe this point to an interesting book by Dr F.W. Bateson.

of outward nature at all, but rather a symbolic transformation of it, and the latter criticism is also irrelevant to the particular form of these later poems: a form which has, for instance, fundamentally something in common with that of Whitman, a certain expansiveness and iteration being an integral part of the total effect.

There is not, certainly, in Miss Sitwell's work the intellectual tautness which we find, for instance, in different ways, in the work of Mr Eliot or Mr Empson; her approach to the world is not through concepts but rather through feelings and images, and it is again a critical error to attack her for being a kind of poet she does not set out to be. It does remain a critical question, of course, whether a poet who does not present (or rather who does not use as a mode of apprehension) some fully coherent philosophy of life can claim major rank to-day. (I say to-day, because to-day the sensitive reader has a special need for exact and applicable formulations of 'the situation.' The poet of a settled society, like Chaucer, does not seem to need any conscious philosophy at all. Shakespeare, the poet of an expanding but disturbed society, seems to have had no philosophy that we can point to as specifically his, and a metaphysical poet like Donne plays with fragments of broken philosophies. But both these could use in their poetry philosophical material, arguments, statements of a general case, and the critical question about a poet of Miss Sitwell's type is whether to-day, with the complexity of our modern world, and the different levels of response among different groups of readers, the symbolist method can provide for the poet an adequate way of handling the whole situation.) Can, in our world to-day, a temperamental response, massive but necessarily confused, integrate a major body of work? That question must be asked but, however it is answered, Miss Sitwell is a poet who cannot be ignored and who has made her own distinct, individual, and on occasions most memorably beautiful contribution to the poetry of our time.

Miss Sitwell's brother, Sacheverell, does not seem on the other hand to have yet progressed beyond the stage at which he was writing some twenty years ago. Skilfully and beautifully written as his poems are, they have a touch of that coldness and remoteness which belongs to all works of art whose inspiration is other works of art rather than the life of the poet's time. Sir Osbert Sitwell, in later life, has confined himself mainly to prose writing, as in his vivid autobiographies. In a satirical cantata, Demos the Emperor, published four or five years ago, he showed in the detail of his writing the rich feeling for texture that is common to all the work of the Sitwells, whether in prose or verse, but at the same time appeared both petulant and confused in his satirical approach 'to the post-war scene.' One might say that the aristocratic background and the strong family loyalties of these gifted writers have at once helped and hampered them. The background gave them rich material and the loyalties sustained them in their early days of struggle for recognition, but both background and loyalties have shut them off to some extent from the common life, even from the common literary life of the time: background and loyalties, also, have rendered them peculiarly and excessively sensitive not only to hostile but to detached criticism. Not, for the matter, that detached criticism is easy. A reader of the Sitwells has to surrender himself to a peculiarly intense and individual family atmosphere, and it is difficult to compare or contrast that atmosphere, in a critically useful way, with anything outside it. It is doubtful, for the same set of reasons, whether the Sitwells have had the same direct influence on the techniques and attitudes of younger writers as Eliot, Pound, or Yeats, whose themes have had a wider general relevance. At the same time, the work of the Sitwells has a peculiar and inimitable charm of its own, and modern English literature would be very much poorer without it.

Roy Campbell, whom I mentioned above, is another important poet whose approach to the world is through his senses and emotions, and one should add emphatically his will, rather than his intellect. He is notable among modern poets for his strict traditionalism of form and vocabulary, only mitigated (but more often in his satires than in his lyrical poems) by a certain expansiveness and a vigorous use of colloquial expressions, particularly army slang. Generally speaking, however, his rhetoric has more in common with that of some of the early French and English romantics – with Byron and Victor Hugo, say – than with that complex and allusive diction of modern poetry which, in our last section, we examined in some detail. He is able to write in this romantic-rhetorical tradition (and sometimes one does, in Mr Campbell's less felicitous moments, remember Keats's snarl at Shelley and Byron,

> . . . large self worshippers
> And careless Hectorers in proud bad verse),

without affectation, partly because he does not really belong to the modern world of great grey cities, but rather to the traditional pastoral

225

8

communities which still exist, relatively undisturbed in their old ways, on its outer edges.

Born in South Africa, Roy Campbell has lived an adventurous life as cowboy, fisherman, farmer, hunter, soldier, in many parts of the world, has for much of his life earned his living with his hands, has fought bravely as a common soldier in the Spanish Civil War (on General Franco's side) and in the last war, and has therefore a direct and simple approach to life which makes him impatient of the subtleties and hesitations, the qualifications and self-corrections, which are so typical of the tone of much modern poetry and criticism.

Mr Campbell's attitude, in fact, to the modern urban scene is a little like that of Rousseau's 'noble savage,' though at the same time, as a satirist, he perhaps deliberately exaggerates the naivety of his responses for rhetorical effect. Campbell's very great gifts as a poet tended to be denigrated in the 1930s, partly because, almost alone among the English poets of his generation, he espoused the cause of General Franco in Spain and indeed fought on that side. He was denounced as a 'Fascist,' though his fine war record with the Allies in the last war shows that to have been an unfair accusation. It would be truer to describe him as a strong traditionalist (he is a fervent Roman Catholic), who has an instinctive dislike of all sorts of political interference with healthy local habits and customs. His feeling about politics, he wrote in a recent article, is that there should be as little politics as possible, and in fact he has strong temperamental affinities with, and is a close friend of, English anarchist poets, like Paul Potts. He likes the common man and distrusts intellectuals, and when he was once asked in a questionnaire in what ways he differed, as a poet from the ordinary man, he wrote, 'In nothing at all . . . in which, however, I differ very much from *the ordinary poet*.' Campbell has a strongly combative temperament and in the last five years, since he left the Army, has been briskly continuing his feud with the English radical poets of the 1930s, in spite of the fact that in the last ten years most of these have fundamentally revised their former attitudes. This combative attitude is his strength and weakness as a poet. He has wonderful vigour, but everything he writes is very much on one note, and his poems never work up to the passages of concentrated meditation which, in poets like Yeats or Eliot or Graves, give one an impression of deep contemplative wisdom. The verse goes at a steady and exhilarating gallop but never comes to a halt from which we could take in Mr Campbell's whole spiritual landscape at a glance. Mr Campbell presents himself dramatically, as a figure in action, in conflict with others, but if this man on horseback has ever any inner doubts and worries, they are not communicated to the reader. A lack of inwardness and concentration in this sense is Mr Campbell's great limitation. It breeds a certain hardness. One of his most striking lines is,

I learned to inflict and suffer pain,

but, in spite of his Christian beliefs, there are few passages in his poems which suggest that he has learned to inflict or suffer forgiveness. Mr Campbell has nearly all the gifts of a major poet, but it can be questioned whether he has sufficiently chastened his irascible appetite to make the tenor of his thoughts and feelings a sufficiently noble content for the grand vehicle of his verse.

A poet who makes an interesting contrast to Mr Campbell, for he has a certain similarity of natural temperament, is Robert Graves. Like Campbell, Graves is vigorous and combative, and he had an excellent record as a fighting soldier in the First World War. His combative nature shows up in his excellent autobiography, *Good-Bye to All That*, with its sharp criticism of much that seemed to him false and dead in the English tradition, and in such literary polemics as his *Pamphlet Against Anthologies*, written in conjunction with Laura Riding. Like Campbell, Graves is, too, on the whole a traditionalist in his metres and his diction, but with a much more subtle feeling for delicacies of implication and proprieties of usage – with, in fact, a much more intrinsically complex and interesting mind. And Graves began his poetic career, again rather like Campbell, as a poet mainly of the outer world. His subject was the English country scene and then he became one of the most typical, though not one of the best, poets of the First World War. That war, however, left him with an inner enemy to struggle against, and his poetry, first conventionally Georgian, has become more and more subtle and interesting the more directly it has engaged the inner enemy. Graves all his life, deeply though humbly confident of his vocation as a poet, has been searching for the proper poetic theme, and that theme, as his work has matured, has gradually revealed itself as that of a sense of complex maladjustment between the mind and the body, between the human spirit and outer nature, between the sexual appetites and romantic love, between the joy of romantic love itself and the vague and fearful forebodings that accompany it, between the special importance which the poet, as such, sets upon the experience of romantic love and his wish as a man for an ordinary, stable, happy existence.

In his important book, *The White Goddess*, Graves asserts that the true traditional theme of all good poetry is the love and fear of the poet for a beautiful woman, who is for him the Muse and the representative of a primitive Goddess; this Muse will return his love if he is a true poet, but in the end she will betray and destroy him. Mr Graves traces this theme back to primitive Greek and Celtic mythology and ritual, and suggests that it is ultimately the theme (which we have touched on already in connection with *The Waste Land*) of the sacrificed God, Adonis or Attis or Osiris, who, after having become for a short time the Sacred King and lover of the Sacred Queen who represented the Goddess, was sacrificed so that the fertility of the land – magically bound up with his youth and strength – might be preserved and not weakened by his growing sick or old. The theme of all true poetry is, according to Mr Graves, this 'pre-historic or posthistoric theme,' based partly on obscure racial memories or garbled traditions of these early sacrifices, and partly on a natural, or supernatural, mixture of love and awe which man feels for woman as the mother who bears him, the lover who awakens him to manhood, and the old hag who closes his dead eyes. The destruction of the old matriarchal Cretan civilisation by the early Greek invaders from the north was, according to Mr Graves, in the long run very damaging to poetry because it substituted a society dominated by men and worshipping a destructive and warlike Father God for the old society dominated by the Threefold Goddess, who, in spite of the cruel sacrifices she demanded, was the symbol of beauty, the inspirer of the poet, the guarantor of social peace and natural fertility.

This theory is perhaps more interesting as reflecting experiences in Mr Graves's own life than as a tenable theory about poetry or about society in general, and the idea of reinstating to-day a bronze age matriarchal society with its static social order, its superstitions, and its human sacrifices, is obviously not either a very practical nor, from most ordinary points of view, a very attractive idea. But Mr Graves seems to me to be right in assuming that behind all true poetry there do lie certain primitive feelings of adoration and awe (they need not be directed towards anything so concrete as the image of woman as a goddess, and in a poet like Rilke, for instance, they are directed towards the mystery of life and death, in a poet like Mallarmé towards the mystery of poetic creation itself). In a civilisation which wholly eradicated these feelings of awe and adoration, that sense, which the poet has, of being in touch with mysterious presences, poetry could not survive and perhaps the wish to live – which is also a mysterious thing, and which has something in common with the impulses that produce poetry – might wither away quite generally.

When poets speak of 'keeping tradition alive,' or of the function of the poet in society, they are thinking of this sense of the sacred mystery of life and of the old customs and ceremonies (of which the composition of poetry is one of the very oldest) that subserve it. But though we recognise the sacred mystery, we cannot adopt an irrational or a superstitious attitude. I myself think like Mr Graves that our world would be a better and happier world if women played a larger part in the ordering of it. As Miss Laura Riding, who collaborated with Mr Graves for many years, pointed out in an interesting book, in the interior of our homes civilised behaviour prevails, because there, on the whole, women, with their feeling for harmony, love, and order, are dominant. On the street, in the factory, in the office, on the benches of parliament or on the battlefield, civilised behaviour does not on the whole prevail in the same way: for there the competitiveness and the aggressive self-assertion of the male are dominant. But if women should play a larger part in our social life, it is not to take us *back* to a in many ways cruel and superstitious primitive society (for if the myth of Adonis is lovely the primitive ritual of sacrifice on which the myth was based would strike us as horrible): no, it is to take us *forward* to a more civilised society. Similarly, poetry must become more civilised. It cannot purify itself and regain a lost force merely by aping primitivism. The themes, in fact, as I have already suggested, of Mr Graves's own poetry are much more complex and interesting (and much more contemporary) than the 'single pre-historic and posthistoric theme,' which, in *The White Goddess*, he imagines himself to have discovered: much of the interest of his poetry lies in the fact that it does exhibit so sensitively the malaise of a fine traditional poet in the complex, mechanical, and destructive modern world. His poetry lacks the social force of Eliot's or Auden's because the malaise is related strictly to the poet's personal rather than to man's general contemporary situation: but for that reason, there is a real sense in which Mr Graves might be considered a 'purer' poet (or one whose work can be judged more easily out of the context of the critic's own religious or political opinions) than either of his two more famous contemporaries. For the skill and integrity of his poetic workmanship, in particular, and for his sensitive and exact restraint of language, he is an ideal model for young poets: it is these which enable him to handle, and to transform into material that gives us the highest poetic pleasure, what might otherwise be the almost unbearable sadness of his themes.

Section 3: The 1930s and the War Years

Before we deal in detail with the poetry of the 1930s, we should say something about one predominating technical influence on the writers of this decade. Gerard Manley Hopkins was born in 1844, went to Oxford where he took a very good degree, was received into the Roman Catholic Church by Dr Newman, became a Jesuit priest, and when he died in 1889 was Professor of Classics in University College, Dublin. He published nothing in his lifetime, but corresponded about poetry with his Protestant friends, Canon Dixon and Robert Bridges, and sent Bridges, in particular, copies of his work. After Hopkins's death, Bridges put some of his work into anthologies and in 1918 published a selection of it (omitting much early and unfinished work) with a rather patronising editorial preface in which, while stressing Hopkins's genius and originality, he had also a good deal to say about his obscurity and oddity, his bad rhymes, and his 'faults of taste'; the 'faults of taste,' from Bridges' own point of view, which was that of a rather chilly agnosticism with a faint Broad Church Anglican flavour, arose largely from the fact that Hopkins in his poetry takes his own religion seriously. Otherwise it is hard to see what Bridges could find amiss in such a phrase as 'the Holy Ghost with warm breast and with ah! bright wings.' The 1918 edition, though a fairly small one, took ten years to sell out; during the 1920s Hopkins was perhaps on the whole regarded mainly as an interesting curiosity. In 1930, however, a second edition with a more whole-heartedly enthusiastic preface by Charles Williams found a generation of young poets eager for a new voice. On these young poets, Hopkins's influence was partly a technical and partly a moral one. In his poetic theory and practice he emphasised the importance of counting the stresses rather than the syllables in English verse. His theory of sprung rhythm allowed for the use either of monosyllabic stressed feet or of stressed feet 'with any number of weak or slack syllables'; his theory of 'common rhythm counterpointed' allowed not only for the normal variations in the iambic line (roughly, a trochee for an iambus in any foot but the second or the fifth), but also for the deliberate mounting of a trochaic metre on a basic iambic pattern, even if that involved inverting the sensitive second foot: to quote the example given by

Dr Gardner, in the third and most scholarly and inclusive edition of Hopkins's work,

Géne̊ | rátions | have tród, | have tród, | have tród . . .

Hopkins was also influenced in his poetic practice by the elaborate alliterative devices of Welsh poetry; and his fondness for Latin and Greek poetry led him to take great liberties with English syntax (particularly, as Bridges noted, in omitting relative pronouns) for the sake of a forcible concision. The total effect of his technical innovations was to give his verse a quite unusual concentration of energy, at the expense, perhaps, of the conversational suppleness of which the ordinary iambic line is capable: his verse asks to be intoned, to be chanted or declaimed. To young poets of the 1930s it seemed to offer a fascinating combination of freedom and order, of an easy and expansive handling of the line with strong and regular rhetorical emphasis. To young poets, also, reacting against more immediate influences (the muted despairs or defeated ironies, as the young might see them, of Mr Eliot's work) the positive assertive force of Hopkins's poetry was peculiarly inspiriting. (Mr Eliot, more cautiously, felt that Hopkins's technical innovations were extremely interesting, but some-how off the main line). The faith of most young poets of the 1930s was very far, in fact, from being that of Hopkins; but they were in need of a faith of some sort, and they wanted to hold to their beliefs, as he held to his, with concentrated fierceness. There was, of course, a great deal more in his poetry than his peculiar rhetoric; there was the striving, grasping, individuating quality of his mind. But rhetoric, or what Hopkins himself had called the common teachable element in poetry, was what a new generation strove to learn from him. It was rhetoric, not the spirit of poetry, that he himself thought the English tradition weak in. His own rhetoric, splendid as it was, had its limita-tions; the limitations of firm and definite emphasis, that cannot com-prise half-tones. The crudity as well as the vigour of some of the early work of Mr Auden, for instance, derives from that rhetoric. And it was because they could not also learn the *unteachable* element – the peculiar vividness of Hopkins's vision, his sense of the individual stress and distinction of things, the sincerity of his self-searchings – that a fair amount of work by the young poets of the 1930s tends to strike us, to-day, as being Hopkins-and-water. Auden's own larger develop-ment, by which he surmounted this danger, was largely one in the direction of wit and humour; neither of which qualities Hopkins possessed; and the models there were very different ones, like Byron's *Don Juan*.

The 1930s in poetry as in the novel are a decade more easy to characterise and more completely dominated by a single group of figures than any of the previous periods with which we have been dealing. The leading figure in the English poetic world in these days was Wystan Hugh Auden and with him there were always associated in the public mind, as his friends and constant associates, Stephen Spender, Cecil Day Lewis, Louis MacNeice, and the novelist Christopher Isherwood. This notion of a group of poets going about in a sort of 'gang' is, as Mr Spender has pointed out in some recent articles, rather exaggerated: he writes that he was never together with Auden and Day Lewis at one time throughout the 1930s and that in the fact the first time the three of them forgathered was at the P.E.N. Conference in 1949 in Venice. The public also exaggerated, perhaps, the similarity of views of these young men. They were thought of as all either Communists, or on the verge of becoming Communists. But Auden described himself as a 'pink Liberal'; there was always a religious note in his poetry (he is now a loyal and orthodox American Episcopalian). MacNeice made it very clear in his pre-war poems that he could not accept Communism and that in many ways he was an old-fashioned individualist. Day Lewis was nearer to the orthodox Communist position, and Spender was a member of the Party for a very short time – his joining up coincided with the publication by him of a sharply critical article about some aspect of Communist policy, and so after paying his admittance fee, he was not asked for any further dues or asked to join a 'cell.' His membership quietly lapsed. To-day Auden is a religious poet, Spender a poet of the inner life, Day Lewis a poet of civilised irony leaning more and more on Clough. The only one of these poets who has *not* retreated from political and social themes is MacNeice, the least radical of them all, the 'liberal progressive'; and even he, in his more ambitious recent poems like *The Kingdom*, has tended to state his humanist beliefs in moral rather than political terms.

If these four writers did not have, in the strict sense, a common belief, neither did they have a common style. Auden and MacNeice had certain resemblance to each other in their fondness for colloquial language, urban imagery, a certain monitory tone: but MacNeice was much more of a sensualist, delighting in the visible world for its own sake, making precise catalogues of sensation – as in this line about a great London station,

> Euston, the smell of soot and fish and petrol,

and holding, in another phrase of his, 'the moment cradled like a brandy glass.' For Auden the outer world was interesting not so much in itself, as for the symptoms which it presented of social decay. Spender was a much more lyrical and subjective poet. His verse techniques, also, were quite different from theirs. They used a fairly regular if slightly roughened and jolting blank verse, or fairly strict stanza forms, but Spender's favourite medium was a free verse in which long and rather contorted sentences, expressing a painful groping of the mind, would lead up suddenly to lines of great lyrical beauty:

> Eye, gazelle, delicate wanderer,
> Drinker of horizon's fluid line . .

Day Lewis does not seem to me, in the 1930s, to have had such an individual style as these other three writers, and some of his poems, addressed to Auden and imitative of Auden's more boisterous or scout-masterish manner, are frankly bad. In his more original and lyrical poetry, he owed something to Yeats. He felt that the time had come to revive the heroic narrative poem, but his attempts at this, like the account of an early flight from Great Britain to Australia,

> Sing we the two lieutenants, Parer and M'Intosh,

are admirable rather *as* attempts, than as achievements.* One cannot help feeling that for Day Lewis Auden was rather an overshadowing influence, and one that distracted him from the proper development of his own talent. Since the end of the war, his style has become much more subtle and complex though still very fluent (as in his recent long poem, *An Italian Visit*) and it has become strengthened perhaps by exercises in translation, of Virgil's *Bucolics,* and of Valéry's *Cemetery by the Sea.* To-day, in fact, it is hard to find between the

---

* Mr Day Lewis's vigorous, rapid, and very readable translation of the *Aeneid* shows what splendid gifts as a narrative poet he has, if in the 1930s he could have found a substantial theme. His translation of one of the speeches of Turnus, into terms of modern tub-thumping but also heart-warming political rhetoric, shows that even the cruder aspects of the 1930-ish manner can make fine poetry *in the right setting.*

work of these four poets that family resemblance which seemed so obvious in the 1930s. Each has gone his own way.

Yet the resemblance *was* there, and the habit of grouping these poets together made sense in relation to the time. They did work together and influence each other. MacNeice and Auden visited Iceland together and wrote a book about it, Auden and Isherwood wrote plays together, as well as a book about a visit to China. They would dedicate poems or volumes to each other. They appeared in the same magazines and anthologies. The work of these young men first became familiar in an anthology, *New Signatures*, edited by Michael Roberts, an important critic and interesting poet, rather older than the rest of the group, who died prematurely, much regretted by many friends and admirers, in 1949. Roberts did more for them than merely publish their work. To many of them he was a sort of father-figure or at least elder-brother figure, and his approval and admiration mattered a great deal to them. Roberts was a skilled mountaineer, and it was largely under his influence (though both Auden and Spender had also brothers who were well-known climbers and explorers) that the image of the hero as pioneer, as explorer, as the leader of some lonely and forlorn expedition plays such an important part in the poetry of the Auden group. Some of their typical imagery comes also from their close emotional attachment to the atmosphere of English public-school life. There is sometimes what one might call a 'boy scout' flavour about their writing, an emphasis on the small group and its daring leader with a background of the boy's adventure story. Another image that gripped them was that of the solitary airman, a hero of the machine-age who has, however, escaped from the mass discipline, or mass despair, of the machine-age. (Or who seems to have.)

One might say that these poets saw around them a world of apparent safety and real drift (they were aware of the dangers of Fascist aggression, and the probability of a new war, long before the mass of the public, and even before all but the best and the most honest of the journalists and the politicians). They turned naturally from that apparent safety and real drift to images of danger courageously faced and of conscious human purpose. They felt a certain deadness in the England around them (an England slugged by the slump, full of the unemployed, leaning against walls, reading papers, and sharing between two of them perhaps, with delicate cautious puffs, a single cigarette). They wanted to make men more alive to the tensions and dangers of the time – to the possible power and purpose and beauty of the time, also. Thus the image of machinery, with its controlled power, fascinated them: and Spender wrote about pylons and railway engines lyrically, as older poets might write of clouds and roses. Machinery signified energy, and what a weak and drifting decade needed was energy more than anything else. 'Drink here of energy, and only energy': from some points of view, that phrase of Spender's might be taken to sum up the attitudes of the whole group.

What is also notable about the atmosphere of the poetry of this group (though this applies with qualifications to Day Lewis and hardly at all to Louis MacNeice) is what might be called an exclusively masculine tone in much of their poetry – their world is one which largely excludes family life, the domestic affections, and even what Mr Graves thinks, as we have seen, the great traditional theme of all true poetry, the romantic love (romantic because mixed with fear and despair, and seeking an ecstasy which it will not be able to sustain) of man for woman. Auden makes much use, in all his poems, of the moving, effective, ambiguous word 'love,'

> O love, the interest itself in thoughtless heaven,

but by 'love' he means the larger social love of man for man, the love of which it can be said that (to quote him again)

> Hunger allows no choice
> To the citizen or the police:
> We must love one another or die.

But it is only in 'thoughtless heaven' (or in a state of innocence) that 'love' in this sense, the sense of a proper and not excessive regard for others based on a proper and not excessive regard for oneself, is 'the interest itself' – is what makes life interesting, or more probably (Auden would be thinking of phrases like 'vested interests,' 'selfish interests') is what we naturally and selfishly, without putting any constraint on ourselves, act by. In man's fallen state, on earth which is not 'thoughtless' but full of care, 'love' and 'interest' in these two senses are always at war with each other. Every individual, whose claim to love is on all fours with the claims of other individuals, wants secretly to be treated as an exception, to absorb all the love available, to be loved 'for himself alone.' This type of statement runs through all Auden's poetry from the beginning, and it should be noticed that it is

POETRY

Christian rather than Marxist. It is based on the dogma of original sin. But on the whole this set of ideas is not, in Auden's earlier poems, expressed theologically, nor is the Christian basis of the thinking obtruded on the reader. The language is often not that of theology or even of politics but of the psychology of unconscious impulses. This comes out very clearly in a famous sentence from Auden's important fantasy in prose and verse, *The Orators*: 'What do you think about England, this country of ours, *where nobody is well*?' Auden, influenced not only by Freud, but by the more curious and fantastic speculations of the less well-known German psychologist, Groddeck, tended to look on most types of illness as the physical expression of some psychological failure courageously to confront the world. Like Samuel Butler, he tended to think of sickness as a sort of crime, and crime as a sort of sickness.

Thus Auden's attitude to man and society is clinical. He diagnoses a disease and suggests a remedy. England seemed to him diseased in the 1930s because of the growth of unemployment, because of the advance of Fascist aggression in Europe and Africa, because of the failure, as it seemed to Auden, of the traditional English ruling classes to live up to their responsibilities. In the writings of Freud, he found what seemed to him the clue to the inner failure of individuals of the upper classes: a traditional puritanism and a conventional decorum had prevented them from being true to their own passions and desires, their 'goodness' had withered into mere 'respectability' and gone sour on them (this is also what D.H.Lawrence felt), and they tended to become neurotics, cranks, eccentrics, men obsessed with the details of some obsessive hobby like stamp-collecting or bird-watching: hiders away from life. All evasive and self-protective attitudes of this sort were for Auden characteristic of what he called 'the enemy.' And the 'enemy' was, in short, a person who shirked coming to grips with the painful realities of his situation and whose mental malady, leading in the end to some physical malady, therefore got progressively worse.

On the other hand, it was in Karl Marx that Auden found what he regarded as the clue to the inner failure of the ruling classes as a *group*. Freud only explained their failure as *individuals*. As individuals, the ruling classes became morally ill because they refused to recognise the reality of passion and desire. As a group, they refused to recognise the running down of an old type of society and the existence of social forces that were clamouring for the birth of a new type. It has often been remarked upon as paradoxical that these young poets, in many ways so much more radical in their notions than the British working man, should themselves have been members of the ruling classes, and also that they should have appealed mainly to young readers of their own class. To working-class readers, Auden's poetry and that of his friends appeared cryptic and obscure and not what they expected poetry to be: poetry like Dylan Thomas's or George Barker's, more intellectually confused often, but more emotionally direct, more florid with imagery, came home much better (as I discovered during my army years, when lecturing and reading to soldiers) to a working-class audience. There was a certain deliberate austerity in the poetic diction of Auden and his group – an avoidance of worn-out 'poeticisms,' a clipped colloquialism, almost a bleakness – and the beauty of austerity is the last kind of beauty which the poor, who have been starved of beauty but still hunger for it in their hearts, are likely to appreciate. They much prefer floridity, exuberance, a touch of 'life and colour.' This, however, is a digression. The main reason why the poetry of Auden and his friends appealed mainly to their own class was that it both sprang from, and spoke to, a sense of guilt and responsibility. Working-class readers might feel a strong sense of *resentment* in the 1930s at the condition of their country and at the insecurity of their own lives. They did not feel either this guilt or this responsibility: they felt that if things were in a bad way it was not pre-eminently, or perhaps at all, the fault of the working man. But readers of Auden's own class might feel that the fault was chiefly theirs and their fathers'. Radical and revolutionary leaders in all ages have in fact tended to spring from the more sensitive members of the ruling classes rather than predominantly from the working class itself.

Thus at the very time when Auden and his friends were regarded by readers of their own class as on the verge of Communism, strictly orthodox Communist intellectuals were already beginning to distrust them. And I even remember reading a review, in a Marxist paper, of one of Auden's most impressive if most obscure works of the 1930s, *The Orators*, which denounced its ideology as 'Fascist.' This was in one sense a ridiculously inaccurate and unfair accusation, and yet what we may call the mythology (or more modestly, the poetic stage properties) of the Auden group, as opposed to their ideology, had perhaps more in common with Fascist mythology than with Communist mythology. Auden wrote about *leaders*—lonely heroes, explorers, airmen, mountaineers, small isolated groups of scouts crossing an enemy frontier, bands of conspirators with secret passwords. As *symbols*, these would have a direct appeal to romantic young German or Italian Fascists, though their ideological interpretation of the symbols would be quite different from Auden's. Communist poetry requires a use of the symbolism of the great suffering masses: or rather it does not require symbolism or allegory at all but a direct appeal to these masses, a direct praise of them, and a tone of practical exhortation, a direct description of their activities and sufferings. And it must not be cryptic or allusive or obscure, it must make no cultural demands on the masses that would give them a sense of inferiority or weaken them in the struggle. This is why strictly orthodox Communist poetry is so hard to write, or why when something is written which, from the Communist point of view, answers this prescription, it more often than not does not appear to us to be poetry: but something else, rhetoric, propaganda, an official hymn. . . .

It would be wrong to call the poetry of Auden and his friends 'Fascist' (except as the Communists use that word, to describe everything that fails either in the short or the long run to serve the interests of Communism, including even, in certain circumstances, objective thought) but it is likely that in the long run the practical importance of the poetry of Auden and his group was rather in awakening a sense of social responsibility among young men of their own class, than in stirring up the consciousness of the working classes. Also latent in the work of all these poets, even in the 1930s, was the strong feeling for tradition which has emerged more clearly in their later work. The poet of all four, as I have said, who has least obviously altered his direction (who has perhaps not altered at all, but merely matured) since the 1930s is Louis MacNeice.

MacNeice was never a Marxist and never showed much sympathy with Marxism. His attitude was and is what we would call in England that of a 'liberal progressive'—that is, of a man who probably votes for the Labour Party but who does not regard certain traditional social differences of function, status, or manners as in themselves undesirable: (rather the opposite in fact, for variety within unity is desirable, imposed uniformity is bad): and who does not want to see the State controlling thought or art or the patterns of the free and adventurous individual life. For this kind of radical (MacNeice is still a radical in a sense), the business of political reform is to mitigate or if possible to abolish real existing evils, it is to keep the public machinery of life oiled and trim and in working order, but it is certainly not to abolish all existing institutions, and to wipe out all existing social distinctions, so as to build a new world from the ground up. This position just 'left of centre' is almost the typical position of the English intellectual since the war, and that is why MacNiece (who had been of course a pioneer of the position in more difficult times, when it looked almost revolutionary) has been able to sustain it, while his companions have had to retreat from their own more dramatic but less realistic positions of the 1930s.

Auden, Spender, Day Lewis, MacNiece have been perhaps generally too exclusively considered from the point of view of their common militant anti-Fascist approach to the contemporary situation in the 1930s. Their decade is still a bone of contention, and I do not think there is any purely *literary* criticism on their work which has much value. Everybody who writes about the 1930s is a partisan one way or the other, nobody has been able to forget the poets and look at the poems. Yet it is a permanent ordering of words, rather than a passing topicality of appeal, which makes poetry last. Let us look for such an ordering of words in some quotations from these poets: and at the same time let us use our examination of these quotations to clarify our sense of each poet's individual distinction.

Here are four passages, one from Auden, one from Spender, one from Day Lewis, one from MacNiece, in that order:

1) Lucky, this point in time and space
   Is chosen as my working-place,
       Where the sexy airs of summer,
   The bathing hours and the bare arms,
   The leisured drives through a land of farms
       Are good to the newcomer.

   Equal with colleagues in a ring
   I sit on each calm evening
       Enchanted as the flowers
   The opening light draws out of hiding
   With all its gradual dove-like pleading,
       Its logic and its powers.

   That later we, though parted then,
   May still recall these evenings when
       Fear gave his watch no look;
   The lion griefs loped from the shade
   And on our knees their muzzles laid,
       And Death put down his book . . .

239

2) I think continually of those who were truly great.
   Who, from the womb, remembered the soul's history
   Through corridors of light where the hours are suns
   Endless and singing. Whose lovely ambition
   Was that their lips, still touched with fire,
   Should tell of the Spirit clothed from head to foot in song.
   And who hoarded from the Spring branches
   The desires falling across their bodies like blossoms.

3) Yet living here,
   As one between two massing powers I live
   Whom neutrality cannot save
   Nor occupation cheer.

   None such shall be left alive:
   The innocent wing is soon shot down,
   And private stars fade in the blood-red dawn
   When two worlds strive.

   The red advance of life
   Contracts pride, calls out the common blood,
   Beats song into a single blade,
   Makes a depth-charge of grief.

   Move then with new desires,
   For where we used to build and love
   Is no man's land, and only ghosts can live
   Between two fires.

4) Then the curtains in my room blow suddenly inward,
   The shrubbery rustles, birds fly heavily homeward,
   The white flowers fade to nothing on the trees and rain comes
      Down like a dropscene.

   Now there comes the catharsis, the cleansing downpour
   Breaking the blossoms of our overdated fancies
   Our old sentimentality and whimsicality
      Loves of the morning.

   Blackness, at half-past eight the night's precursor,
   Clouds like falling masonry and the lightning's lavish
   Annunciation, the sword of the mad archangel
      Flashed from the scabbard.

   If only you would come and dare the crystal
   Rampart of rain and the bottomless moat of thunder,
   If only you would come I should be happy
      Now if now only.

In the first passage, that from Auden, notice the strong and regular movement of the stanza, so that the poem seems to be asking to be read aloud. The movement is a simple one, iambic with only the usual substitutions,

> Lucky, this point in time and space
> Is chosen as my working-place,

of a trochee for an iambus. There is no wrenching or jolting, there is even a rather lulling rocking-horse movement. There are no difficulties about word order except

> Lucky, this point in time and space,

which means either

> This point lucky in time and space,

or elliptically

[I am] lucky . . . [or lucky (I am)!] . . . [in that] this point in time and space,

or, what is most probable, is intended to suggest both of these ideas. If the word order is almost that of conversation, so is the choice of words. The choice of words, in fact, wakes up the reader who might be too much lulled by the metre; but the rocking motion, at the same time, lets him accept the occasionally startlingly prosaic or pungent choice of words. The phrase 'equal with colleagues' might seem more in place in a speech at a school prize-giving than in a poem: the metre 'carries' it and adds a certain romantic feeling to it – so also to the 'leisured drives' which suggest some phrase from a prospectus about a seaside hotel. If such phrases are as deliberately and reassuringly banal, the lines

> Where the *sexy* airs of summer,
> The bathing hours and the *bare arms* . . .

take us aback a little. The conventional metre and movement of the piece have awakened what Dr Richards calls our 'stock responses.' We expect the 'airs of summer' to be 'mild,' 'soothing,' or even 'balmy.' Auden reminds us that one of the reasons we like summer is because bathing with other people, if they are handsome people, is mildly erotically stimulating. At the same time, the slightly slangy or facetious word 'sexy' and the emphasis on the relatively non-erotic, or only innocently erotic, 'bare arms' ('bare legs' would have another and sharper effect) means that this eroticism is only something mild, dreamy, and contemplative, part of the general atmosphere of pleasant summers. It is not to be over-emphasised, it is to be kept in place. The real pleasure that Auden is thinking of is that of free and frank conversation between a group of friends, who are 'drawn out,' as they sit in the open air in a circle, by the mild delightfulness of the evening. This is what is to be remembered, rather as Wordsworth remembered his moments of quiet and solitary ecstasy in the hills, in more difficult later situations. And what is essential to it is the momentary conquering by the fine weather and the friendly atmosphere of the typical neuroses and inhibitions of clever young men in our time,

> . . . these evenings when
> Fear gave his watch no look;
> The lion griefs loped from the shade
> And on our knees their muzzles laid,
> And Death put down his book.

These lines are examples of Auden's magnificent revivification of what, when he began to write, must have seemed to most poets and critics the quite dead eighteenth-century poetic device of *personification*. It is alive in Auden because he finds exactly the right image for it – a constant nervous looking at one's watch is not only the mark of a frightened man, but becomes in Auden the emblem of Fear itself. It makes the *idea* of Fear more concrete and real to us. The lions, beautiful and terrible creatures, allowing themselves at last to be soothed, somehow make more real our idea of grief. And the wonderful line,

> And Death put down his book,

recalls to us the young student, sitting lonely in a corner and pretending to be reading, hiding rather behind his book, because he is too shy or not brave enough to break into a conversation: the kind of 'Death' Auden has in mind here is not so much physical death as a frightened and neurotic retreat from life. Thus in these lines we are given an atmosphere, a scene, a moral commentary of a very original kind. We are forced to revise our attitudes about several things, first of all about what is really enjoyable in a summer holiday – we must first of all admit that there is more sensuality in it than we thought, but then that the sense of comradeship is the main thing: but then what is the use of this sense of comradeship, Auden asks. It is, he replies, to enable us to conquer our fears and neuroses, to share our sorrows.

Auden, therefore, we may be tempted to generalise, likes to start with a concrete situation: likes to draw a general moral lesson from that: but likes to convey the lesson in a concrete fashion, less by abstract statement than by the use of emblematic or allegorical images. He prefers, on the whole, fairly strict verse forms and the regularity of the movement of his poems may even become a little mechanical. There is a slight suggestion, in these stanzas, of a seesaw movement. The very regular metres are used to lull the reader and to take him off his guard: he is reassured also by the use of slangy or colloquial or sometimes deliberately trite phrases – 'the leisured drives through a land of farms' – and thus Auden, having established a situation of confidence, is able gradually to shift the reader's perspective and make him criticise his previous point of view. Auden is a poet of wide and various gifts, but these generalisations apply at least to a large part of his output.

The second passage, by Spender, is completely different in tone. It is written, first of all, not in rhyme but in a kind of very free blank verse, which can include at once lines like

And who hoarded from the Spring branches,

of nine syllables, and others like

Should tell of the Spirit clothed from head to foot in song,

of thirteen. We can find one or two lines that can be scanned fairly regularly,

Endless | and sing | ing. || Whose | lovely | ambi | tion,

but on the whole we are not looking for a regular recurrent *beat* as in the Auden passage, and we think perhaps rather of the irregularity of a blank verse speech in a play: where the ten syllable line can be tightened or loosened according to the demands of rhetoric. It helps us to define Spender's difference from Auden if we say that this passage is rhetorical, or like a speech, in a way that Auden's is not, and that when we say, as critics often say, that Spender, when contrasted with Auden, is a typically *lyrical* poet it is not exactly his verse-movements we have in mind. What we have in mind perhaps is rather the use of a kind of imagery that is traditionally associated with lyrical poetry, and of a kind of vocabulary, too: the repetition of the *idea* of lyricism here – 'song' and 'singing' – the use of rather worn emotive phrases, like 'lovely ambition,' 'lips . . . touched with fire,' 'desires . . . falling like blossoms.' The triteness of these phrases is not like the triteness of 'leisured drives.' Auden is using in a poem a phrase that might come from a hotel prospectus: Spender is using phrases that we are familiar with, and rather tired of, in other kinds of poetry, but setting them in a new rhythmical and rhetorical pattern. His rhythms give an effect of slow sincerity, and we feel that the use of worn phrases may be even a part of that sincerity: why should he coin a new phrase for an old idea?

Another notable difference between the Auden passage and the Spender passage is the lack of concreteness, or of definite answers to such questions as, 'Who? When? What? Where? How?' in Spender's passage. Who were those who were truly great, when did they flourish, what sort of thing did they do (is it poets, philosophers, scientists, soldiers, humanitarian reformers, or just ordinary unusually sincere and good people that Spender has in mind)? We are told that from the womb they followed the soul's history, which does not mean much more than that they followed their proper way of development, but we are not told what that was. We may ask ourselves about the beautiful (but bewildering?) lines

> Through corridors of light where the hours are suns
> Endless and singing, ___

whether we can imagine suns in corridors, or suns as singing, or hours as endless – though this is a carping and false criticism, and it is easy to sort out the prose sense, 'Along the bright corridors of their lives, each hour, full of song, did not seem something that would pass but as endless as the sun.'* It is strange, and I would not like to explain on general principles why it *is* so, that the logical rearrangement of the statement is not nearly so poetically moving as the illogical, or at least fantastic juxtaposition of the images. One should note a slack relation between the lips, touched with fire, that tell of the *spirit* and the *bodies* across which desires fall like blossoms: 'the truly great,' Spender means, 'do not sacrifice either the body to the spirit or the spirit to the body,' but the lines skirt the tensions between these two poles that exist in most men, even great men, and it is notable that the desires in one line are spoken of as 'hoarded' while in the next they fall lightly, and presumably drift and vanish away, like 'blossoms' from a tree. One might say, in short, that in this passage Spender expresses,

---

* Yet in prose, surely, this is rather a sentimental and inflated sentence? Or one that would need a backing of concrete detail?

in dignified rhetoric, his sincere and deep emotions about a general concept, that of true human greatness, but that the application of the concept is left to the reader: and that even so the reader feels it would be tactless to bring the argument down to particular cases. The atmosphere is like that of a public speech, perhaps a patriotic one, or one in honour of some great man retiring from public life: on such occasions we thrust our awareness of the faults of man or country being praised to the back of our minds – what is being praised is not so much an achievement, as an ideal. Spender is rousing our emotions not so much about individual great men as about our dreams* of human greatness. And what one might be at first inclined to criticise as the vagueness, the indefiniteness, in his presentation is, in fact, essential to the particular poetic effect he is aiming at. The more *general* criticism that some people might be inclined to make of the effect aimed at, itself, is that it seeks to rouse poetic emotions without presenting an 'objective correlative' for these emotions – or to make us share Spender's poetic response, without putting us in his full situation. The contrast with Auden, in whose work the presenting of the situation is often very dense and factual, but the response we are intended to make dubious, is striking. And we should note that this grave, rhetorical manner of Spender's puts out of his reach certain devices which Auden can use with great effect – flippancy, humour, irony, and in particular *ambivalence*, the device by which, judged by different standards, the same set of events can be seen as funny and sad, ignoble and heroic, touching and silly, petty and significant, at once.

Day Lewis's passage, again, like Auden's is not a poem about a mood (one might call Spender's poem one about a mood) but about a situation, the typical situation of the young intellectual of the 1930s caught between the two fires of Fascism and Communism and sensing an emotional or practical inadequacy in his traditional liberal attitude. Unlike Auden, however, Day Lewis presents his 'situation' not in terms of the personal and concrete – the country roads, the bathing beaches, the group of friends round a table, and so on – but in phrases such as we find in the newspapers, abstractions, faded metaphors, or metaphors that do not cohere. Notice the abstractness of 'massing powers' in the first stanza quoted – it suggests at once armies mobilising and states preparing for war, and yet we do not *see* the armies or conceive the states as communities of people, we think of them in terms of abstract *force*. The hero is like a buffer State, like Poland, say, due

* Our dreams, I think, of a greatness which is essentially *innocence* and *happiness*.

to be crushed between Russia and Germany. Taking up a neutral attitude will not save him nor will 'occupation' – distracting his mind from public affairs and getting on with his job – cheer him up: I do not know whether Day Lewis had also in mind the *other* sense of 'occupation' (being occupied by a hostile power), which was not in very common use in the 1930s, but in retrospect it enriches his meaning. Taking up a neutral attitude will not allow the liberal tradition to resist the pressure at its edges from Communism and Fascism: their emotional force is too strong: but *being occupied* – allowing himself to be conquered by one or the other of these irrational creeds – will not be a cheering experience for the ex-liberal either. The next two stanzas are weaker, because they move from relevant abstraction to stale metaphor. The hero who is appropriately and accurately represented as a buffer State becomes rather sentimentally idealised as 'the innocent wing.' If 'private stars' fade in the 'blood-red dawn,' they arise again when evening falls, as of course it will by and by. In what sense are stars 'private'? Day Lewis is thinking of metaphors like that of 'hitching your waggon to a star' and by 'the blood red dawn' of course he means the Communist revolution. In a revolutionary period we must give up our private dreams and ambitions. But what Dr Richards calls the vehicle of a metaphor should make sense as well as the tenor of it: and these 'private stars' that disappear for ever make no sense in themselves any more than 'the red advance of life' which 'contracts pride, calls out the common blood,' and so on, in the next stanza. We know that Mr Day Lewis means that the revolution will do these things, will humble the pride of the individual, bring about a sense of common purpose, make poetry into the instrument of revolution, use the pent-up sorrow of the masses explosively, and so on. But the '*red* advance,' the reference to 'the common *blood*,' suggest that this political process is analogous with some natural or biological process: and there is no such process. But if these two stanzas are bad, the last stanza, like the first, is beautiful,

> Move then with new desires,
> For where we used to build and love
> Is no man's land, and only ghosts can live
> Between two fires.

Here the metaphor is again that of being 'caught between' – between two armies now, not two states, in the no-man's-land, or space between the trenches, of the positional warfare of the First World War. The liberal to-day, trying to carry on his old habits of life, is like a man being shot at from both sets of trenches. He must acquire a new philosophy, 'move with new desires,' for only a ghost could survive the firing from both sides. That is what the stanza *says*, but it seems to me emotionally to add up to more than that. I think that Mr Day Lewis is conceding more to the liberal attitude than he intends to. The liberal no-man's-land has after all the quality of being where we 'used to *build and love*,' where the Communist and Fascist trenches are, where we are now trying to kill each other, full of hate. The association of the word 'ghosts' with the word 'fire' is bound (though this pun may be quite as unintentional as the pun on 'occupation') to suggest a ghost come from purgatory fire to witness the gunfire at our wars. And the judgment of the ghost might be, from his point of vantage in no-man's-land, that to-day it is the *living* who are in hell. The movement of the verse with its effect of great sadness, coming partly from the repetition in two contrasting sense-positions of a long, lingering vowel,

> Move then with *new* desires,
> For where we *used* to build and love,

gives also an effect of a decision to abandon the liberal position made with slow dragging reluctance. We can say in fact that Mr Day Lewis's special quality as a poet is perhaps a gift of handling abstract ideas, and their relations to each other, poetically, and a subtlety, conscious or unconscious, of complex statement that has something in common with metaphysical 'wit.' His weakness is a certain thinness of texture— so that these stanzas have neither the physical reality of Auden's nor the emotional density of Spender's – and a readiness to accept current jargon (the 'blood-red dawn,' the 'red advance of life,' and so on) without asking himself whether it is properly translatable into poetic metaphor. Since the war, Mr Day Lewis's diction has become more concrete and coherent, and he is indeed one of the poets of the 1930s whose development since 1940 shows an undeniable advance.

Mr MacNeice's passage obviously contrasts with all these quoted so far in its sensuous vividness. He is not merely like Auden summarily cataloguing the elements of place,

> The bathing hours and the bare arms,

but evoking one particular place, time, and event: a summer thunderstorm seen from his room across the garden of an English country house. The observation is exact—the curtain blowing in, the birds flying heavily homeward, the white flowers fading to nothing on the trees – and we stand with him by his window and feel this is *happening*. But the scene is not left by itself – the coming of the thunderstorm, of the lightning and the heavy rain, suddenly blotting out the garden, is like the dropping of a painted backcloth in a theatre. It is a change of scene, of emotional scene as well as outward scene. Like high moments in the theatre it induces catharsis or purgation – release from all the tensions that have been pursuing the poet on this June day, like the feeling of tightness in the hot air itself, waiting for the thunder. Just as the rain sweeps away the white blossoms of the trees, so this new mood sweeps away the blossoms of

> our overdated fancies
> Our old sentimentality and whimsicality
> Loves of the morning.

The next stanza sums up the 'tremendous drama' of the scene in terms of baroque religious imagery,

> Blackness at half-past eight the night's precursor,
> Clouds like falling masonry and the lightning's lavish
> Annunciation, the sword of the mad archangel
> Flashed from the scabbard.

The storm is seen as a *spectacle* of awe, which the poet regards half ironically ('the *mad* archangel') as he might regard the swirling angels in a painting by Rubens: but in spite of the irony, he participates in the awe – just as in the end the masterly composition of a painting by Rubens makes the spectator something more than a mere spectator, catches him up in the painter's grandiose dream. But Mr MacNeice is above all things a humanist, and it is not nature itself, but nature's human relevance, that moves him. He has found outward natural symbols for his state of mind, but it is an inner state, the tensions and the release both connected with his love for another person:

> If only you would come and dare the crystal
> Rampart of rain and the bottomless moat of thunder,
> If only you would come I should be happy
> Now if now only.

This is the moment of release from tension, of the sense of human dignity, of the proper natural background for the noble drama of human love. This, if only she would come, would be the moment of resolution. But Mr MacNeice is a realist. He does not think that our emotional tangles can be resolved once and for all: he knows that we must begin building our lives afresh every day, that old misunderstandings that we have cleared up tend to crop up again in new forms, and so he says

> If only you would come I should be happy
> *Now if now only.*

Mr MacNeice, we can say, is more concerned than the other poets of his group with the merely personal, or with the truly immediate: with what we see and feel, with our particular ties to places and people and the complex momentary knots these form. He is the least obviously abstract of them. Auden has been writing about group happiness, Spender about the emotions connected with the idea of greatness, Day Lewis about the plight of the liberal: MacNeice is writing about his own complex responses in a particular place, time, relationship – but in all his vividness and immediacy a general and exact evaluation of human life is implied. Purely humanly I would say, he is the sanest, the most balanced of these poets. His special weaknesses do not appear at all in the stanzas I have quoted. They are an occasional affectation of sophistication: a failure sometimes to make vivid images or witty lines cohere in a convincing whole: and in some of his later longer poems, where he is not disciplined, as here, by a strict and difficult form, a tendency to write in a slapdash fashion and to moralise rather obviously, without proper application or qualification, and at too great length.

One of the most original and skilful poets of the 1930s (and it is a mark of his originality that, in a period which ran to groupishness, he stands quite alone) was John Betjeman. Mr Betjeman is a poet who, like certain wines, will not carry; he makes so much of his effect by precise local allusions that it would be very hard to explain to a Frenchman (or even, say, to a Scotsman who had not a fairly intimate knowledge of Southern England) how good he is. It is not merely that he requires his readers to carry in their heads something like a map of London so that 'the curious Anglo-Norman parish church of Kentish town' or the now vanished trolley-buses diminishing towards Highbury, or the polychromatic wall of a Victorian church, St. Saviour's, Aberdeen Park, must ring at once some sort of bell, but that his feeling for social settings is as exact and specialised; in the Cornish seaside bungalow, the children of Mrs Hanks are preparing for a dance:

Norman and Gordon in their dancing pumps
Slide up and down, but can't make concrete smooth.
'My Sweet Hortense . . .'
Sings louder down the garden than the sea.
'A practice record, Phoebe. Mummykins,
Gordon and I will do the washing-up.'
'We picnic here; we scrounge and help ourselves,'
Says Mrs Hanks, and visitors will smile
To see them all turn to it.

Just as the record, for instance, for an expert in popular music probably fixes the date of this little episode, so the very names Norman, Gordon, and Phoebe, and the expression 'mummykins,' and Mrs Hanks's perhaps faintly forced cheerfulness about doing without servants, about all the family lending a hand, for an English reader place the Hanks family in their exact social stratum; the sons, for instance, I think probably went to a good minor public school but would not go to a university. The family income was perhaps something like a thousand pounds a year, which in the 1920s was worth more than it is to-day. A mention later on of polishing 'dulled Benares ware' might suggest that Mrs Hanks is the widow of an Indian public servant, and that the Hanks family generally are the nicer type of cheerful and decent philistine. Mrs. Hanks, too, is the 'jolly' type of mother, a companion to her children, but she does keep them and their friends in order: the use of 'we' in her one recorded statement does seem to imply: 'And *you*, for the time being, had better fall in with our ways.' This elucidation of a perfectly uncomplicated passage may appear extremely pompous and silly, but it does show the kind of background of experience which Mr Betjeman's readers must take for granted if they are to pick up his points. More generally, the reader must accept, sympathetically, for the time being, Mr Betjeman's profound conservatism, even when what it is concerned with is no longer there to conserve. Thus in *Sunday in Ireland* the 'native Irish,' the Julias, Maeves, and Maureens going to mass, are summed up with what for Mr Betjeman is almost a harsh statemen :

Stone-walled cabins thatched with reeds,
Where a Stone Age people breeds
The last of Europe's stone age race.

His regrets, his deep and poignant regrets, are for the dead and buried Protestant Ascendancy:

There in pinnacled protection
  One extinguished family waits
A Church of Ireland resurrection
  By the broken, rusty gates.
Sheepswool, straw and droppings cover
Graves of spinster, rake and lover,
Whose fantastic mausoleum
Sings its own seablown Te Deum
  In and out the slipping slates.

The conservatism again comes out in the moving poem on the death of King George V:

Old men who never cheated, never doubted,
Communicated monthly, sit and stare
At the new suburb stretched beyond the runway
Where a young man lands hatless from the air.

'Communicated monthly': the reticent, precise, very Anglican phrase reflects the quality of Mr Betjeman's own religious experience. *Before the Anaesthetic, or a Real Fright*, one of his most moving poems, distinguishes it sharply from his aesthetic experience:

Illuminated missals – spires –
Wide screens and decorated quires –
All these I loved and on my knees
I thanked myself for knowing these
And watched the morning sunlight pass
Through richly stained Victorian glass
And in the colour-shafted air
I, kneeling, thought the Lord was there.
Now, lying in the gathering mist
I know that Lord did not exist;
Now, lest this 'I' should cease to be,
Come, real Lord, come quick to me . . .

And in what is perhaps his *most* moving poem, *On a Portrait of a Deaf Man*, he distinguishes with a similar honest sharpness between the consolation which is formally present in religious belief, and that which, faced with real loss, we actually find there:

He would have liked to say good-bye,
  Shake hands with many friends,
In Highgate now his finger-bones
  Stick through his finger-ends.

You, God, who treat him thus and thus,
Say 'Save his soul and pray.'
You ask me to believe You and
I only see decay.

Mr Betjeman is also, of course, an acknowledged master of humorous light verse, but it is on his more serious side, his poetry of personal attachment, that I have preferred to dwell. The seriousness does, of course, also express itself through humour, and the humour even in pieces like *The Arrest of Oscar Wilde at the Cadogan Hotel*, which seem intended for mock-melodramatic recitation, is never wholly shallow. Mr John Sparrow, in his excellent essay on Mr Betjeman, speaks of that poem as 'an attempt to create an atmosphere of "period" by wheeling the old stage properties – the astrakhan coat, the hock and seltzer, *The Yellow Book* – all too conscientiously into place'; he might have added that the third and second last stanzas (entry of the police) are pure burlesque; but then the very last stanza while we are laughing our heads off,

He staggered – and, terrible-eyed,
He brushed past the palms on the staircase . . .

does remind us that poor Wilde's farce was after all a tragical one. We cannot quite laugh off 'terrible-eyed' and the total complicated effect of the poem is to make us first uproariously amused and then a little ashamed of ourselves. What Mr Betjeman does in poetry may look sometimes smartly facile; that it is in fact both subtly sincere, and very difficult to do, is proved by the fact that, though such a tempting target, he has never found a really effective parodist or imitator.

All these poets had been to Oxford. Cambridge in the 1930s also produced its own group of poets, different in their general tone and appeal. Cambridge has traditionally been famous for the attention it pays to science, to mathematics, to the analytic faculties of the mind generally, where Oxford is traditionally famous rather for the regard it pays to the study of Latin and Greek and literary and humane disciplines in general. Two teachers at Cambridge in the late 1920s and early 1930s had a great influence on young poets there, Dr I. A. Richards and Dr F. R. Leavis. Dr. Richards was more scientific in his approach, Dr Leavis more purely literary, but both insisted on the paying by students of a very close attention to the *meaning* of poetry. Dr Richards in his famous book, *Practical Criticism*, has shown that when a sample group of fairly intelligent undergraduates were confronted with a set of unsigned poems, they found it very hard not only to arrive at a confident judgment about the value of the poetry but to follow the mere prose argument of a poem of any complexity, and to avoid projecting their own personal and private associations into that argument. Thus there might be students who liked a poem because it was about winter, and they liked winter: or who disliked a poem because it was about religion, and they were anti-religious. Dr Richards taught a whole generation of students to regard a poem as a complex structural object, existing in its own right, and demanding sensitive and intelligent exploration before any confident judgment could be made about it. He taught students to use poems as instruments to test and if possible to correct their own deficiencies of grasp, sensibility, and inward coherence.

Dr Leavis, from his more purely literary point of view, taught students to question the accepted conventional judgments about poets of 'established reputation,' like Milton or Shelley, and not to be afraid to record the fact that some famous or esteemed poem had in the long run failed to yield them adequate satisfaction: and to ask themselves from what that failure sprang. Like Dr Richards, Dr Leavis tended to instil into his pupils the feeling that a good poem is a very complex and delicately balanced structure, indeed, and that success in writing a poem is related to the complexity and the delicate equilibrium of our grasp of the world around us.* Both teachers felt that in poetry a gross appeal to stock sentiments, a flattering use of familiar images, a mechanically lulling and hypnotic use of metre, are immoral. The young poets who studied under Leavis or Richards thus tended to have an extreme self-consciousness about the very act of composition, lacking in the Oxford poets of the same generation. Indeed, Auden's fluency, and his readiness to write light verse or burlesque on occasion, as well as to appeal most obviously to 'stock responses,'

> Now north and south and east and west
> Those I love lie down to rest;
> The moon looks on them all ...

are some of his most striking characteristics. He was not at all a self-conscious writer. But the Cambridge poets were. They were very

* Dr Leavis is very sensitively concerned with the connection of the quality of literature with that of the reader's – and writer's – life. His judgments are perhaps fundamentally *moral* ones, though by no means crudely or dogmatically so.

much aware of the necessity for a complex intellectual structure to underpin the direct emotional impact of a poem. They wrote, as it were, 'as ever in the great taskmaster's eye.'

The two most famous of these Cambridge poets were Ronald Bottrall, for whom Dr Leavis foresaw a great future, and William Empson, who was more directly influenced by Dr Richards. They were poets of different types and temperaments. Bottrall was a great admirer of Ezra Pound, particularly the Pound of *Hugh Selwyn Mauberley*. Like Pound in that poem, he aimed generally at a complex and erudite ironical allusiveness. Mr Bottrall had an interesting and subtle mind, a wide range of reading, a sensitive feeling for the structure and texture of verse, but this desire of his to be 'complex' and to bring in a wide range of cultural references at all costs does make his work sometimes smell a little of the lamp. The fact is that, even to-day, simple statements and direct responses have their place in poetry. Poetry which always seeks to avoid these may in the end appear often merely to be saying simple things in unnecessarily portentous ways. A tendency to qualify, or to introduce a tone of irony or hesitation into, every direct statement, though it gives an air of precision to a style, in the long run weakens its impact. The use of very many contrasting or diverse illustrations or allusions in a single poem, again, as in Marvell's *Coy Mistress*, may produce a lively and amusing surface, but to be poetically effective it requires, as in that poem of Marvell's, to be counterbalanced by a very clear and direct underlying pattern of argument. It is the lack of such a clear and direct underlying pattern in much of Mr Bottrall's work that one must complain of. Much as he has written, it is impossible to characterise his attitudes in a succinct fashion, or to summarise his main drift. There is a satirical criticism, rather like that of the early Pound and Eliot, of the confusions and vulgarities of modern society; there is an obvious regard for sane and sensitive human behaviour, and a feeling that such behaviour requires scrupulous self-examination and strict self-control: there is a note of melancholy, qualified by a sense of the dignity of the human fate. But there is not, as in Pound or Eliot or Yeats or Auden, any *prescription* for the unsatisfactory contemporary state of affairs – any religious or political or even moral attitude that can be easily defined. Nor is there even an underlying personal theme (like the theme of deep inner maladjustment and unhappy love in Robert Graves) to give, to a large and various body of poems, a unity of coherence. Mr Bottrall is typically the sensitive searcher:

it is as if he still felt Dr Leavis's eye on him, from time to time, and were thus afraid of committing himself in any crude, obvious fashion.

And this suggests a criticism of the Cambridge attitude. In life as in art, we perhaps after all *need* certain 'stock responses,' or certain persistent underlying sentiments and purposes, if we are to make a coherent pattern of our poetry or our lives.* The danger of attempting to preserve a permanent attitude of hesitant and ironic receptivity is that our experience gradually, unless we limit and define the lines we are working along, loses shape. By exposing ourselves on a very broad front to the impact of life, we weaken our own impact on life on a narrower front. The avoidance of 'over-simplification,' in an age like our own, may merely be a way of postponing necessary practical decisions. Yet Mr Bottrall's attempt to avoid 'over-simplification' cannot be dismissed in this fashion: it is an attempt rather, like that of Pound's Mauberley, to find

> his sieve ...
> Ultimately his seismograph,

with which first to sift and then very delicately to *measure* experience. As in Mauberley's case, too, there is an ironic contrast between the delicacy of the poetic instrument and the crude motions which, in our own time, it has to measure. Mr Bottrall has always been a copious poet, and probably he has still much to write. It is not time, yet, to attempt anything more than a provisional judgment on his work. His gifts as a lyrical poet cannot be very suitably exhibited in short quotations, but his gifts as a satirist may. Here is an admirably accurate description of a type common in all societies, the cultural 'hanger-on':

> Eager to embrace every fresh manifestation
> Of intellectual and political snobbery,
> He was nevertheless too watchful for the revelation
> To outlast more recent and more successful jobbery.
>
> His material home was a neutral country,
> His stock-in-trade litmus paper,
> His spiritual home a Laodicean chantry,
> His badge a chameleon couchant on a cloud of vapours.

* The critical case against 'stock responses' is not fundamentally one against persistent sentiments or interests, but against the irrelevant dragging in of them at all times.

Careful to avoid undisciplined enthusiasm,
He always watched for the week-end reviewers
Before committing himself to a criticism
Of new works by even solidly established authors.

Not that he was behindhand in appraising
A really *épatant* technique
Once he had got the appropriate phrasing
From the impressario of the clique . . .

I do not say that the making of such wry observations is one of the most important things the poet can do; but I become a little afraid (for the state of poetry, or for the state of society, or for both) when no poets at all are making such observations. Mr Bottrall is at his best the poet as critic, or the critic as poet. In his higher flights the lack of a definite faith or commitment may make him sometimes seem obscure, hesitant, or too hampered by the scrupulous qualifications with which he loads his words: as the detached and pungent recorder of social follies he is excellent.

William Empson is a much less copious poet, whose great reputation is based on two fairly short volumes of verse. His style is much less overlaid with contemporary tricks and mannerisms than Bottrall's. It has a harsh, strong precision, both of rhythm and statement, that might remind one of the poets of the late Caroline period and the early Restoration – Waller, Marvell, Rochester, the young Dryden. Empson aims at a tone, sharp and exact, fairly near that of lively conversation or of good prose: his lines get their 'poetic' impact from the succession of little sharp shocks and surprises they give us – not by any 'music' that will lull us or by any 'images' over which we are invited to brood in a dreamy fashion. The thought is extremely condensed: the feeling, which is deep and strong, is conveyed by an effect of restraint or compression rather than by an expansive flow. Nevertheless, in spite of the admirable decorum and pose of his poems, and in spite of the extremely healthy and supple state in which he keeps his diction, Mr Empson is for the average reader, even for the average fairly sensitive and intelligent reader, perhaps quite the most bewildering of contemporary poets. He has a training, for one thing, in physics, and mathematics, and the wider theories of logic and language, which most contemporary readers of 'literary' culture still completely lack. As a literary critic, also, he has specialised in the study (in *Seven Types of Ambiguity*) of effective ambiguities of literary language and (in *Some Versions of Pastoral*) of effective ambivalences of social meaning in larger literary structures. From all these interests, there derives the use in his poetry of metaphors from, or allusions to, scientific concepts like those of Einstein and Eddington, and of familiar mathematical paradoxes,

> Two mirrors with infinity to dine
> Drink him beneath the table when they please,

which are puzzling to the ordinary reader, and of structures of double or triple meaning which make many of his poems as hard to work out as cross-word puzzles.

Mr Empson feels that science and mathematics and modern types of general investigation into the structure of language should be part of the common culture of the educated man to-day and part of the currency of poetic diction: just as, for instance, the theories of Hobbes and the discoveries of the Royal Society were of *poetic* interest to Cowley, and just as the relation of the Copernican theory to the mediaeval picture of the universe was one of the recurrent concerns of John Donne. But in fact, Mr Empson himself is, as I say, the only poet of distinction I know who has managed to absorb this new material and to use it with distinction, and also with an air of familiar ease. Most people of mainly literary culture to-day are sadly illiterate as far as the scientific and mathematical picture of the universe goes. Yet there is a growing demand for good popularisations of the discoveries of modern science and one might expect the average intelligent reader, in say twenty or thirty years, to be abreast of Mr Empson.* Even so, there is the other hurdle to cross. Mr Empson is specially interested, as I have said, in poetic ambiguity. In *Seven Types of Ambiguity* he points out that the crude comic pun is only an extreme and obvious case of a use of language very common in poetry, a serious and interesting use. Mr Empson's most elaborate attempt at serious punning is a long poem called *Bacchus* at the beginning of his second volume, in which every key word can be taken, and is meant to be taken, in several contrasting senses. Thus the poem can be read, according to which sense one emphasises, as an account of the myth of Bacchus: as a description of the process of distillation: and as an interpretation of human history, in terms of the progressive stages of drunkenness. And the reader should grasp all these implications

* The atom bomb in fact has given even English poets as unmathematically minded as Dr Edith Sitwell a new awareness of the *poetic* interest of contemporary physics.

9

simultaneously. Mr Empson thoughtfully provides notes to this and others of the more difficult poems in his two volumes, and without the notes it is the case that even the most acute reader might feel lost.

It might be thought that these preoccupations of Mr Empson would rob his work of any very direct emotional impact, that it would merely have the value of a literary curiosity. But this would be a mistaken judgment. In fact, these intellectual complexities are balanced and corrected by an admirable simplicity of human approach (there is no affectation about Mr Empson's *tone*, everything that he writes, in prose and verse, has the run of the natural speaking voice) and by a direct, intense, and sometimes melancholy note of passion (Mr Empson's emotional responses to his private experiences, and to the public life of his time, are very much those of sane normality). Paradoxical as this may be, these tricky structures of words of his do often have the air of being the speech of an 'honest Casca,' a typical 'plain, blunt man.' Here, for instance, is Mr Empson in 1938 or so, contemplating the state of Europe from the vantage point of an earthquake in Japan – the 'same war' to which he alludes in these stanzas was, of course, the 'China incident.'

> I slept, and blank as that I yet would lie.
> Till you have seen what a threat holds below
> The heart of standing is you cannot fly.
>
> Tell me again about Europe and her pains,
> Who's tortured by the drought, who by the rains,
> Glut me with floods where only the swine can row
> Who cuts his throat and let him count his gains.
> It seemed the best thing to be up and go.
>
> A bedshift flight to a Far Eastern sky.
> Only the same war on a stronger toe.
> The heart of standing is you cannot fly . . .

The earthquake for Empson is the symbol of the insecurity of our modern society – which opens under our feet, in wars, and slumps, and revolutions, so that our human courage feels unable to face it. Empson escaped from the earthquake into deep dreamless sleep, and while our world is what it is he would like to sleep for ever like that. The essence of courage, in any case – 'the heart of standing' – is usually simply that one cannot run away. But when something like an earthquake occurs we realise that not even being unable to run away will always give us courage. He had thought that he could fly away from 'Europe and her pains' but in the Far East he found 'only the same war on a stronger toe' . . . the general crisis from which none of us to-day can escape. But his very attempts to escape, his failures to escape, his experience in this earthquake of the individual's helplessness before the forces of nature (and before also, it is implied throughout the poem, the impersonal forces that are ruthlessly shaping history), have taught him the futility of escapism: have instilled into him a certain courage though no sort of complacency. 'The heart of standing is you cannot fly.' The complexity of the sense in these lines is obviously a justifiable complexity: very much of the typical experience of all of us in these years is compressed into them, and generalised into statements that have the ring of moral authority.

In Mr Empson's case, as in Mr Bottrall's, it is difficult perhaps to summarise his main drift. But one might say that there is a sense in all Mr Empson's best poems of the bewildering complexity and precariousness of the human situation, not only in our own particular troubled period, but always and everywhere; yet this is combined with a feeling that the complexity and precariousness are after all what give man his dignity and make life worth living. There is thus a refusal to surrender to what might be called the boom-gloom-and-doom tone of much verse of the 1930s, a refusal admirably expressed in a witty parody called *Just A Smack At Auden*. Mr Empson mocks there the tone of those of his contemporaries who were always writing as if the world were going to come to an end next Tuesday. With his sense of the complex and paradoxical nature of the human situation, Empson did not see, as Auden, the contradictions of contemporary capitalist society in Great Britain as implying that the British type of society was necessarily at an end: looking back through history and literature he found similar contradictions, or a similar ability of individuals and society to take up apparently mutually exclusive attitudes simultaneously, everywhere. And he thought of this illogicality of the human species, its ability to eat its cake and have it too, as a source of moral and poetic strength. Thus he praises in John Donne, a sincerely Christian poet, 'the secret largeness of outlook' which enables him to transfer in two famous poems the praises usually lavished on Christ – particularly the praise that he is the force which holds the universe together – on an unknown young woman. Mr Empson has that same largeness of outlook, but there is nothing 'secret' about it in his case. He differed, for instance, from Auden and Auden's group in having, throughout the 1930s, a deep confidence in the basic soundness of the British people. Whenever, he wrote in one of his poems, the soundness of the British people had been tested by a real international crisis in these years, it had 'answered like a gong.' Yet part of this social sturdiness of his came, again paradoxically, from a much more pessimistic view of the individual case than is common among Auden and his group. He was more aware than any of them of the compromises, the failures of energy, the swallowed bitterness and humiliations, that are involved merely in growing older, in growing towards one's death:

> Not to have fire is to be a skin that shrills.
> The complete fire is death. From partial fires
> The waste remains, the waste remains and kills.

The idea there is of human life as an artificial struggle against a natural inertia, which is bound to conquer in the end. Yet it is the struggle, foredoomed in the individual case to ultimate failure from the start, that carries the race along, and gives human life its dignity and value.

Mr Empson's strict scientific training left little foothold in his mind for orthodox belief, but on the other hand he had a very strong sense of most human values as being very intimately bound up with our ideas about God. He might be thought of as believing (with one of these ambivalent attitudes of which he is so fond) both that the human aspirations, traditionally bound up with religion, are directed towards a fiction, and yet that fictions of this sort are what give life meaning. Something like this seems to be expressed in these lines of his:

> All these large dreams by which men long live well
> Are magic-lanterned on the smoke of hell:
>   This then is real, I have implied,
>   A painted, small transparent slide.

> These the inventive can hand-paint at leisure
> Or most emporia would stock our measure:
>   And, feasting in their dappled shade,
>   We should forget how they were made.

The theory expressed in these two stanzas is something like that expressed by Dr Richards in his famous short pamphlet, *Science and Poetry*, in which he suggests that poetry, unlike science, does not make 'statements' but rather 'pseudo-statements': that is, by the emotive gestures and allusions it makes it enables us to integrate our inner lives, but we must not look in it for 'truth' in the scientific sense. (This is an early and crude pamphlet by Dr Richards, many of the views in which have been much refined and subtilised in his later work. If Mr Empson, for instance, is not making 'statements' in these lines of his which I have just quoted, I do not know what he is doing.) More subtly in this poem, starting from such a theory as Dr Richards's, Mr Empson asks himself if, supposing the poet is playing an elaborate trick on himself, and he knows it, the trick will still work. If our 'large dreams,' by which we hope to live nobly, are mere projections, can we really, when trying to live by their inspirations, 'forget how they were made'? Yes, we must 'imagine . . . by miracle . . . what could not possibly be there' and 'learn a style from a despair.'

This poise between scientific objectivity and imaginative creativeness is a very difficult one to sustain, and it is perhaps natural that in recent years Mr Empson should have largely confined himself to scientific, or quasi-scientific, studies of the structure of language and should have written very little poetry. But it will be a great loss to literature if he abandons poetry altogether and gives up to semantics what was meant for mankind. Mr Empson's output is small: and of the poets of his generation, Mr Auden has a more various invention, a greater range of tones, a generally wider scope. I do not think he has a greater depth or, in individual poems, a harder perfection of form. Mr Auden's work will remain, for the literary historian, the *typical* poetry of the 1930s. But of all the poets of that generation, it is for Mr Empson that I, at least, feel the greatest moral and intellectual respect.

Towards the end of the 1930s there was among a younger generation of poets (say, those born between 1915 and 1920, Mr Auden and his generation being generally born between 1905 and 1910) a general reaction against the dominant tone of the decade. At Oxford, this expressed itself in the work of John Heath-Stubbs, Sidney Keyes, Keith Douglas and other young undergraduate poets of that time in a new interest in the romantic period and a tendency to move away from the colloquial diction and urban imagery of Auden and MacNeice towards something more florid, more lavish, more ornate. With a less scholarly basis, there was a very wide parallel reaction elsewhere. There was a group of young men of whom the more important were Henry Treece, Nicholas Moore, Tom Scott, Norman McCaig, who were all at one time, as I was myself, connected with an ambitious but vaguely defined movement called 'The New Apocalypse.' The title was an unfortunate one as it lent itself all too easily to jokes about epileptic, apoplectic, elliptical, and apocryphal writing. Indeed, as the movement widened and drew in new adherents like the pacifist and anarchist poet, Alex Comfort, it became more usual and more tactful to describe it as Neo-Romanticism. Three great influences behind it were Herbert Read, George Barker, and Dylan Thomas, all in their different ways poets of the image rather than the statement (where both Auden and Empson, for instance, were poets of the statement rather than the image).

Another more general influence was that of Surrealism with its experiments in automatic and semi-automatic writing, its contempt for obvious logic and traditional form, its use of unrelated or violently incongruous, apparently meaningless, juxtapositions of phrase. The English Neo-Romantics did not, however, go all the way with the Surrealists but felt rather that there was an inner logic, or a dream logic, in the images that emerged from the subconscious mind and that it was not the business of the poet to interpret these images intellectually (or at least to do so in the poem itself), but that the task of the conscious mind should be confined to rejecting those among the unconscious images presented to it which seemed trivial or incoherent and to moulding the rest into a pleasing metrical shape.

There was also behind this movement a feeling that the cult of objectivity, of exact reportage, of a critic and poet like Mr Geoffrey Grigson (who edited *New Verse*, a periodical in which Auden, his friends, and his followers, published some of their best work), or the insistence of poets like Auden on abstract Freudian or Marxist formulations of the current crisis, was in either case due to a fear of the complexity and richness of the organic universe and of the depths and tangles of the subconscious mind. 'In the destructive element immerse – that is the way': the neo-Romantics, like earlier poets who interpreted it differently, might have taken that phrase of Conrad's as their motto. It was the business of the poet to express rather than to communicate what he came upon in his own dark depths: and to let his feeling and imagination, working out from within, find their own form, rather than to impose a preconceived form upon them. The strength of this movement was that it did enable young poets to use with conviction the confused and painful material of the inner life and that it rescued them from a mere imitation of Auden (the close imitators of Auden, like those of Pope, have all his mannerism and none of his genius). Its weakness was that it slackened the poet's grip on the reins. It is difficult to control critically material which the mind does not analyse: it is almost impossible to relate that material, tangled stuff of dreams, to waking experience. Neo-Romanticism, in fact, lent itself to various kinds of faking. For the young poets of the 1940s, the subconscious mind did not prove quite the treasure-house it was supposed to be. It tended to offer a somewhat narrower, a more monotonous, range of images than might have been expected. Nor did these images always, or even often, cohere convincingly around a single theme. Thus the movement lent itself to slack and imitative writing: in some of the leaders, to the most vicious and enervating type of imitation, imitation of *oneself*.

Thus the better Apocalyptic or Neo-Romantic poets (I might mention Nicholas Moore, whose development has been extremely individual and interesting) tended as they matured to become less and less typical of the 'group.' Those poets who retained their loyalty to the 'group' tended, as individuals, to mark time. For all that the new romantic reaction had its usefulness, and indeed its inevitability, in its period and place. I shall deal with it in more detail, with illustrative quotations, in my final section.

In general, it may be said that the outbreak of war in the late summer of 1939 caused, quite apart from these special movements, a widespread shift in the themes of poetry from public events to personal experience (which, however, would often have a certain relative public interest, as being the experience of a soldier, or of an Englishman exiled by the war – it would be a kind of experience many people had shared). Of the three most famous of the young British poets killed in the war, Sidney Keyes, Alun Lewis, and Keith Douglas, only the last carried into his descriptions in verse of fighting in the Western Desert and of sour leaves in Cairo something of the objective vividness, the harsh satirical attack, which had been typical of poets like MacNeice in the 1930s. But his nobler note was a kind of clinical compassion: as in these lines about a dead German soldier, in the Western Desert, beside whom Douglas found a photograph of the dead man's girl, with 'Forget me not' in German on it:

> But she would weep to see to-day
> how on his skin the swart flies move;
> the dust upon the paper eye,
> and the burst stomach like a cave.
>
> For here the lover and killer are mingled
> who had one body and one heart.
> And death who had the soldier singled
> has done the lover mortal hurt.

Lewis was a quieter and more tender poet, full of nostalgia for Wales: he had something in common in his tones and techniques with Edward Thomas – some of his poems are on very simple subjects, like a wet day in a soldiers' camp in a beautiful countryside – but could be more direct and passionate in his love poetry than Thomas. Sidney Keyes, younger than either of these (he was only in his twenty-first year when he was killed in North Africa) and more obviously technically accomplished, was also less direct: an extremely 'literary' poet, whose themes were metaphysical or bookish rather than drawn from observation of the outer world. Keyes' great models, his sources of inspiration, were Wordsworth and Rilke, and he aimed in his poetry at a sort of Wordsworthian acceptance of the natural universe which would include, however, a Rilkean acceptance of the mystery of death. The emphasis on pain and death in many of his poems would be very distressing, but for a certain polished frigidity of language, which stops his work from coming too brutally and crudely home. It is about the *ideas* of pain and death, rather than the harsh observed facts. But Keyes had astonishing talent for so young a man, the limitations of his work are those of immaturity (one has the sense that he had not, when he died, really been awakened to the ordinary world around him, or to the sense of everyday companionship, affection, or love) and if he had survived he might have done really fine things.

Perhaps the most pleasurable poetry written during the war was that by a group of civilian friends in Cairo, Lawrence Durrell, Bernard Spencer, and Terence Tiller. This was primarily personal in tone and descriptive in manner. Durrell and Spencer, who had both lived in Greek islands in the years before the war, were chiefly concerned with the landscape and the atmosphere of the eastern Mediterranean, particularly the Hellenic, world. Of the two, Spencer was the better poet of pure landscape, but Durrell could perhaps convey historical atmosphere in a richer fashion. Tiller, who did not know Greece, whose arrival in Egypt as a teacher had in fact almost coincided with the outbreak of the war, was a more introspective poet than either of these and was specially concerned perhaps with the sense of decay and melancholy, of exile and maladjustment, which was one of the penalties of prolonged sojourn in Egypt in these years.

Cairo, during the war, was in some ways, at least in so far as poetry was concerned, a livelier literary centre than London. Among those who passed through, or who found themselves permanently stationed there, one might mention Hugh Gordon Porteous, a fine scholar and poet (an expert on Chinese art and literature, he has written some beautiful translations of Chinese classical poetry) and a pungent critic of his contemporaries, whose work has somehow never quite received its proper due; John Waller, a poet of moods, of humours, and of personal relationships, whose romantically sensuous poetry had a smooth ease and naturalness of style; Iain Fletcher, an elaborate and rather mannered poet in a neo-metaphysical vein, whose early poems anticipate that cold and intricate but structurally impressive 'baroque' diction which Mr Auden has adopted for some of his later poems; John Gawsworth, a sturdy traditionalist of the school of Hardy and the great romantics, quizzically sceptical about but always courteous and receptive to the more experimental work of younger poets. Many of us who grumbled at the heat, discomfort, and other draw-backs of Cairo in these years now find ourselves sometimes looking back on it a little wistfully. For somehow, though the exploration of London after the war has been exciting, we have not in the last few years done quite the things that, in those days of young enthusiasm, we imagined ourselves as doing.

At the end of the war, a critic's picture of the contemporary situation would be bound to be a confused one, but, as we shall see in our final section, in the last five years a fairly definite and clear new tendency has announced itself in English poetry, a tendency towards what one might call visionary writing, making a new and interesting use of the symbols of ancient mythology. The psychologist Jung has drawn attention to the fact that myths have a kind of permanent validity, that they represent stages through which the conscious attitudes of each individual life-history must pass, and that they are our best means of dramatising these stages to ourselves and making them aesthetically objective. With this new interest in myths, there has come a new interest also in the only English poet who ever invented his own mythology, William Blake. For a leading woman poet of our own decade, Miss Kathleen Raine, Blake is the poet to whom she instinctively turns, just as Mr Eliot in his early days turned to Donne, and Auden and MacNeice to those socially alert and satirically aggressive poets, Byron and Pope.

One might say, in fact, that the re-exploration of English poetic culture, which has been one of the most fertilising influences on the original poetry of this century, has in the last thirty or forty years worked forward from the early seventeenth to the early nineteenth century and that the time is now ripe for an objective revaluation of the later romantics and even the great Victorians. At the middle of our own century, we are perhaps beginning to see the English poetic past in something like its due and proper proportions. We are also, after half a century of technical and psychological experiment of every kind, perhaps beginning to digest the experiments: and we find ourselves looking once again for a set of common standards about diction, decorum, and the formal aspects of poetry generally. This, in itself, is a hopeful sign. For poets, if they are not prophets, are often precursors, and the fact that poets of the 1840s, like the young Arnold or the young Tennyson, if less inventive and original than their great romantic predecessors, were more concerned with balance and form, with the avoidance of a one-sided emphasis and the securing of a widely acceptable tone, was a sign perhaps that a very stable period of history – the high Victorian age – lay ahead. Not, of course, that either of these poets was without deep inner doubts or worries, any more than the high Victorian age was itself. But the poets were able to integrate these doubts and worries, these questions and uncertainties, into a stable and imposing body of verse, just as the high Victorian age itself was able to integrate elements that might seem, on the face of it, to make for social disorder, revolution, or a basic loss of faith. A common ideal sustained both age and poets, the ideal of liberalism understood in its broadest sense.* It seems to me that both poets and men of good will generally now are groping towards the formulation of some similar broad, sustaining ideal. This, in a period of immediate crisis like the present, may appear a risky generalisation, or a strained analogy: but we may be permitted at least to hope (and the present tendency of poetry, at least, does not forbid us to hope) that some such deep integrative process is at work to-day under the confused and troubled surface of our time.

Section 4: Poetry Since the War

Even before the outbreak of the war in 1939, various reactions (as we have seen) were setting in against the dominance of Mr Auden's group, and these reactions were strengthened by Mr Auden's own absence during the war in the United States and also by a general turning away of his companions who remained at home, Mr Spender, Mr Day Lewis, and Mr MacNeice, from overtly political themes. When Mr

* Arnold, of course, is a sharp critic of the actual *failures* of Victorian Liberalism; but not from an anti-liberal point of view – rather from the point of view of a Higher Liberalism, or Liberalism's 'best self.'

Roy Campbell, in 1946, published his book of lyrical and satirical poems, *The Talking Bronco* (it was Mr Geoffrey Grigson, I think, who had said that Mr Campbell's poems were of the kind that would be written by a horse, if a horse could talk), he invented a composite character called 'McSpaunday' (out of the names of MacNeice, Spender, Auden, Day Lewis, in that order) and fought the old battles of the 1930s over again, from the other side. But the live horse was flogging a dead horse; or in other words, not one of the poets whom he was attacking was still defending the old positions.

And in fact the general reaction against the tone of 1930s poetry in the last decade was not, originally, a political reaction at all. It began in the 1930s themselves with the poetry of George Barker and Dylan Thomas and with the interest in the French Surrealist movement that was aroused by a brilliant short book written by the young poet David Gascoyne and by an anthology of Surrealist pictures and poems edited by Herbert Read. It could, generally, be described as a romantic reaction against certain neo-classical tendencies in the 1930s.

Mr Grigson, when editing *New Verse*, had emphasised the need for the poet to make clear statements, to keep his eye on the outer world, to be objective in his descriptions, easy and colloquial in his language; he emphasised, in fact, the part played by the conscious designing mind in the poem as against the part played by what, in the romantic period, was called inspiration, and what to-day might be called the 'given' element in a poem. The Surrealists, on the other hand, were interested in the possibility of producing poetry not by any kind of conscious design at all but by a sort of semi-automatic writing which would gradually loosen up the inhibitions of the conscious mind and allow all sorts of submerged material to come to the surface. They thought the great source of poetry was the dream image, in the Freudian sense (the image as a confused but rich symbol of suppressed desires), and they sought in their writing as in their painting not to *record*, to *comment upon*, or to *interpret* life but rather, like Rimbaud, to *transform* it. That is, in fact, the literal meaning of the word Surrealism or Superrealism; the wish to get above reality, or to transcend it, or to set it at a higher key. Outer reality (that is to say, the physical world around us, our perception of that, the social world around us, our responses to it and explorations of it) was of no interest in itself to the Surrealists but was merely material for transformation, for various acts of creative fantasy or radical metamorphosis; perception was to become hallucination, emotion paranoia, thought the most arbitrary and obscure set of private associations; and though the Surrealist had to start off, like the rest of us, from brute fact or crude reality his ambition was to reach a stage where he would be cut off from it for good. The results of such an ambition can be seen in the long, often obscene and blasphemous, always incoherent, sometimes momentarily powerful poems of a French poet, who died a year or two ago, Antonin Artaud: poems sometimes written in a state of alcoholic delirium and sometimes in lunatic asylums. With ruthless French logic, the Surrealists were willing to become alienated from the world and from their rational selves, to pursue, from a worldly point of view, their own destruction, if they could only in this fashion arrive at a state of pure, uninterrupted, uninhibited creativeness. No more striking contrast with the tense conscientiousness of Mr Grigson's prescriptions for poetry in *New Verse* could well be imagined.

To accept *all* the implications of Surrealism was not in the English temperament but on the other hand it was impossible to deny the power of certain Surrealist texts and paintings. The 'neo-romantic' movement that stemmed from Surrealism, and from the work of Thomas and Barker, embodied, then, a typical English compromise. It accepted the idea that the poet should use images that arose spontaneously in his mind, without trying to 'understand' them, and should let one image suggest another image, without trying to work out the pattern of a poem logically; on the other hand he should be, as the Surrealists were not, selective, he should reject images that seemed to him trivial or jarring, accepting only those which seemed to have a certain massiveness and an emotional coherence with the other images in the poem; and – this above all was the great contrast with the French Surrealists – he should shape his poem as a work of art, with a regard for rhyme, and metre, and the amenities of diction, and in fact for the traditional formal demands made on the English poet. Even if the material of the poem all came straight from the subconscious mind, at the aesthetic or formal level there must be conscious control. For the true Surrealist, on the other hand, 'aesthetic' or 'formal' demands are just another *bourgeois* superstition; a Surrealist text or picture has not the purpose of being a beautiful object to be contemplated or a psychologically harmonious whole. On the contrary, it aims at disruption; it has the purely practical purpose of loosening the reader's or the spectator's grip on the everyday world, boring a hole, as it were, in reality that will let the great floods through, and thus playing its small part in the grand task of the total transformation, or metamorphosis, of the world. It is there to remind us how near we all are, under the surface, to what is generally called madness, and to push us a little nearer that brink. Once the concepts of form and control are introduced, however, the case is entirely altered; and a poet like Dylan Thomas, who uses confusing dream material, very like that of the Surrealists, does not see himself as embracing confusion for its own sake but as pushing up through it towards the light.

The main scientific basis of the Surrealist movement is the psychology of Freud according to which dreams, verbal errors, neurotic obsessions, accidents, and so on, are all means by which suppressed sexual desires (desires of a sort which seem to the adult mind shocking or criminal, but according to Freud based on the emotions and appetites of infancy) force an awareness of their presence, in a disguised form, on the conscious mind. The difference between Freud and the Surrealists, however, was that he wrote in the interests of rationality, of normality, he sought to understand and control this material; the Surrealists wrote rather in the interests of the material itself. In recent years, Freud has become a much less popular psychologist in England than his rival, Jung, who thinks that much dream imagery, and much traditional poetic imagery, does not represent so much the suppressed desires of the individual as a kind of latent race memory in the individual; in some obscure way we each of us recapitulate in the sunken depths of our mind the whole history of the race, and that explains the almost universal validity of certain images, which Jung calls archetypal images, and in particular it explains the effectiveness in poetry of *mythological* imagery long after we have ceased consciously to believe in myths. The poetic use of images in Jung's sense takes the poet back to a sort of symbolism, though no longer the enclosed and purely literary symbolism of Mallarmé; the symbol is now the way of expressing certain universal emotions and aspirations which cannot be expressed in any other way.

Let us illustrate these points by considering in turn some texts from recent poetry which illustrate: (1) the Surrealist method; (2) the 'neo-romantic' attempt to impose a formal or aesthetic order on the Surrealist method and to struggle up to the light out of the confusion of dream images; (3) the conscious use of images as symbols of some otherwise inexpressible human experience.

Here are some examples of (1):

a) Sisters of nothing ready for everything
    Sisters of flowers without roots
    sisters of rebel children
    tiny
    indifferent
    reduced by the intellect
    to reason to die of it
    reduced in your secrets
    abandoned strangers
    my distant companions
    with sentimental flesh
    beautiful hardly beautiful but always beautiful
    more simple than misfortune
    more precious than the beauty
    of your slaughtered lips
    of your undermined smile
    you entrust your poisons to me
    O mithridatised ones
        and I oppose to love
        ready-made images
        not images still to be made

                                        PAUL ELUARD

b) the aeroplane weaves the telegraph wires
    and the stream sings the same song
    at the pull-up for cabmen they drink orange drinks
    but the railway mechanics have white eyes
    and the lady has lost her smile in the woods

                                    PHILLIPE SOUPAULT

c) Last night the wind blew so hard that I thought
    it was going to batter the rocks into pasteboard.
    Throughout the time of darkness the electric lights
    burned like hearts;
    in my third sleep I awoke near a lake
    where the waters of two streams were coming to die.
    Around the table women were reading.
    And the monk was silent in the shadow.
    Slowly I crossed the bridge and at the bottom of the turbid water
    I saw the slow passing of big black fish.
    All at once I found myself in a big square town.
    All the windows were shut, there was silence everywhere,
    Everywhere meditation.
    And the monk again passed beside me. Through holes of his rotten robe I
        saw the beauty of his body pale and white like a statue of love.
    On waking happiness once again slept beside me.

                                    GIORGIO DI CHIRICO

d) give tear twist and kill I traverse illuminate and burn caress and lick embrace and look I sound at every flight the bells till they bleed frightening the pigeons and I make them fly around the dovecot till they fall to earth already dead of weariness I will rase all the windows and doors to the earth and with your hair I will hang all the birds that are singing and cut down all the flowers I will take the lamb in my arms and give it my breast to eat and I will go to sleep alongside the song of my solitude by *Soleares* and I will etch the fields of wheat and hay and I shall see them die supine with their faces to the sun and I will wrap the flowers in the newspaper and I will fling them through the window in the gutter-stream that is hurrying by with all its sins on its back but laughing all the same to make its nest in the sewer and I will break the music of the woodlands against the rocks of the waves of the sea and I will bite the lion on the cheek and I will make the wolf cry for tender pity in front of the portrait of the water which is letting its arms fall slackly into the wash-hand basin.

PABLO PICASSO

None of these passages, indeed, is completely uncontrolled (Picasso's, for instance, however wild and formless it seems, has nevertheless a density that suggests it has been carefully worked over). Eluard, in fact, is almost classically lucid, and the passage I have quoted from him is rather a meditation on the bewildering nature of the image than an evocation of the bewildering image itself. The 'sisters of nothing ready for everything' *are*, in fact, the images often apparently meaningless and not even strikingly and obviously beautiful ('beautiful hardly beautiful but always beautiful') that come to the poet quite spontaneously, that are 'given.' If he tries to explain them rationally he destroys their poetic power ('reduced by the intellect to reason to die of it'). The images come from the subconscious depths of the mind, from our repressed sufferings and desires there, and therefore from the point of view of the highly moral conscious mind (or of what Freud calls the superego) they are 'poisonous,' though, like the Eastern King Mithridates, who in fear of ultimate assassination took small daily doses of arsenic and other venoms, they have gradually become accustomed to the poisonous atmosphere surrounding them and immune to it. That is to say that the fact that dream images may, from the point of view of the conscious mind, have a sordid hidden meaning does not prevent them also from having a true and mysterious poetic beauty. The poet equates these 'images still to be made' – images, that is, which have not yet been poetically destroyed by being given too firm an outline – or set in an intellectual context – with the idea of love, which he opposes to the idea of the 'ready-made image' (our conventional perceptions, and more widely the traditional images of mere rhetoric, of mere literature, as opposed to the sacred poetic mystery). Love, for him, that is to say, is the sense of endless potentiality, as opposed to any limiting act. Here again we can see Rimbaud's leading idea of the transformability of the world through poetry. One might compare an English poem by Robert Graves:

> He is quick, thinking in clear images;
> I am slow, thinking in broken images.
> He becomes dull, trusting to his clear images;
> I become sharp, mistrusting my broken images . . .

In Soupault's little poem, on the other hand, the images have been a little too consciously 'broken.' It is a series of statements of the type, 'The X is Y,' or 'The X does Y,' where Y is a property one does not think of X as having or an action one does not think of X as performing. The effect here is one of lyrical fantasy, but obviously with sufficient repetition the trick would become unbearably monotonous. In many Surrealist poems it does.

Chirico's poem, on the other hand, has the same atmosphere as many of his paintings, the transformation of dream material into a solid and objective-looking landscape which conveys however a strong feeling of loneliness and frustrated desire. Picasso's passage is an imitation in language of some state of delirious excitement, probably erotic in its origin: 'Picasso's dazzling and disconcerting flow of colours and materials,' says Georges Hugnet, 'is transformed in his poems into aggressive, highly coloured, flamboyant images used in continuous passages worked and reworked until they become a strange kaleidoscopic saraband.' There is the same formal drawback to this type of writing as to Soupault's; at first vivid, startling, and bewildering, it gradually loses impact, since it is not a development but simply an endless repetition of the same sort of thing. One short passage of this sort of thing is exciting; a longer passage would soon become unreadable; and a series of short passages, once the reader had grasped the trick, would become a bore. Chirico's transcription of a dream landscape has not these faults, it is evocative, and as a series of statements about an imaginary scene perfectly clear; but it is a kind of poetry only possible for the poet whose imagination is *primarily* that of the painter, for whom words serve merely for transcription. Thus of all these passages only Eluard's is primarily poetical and formally satisfactory; and it is untypical of the Surrealist purpose.

Here are some examples of (2):

a) Turn on your side and bear the day to me
  Beloved, sceptre-struck, immured
  In the glass wall of sleep. Slowly
  Uncloud the borealis of your eye
  And show your iceberg secrets, your midnight prizes
  To the green-eyed world and me. Sins
  Coil upwards into thin air when you awaken
  And again morning announces amnesty over
  The serpent-kingdomed bed . . .

                                        GEORGE BARKER

b) The season's anguish, crashing whirlwind, ice,
  Have passed, and cleansed the trodden paths
  The silent gardeners have strewn with ash.

  The iron circles of the sky
  Are worn away by tempest;
  Yet in this garden there is no more strife:
  The Winter's knife is buried in the earth.
  Pure music is the cry that tears
  The birdless branches in the wind.
  No blossom is reborn. The blue
  Stare of the pond is blind.

  And no-one sees
  A restless stranger through the morning stray
  Across the sodden lawn, whose eyes
  Are tired of weeping, in whose breast
  A savage sun consumes its hidden day.

                                        DAVID GASCOYNE

c) The force that through the green fuse drives the flower
  Drives my green age; that blasts the roots of trees
  Is my destroyer.
  And I am dumb to tell the crooked rose
  My youth is bent by the same wintry fever.

  The force that drives the water through the rocks
  Drives my red blood; that dries the mouthing streams
  Turns mine to wax.
  And I am dumb to mouth unto my veins
  How at the mountain spring the same mouth sucks . . .

                                        DYLAN THOMAS

d) They are like scarlet moths
  With heads of gold
  and bright eyes peeping out from vats of flowers.

Their glowing hearts
make a restless masque of torches.
Moving like danger through the summer dusk
they light each theatre of immense desire . . .
And should you touch them
they would melt like honey,
drop at your feet in a wreath
of rotting lilies,
or burst into flames
like the nitrous core of a star.

DEREK STANFORD

Sprung on the reader at once, these passages might appear obscure but when he has been prepared for them by reading Surrealist texts they probably seem to have, at least by comparison with what has gone before, a refreshing clarity. They are composed, like the Surrealist texts, in images rather than in conceptual statements, but they have a conceptual background: it is fairly easy to relate them to our ordinary realms of discourse. They start from the reality of experience, not from an attempt to transform it utterly, and can be referred back to that realm. In a certain brilliant incoherence of imagery, Mr Barker is probably most like the Surrealists and it would be useful to compare his passage here with Picasso's. We do not see why a result of being sceptre-struck should be immurement in a wall of glass though we can see how glass could suggest the iceberg image and the iceberg image, in its turn, the green-eyed world (we remember the ice as green as emerald in *The Ancient Mariner*). The fact that sins 'coil upwards' in one line (like wreaths of smoke or mist) suggests the serpents in the next line as does, also, of course the poet's remembering that a serpent introduced sin into the garden of Eden. And 'kingdomed' in the same line refers back to 'sceptre-struck' in the second line, makes it look less arbitrary, and gives it a context. But where in Picasso's passage there is nothing but these arbitrary associations of imagery held loosely together by the theme that love is both delightful and sinful, here that argument is coherently worked out in such a way that the images, a set of loose word associations if we take them by themselves, justify themselves in detail in relation to separate parts of the argument. It is early morning, the poet is awake in bed, waiting for his loved one to awake also. He is worried by a sense of the sinfulness of his love, and the sceptre which has struck his love so deep asleep is that, he thinks, of a serpent kingdom, a kingdom of sin. He is worried also because of her remoteness from him in sleep as if shut in a wall of glass

274

and he thinks of the world of sleep as a remote and icy one of which he will catch a sudden glimpse when she opens her eyes on a world that is green-eyed with jealousy, as perhaps he is too, of her distant beautiful self-containment, of that coldness of hers, which is part of the quality of all beauty. But when she wakens all these night-waking worries of his and his gnawing sense of sin will vanish away in the normal atmosphere of morning, though his ability to forget it for a time will not make his sin any less real: the bed is still serpent-kingdomed, it is only the haunting ghosts of the serpents that coil away in the morning, but still the lovers are going to get out of bed and begin a new day. . . .

Mr Gascoyne's poem, on the other hand, should be compared with the landscape piece from Chirico. It is a more solid poem, in that the landscape is a real, not an imaginary one, a garden or a public park in winter, and in that what it symbolises for the poet is not some special obsession of his (as the monk, the ladies, the pond do for Chirico) but rather the general weariness, sadness, and barrenness of our time. Everything that is said about the garden is true of the poet's state of mind, and on the other hand everything that is said about the poet's state of mind is true of the garden. It is a harsh winter in the war years. Nature, and the poet, and perhaps human history itself, are at the saddest stage of dead mid-winter and longing for a new spring. Thus this poem is more than a mere transcription of a possible painting: it expresses a set of complex interrelations which can be expressed only in words.

Mr Dylan Thomas's passage can be compared with Soupault's, in that its form is a set of statements of the type, 'The X is Y' or 'The X does Y'; but Mr Thomas is not aiming at trivial surprises but at massive identification. The forces, he is saying, that control the growth and decay, the beauty and terror of human life are the very same forces that we see at work in outer nature. This is a statement which most of us would accept up to a point, or with qualifications, or as a platitude but the fine, strong shape of Mr Thomas's stanza and the wonderfully concrete nature of his imagery gives it a freshness of discovery and an emotional force, and it also gains strength from an intertransference of qualities between man and nature; we feel a human pity for the 'crooked rose' and on the other hand the 'wintry fever' of the young man's unsatisfied desires acquires something of the impersonal dignity of a natural process. Mr Thomas's approach to nature has not anything very obviously in common with Wordsworth's; but in both cases it does at least seem true that both man and nature, at the poetic level, gain by the transaction.

The extract from Mr Stanford is from a poem about women and there, too, we notice the succession of apparently disconnected images that remind us of the Surrealists. But again, as with Mr Barker, there is an implicit logic of statement, not about women as such, but about Mr Stanford's attitude to them, which lies somewhere between attraction and terror. They are like moths, elaborately described, because they are at once beautiful and, to Mr Stanford, sinister. But he himself is like a moth – again one sees new images arising through association – because he might be burnt up if he approached too near their torchlike glowing hearts; but he is not really like a moth for he sees them as a 'masque,' they light up a 'theatre of immense desire,' which is to say that they are to be longed for, watched, but not approached. If they were approached, they would melt like honey, drop like rotting lilies, or explode like stars, but Mr Stanford does not really mean that they would do this, but rather that *he* would, or rather that he has longed so much for woman's beauty, brooded about it so long, that if it were to be put into his hands at last, he would not be equal to the occasion, he would suffer a kind of nervous collapse. Here, too, we have as in Mr Barker's case an inner argument about love—not so much about delight and sin, now, as about fear and desire.

I hope this psychological approach to the content of poetry does not distress the sort of reader who has been accustomed to think of poetry as dealing mainly with what one might call *the ideal*: like other types of literature, though it can treat of the ideal, it also takes reality as its province, particularly the reality of the inner life. Fear and desire, delight and the sense of sin, do tug against each other in most human hearts: in the difficult world we live in to-day, we are often overcome, like Mr Gascoyne in the poem I have quoted, by an almost hopeless sadness; the affinities and relations between man and nature have also, as Mr Thomas is wise to point out, their frightening as well as their comforting side. By giving a satisfactory formal shape to all this disturbing material, the poet helps himself to control it, to get into a dignified human perspective; and, if we read him with sufficient alertness and intelligence, he can help us to perform the same feat.

Here are some examples of (3):

a) There is a fish that quivers in the pool
    itself a shadow, but its shadow, clear.
    Catch it again and again, it is still there.

Against the flowing stream, its life keeps pace
with death – the impulse and the flash of grace
hiding in its stillness, moves, to be motionless.

No net will hold it – always it will return
when the ripples settle, and the sand –
It lives unmoved, equated with the stream,
as flowers are fit for air, man for his dream.

KATHLEEN RAINE

b) Strange that the self's continuum should outlast
The Virgin, Aphrodite, and the Mourning Mother.

KATHLEEN RAINE

c) Swordsman of the narrow lips,
Narrow hips and murderous mind
Fenced with chariots and ships,
By your joculators hailed
The mailed wonder of mankind,
Far to westward you have sailed.

ROBERT GRAVES

d) So soon as ever your mazed spirit descends
From daylight into darkness, Man, remember
What you have suffered here in Samothrace,
What you have suffered.

After your passage through Hell's seven floods,
Whose fumes of sulphur will have parched your throat
The Halls of Judgment will loom up before you,
A miracle of jasper and of onyx.
To the left hand there bubbles a black spring
Overshadowed with a great white cypress.
Avoid this spring, which is Forgetfulness;
Though all the common rout rush down to drink,
Avoid this spring.

To the right hand there lies a secret pool
Alive with speckled trout and fish of gold;
A hazel overshadows it. Ophion,
Primaeval serpent straggling in the branches,
Darts out his tongue. The holy pool is fed
By dripping water; guardians stand before it.
Run to this pool, the pool of Memory,
Run to this pool.

ROBERT GRAVES

e) 'O Dionysus of the tree – you of the beard, you of the ripeness
Among the branches of my arms and hair
As the boughs of the vine hold the plane-tree
You came like the wind in the branches.'

277

'And to the earth of my heart, O golden woman
You are the corn-goddess.'
'O wind, come again to my branches.'
'O darkness of earth – O ripeness.'

DR EDITH SITWELL

f) I who was once a golden woman like those who walk
In the dark heavens – but am now grown old
And sit by the fire, and see the fire grow cold,
Watch the dark fields for a rebirth of faith and wonder.
The turning of Ixion's wheel the day
Ceased not, yet sounds no more the beat of the heart
But only the sound of ultimate Darkness falling
And of the Blind Samson at the Fair, shaking the pillars of the world and
   emptily calling.

DR EDITH SITWELL

g) The ultimate dream. Arms, eagles, broken banners,
And the blind battle in the naked wood
Over the brazen birds
Those with black shining feathers that scream and tear:
The angels rending their bright hair
Amid the fog and babel of crying voices,
Where Cyril and Methodius clitch at their split hearts.
Look now, this
Is the last Emperor, whose crown of iron and gold
Drops diamonds like frozen tears, like those smooth stones
The glacier bears from mythological mountains . . .

JOHN HEATH-STUBBS

h) Since I emerged that day from the labyrinth,
Dazed with the all and echoing passages,
The swift recoils, so many I almost feared
I'd meet myself returning at some smooth corner,
Myself or my ghost, for all there was unreal
After the straw ceased rustling and the bull
Lay dead upon the straw and I remained . . .
      . . . since I came out that day
There have been times when I have heard my footsteps
Still echoing in the maze, and all the roads
That run through the noisy world, deceiving streets
That meet and part and meet, and rooms that open
Into each other – and never a final room –
Stairways and corridors and antechambers
That vacantly wait for some great audience,
The smooth sea-tracks that open and close again,
Tracks undiscoverable, indecipherable,
Paths on the earth and tunnels underground,

And bird-tracks in the air – all seemed a part
Of the great labyrinth. And then I'd stumble
In sudden blindness, hasten, almost run,
As if the maze itself were after me
And soon must catch me up.

EDWIN MUIR

In this sort of poetry we have not the puzzles about detail, the bewildering associative growth of imagery, that confront us in the Surrealists and in the recent romantic English poets who partly derive from them. The structure of language and thought is logical, and in one sense one might almost say there is no imagery, for the image has ceased to become something that enriches the texture of the poem, it has become instead intrinsic to the poem's structure: a symbol, what the poem presents. We are given the myth in itself, not the comparison of private experience to the myth. Once more poetry is becoming objective. Puzzles are likely to arise only out of the unfamiliarity of this or that myth, or out of the unfamiliarity of the poet's interpretation of it. Thus, Mr Graves, in my first quotation from him, is talking of Perseus who slew the Gorgon; but the Gorgon for Mr Graves is merely one terrifying aspect of the triple Goddess (mother, lover, and destroyer of man) who for him is the inspiration of all true poetry: and Perseus represents a spirit of male dominance that is hostile to all true poetry, represents the northern invaders, fierce and barbarous, who destroyed the woman-dominated civilisation of Crete. Hence the tone of satire,

Swordsman of the narrow lips,
Narrow hips and murderous mind,

and hence the fact that Perseus, type of the conqueror, is surrounded not by true poets but by flatterers, 'joculators.' He has sailed 'far to westward' in the sense that his man of action's philosophy dominates modern Western Civilisation. Feminine magic is at a discount in our world and obtuse male vanity, masculine 'practicality' and 'realism', leaves almost no place for poetry. The true poetic theme (the theme of woman as a goddess, creative, lovely, and fatal) is, according to Mr Graves, a 'pre-historic or a post-historic theme.' It has been carried on through the centuries by a sort of unconscious conspiracy among poets, who have never, in their heart of hearts, accepted at any time the current beliefs and standards of civilisation. All these ideas are worked out in great detail in Mr Graves's fascinating book, *The White Goddess*. The second quotation from him (which is largely a translation from

Orphic texts) I cite partly for its great intrinsic beauty; partly to show how to somebody with an attitude like Mr Graves's mythology is far more *true* than history (mythology preserves the memory of ancient rituals, it is about what many people, under a very deep emotional compulsion, were always doing, where history is about what individual people did *once*.)*

In the quotations from Miss Raine and Dr Edith Sitwell we see the other side of this picture. If the male poet is the votary of woman as the goddess or Muse, the female poet is the actual representative of the goddess. Thus Dr Sitwell, in the second of my two quotations, identifies herself with the corn-goddess whom she represents (using familiar material from Sir James George Frazer) in the first. Miss Raine rather sees the various types of the mother goddess as stages through which the individual woman grows,

> Strange that the self's continuum should outlast
> The Virgin, Aphrodite and the Mourning Mother,

and which she may outgrow, but which nevertheless have a more poetic significance than her mere individuality; they are parts, as it were, which she has to play in a sacred drama. They are perhaps not *actual* except when embodied in the individual woman, but they are nevertheless more *real* than she. They are archetypal roles that give the individual existence shape and meaning. That is the sense of the first, very simple and very elusive and subtle poem I quote from Miss Raine – a poem which again and again slips through the fingers, like the fish it describes. The fish is neither the abstract idea of a fish, which one knows one cannot catch, nor the individual fish, which one knows one can; it is rather the archetypal role of the fish, which every fish assumes, but which it loses when it is caught. Similarly, if one were to domesticate a poet, and then to ask him his secrets, he would be able to tell us nothing; the god that had once inhabited him, the youthful Dionysus in love with the Corn-Goddess, would have left him for ever.

In the quotations from Mr Heath-Stubbs and from Mr Edwin Muir we see this same pursuit of archetypes working outside the strict pattern of poet as worshipper and woman as goddess, which for Mr Graves

---

* The poetic 'truth' of the myth of the Orphic heaven lies in the psychological efficacy of the rituals of purification on which the myth was based. What seems permanently valid in the passage is the advice that if we wish to be pure we must *remember*, not *forget*. Psycho-analysis is a similar modern purifying ritual. Freudian theory is the much less beautiful 'myth' derived from the 'ritual.'

is the only true pattern of poetry. Mr Muir takes the story of Theseus
in the labyrinth as an archetype of our bewilderment in the maze of
the world, and gives the story a new twist, by suggesting that the maze
is the essential clue to the story of Theseus, that he never really escaped
from it, and neither do we; either the maze was a reality and the real
world a hallucination, or the maze was a hallucination that expressed
the essential nature of the real world.* We seek a way out of the
limitations of the real world, as Theseus sought a way out of his
labyrinth, and perhaps there is no way out, and yet the whole 'meaning
of life' is probably in our seeking.

In Mr Heath-Stubbs, we see a perhaps simpler use of historical, not
mythological material (yet historical material so ancient and picturesque, with the characters in it reduced so completely to mere ritual
roles, that it has acquired some of the prestige of mythology) to
illuminate the present state of the world. The Roman legions making
their last stand, their brazen eagles cast down, the barbarians closing
in on them, the ravens closing over, the distress of the Christian
Fathers, the angels weeping in the Christian Heaven, are in one sense
frozen and archaic symbols, in another disturbingly contemporary.
There is a sense in which this last stand for a doomed great cause *is*
an 'ultimate dream'; there is a sense, also, in which it should encourage
us, for though the picture which Mr Heath-Stubbs paints is so terrifying
it has also its own heroic value and, in point of fact, the victories of
the barbarians did not in the long run mean the end either of religion
or civilisation. So we might almost imagine Mr Heath-Stubbs to be
indirectly exhorting us: 'Fight bravely for your beliefs, even in the last
ditch, even against hope. There is an exhilaration in that last ditch
fight. But do not imagine that your own defeat, if you are defeated,
can really be the end of what, most profoundly, you were fighting
for.'

We can see then that this new feeling for myths and for archetypes
has enabled English poetry to move in the last ten years from a comparative obscurity to a comparative clarity, and from an obsession
with the personal life to a wide general relevance; at the same time
in this rediscovery of the wider uses of symbolism, there is a real
danger of the imagery and diction of poetry losing touch with the

* In Mr Muir's autobiography, we learn that he first felt this sense of being in a labyrinth
while walking to work through the slums of Glasgow – and, he says, 'if I was tired or ill
I often had the feeling ... that I was deep down in a place from which I might never be
able to climb up again.'

everyday surface of contemporary life. There is a sense in which occasionally, in reading nearly all the poets I have quoted here, one longs occasionally for the 'common touch,' for an ability in the poet to handle everyday experiences and emotions; but some young poets are regaining this touch. Let me quote in conclusion this from Peter Russell,

'O Mother Venus,
What can your poor sons do deserted by girls
They have ever taken for granted. It hurts.
Send either another Greek courtesan
Who is tired of life in the brothels, and is seeking a home
Modest enough for dull me to provide for,
Or end this unnecessary slowness of days.
I'll make her a good husband I promise you;
Just show me a house and a field at the edge of the city
With room for chickens, a cock, a pig and a cow:
Let it have three or four gnarled olive-trees
With ripe berries in early November; let it
Have ample room for the winter wheat and a terrace
Of large-leaved vines for the summer months.
And don't forget to remind your old father
To make sure there's rain when it's needed. Dear Goddess
I'd soon take root at the edge of the city of Sfax
Provided my new wife doesn't turn a scold
And further invasions don't interrupt the hours
With parties of homeless and hungry looking for food.'

There we have the use of archetypal material, with, however, a homely ring of humour and pathos and a complex rather than a simple relevance to contemporary life – the desire for a quiet life, the readiness to make do with a second best, the fear of disruption of order by war, the tendency to cajole, coax, and badger one's gods, if one really believes in them, rather than to treat them always with too much solemnity and awe. It is the extension of that 'human note' that one is looking for in contemporary English poetry; it will, when it comes, be one of the most certain signs of renewed national confidence and health.

In this final section of this chapter I have adopted, the reader will have noticed, a method rather different from my method in other sections. I have not attempted to characterise or to judge poets of whom many are my friends and contemporaries. I have simply assembled quotations to illustrate one main pattern of development in poetry in the last ten years, and I have tried to bring out common factors in these groups of quotations. There are excellent young contemporary poets who do not illustrate this pattern of development, and these I have simply ruthlessly left aside. One cannot really, without some harsh simplification of this sort, get one's own decade, the decade in which one has done most of one's own work, into any sort of perspective. I shall be happy if I have pointed out to the reader, at least, some paths to explore; and if I have left him also with the feeling that English poetry in the last ten years, in spite of all the discouragements that the troubled times have put in the poet's way, has been carrying on the great tradition; not copying merely, nor going back to the past, and not trying to cut away from the past; but growing and putting out feelers, as a living plant does, towards a future of which the poet, by his very nature, however hard the times are, will always refuse to despair.

CHAPTER FIVE

THE TRENDS OF CRITICISM

Section 1: The Victorian Tradition

The romantic revolution in English criticism, like many revolutions, resisted effective consolidation. It represented too complete a shift of the traditional point of view. For the critics of the eighteenth century the question about any poem was, fundamentally, how far it satisfied the reasonable expectations of the reader. There was a hierarchy of kinds of poetry, with the epic at the top, tragedy not far below, didactic poetry and serious satire fairly high up, and the slight lyric and the epigram at the bottom, well below that extinct bird 'the great ode'; each kind had its own appropriate beauties. There were accepted standards of good sense, of good taste, of correct, easy, and forcible expression. There were rules. For the great romantic critics, the rules had vanished. It was no longer the poet's business to satisfy expectation; it was the reader's business to strive to comprehend the workings of the poetic mind. The mind in creation, 'like a fading coal,' was what interested Shelley or Coleridge and the poem itself was thought of almost as a by-product. Where criticism had been social and external and concerned with particular works, it now became psychological, subjective, concerned with the general poetic process. The history of Victorian criticism, both as a consolidation of and partly as a reaction against the romantic revolution, is the history of various attempts to restore external standards, to find generally acceptable methods of judging particular works, without reverting to the rigidity and pedantry of the eighteenth century. The natural tendency, in an age which was both full of doubt and anxious to believe, was to seek these external standards in moral and religious principles; but to adapt these principles, as far as possible, to new scientific knowledge. In criticism, as in other fields, the Victorians were looking for a working compromise. But a latent fear that new scientific knowledge might prove *all* moral and religious principles to be illusory, a fear that everything might be swept away, led in most of the great Victorian thinkers, in Carlyle and Ruskin notably, to a strained and excessive emphasis; they have the preacher's tone because they are seeking to convince themselves. They have not the true critic's tone; men in the grip of such a fear cannot be detached and objective.

Matthew Arnold strikes us as the great and typical Victorian critic largely because, unlike so many of the others, he has that detached and objective tone. Yet he shared the doubts, the hopes, and the fears of men like Carlyle and Ruskin; and for him as for them the criticism of literature was only one aspect of a wide 'general censure' of the age. He was a preacher and even a prophet in his own way – 'an elegant Jeremiah.' But Arnold was at least less insular and flurried than Carlyle or Ruskin, and had not their fear of detachment. He did manage to state, not in philosophical, but in lucid and sensible terms, what was emerging as the central problem of the Victorian age. Standards of criticism, for him, depended upon standards of conduct; our perception of fineness or coarseness in literature was not essentially different from our perception of fineness or coarseness in life. But, to breed respect for, and imitation of, moral fineness, the Victorian emphasis on political and economic liberty, on 'doing what one liked,' needed to be balanced by emphasis on social order, and on the wider order of what Arnold called 'culture' – the influence everywhere, on educated minds, of 'the best that has been thought and felt.' Here the central problem arose. That order, in so far as it still persisted through the Victorian age, was a Christian order; and yet Christian belief, in a hard and literal sense, was becoming more and more difficult for the educated man. Arnold's ideas about purely literary criticism cannot be properly understood unless we relate them to his ideas about Victorian religious difficulties.

There was a solid middle-class Evangelical Christianity which simply ignored these difficulties. It was a source to the nation of moral strength of a kind, but to Arnold narrow, stupid, and the enemy of 'culture.' There was the subtle argumentation of the Oxford Movement which tried to get round these difficulties, or ingeniously to evade consideration of them, by concentrating on difficulties of another kind; Arnold was sympathetic, he recognised the genius of Newman, but he did not find the High Church case either quite honest or quite convincing. There was the possibility of rejecting Christianity altogether, as Mill and his followers had done. This seemed to Arnold to involve a fatal impoverishment of life. It rejected our only real existing source of moral instruction, and could offer only an ideal source in its place; it was likely, in practice, to pave the way for crude materialism. What, then, was Arnold's own solution? He was a genuinely religious man; prayer, meditation, scrupulous self-examination, were part of his daily life; but he was willing to believe neither more than he felt reasonably able to, nor less than he felt emotionally inclined to. He thought that the educated man should adhere to the outward usages of established Christianity but should interpret the meaning of these in his own way; he should adhere to the forms without feeling bound by their hard and literal sense.

What was new was not so much this position in itself as Arnold's frank statement of it and his tactful vagueness about what it fundamentally implied. To men whose belief or unbelief was more definite he appeared to be anxious to preserve a mere empty shell of Christianity; to himself he appeared to be preserving its essence. Yet, one might, it seemed, almost be an Arnoldian Christian without even believing in a hard and literal sense in the existence of God. God, for Arnold, was 'the Eternal not ourselves that makes for righteousness.' The philosopher Bradley, who had found a substitute for traditional Christianity in the theory of the Absolute, accused Arnold of worshipping hypostatised copy-book headings. Arnold's God, he said, was not much more real or more adorable than a personification of the maxim: 'Be good and you will be happy.' Arnold's God was not what any religiously minded person meant by God. Arnold might have retorted that neither was Bradley's Absolute; he had a peculiar and perhaps excessive contempt for metaphysics, and no dry and abstract scheme of notions, for him, could ever be a source of moral nourishment. There is a criticism of Arnold's religious scheme, however, to which he might have paid more attention. Arnold hated and distrusted individualism, and yet his religion was an extremely individualistic one. He did not so much find authority in the Church or the Bible as provisionally lend them an authority which he found in himself; he was his own final rock and sanctuary. The very possibility of his own kind of outward deference and wistful half-belief depended on the persistence of a more definite assent in others; a Church which consisted wholly of Arnolds would soon drift apart.

Moreover, a similar fundamental individualism, combined with an outward deference to authority, is to be found in Arnold's purely literary criticism. Though he is always wishing that outward sources of authority, like the French Academy, existed in England, his final court of appeal is really his own sensibility; he does not really need an Academy to tell him what to think and feel, but merely to lend his own judgments its moral support. The function of Arnold's ideal Academy, as of his ideal Church, would be to assure him that he was always in the right. The importance of such imaginary props in Arnold's inner life explains, perhaps, the calm assurance of his tone of voice, so different from the passionate, emphatic assertions of Carlyle and Ruskin, or the dogged grey argumentation of Mill. It is as if in the background a throng of ghostly pontiffs and senators were murmuring, 'How right, how right!' The assurance is combined with what Arnold himself called his 'vivacity' – a demure, malicious wit; a habit of repeating favourite phrases of his opponents two or three times, till they acquire an air of pompous absurdity; and a manner which suggests, though with the utmost urbanity, that he is not going to waste time arguing with fools. Arnold's tone involves both a flattery and an intimidation of his readers; if they accept what he is saying, they are members of an inner circle; if they want a kind of detailed reasoned proof, which questions of taste and feeling do not admit of, they may be very worthy persons, but they are 'outsiders.'

How far does this implicit claim to a kind of unarguable personal authority weaken Arnold's criticism? It certainly weakens it logically, though for merely logical, as for merely metaphysical, arguments Arnold himself had always a certain contempt. One of his most famous notions, for instance, is that of the 'touchstone' – the short passage, even the single line, from the great poetry of the past, against which we can test the ring of the poetry of the present. But, as Lytton Strachey in an otherwise bad essay sensibly pointed out, if we can immediately recognise the quality of these touchstones from the past, might we not similarly immediately recognise a comparable quality in contemporary poetry? And if we cannot recognise the quality, if we must accept the fact of its presence on Arnold's authority, will the touchstones be of any real use to us? More widely, this approach to poetry through the quality of the detached single line has its critical dangers. It prevents Arnold from considering a poem as a complex living structure; it narrows his field of practical appreciation to poets, like Milton, Gray, or Wordsworth, who can offer him the moments of concentrated elevation that he is chiefly looking for. His wish to have the 'grand style' at all costs makes him reject a great deal in the English tradition that ought not to be rejected. He has a peculiar animus against the ballad-style, and by cunningly quoted examples of it at its most jogtrot, and by the use of epithets like 'Lowland-Scotchy,' he usually manages to make it appear ignoble and ridiculous. He dismissed Dryden and Pope, and their whole tradition, without really representative quotation, as 'classics of our prose.' Chaucer is too homely, Burns too plebeian, for real greatness. Shakespeare's greatness must be admitted, but the loose, easy, inclusive sweep of it is faintly embarrassing. The great romantics do aspire towards and achieve the loftiness that Arnold admires; but most of them are socially deplorable – 'What a set!' – and even the best of them do not 'know enough.' Not even Dr Leavis, among critics of our own day, has been more thorough in his rejections. Like Dr Leavis, Arnold is fundamentally a moralist, and, like Dr Leavis again perhaps, thinks that good conduct is nourished less by general rules and abstract principles than by an alert and chastened sensibility. The 'highest' poetry is that which can nourish the 'highest' life. Indeed, one could go further, and say that if Arnold's approach to specifically religious problems was too much, often, that of a literary dilettante, his approach to purely critical problems is sometimes too much that of a sternly Jansenist director of souls. To admire *The Lays of Ancient Rome*, even for what, at their schoolboy level, they so admirably are, is the equivalent, if not of heresy, at least of 'worldliness'; to fail to recoil from the 'brassy, Corinthian' style of Kinglake or the *Daily Telegraph* is to be deliberately obdurate to grace. Arnold's horror of bad taste is like a horror of sin, and for him vulgarity is the root of all evil.

This religious approach to criticism is exemplified most clearly in Arnold's essays on writers, like Marcus Aurelius or Joubert or Spinoza, from whom he himself drew direct spiritual nourishment. Two of these were great, and one a rather middling man; only one was strictly a 'great thinker.' But Arnold does not attempt to 'place' such writers, as the comparative critic might. He is not interested in their scale or originality, but in the practical help he finds in them. He can find that help in very minor figures, like the Guérins; and where a generally accepted originality and greatness, like that of Victor Hugo, does not offer him that help, he is openly contemptuous of it. The acceptance of a writer as edifying is, in fact, for Arnold a minor religious assent. Thus, in spite of his genuine effort to be detached and objective, he is never impersonal. We feel that he is always, fundamentally, talking of a subject much more urgently important to him than the place some particular writer might have in general history of literature. He is quite conscious of his prejudices, without feeling it necessary to make more than an outward, polite, and always slightly ironical allowance for them. He tactfully avoids subjects that do not arouse his sympathy (except as 'dreadful examples' in passing), but where he is unsympathetic he does not make any very strenuous effort to muffle his negative responses and 'be fair.' Arnold was a very great man; but it is not unjust to say that the extraordinary self-confidence of the Victorian age, which he mocked so much for its obtuseness, does in a peculiarly indirect and unconscious way express itself in his own criticism.

Arnold's criticism can be usefully contrasted with that of a contemporary of his, Walter Bagehot, an equally typical Victorian of another kind. For Bagehot, as for Arnold, the criticism of literature was again one aspect only of a general criticism of life, but unlike Arnold he was immersed in practical affairs. He shared, with Arnold, the typically Victorian interest in religion, but from another point of view; he liked to discuss queerly indirect arguments for the truth of the Christian religion, like those of Bishop Butler, who thought that the world as we know it is so odd that the supernatural world, as the Bible reveals it to us, may be, very properly, extremely odd too; and he had a great sympathy with Victorian agnostics like Clough who combined 'honest doubt' with an incurably religious habit of mind. He might, though he never did, have written a very good essay on Pascal. But his special subjects were economics and politics and his two books on these, *Lombard Street* and *The British Constitution*, though naturally out of date on many details, are still classics of their kind; they are perhaps the last important books on their subjects addressed to the intelligent general reader and not to the specialised student. They have a summary precision and a gay speculative ease. The book on the British constitution, in particular, exemplifies that harsh but tangy 'realism' which is a mark also of Bagehot's purely literary criticism. For Bagehot, the stability of the Victorian compromise depended on the forms of political democracy continuing to be combined with the actuality of rule by the upper classes. In other words, he was an aristocratic liberal, and almost his favourite politician was Palmerston. He was not quite a Whig, because though the Whigs represented the sort of compromise he supported, they did not take his objective view of their own position; they were very conscious of being liberal, but took the fact that they were aristocrats for granted. What would be fatal, Bagehot felt, would be if – as has actually happened – the lower classes should use their new voting power, acquired through the mid-Victorian Reform

Bills, to push their sectional interests. That the upper classes should use their strategic position to push *their* interests was, on the other hand, right and proper; for, as an orthodox Victorian economist, Bagehot felt that such prosperity as the lower classes could ever enjoy could only be a spill-over from the prosperity of their betters. The function of monarchy, for Bagehot, was essentially what modern writers would call an emotive one. A constitutional monarch like Queen Victoria did, of course, in the long run acquire more experience than any of her ministers and could give them in the long run sound advice; but the main business of monarchy, in a modern state, was to reconcile the lower classes, by a kind of poetic symbolism, to the hard and dry facts of economic and political life. The monarchy was the decorative part, the façade, of the constitution.

Bagehot's view of poetry or literature in general in relation to life was perhaps not unlike his view of the institution of monarchy in relation to politics. His whole attitude reflects a fundamental division of interests which Arnold nobly sought to transcend – a division between the true and the useful, as hard, dry fact, and the beautiful as a kind of decorous façade. He loved poetry, and was one of the most acute critics of poetry of the whole century (a better 'close' critic than Arnold), yet it is doubtful whether he found in poetry any real organic connection with life's basic needs. At the same time, he is a good critic of poetry because his sharp destructive common sense, his irreverent humorous realism, does not desert him even in this field. His criticism of the moral balance of *Paradise Lost* in terms of the power-politics of Heaven and Hell is even to-day the soundest thing that has been written on the subject:

Paradise Lost, as a whole, is radically tainted with a vicious principle. It professes to justify the ways of God to man, to account for sin and death, and it tells you that the whole originated in a *political event*; in a court squabble as to a particular act of patronage and the due or undue promotion of an eldest son. Satan may have been wrong, but on Milton's theory he had an *arguable* case at least. There was something arbitrary in the promotion; there were little symptoms of a job; in *Paradise Lost*, it is always clear that the devils are weaker, but it is never clear that the angels are better.

Similarly, in some very amusing pages on Tennyson's *Enoch Arden*, Bagehot points out that a man who goes about in a cart selling fish, however honest and ill-used, is not really a 'noble' subject, and that Tennyson is uneasily aware of this, and uses the most inappropriately ornate language to disguise the fact from himself and his readers. In a sense, Bagehot is the *enfant terrible* of Victorian criticism; he lacks the typical deep anxiety of his age, and is so sure of the solidity of the ground under his feet that he can risk the tactless and acute remarks that everybody else is afraid to make. His voice, even to-day, has a contemporary ring; it is the voice of a frank conversationalist, at ease among equals in his club, where Arnold's is the voice of a brilliant but condescending lecturer. Yet we may feel that Bagehot's realism in the long run was more short-sighted than Arnold's idealism; apparently more harshly in touch with the world as it is and must be than Arnold, finding a source of national strength even in British coarseness and stupidity, Bagehot was nevertheless unduly complacent about the permanence of his world. Practical, sceptical, and sensitive, the sort of public-spirited cynic who becomes a reformer with a sigh and never on any account a revolutionary, himself the perfect product of the Victorian compromise, he assumed a stability in that compromise that was simply, in the long run, not there.

Yet Arnold and Bagehot are both much better critics than Walter Pater, who neither accepts the wider world nor seeks to reform it, but who beats a conscious retreat to the realm of subjective sensibility. The great romantic critics of the beginning of the century, poets like Coleridge and Shelley in his *Defence of Poetry* and Keats in his letters, were perhaps equally subjective: but they described the subjectivity of the creator; Pater described the much more sterile subjectivity of the *connoisseur*. The life of his mind was a secondary life, drawing its strength from works of art which more primary energies had created. Comparing him to Coleridge, Dr Richards rightly describes him as a 'supple' rather than a 'subtle' mind. Pater, too, like all the great Victorian 'thinkers,' was, as Mr Eliot has pointed out, a moralist; but a moralist for men who were willing, as they withdrew from the ordinary duties and interests of life, to exist enclosed in their own sensations. Pater's refined hedonism, his cult of the intense moment, is a practicable morality only for sheltered minorities; dandies of life and literature will soon find their schemes upset if policemen, servants, artisans, and shopkeepers, all those who prop up the gross outer framework of life, begin to live for the intense moment, too. Any non-universal scheme of morality must be always extremely vulnerable; the mere existence of an attitude like Pater's in a sense justified, as a counterbalance, the crudities of Kipling and Henley. More specifically, in Pater's own criticism, even writers so different from him as Wordsworth and Shakespeare tend to be made over again in his own image;

and in his cruder disciples, like Wilde and George Moore, the cult of subjective appreciative sensibility becomes one of gaudy self-display.

It is, of course, of writers like Wilde and Pater and Moore – and of the faintly false heartiness of Henley and Whibley as a counter-balance – that one first thinks when attempting to sense the critical climate of the 1890s. Yet perhaps the really new, or at least the continuingly fruitful, tendencies of the period are to be found rather in the work of a man like George Saintsbury, who is by no means a typical '90s man at all; Frank Harris, for instance, was a typical '90s man, and one of *his* first steps on taking over *The Saturday Review* was to remove Saintsbury from the panel of regular reviewers. Yet Saintsbury was the first and in many ways the greatest of the long line of academic critics who, in the last fifty years, have turned the study of English literature into a humanistic discipline for undergraduates which may, in the long run, largely replace Latin and Greek. Saintsbury was at first a very hard-working London literary journalist, almost a hack; in early middle age, with Henley as one of his rivals, he became Professor of Rhetoric and English Literature in Edinburgh University. The traditional interest in rhetoric, or in the art of writing as opposed to the history of literature, of those who held that chair encouraged him to do pioneer work in examining the metres of English poetry and the rhythms of English prose. For Saintsbury, the first great 'professional' in this field, literature, particularly though by no means exclusively English literature, was in itself a sufficiently exacting field to demand a lifetime's devotion; with nothing of Pater's finicky subjectivism, he had nothing either of the urge of Arnold or Bagehot to relate purely literary criticism to a general 'censure of the age.' He could not, in fact, repress a certain contempt for Arnold's 'wide-ranging scatter of sometimes rather haphazard arrows.' Saintsbury himself was an old-fashioned Church-and-State High Tory; almost a pre-Victorian in temperament, in that he had nothing at all of the common Victorian taste for adapting oneself gradually to broad changing views; from his youth onwards, he must have disliked the general tendencies of his time; but he was much too 'professional' to wish to impose his critical authority outside his chosen field. His Toryism gives a personal flavour to his books, but never makes him unfair to writers, like Shelley, whose genius he admires and whose opinions he deplores; nor does he attempt to rehabilitate such victims of Whiggish invective or irony, such proper victims, as William Gifford or John Wilson Croker.

In thus narrowing his range, Saintsbury knew what he was doing. Of Arnold's effort of general censure, especially in relation to religious topics, he remarks that 'it underwent the very curse, on speaking without qualification and without true culture, which Mr Arnold had himself so freely pronounced.' Arnold, without meaning to be, and indeed meaning the opposite, seemed to Saintsbury to have been the enemy, in literary criticism, of scholarship, seriousness, and simplicity. Unlike Arnold, Saintsbury had the historical sense; he judges any work of literature in its setting, and according to its intention and its kind. If he has a major weakness, it is that in reaction against Arnold's system of fastidious rejections he is sometimes too inclusively tolerant. He is so eager to be fair to the foothills that the high peaks behind them sometimes do not get all the emphasis they might. 'We cannot,' he will say regretfully, 'talk here of *Emilia Wyndham* or *Paul Ferroll*, both emphatically novels of their day. . . .' But certainly, if space and time allowed, he would like to. The fact that reading was the main business of his life gives his critical approach an almost alarming leisureliness; Bagehot's banking, Arnold's school-inspecting, the busy, worried lives which both led, did, at least, force on them a drastic necessity of choice.

Saintsbury, on the other hand, seems to write sometimes as if he had been set down in the British Museum with eternity before him. Thus his style, with its long, loose, outstretching sentences, is parasitic on the literature it deals with; in its way it is lively, but its life is less in its own rhythms than in the quotations embedded in it, or in its appeal to the reader's alertness to spot an oblique allusion. Henry James's splenetic description of some great Russian novels as 'fluid puddings' might apply very neatly to Saintsbury's prose, with the proviso that the plums in the pudding are almost never Saintsbury's own. No ideas or sentences stand out; the writer's personality, though it comes over strongly, comes over largely through an old-fashioned formality and reserve. Thus Galt, we are told, 'had some of the national characteristics which have not always made Scotsmen popular,' and we are left wondering: 'Was he quarrelsome, dogmatic or pragmatic, a heavy drinker, mean about money?' It is too late to know now; a friend of Saintsbury's, like Andrew Lang, would probably catch the allusion at once. Modern undergraduates, alas, tend to be exasperated by these knowing hints and that rigid courtesy. Yet within Saintsbury's labyrinth a young student may hit on something to fire his imagination – I remember, for instance, a phrase about the 'sad clangor' of Donne. And a very modern critic, like Mr Edmund Wilson, finds, in the early middle age of a life devoted to literature, that he has reached a point at which he finds Saintsbury pleasant light reading.

Saintsbury does remain, in fact, for all the distinction, the greater expertness or sensitiveness in particular fields, of worthy successors of his like Raleigh, Kerr, or Grierson, the greatest of the professorial critics – and the greatest perhaps, paradoxically, just because, being the first of the really notable 'professionals,' he did always remain at heart so much, in the good sense, an amateur: reading for pleasure; covering enormous fields, of which a more cautious man would have tackled only a section; refusing to be trammelled either by theories about the best methods of research on the one hand, or by doubts about how much the average undergraduate can absorb on the other. As a textual scholar, for instance, he was, as the scathing introduction to the Oxford 'Dryden' shows, extremely vulnerable; as a lecturer in Edinburgh by all accounts, besides having a rather unimpressive delivery, he conveyed to his students too many brute facts and too few leading ideas. But if there have been better scholars and teachers among his successors, it is doubtful whether there have been better critics. And for the ordinary reader, Saintsbury and his successors – in their immense and in his own case almost incredible labours – have performed a preliminary task, without which criticism by the creative writer, that is sane as well as intense, would be impossible. For even about Arnold, even about Bagehot, as critics, we have in the end to say what Arnold said about the romantics; that even of the facts of the case, even of the outlines of the history of their subject, they literally, for all their immense gifts of penetration, 'did not know enough.' It is due to Saintsbury and his successors that we to-day almost instinctively think of works of literature as parts of a complex historical process; and therefore, by being able to place them, however approximately, in their real settings, are also able to attempt to see them as they are 'in themselves.'

Section 2: The Edwardian Interval, and the Revolution of the 1910s

The Edwardian age was not an age of major criticism. It saw the consolidation, in the universities, of the professorial tradition; but men of letters, in general, were briskly reacting against the melancholy and decadent atmosphere of the 1890s, and unconsciously reacting at the same time, perhaps, against the critical attitude, too. Perhaps the typical literary critic of the period was G.K. Chesterton, for whom criticism was a sideline; he was essentially a journalist of ideas. Gide, giving qualified praise to his book on Browning, noted one of the most irritating mannerisms of Chesterton's style: a habit of setting up dummies for the sake of knocking them down. He would often begin a paragraph with some such phrase as, 'It is a commonly accepted opinion that . . .,' and the 'commonly accepted opinion' would be some obviously absurd point of view of his own invention, whose absurdity he would then proceed pugnaciously to demonstrate. About writers with whom he was in sympathy, Dickens, Browning, Stevenson, Chesterton could write extremely well. His little book on Victorian literature is an extraordinarily lively performance; but it is, like all his writing on general themes, a performance in more senses than one – we can see what Mr Eliot, a young critic who in the 1910s had not acquired his present urbanity, meant when he described it as a 'Lord Mayor's show.' Mr Eliot added: 'Mr Chesterton's brain swarms with ideas; I see no evidence that it thinks.'

Mr Eliot in later years learned to think and speak of Mr Chesterton more respectfully; but in his youth he regarded the 'ideas' of Chesterton as a very poor substitute for the 'observation and inference' which he admired in Henry James. James, as a novelist, draws out of a situation not more and not less than what is implicit in it; Mr Eliot no doubt felt that what Chesterton, as a critic, drew out of a situation was what he had put there himself. Chesterton's general critical method is perhaps reasonably well exemplified in a volume of essays like *Heretics*, which is, of course, only incidentally a volume of literary criticism. He takes an author and gives him a label: Shaw the puritan reformer, Moore the hedonistic dilettante, Kipling the romantic militarist, and so on; then he writes an essay not so much on the man as on the weakness of the attitude, the weakness of puritanism, hedonism, the cult of power. In this particular book, the essays would be as relevant, with the alteration of two or three introductory paragraphs and a few sentences elsewhere, to, say, Bunyan, Wilde, and Nietzsche. The level of discussion is, in fact, as Mr Eliot had shrewdly noted, that of 'ideas,' in detachment both from their social setting and their philosophical basis; ideas as rather irresponsible forces in themselves. Perhaps ideas often are that. But Chesterton's approach does on the whole preclude his getting to actual grips with complex problems. The notions discussed would often seem very abstract, but for the fanciful felicity of the way in which they are illustrated. Yet even that felicity leads, in the long run, to a rather wearying effect. Every sentence, as in Emerson or Wilde, has to tell; and a writer who composes with the individual sentence as his unit will never write very concise or coherent paragraphs. Chesterton, in fact, tends to repeat himself with variations; the surprises become monotonous, the reader feels a drastic desire to compress. Yet at his best he is both serious and perceptive. He can, when he is writing about Browning or Dickens, seem, at least, to recreate a writer and his point of view for us. He is trapped by his own mannerisms, by his terrifying facility, but we continue to read him waiting for the moments, which do occur, when the Chesterton-machine stops working and the Chesterton-creature speaks.

Among other Edwardian men of letters, Chesterton's friend, Mr Belloc, had certainly the makings of a very fine critic. His little book on French Renaissance poetry, *Avril*, sturdily 'mannered' though it is, has permanent charm. But that 'sturdiness' of Mr Belloc's style, like Chesterton's paradoxes, is again symptomatic of a decade which does not appear to have had a tone of voice quite properly (or at least, quite naturally) its own. The best discursive prose, within its frail and tiny limits, of the later 1890s and the Edwardian decade is Sir Max Beerbohm's, and Sir Max is a writer who is all 'manner,' and nothing but 'manner'; his style, like his personality, is artificial, a conscious construction. It may be simply that we are no longer near enough to, and not yet far enough away from, the Edwardian decade, but I think that on most modern readers the mannerisms of Edwardian prose have a faintly disquieting effect, like that of watching adults, instead of children, dressing up in old clothes from the attic – a kind of embarrassing middle-aged infantilism (the Edwardian age was also, of course, the age of Barrie's *Peter Pan*). What is important, however, in our present context is that a false style – even if it is assumed with the same gaiety as a false nose – leads to false thinking. When Wilde described Kipling as a man who had seen wonderful things through keyholes, or Chesterton described Hardy as the village atheist brooding over the village idiot, their very gift for epigram made them cartoonists rather than critics. In his book on Milton, written many years later than the Edwardian period, Mr Belloc's sturdiness (and his habit of imposing a pattern of ideas on his material, rather than persuading them to emerge from it) prevents him from qualifying, from putting in nuances. He is determined to see Milton as the solitary great English example of that austere thing, the 'classical' tradition; where Milton in truth is a great, extravagant poet of the baroque age, who largely invented his own idiom; and in fact where Milton might possibly be described as 'classical,' in the sober design and diction of *Paradise Regained*, Mr Belloc does not really admire him.

In considering the critical revolution against the Edwardians, the revolution of the decade of the First World War, we ought to bear in mind the background and temperament of the young rebels. It was important that two of them, Pound and Eliot, were American, with the American inclusive view of European culture. Pound had come to Europe to escape from the philistinism of the Middle West and Mr Eliot to complete a typical mandarin education of the New England sort, at Oxford, at the Sorbonne, and in Germany. Both had a range of interests very unusual among English writers of that time. Eliot had been regarded by Bertrand Russell, when he taught at Harvard, as his most brilliant pupil; Pound himself had been a teacher of romance languages at an American university, and had lost his job as being too much of a 'Latin Quarter' type. To both of them the hearty and shallow approach of the typical Edwardian man of letters was likely to seem boring, and the general literary atmosphere of England before the Great War stuffily provincial. Mr Eliot has admitted that the poetry that was being written in the United States and in England in his youth simply wearied him; to find anything interesting he had to go back to the 1890s and to the French Symbolist tradition. Pound was an admirer of Hardy and Swinburne and Henry James, which is to say that his own roots were in a sense in the 1880s; his attitude was rather that of a belated Pre-Raphaelite, or of an admirer of the aesthetic movement before it had become consciously decadent. Both of them again differed from typical Georgian poets, even Georgian poets of the country week-end like Harold Monro, by being consciously metro-politan. The setting of *Prufrock* and *Portrait of a Lady* is the evening party and the drawing-room full of bric-à-brac; the setting of the short poems in Pound's *Lustra* may range from the tea-shop to the art-gallery, but it is a town world, too; and *Hugh Selwyn Mauberley* is a poem, among other things, about London literary politics. Uprooted in a strange setting, and a man full of generous energy, Pound was always whipping into being new literary 'movements' and writing programmes, for instance, for Imagism. In the two Englishmen who had most to do with the critical revolution, Percy Wyndham Lewis and T. E. Hulme, the most notable characteristic, to an outside observer, would probably seem to be a certain violent impatience. A great deal has been said about Hulme as the rediscoverer, for the literary world, of original sin and the notion of man as a finite creature; in fact, his reading was very largely in German art criticism and philosophy. He was a pugnacious person, a militarist who had been sent down from

Oxford for a brawl, and he translated Sorel on violence. It is hard not to see a Nietzschean touch in him, and also in the title of Wyndham Lewis's explosive magazine, *Blast*. These four young men in fact had no philosophy in common; they had in common a youthfully contemptuous attitude towards the living dead.

As a critic, Mr Eliot is more important than Hulme or Pound; and his criticism, in its quieter way, has effected as profound a revolution as his poetry. It is to him that must be attributed the general reaction among English undergraduates for some years (and I allude to undergraduates because, when they go down, they become 'carriers' of shifts of taste to a wider public) against the romantic movement, against the great Victorians, and in favour of 'difficult' poetry generally, whether it is that of Donne or that of Hopkins. To Mr Eliot also must be attributed the current critical questioning of the reputation of Milton. His excellent essays on Dryden and on the poetry of Dr Johnson perhaps largely account for our new sympathy with, and understanding of, the eighteenth century. In a narrower field, the current critical view of the Elizabethan dramatists other than Shakespeare – of Marlowe, Jonson, Middleton, and Tourneur – is largely his view, expanded and qualified. He has written the best short English introduction to Dante, and good essays on two writers whom Englishmen find it hard to get morally to grips with, Pascal and Baudelaire. But he has also (and this in the long run may be even more important) thrown out, in the course of such close and sensitive examinations, a number of suggestive or disturbing ideas – ideas often compressed into a single phrase – which have had a fertilising effect on the work of other critics. Mr Empson has wittily described him as a penetrating and inescapable influence, rather like an east wind.

Some of these ideas are connected with the notions of tradition and originality. For Mr Eliot, an emphasis on the idea of tradition had originally two tactical uses; as an alternative to the romantic emphasis on 'inspiration' and on poetry as the expression of the poet's 'inner being'; and as a clarification of the fact that, in his own poetry, he was not merely making, as his early critics tended to think, a clean break with the past. He wanted to deflect attention from the poet's personality (from the dying Keats or the drowning Shelley) to the poem itself; he wanted to suggest that the poem itself, if it is a good one, fits into, extends and alters a pattern of other existing poems. In a preface to a selection of Pound's earlier work, Mr Eliot points out that a *merely* traditional poet would be an imitator, doing over again what had been done better already, while an *utterly* original poet, who derived literally nothing from his predecessors, would not be able to communicate anything at all. Thus 'the tradition' is a kind of large and changing order which works of literature make among themselves. We might almost think of it as an order in space rather than in time, spread out like a map; for there is a sense in which all great works of literature are eternally contemporary with each other. Thus, if we know more than the ancients, it is because 'they are what we know'; and the importance of the emotions expressed in poetry has relation to an ideal order (the order of emotions properly expressible in poetry), not to the poet's own life.

Eliot, moreover, in his fascinating if faintly perverse essay on *Hamlet* (it is arrogant to dismiss what generation after generation has at least found Shakespeare's most 'interesting' play as a comparative failure), has something even more profound to say about the poetical expression of emotion. Such expression, he thinks, if it is to be poetically effective, cannot be a mere direct statement of subjective feeling; it must be provided with, and ideally at least it should be elicited by, an 'objective correlative.' No phrase of Mr Eliot's has been more discussed by critics, but it may help a little to expand it into simpler English: an 'objective correlative' of an emotion would, in such plainer words, be something actually there corresponding to our feelings, something which our feelings were feelings *about*: and it would be something that would arouse similar feelings in most normally constituted people. Thus what Mr Eliot may have had in mind was that the emotions of poetry should be provided with motives (not just, 'I feel sad,' but, 'I feel sad because ...'), or that the responses of the poet should be responses to a defined situation. The situation may be complex: when Pascal said, 'The eternal silence of these infinite spaces frightens me,' the 'objective correlative' of the emotion he expresses was the universe, but when Paul Valéry said, 'The eternal silence of these infinite spaces does *not* frighten me,' the 'objective correlative' of his more trivial and secondary remark was what Pascal felt about the universe. Eliot may have had in mind also the occasional possibility in poetry of eliciting emotion without directly expressing it, by evoking some situation which by itself arouses emotion:

No, all is hush'd, and still as Death – 'Tis dreadful!
How reverend is the Face of this tall Pile,
Whose ancient Pillars rear their Marble Heads,
To bear aloft its arch'd and pond'rous roof,

By its own Weight made stedfast and immoveable,
Looking Tranquillity. It strikes an awe
And Terror on my aking Sight; the Tombs
And Monumental Caves of Death look cold . . .

Dr Johnson enormously admired these eloquent but rather stilted lines of Congreve's, as they may strike us as being now: and his reason for his admiration, as reported by Boswell, has something in common with Mr Eliot's notion of the 'objective correlative': 'What I mean is, that you can shew me no passage where there is simply a description of material objects, without any intermixture of moral notions, which produces such an effect.' The fact that to a modern reader the passage seems anything but a simple description, and full of 'moral notions' – full of emotive words which help the poet to project into his gothic scene our conventional sentiments about death – shows what a tricky business precise critical judgment is. It is all very well to demand an 'objective correlative' for poetic emotions, but what if in most of the language of poetry (in words here like 'hush'd,' 'stedfast,' 'pond'rous,' 'still,' 'weight,' 'cold,' as well as in the more obviously emotive 'dreadful,' 'awe,' 'terror,' 'tranquillity') our emotions are pretty firmly embodied already? Yet the notion of the 'objective correlative' is very useful if we apply it to a poem of Mr Eliot's own, like *The Waste Land, where the emotions aroused in the reader are not expressed* directly by the poet but must be evoked by the reader's own sense of the complex relationships between various objectively, or at least dramatically, presented and at a first glance almost totally disconnected ideas and images.

Mr Eliot's prose should be read, however, not only for such seminal ideas, or for its admirably acute examinations of particular writers, but also for the general attitude of mind that underlies it. As a censor of the age, Mr Eliot has inherited, with a very different theology, some of the preoccupations of Arnold. But if he is a better pure critic than Arnold, he is perhaps not such an effective critic of general manners. Pamphlets and small books of Mr Eliot's like *After Strange Gods, Thoughts After Lambeth, The Idea of a Christian Society*, and *Notes Towards the Definition of Culture* lack the urgency that makes Arnold's *Culture and Anarchy* for all its faults (flimsiness of construction, padding by repetition, condescension and flippancy, a too genial self-regard) one of the central social documents of its period. Mr Eliot has, indeed, an air of coming to grips with his subject which Arnold, in his elegant airiness, lacks. This appearance is often deceptive. Mr Eliot plays with two senses of the word 'culture,' for instance – culture as mental cultivation, and culture as the general pattern of a society's traditional habits. The two senses are indeed related, but in a more complex fashion than Mr Eliot allows. Boiled cabbage, to use an amusing illustration of Mr Eliot's own, is part of English 'culture,' just as dating or drugstores are part of American 'culture.' But every society that continues to exist will have its habits, good and bad, and to call our habits our culture is no reason for being automatically cheerful about them. And in the intermediate sense of culture (about which writers in *Scrutiny* have had a great deal to say) in which culture means a traditional rhythm of life, fed by, and feeding, higher values, culture may be pretty generally in decline except in small communities like country villages; the modern metropolitan substitute for it (working from above, downwards) may be popular education. More generally, it may be said that while Arnold was the spokesman of a rather formidable central body of opinion, Mr Eliot, when he writes on religious and social topics, is the spokesman of a respectable minority; he speaks for what is no longer, in fact, the conventional educated point of view, but for a point of view which, because of the extraordinary social peace which these islands have enjoyed in this century, can still think of itself as being so. Perhaps to a continental Catholic Mr Eliot's Anglicanism might seem largely a religion of 'good taste' and similarly to a continental Conservative his politics might seem more concerned with keeping façades in repair than with renewing foundations. Perhaps if we are indeed, as Mr Eliot has himself acutely remarked, moving towards a period of 'lower-middle-class culture,' the cruder perceptions of a writer like George Orwell – in his essays on popular fiction, on boys' comic papers, on seaside postcards – may be more in touch with the real roots of contemporary sensibility than Mr Eliot's cautious and dignified rearguard actions.

But there is a final and very important reason for reading Mr Eliot's prose. He is, after all, one of the great artists in prose of our time; an artist even in his evasiveness. His style is a fascinating, sometimes dry and forbidding, but always severely graceful one. It is full of hints and implications, but never becomes curt or breathless. Its sometimes slightly misleading air of precision comes partly from Mr Eliot's frequent anxiety to make clear not quite so much what he does as what he does *not* want to say. There is a decorous subacid wit; and behind the measured and cautious sentences, the enthusiasms ridden on a tight rein, the prejudices politely flaunted, and the insights reduced to formula with scholastic tidiness, one can sense a ranging intelligence and profound sensibility, both habitually stretched to almost painful alertness. No critic of our time respects his readers more. Mr Eliot's *Selected Essays* is one of the few critical works of our time that can be read, with profit, over and over again; at each new reading, one is likely to discover subtleties and emphases previously missed.

Mr Eliot's friend and early mentor, Ezra Pound, is a very different proposition, indeed. Mr Eliot affects a severe decorum even when he is profoundly subverting established views; Pound has an air of rebellious dash even when he is repeating a point that is generally accepted. His style is deliberately abrupt; the reader must put in the links between sentences and paragraphs that often look like jottings from a private note-book. Pound's style is perhaps as typically that of the 'little magazine' as Eliot's is that of some dignified and impersonal organ like *The Times Literary Supplement*. And it is, whether surprisingly or not, the superficially livelier style that wears less well. We become tired of the words in block capitals, the comic misspellings, the faintly factitious heartiness (a poet, too, can be one of the boys and a regular guy), and the schoolboy slang. The flaws in Pound's prose style give us a sense that there are gaps also in his argumentation and even in his sensibility – gaps or intermittences concealed by a kind of violent bluffing. His letters, more continuously readable than his essays, are more humanly profound. They consist largely of detailed technical advice to younger writers, and thus demonstrate the great generosity of his temperament. They show also a practical shrewdness, which from his more formal critical pieces one might not always suspect. He warns a young friend in the 1920s that drunkenness and neurosis are not intrinsically interesting themes for fiction; they spring not from anything fundamental in human nature, but from economic and social anxiety – the roots of that anxiety, on the other hand, *are* interesting. Here, Marxist critics, at odds with Pound about everything else, might agree with him; Mr Eliot, with his firm belief in original sin, and his occasional admiration for rather deliquescent novels, like Djuna Barnes's *Nightwood*, might not.

Pound's general critical method is – apart from an insistence, very useful up to a point for younger critics, on proceeding not by abstract generalisation but by example and particular comment – often a hit-or-miss one. To get the sample on the page is a good idea, but it must be the relevant sample; and to be relevant it must illustrate some specific complex of qualities, and therefore even the critic who seems to be concerned with example and comment entirely has (or ought to have) his generalisations up his sleeve. In a book like Pound's *ABC of Reading* the quotations through the Middle Ages and up say to the early Renaissance seem very well chosen indeed; for Pound has a very clear idea in his head of the complexes of qualities that properly belong to the springtime of literature, to the 'first spritely runnings' of any tradition. But mature developments tend to bore him; the great writers, for Pound, are on the whole the great innovators. Thus his two pages of quotation from, for instance, Alexander Pope, a mature writer if ever there was one, seem chosen almost at random; and the commentary is terse but trite. Perhaps the most alarming comment, however, in this short book, is that on Donne's *Extasie*. Pound is writing about the last four lines which, with the four that precede them, are:

> To'our bodies turn wee then, that so
>   Weake men on love revealed may looke;
> Loves mysteries in souls do grow,
>   But yet the body is his book.
> And if some lover, such as wee,
>   Have heard this dialogue of one,
> Let him still mark us, he shall see
>   Small change, when we'are to bodies gone.

The poem is, very roughly, about the relationship between spiritual and physical love; love is of the spirit but, in human beings, can find its fullest concrete expression only through the body; Monsieur Legouis, rather too cynically, has described the poem not as a straightforward expression of intense feelings but as a sophisticated exercise in the rhetoric of seduction. What is, as I have said, alarming is that Pound seems to miss altogether this central and obvious point; he thinks that 'when we'are to bodies gone' means not, 'when we are engaged in the act of physical love' but 'when we are turned to atoms, when we are dead and dust.' With an affectation of learning, he says Donne would have used 'bodies' for 'atoms'; he should have remembered Donne's *An Anatomy of the World*:

> And freely men confess that this World's spent
> When in the Planets and the Firmament
> They seek so many new; then see that this
> Is crumbled out again to his Atomies . . .

Here, as elsewhere, we find that haste, impatience, a kind of careless arrogance, prevent Pound doing himself justice.

More profoundly, writers of the school of Dr Leavis would accuse Pound of an 'abstract' interest in literary handling as apart from literary substance – technique, from their severe point of view, being interesting only in relation to subject-matter. Pound sometimes seems to consider the art or craft of writing quite without reference to the moral ordering of experience. He thinks of writing as a skill which anyone with certain basic aptitudes can learn. And for Dr Leavis the moral content of Pound's own later writing – the opinions on economics, politics, and so on – tends also to be abstract, to exist precisely at the level of wilful prejudice, of a cranky and sometimes violent 'viewiness,' rather than at that of a deeper ordering of the self. . . . But it is probably hard for any skilful practising poet, writing about poetry, not to write to some extent as a technical specialist. General moral notions are often, at least in our own day, just what such a man cannot handle with pleasure; if he wanted to be a moralist, to discuss human conduct in general terms, he would not aim at the implicit and concrete morality of poetry itself; and technical questions are something which he has, if he is such a notable technician as Pound, a right to be dogmatic about. A fine traditional poet like Laurence Binyon was not ashamed to go to Pound for detailed advice about his translation of Dante; and it was Pound's will, more than Mr Eliot's, that imposed its present shape on The Waste Land. A critic who in a sense 'discovered' writers like Pound and Eliot, and who certainly gave them early practical help and encouragement which nobody else could have given them, cannot be airily dismissed. One can think of plenty of critics who have none of Pound's faults of tone, and taste, and emphasis, and also none of his virtues. He is not a 'sound' critic, in the academic sense, certainly; but he is something more important, a man who has helped good and even great literature to struggle into existence.

Section 3: Other Innovators

Two or three other writers who began to make their reputations in the decade of the First World War contributed, though perhaps in a less fundamental way than Pound and Eliot, to a general shift in the critical attitude. Mr Wyndham Lewis, quite apart from his great reputation as a painter and as a satirical novelist, has a well-deserved fame as a general censor of the age, criticising not only literature but art, philosophy, political orthodoxy. What is perhaps his most important critical volume, *Time and Western Man*, is an extremely vigorous attack on the emphasis in contemporary art and philosophy upon the ideas of change, process, becoming, as reflected in subjective experience, rather than on the ideas of the outward apparent permanence of the visible world and the relation of that world of visible appearances, even in so far as it does change, to eternal being. Lewis, however, is primarily not a metaphysician but an artist; if he postulates, or seems to postulate, eternal being, it is not out of any deep philosophical or still less religious need, but as a kind of hidden support for the artist's world of forms. His favourite philosopher is, probably, Berkeley; and for him, as for the earlier Berkeley, the main practical use of a God is to sustain the permanent miracle of the visible world. Painting and the plastic arts, with their stillness, are for Lewis the types of what all art should be. The art which he hates and fears is music, with its powers of magical dissolution; he also hates and fears, in literature, the kind of modern psychological approach, like that of Miss Gertrude Stein at one level and Proust at another, which seems to destroy the apparent outward unity of personality, the unity of the mask, by dissolving for the introspective mind the basis of that unity into a changing pattern of blind and often trivial impulses. For Lewis, everything that is 'inner' and 'changing' is also dangerous and messy. The true artist should behave as if he were already living in eternity.

Lewis's critical point of view is thus very obviously conditioned by his own technical preoccupations. Music is not necessarily such a dissolvent art as he thinks; it can be concerned with eternal relationships, like those of logic or mathematics. And if a painting or a statue does not move, still the eye moves, taking it in; and it can suggest arrested or incipient motion; and we understand the plastic, as we understand other arts, partly historically, that is, by setting them in a context of changing attitudes and styles. It is Lewis's own practice as a novelist, again, that leads him to set, both in prose and verse, a higher value on satire than has been common among literary critics. It is the fact that he himself has a very elaborate and rich vocabulary for describing outward appearances and physical behaviour that makes him distrust the novelist who emphasises inner motives; and yet a short novel like *Adolphe* or a long one like *Les Liaisons Dangereuses*, in neither of which the appearance of anything is really described, possibly represents a higher art-form than Mr Lewis's own *Apes of God* with its terrific but indigestible accumulations of visual detail. One might suggest, perhaps, that Lewis's critical attitude represents a typically 'male' response to the universe; not a 'sexual' maleness like that of Montherlant, nor a 'militant' maleness like that of Malraux, but a spartan desire to tread 'the mob of the senses' underfoot, and to live by the intellect and the dedicated will. Lewis transcends the cults of the seducer or the soldier, transcends, for instance, Hemingway's hero-worship of bullfighters and boxers, not out of humanitarian qualms, but because these cults are not really 'hard' enough for him. But something like a taste for brutality, however disinfected by the external satirical approach, gives an oddly equivocal flavour to many of his fictions; and when he finds himself, as he sometimes does, betrayed in some of his more general books into an expression of humanitarian sentiment, he seems to feel it necessary at once to balance this weakness by a display of cynical 'realism.' Any tendency, however, on Lewis's part to become deeply involved in activist politics has been corrected by a sense of satire as a universal and non-partisan activity; his little machine-gun post is somewhere in no-man's-land, and can swivel round to spray both sets of trenches, with scornful independence. Perhaps all human activity, except the artist's, is fundamentally ridiculous to him. The human person is comic when, through inner inertia, he behaves like a machine; we are *all* comic most of the time, the standard of seriousness being provided by the rare moments (in the work, say, of a Michelangelo or a Plato) when the potentialities of will and intellect are adequately actualised. Thus 'seriousness' occurs only in the life-history of the major artist or philosopher, and only when these are really functioning as such. A Plato drunk, or sentimental, or amorous, is as comic as the rest of us in such a state.

Mr Lewis therefore (though he distrusts the dogmatic absolutes of politics, of religion, and of most philosophy, and is ready to defend the freedom even of those whom he thinks bad or minor artists on pragmatic grounds) in a sense is a critic of human manners from an absolute or non-human point of view. He does not make his negative points about our behaviour having in view some social standard – like the reason, good sense, order, decorum of the eighteenth century – to which, with not too extravagant an effort, we might all ideally attain. His universe consists, his contemporary universe, at least, of a few imperfect thinkers and artists, of Mr Pound and Mr Eliot, for instance, with whom he is at war on matters of principle, but who do at least tower above their fellows; and a crowd, the rest of us, of inferiors who, however hard they try, are bound to betray the human image in a way that would be pathetic and horrible if Lewis did not choose to transcend pity and disgust in frightening laughter. This approach gives Mr Lewis's critical work an uncommon piquancy, but, if it does not narrow its range of relevance, it certainly narrows its range of appeal. The common man thinks (I myself would say, rightly) of the quality of art of an epoch as both nourishing, and being nourished by, the quality of its ordinary social living. About that quality of ordinary social living Mr Lewis has, for our own time, no hopes; he thinks that things are going to get steadily worse, but that art may survive all the same. Will it, however, matter if it does? If, for instance, prisoners in Belsen still in some cases managed to write poems or draw pictures, that would be an admirable testimony to the resilience of the human spirit; but I do not think the actual *quality* of the poems and pictures would matter much – they would be equally morally admirable, good or bad. But Mr Lewis regards morality – except the morality of the artist, his wish to do, in all circumstances, as good a job as possible – as so much humbug. And if the artist to-day is going to regard ordinary life as merely the dung from which his flowers spring, as unredeemable mud, the common man has enough *amour propre* to be an egoist, too, and to think in times of crisis not of culture's survival but his own.

D. H. Lawrence summed up, perhaps unfairly, Lewis's reaction to the human race in the phrase: 'My God, they stink!' Lawrence himself to Lewis was, on the other hand, a dangerous advocate of 'primitivism,' an enemy of Western values. Yet if we consider Lawrence's critical articles and his brilliant, neglected little book, *Classical American Literature*, we find that the central standard by which Lawrence seems to judge is a classical one: 'Nothing too much.' He attacks the great American writers of the last century for what seems to him one-sided excess. 'Oh,' he says of Poe's decadent romantic eroticism, so obscenely 'spiritual,' 'the indecency of all this intimate talk!' He notes Whitman's greatness but also the sinister side of his cult of immersion in the mass: 'It all slides into death. . . . Death, the last merging, that was the goal of his manhood.' He notes how even the transcendental idealism of New England, which represented at least a dilution of what had been a living Puritan tradition, which sprang unlike Poe's attitude or Whitman's from a remembered 'way of life,' has its morbidities: Hawthorne's characters in his *Blithedale Romance*, anxious self-perfectionists one and all, seem to be 'all going slightly rotten.' And he puts his finger on a central and rather terrifying paradox in the American tradition when he contrasts the smugness of Franklin's moralising:

Imitate Jesus Christ and Socrates,

with the very different smugness of his political realism:

And, indeed, if it be the design of Providence to extirpate these savages in order to make room for the cultivators of the earth, it seems not improbable that rum may be the appointed means.

Yet the essential sanity and balance of Lawrence's criticism are probably hidden from most readers by the peculiarities of his discursive prose. Consider such a passage as this:

And the Holy Ghost is within us. It is the thing that prompts us to be real, not to push our cravings too far, not to submit to stunts and high-falutin, above all not to be too egoistic and wilful in our conscious self, but to change as the spirit inside bids us change, and leave off when it bids us leave off, and laugh when we must laugh, particularly at ourselves, for in deadly earnestness there is always something a bit ridiculous.

We are reminded of the revivalist sermon and of the popular soul-stirring article for the Sunday newspapers (at which, in fact, Lawrence was a dab hand). The colloquialisms are just a little too heartily conscious ('stunts and highfalutin,' 'something *a bit* ridiculous') as in a parson's fireside chat. The unscrupulous use of the theological phrase (not really in any profound, even heretically profound sense, of the theological idea), 'the Holy Ghost' exploits our unwillingness to question irreverently what the preacher is saying; we would question it if Lawrence said (which is more on the lines of what he actually means) that *all* our deep unconscious impulses are healthy and that they can always be tapped as a guide to action. The syntax is similarly sinister; the clauses of the long sentences pile up with a breathless eagerness which, again, is too much of the official eagerness of journalist or evangelist. There is 'art' in this passage, of a rather low-grade popular variety, the imitation of spontaneity; and it is not artfully enough concealed. There is 'thought,' but the key ideas – whatever is meant by 'the Holy Ghost' and whatever is meant by 'to be real' – are glossed over with emotive or inadequate phrases; and whatever is meant by 'the Holy Ghost,' finally, is given a false concreteness by calling it 'the thing,' as if it were a tap, a screw, a gadget we could adjust. But the paradox of this and many similar

309

passages is that these intolerable mannerisms, which so often mask a pretence of wisdom, with Lawrence often mask real wisdom.

Let us try to translate the passage into normal English. We find ourselves faced with much flatter statements certainly, but also with statements that invite a broader agreement:

The deep and sane springs of life are within us. They are whatever it is that prompts us to be true to ourselves, not to be self-deceivers, not to yield ourselves to false enthusiasms or factitious ideals. They are, above all, what prompts us not to concentrate too much on self-centred purposeful willing at the conscious level; but to change as deep impulses tell us to change, and to abandon some project when they tell us to abandon it. These deep impulses, if we are really in touch with them, make us ready to laugh at ourselves; for in "deadly earnestness" there is always something a little absurd.

The passage still invites argument; there are other impulses that lie deep in us than the sane ones; there are those that come to the surface in panic or cruelty; or in the kind of language that Lawrence appropriated all too easily, in our depths we can be possessed by devils as well as touched by grace. Yet the passage does express Lawrence's profound and religious respect for life; and what he attacks most vigorously in his criticism are the excesses that lead to death. In classical American literature, nevertheless, he recognises the life-building forces under a dangerous surface. Whitman's lust for death as the great sea is wrong, since life, not death, for Lawrence is the ultimate; but what is right in Whitman for Lawrence is 'a recognition of souls, all down the open road' – 'the great riches, the great souls.' Again the vocabulary – 'souls,' 'the open road' – smacks of the battered literary ornament, the wayside pulpit; and again the substance of what is being said, within its setting and limits, is profound and sane.

Lawrence did not consciously 'react' against the new critical orthodoxy of Hulme, Pound, and Eliot, the 'new traditionalism' or 'new classicism'; he had no real interest in any of these writers, his own thought was enough for him. But a friend and admirer of Lawrence's, Mr John Middleton Murry, carried on for years a kind of public debate, in his magazine *The New Adelphi*, on behalf of 'romanticism' with the 'classicism' of Mr Eliot; and in the last ten years or so Sir Herbert Read has become, particularly for young poets, a similarly authoritative spokesman of the romantic attitude. Mr Murry's early critical essays are thoughtful, thorough, and sensitive: that on *Coriolanus*, for instance, is perhaps still the best short treatment in English of that puzzling and splendid play. He could be wrong about his contemporaries, as when he dismissed the Yeats of *The Wild Swans at Coole* as a used-up aesthete; but always interestingly and sensitively wrong. Unfortunately, perhaps, his wide range of general interests tended to lead him more and more into dealing with religious and political topics for which he lacked, as he did not lack in dealing with purely literary topics, the philosophical equipment. He had the art of reconstituting both traditional and contemporary beliefs in such a way as both to meet current objections to them and to deprive them, from another point of view, of their *raison d'être*. Thus his followers were presented from time to time with a version of Christianity which left both the divinity of Christ and the actual existence of a God, in any traditional sense, rather doubtful; and with a version of Communism which met the moral objections to that creed by excluding the class struggle and the necessity for revolutionary change. Serious and thoughtful, making a great appeal to the emancipated middle classes, these new creeds were rather like the chassis of an expensive motor-car from which the engine had been quietly removed; they were comfortable to sit in, but would not get you anywhere.

Mr Murry, to some of his critics, has seemed in his intellectual development to tend to move, not quite consciously, from a given position to its opposite. He made a cult of the memory of Lawrence; yet his writings about Lawrence both threw a rather cruel light on the dead man's personality and expressed a radical disagreement with his beliefs. As against Mr Eliot in the 1920s, Mr Murry seemed a man of the Left; as against the fashionable writers of the 1930s, and even more as against such a magazine as *The New Statesman* to-day, he seems a man of the Right. Before and during the last war he was a pacifist; to-day he emphasises with great eloquence the necessity for the military defence of Western Europe. Perhaps the various poles between which he has moved have forced such changes on him by their internal inconsistencies. One cannot call him a 'muddled' writer in the ordinary sense, but it is typical of him, for instance, that when he wants to select a figure to typify the traditions of English liberty he chooses Cromwell, who was a military despot and who is thought of in Ireland at least as a bloody tyrant. In all his explorations, a subtle and sensitive mind has been at work, but without the rigour that derives from a philosophic training or the 'tact of the possible' that comes from immersion in practical affairs. And in the earnest and voluminous publicist the acute and sensitive young critic has almost vanished; one might almost cite Mr Murry as an example for critics of the dangers of too much 'thinking,' or at least of too much thinking at large.

Sir Herbert Read, like Mr Murry, is much concerned with general ideas; but he handles ideas, on the whole, with less of the preacher's unction and more of the professional touch. His main interest as a critic has always been less in communicating the specific quality, as he finds it, of some work of art or literature than in examining the pattern of ideas that gives rise to a general literary movement. His book on Wordsworth, for instance, is excellent both on Wordsworth's personal history—including his reactions to the French Revolution and his affair with Annette Vallon – and on the sources of Wordsworth's thought in philosophers like Hartley; what one does not recall from it are the remarks on individual poems. Similarly, his famous essay, *In Defence of Shelley*, directed against the depreciation of that poet by Arnold and by Mr Eliot, contains a profound examination, based on the latest findings of modern psychology, of Shelley's temperament; it demonstrates cogently that Shelley being the sort of person he was would write the sort of poetry he did. It does not really answer the case of those who still find themselves unable to like the person or the poetry.

Sir Herbert has a much greater interest than any of the critics we have previously mentioned in groups, movements, and trends. There can be few modern ideologies, from Marxism to Surrealism, and from Surrealism to Existentialism, in which he has not discovered some sympathetic and positively valuable aspects; similarly with all schools of painting from pure Abstraction to German Expressionism. With his gift for grasping leading ideas, Sir Herbert in fact is essentially a philosophic critic. But where the great philosophers, like Descartes or Spinoza, have sought to construct their universes out of as *few* leading ideas as possible – the 'beauty' of a philosophic system consisting in its economy – Sir Herbert, with his genial wide-ranging hospitality, seeks to welcome as *many* as possible. This wide and fluid receptiveness to some extent robs his lucid prose of personal flavour; it is, for many of us, mainly the transparent medium through which we apprehend the newest notions. Perhaps also when, as in his essay on Surrealism, he equates classicism with tyranny and romanticism with freedom, we should make allowances for a man with a natural gift for the manifesto's making all that is rhetorically possible out of his case. At other times, as in his admirable essays on Hopkins, Bagehot, Benda, or Froissart, Sir Herbert shows that he understands that both 'romanticism' and 'classicism' are at the worst labels and at the best banners. His own work, whether in prose or verse, never lacks a discipline and a sensitive severity which belong to 'the classical tradition' in the broader sense. His mind is orderly, whether that order is imposed or spontaneous; and the whole current discussion about 'romanticism' and 'classicism' is really, perhaps, a debate on whether the order of art should be imposed or spontaneous; a debate which ignores the fact that iambic pentameter couplets come 'naturally' to a poet like Roy Campbell and that the free verse of Pound has, just as obviously, been 'worked on.' To write in words, in sentences, in a regular grammar, with some regard for what one has read already, for what the language is, is to accept an 'imposed' order; and the poets of the greatest romantic period, Coleridge, Wordsworth, Byron, Shelley, Keats, expressed themselves 'spontaneously' in sometimes very elaborate forms. But Sir Herbert is at his best as a critic when he gets away from doctrinal presuppositions; and yields himself, instead, to the admirable candour and sincerity of the motions of his own mind.

Section 4: The Bloomsbury Tradition

If the group of critics considered in the last two sections can be thought of as having, over a long period, effected a rather massive revolution in general literary taste, the group we are now to examine – the Bloomsbury group and their spiritual heirs – can be said for the last twenty or thirty years to have presided over many of the more rapid and superficial shifts of literary fashion. Even to-day the tone and manner of the reviews in the greater English literary weeklies – in *The New Statesman*, the *Observer*, or the *Sunday Times*, though not to anything like the same degree in the graver pages of *The Times Literary Supplement* – is often in its essence the Bloomsbury tone and manner. It is, of course, among other things, a more *amusing* tone and manner than that, say, of Mr Eliot, Mr Murry, or Sir Herbert Read; it has a lightness and gaiety that lend themselves excellently to the purposes of literary journalism; it does not need, as more heavyweight types of criticism often do, a great deal of space in which to turn.

When one thinks of the Bloomsbury tradition one thinks first of all of the 1920s, and of a group of critics of whom the most important, in relation to pure literature, were probably Mrs Woolf, Mr E. M. Forster, and the late Lytton Strachey; though as a writer on art the late Roger Fry showed more original and profound critical gifts than any of these. Literary journalists like the late Sir Desmond MacCarthy and Mr

Raymond Mortimer could be considered as outlying members of this group; and in a younger generation their tradition is carried on by Mr Cyril Connolly. Mr V. S. Pritchett and Mr Edwin Muir are two very different critics and reviewers of books who rather stand out, among the leading figures in English literary journalism, by *not* belonging to the Bloomsbury tradition. But before we deal with particular names we ought perhaps to attempt to describe, if not to define, that tradition in general terms itself.

The Bloomsbury tradition has been criticised from two respectable points of view, that of the sturdy lowbrow and of the real stern and unbending highbrow. In common parlance, say in a saloon bar, the epithet 'Bloomsbury' still connotes something like 'la-di-da, high-falutin, above the plain man's head'; even though the rather battered and shabby Bloomsbury of the years since the war is no longer a centre for any writers as wealthy, as successful, or as exclusive as Mrs Woolf and her friends. On the other hand, the attitude of D. H. Lawrence, on being introduced to Lord Keynes and his circle at Cambridge – and Keynes was in a sense the moral centre of the brisk, fastidious Bloomsbury of the 1920s – was not profoundly different; he found in them a sterile and aggressive cleverness, what Keynes himself was retrospectively to describe as a 'brittleness' of tone. In dealing with the novels of Mrs Woolf and Mr Forster, I have already referred to the general philosophical standpoint of this group. In a sense, and to put it very crudely indeed, they were belated upper-middle-class Victorian agnostics, consciously emancipating themselves from Victorian puritanism. At the conscious level, they rejected both traditional religious belief and conventional moral standards; but in a sense also, and again very crudely indeed, it was safe for them to do so, since they had inherited both the instinctive decorum and restraint and even, in the case of Lord Keynes at least, the strenuous public spirit of their class. Morally, as well as financially, they could live on the interest from their inherited capital. Lawrence reacted against them because he knew he would have to accumulate his moral capital for himself. He could not afford to be irreverent as they were, or at least not to be irreverent in their way. He felt the deep need, which they did not feel, for some kind of religion; and he did not perceive that what struck him as their petty and malicious discriminations about conduct sprang from a kind of unconscious religion, too.

It was the religion of the good life, derived from G. E. Moore; of the good life as consisting of affectionate and pleasurable but discriminating personal relationships, and of the enjoyment of natural beauty and works of art; everything else was either an illusion, like religion in any more orthodox sense, or machinery, like economics and politics. To the outer observer, this religion of the good life was perhaps hard to distinguish from a refined but complacent hedonism; and the sense which the Bloomsbury group very strongly had of being a distinguished set, of 'there being really no one else,' may have encouraged them to adopt, as their habitual mode of address to the outsider, a flippant or ironic condescension. On the other hand, the sense of writing for an appreciative small group, that would pick up their points without these having to be laboured, does give their work a grace and ease. Mrs Woolf and Lytton Strachey, the two most prominent literary critics of the group, had neither the taste for close examination of literary texts nor the aptitude for very profound general theorising. They could, however, unlike some deeper and duller writers, communicate their own enjoyment. And they used their narrative gifts, within the critical essay, to recreate a personality, a scene, an atmosphere. We remember portraits from their essays rather than judgments. Mrs Woolf was better at light and shade, at suggesting an ambience; Strachey at the bold flat outline, verging on caricature.

Strachey is at his worst, however, when he relapses completely into caricature, indulging in silly exaggeration and simplification for their own sakes, and in a parody of his own better manner. His Leslie Stephen lecture on Pope, for instance, exemplifies almost everything in the Bloomsbury approach that raises the hackles of readers so different as D.H. Lawrence, Dr Leavis, and the plain man in the pub. Alexander Pope, a great and unhappy poet, with an unusual capacity for resentment but also for affection, with a profoundly complex sensibility to the whole life of his time, is caricatured by Strachey as a malignant monkey spooning hot lead from a window on casual passers-by; and at this repulsive image we are supposed to titter and say, 'How amusing!' Moreover, all the subtleties of Pope's verbal art within a medium that, like the tight swaddlings into which he was bound every day, at once constricted and upheld him are reduced by Strachey to the mere mechanism of the medium itself: to the heroic couplet when that contains four phrases divided into two antitheses. Such couplets, of course, have special uses; they clinch a passage; if all Pope's couplets had been of this type, the result would be, as it is not, intolerably monotonous; and moreover anyone who takes a little pains can produce a few couplets of this sort. What is exasperating is that Strachey does insist throughout his lecture on Pope's greatness; and yet he leaves us to suppose that the main constituents of that greatness are a petty malignancy of attitude and a mechanical adroitness in versifying. It will not do. . . . But it is unfair to judge Strachey as a critic on the strength of such lapses. On French literature in particular, he could speak with knowledge and taste. Nobody has written better in English on Voltaire and such a distinguished judge as Gide found admirable qualities in his essay on Racine, even though he felt that Strachey could have chosen his quotations better. It is certainly almost the first essay in our language to make the common reader aware that Racine was a great poet. More widely, if there are things about which Strachey seems shallow and flippant, there are also real values – those of liberty in general, of intellectual sincerity, of the free play of the intellect – which he has very much at heart. He is a consistent writer.

Mr E. M. Forster's occasional critical essays, and his short book on the novel, are a minor part of his work. They have the modesty and charm of all his writing, but the limitations of the Bloomsbury attitude can be seen both in his rejection, from a too narrowly 'civilised' point of view, of Joyce's *Ulysses* and in his acceptance of Mr Eliot's early poems on the same basis as Firbank's novels, as pleasantly independent escapist literature, the raising of 'the private voice' in crude times of war. For Mrs Woolf similarly both *The Waste Land* and even *Ulysses*, such a much more massive creation than any of her own, were chiefly interesting as illustrations of a tendency towards the 'fragmentary' in modern literature. One might say that as critics both Mrs Woolf and Mr Forster are at their best when dealing with figures of moderate size; Mrs Woolf, indeed, can distil a small work of art out of books that are not themselves works of art at all – old diaries, old letters, or a rambling and padded biography like Captain Jesse's *Life of Brummell*. The Bloomsbury group hated the ponderous and the obvious and it is difficult to deal with the major figures of literature – with Homer, or Milton, or Shakespeare, or Dante, or Tolstoy – without repeating respectfully a great deal that many worthy persons have said before one. Minor figures gave writers like Strachey and Mrs Woolf and Mr Forster a better scope for their wit and humour, for their gift of oblique self-revelation. They were writing, after all, neither for undergraduates nor professors but for their own sort of *honnête homme*; and it is ponderous and obvious, indeed, to blame them for failing at another sort of critical task which they never attempted.

What they offered in fact was pleasant, vivid, and cultivated conversation about literature: not academic 'sound approaches' or new lines for research. That was why their approach, stretched a little wider and thinner, lent itself so admirably to the purposes of literary journalism. Sir Desmond MacCarthy resembled Mr Forster in the conversational ease of his tone, less precious than Mrs Woolf's, less mannered than Lytton Strachey's. He could not write on any subject from George Meredith to a boxing-match without making it charming; and the charm is never forced. In his case, again, his portraits of persons, such as Samuel Butler or Lord Asquith, are on the whole more memorable than his particular literary judgments. Of all literary journalists writing now, perhaps Mr Raymond Mortimer has most of Sir Desmond's tone; the same charm, the same quiet air of authority, and the same gift for saying a great deal in a short space without the appearance of hurry and congestion. Like Sir Desmond, who published such volumes of selected essays as he did mainly at the instance of his friends, Mr Mortimer seems to have no great desire to produce books. His one volume of selected pieces, *Channel Packet*, is a delightful but a slim one.

Mr Cyril Connolly as a critic stands somewhere between the Bloomsbury tradition and that of the young 'socially conscious' writers of the 1930s. His partly autobiographical *Enemies of Promise* deals vividly with the dangers to the young writer of commercialism, the pursuit of fashion, marriage, bohemianism, and hack work. His volume of critical essays, *The Condemned Playground*, has a bitter melancholy and a boyish high spirit that, in combination, are peculiarly his own. Some of his best criticisms have been in the form of parody: of the typical post-undergraduate autobiography or of Mr Aldous Huxley enlivening a mildly erotic narrative with reflections on mysticism and extracts from his wide reading in the *Encyclopædia Britannica*. Mr Connolly's book of short sentences, short paragraphs, and quotations, *The Unquiet Grave*, reveals more than any of his strictly critical essays the range and sound taste of his reading: particularly in the great French moralists and the great Latin poets. It is also an astonishingly honest and effective portrait of a temperament, and perhaps the most readable bedside book of our time. But it does show the collapse of the religion of the good life into a rather melancholy and remorseful hedonism. And it is notable that in Mr Connolly's work (apart from an acute essay on A. E. Housman, who hardly represents 'greatness' in the sense that I have in mind) it is perhaps, as with the Bloomsbury group generally, impossible to find a really good essay on a really great writer.

Has the Bloomsbury tradition come to a dead end, then, as *The Unquiet Grave* might suggest, in something like self-pity and self-regard? Mr Connolly's brisk, combative temperament, and his searching honesties with himself, make him, in fact, a more inspiring writer than such a criticism would suggest. Like the earlier writers of the Bloomsbury tradition, he feels that he has a complex set of duties towards his readers, which includes the duty of keeping them amused. His magazine *Horizon* had not only a very wide cultural range, it was more consistently readable (even on, say, a long and tiring train journey) than most such magazines are; so that those young writers who reacted violently against him may seem to have been claiming, among other things, the right to be bores. Some great and serious literature, however (parts, for instance, of Tolstoy, of George Eliot, of Wordsworth, of Walter Scott) *is* sometimes boring. The quality of amusingness *can* sometimes be bought at too high a price. Readers are likely to go back to the Bloomsbury group for their wit, ease, and charm. They may nevertheless feel that the Bloomsbury approach does not and cannot offer us criticism of the most ambitious kind – criticism as theory and method, as elucidation of structure, as the raising of fundamental questions about the values of life. The next group of critics we are to consider, those of the new Cambridge school, often lack wit, ease, and charm; one of the most distinguished and influential figures among them, Dr Leavis, writes in a quite peculiarly awkward and contorted prose, and has a manner, in rebuking other critics, of disagreeable acerbity. Dr Richards, another leading critic of the new Cambridge tradition, can write exceedingly memorable sentences and even paragraphs but is on the whole too much taken up with the complicated things he is saying to bother much consciously about superficial graces of style. Mr Empson, the third important Cambridge critic we shall be dealing with, writes beautifully witty and sinewy conversational prose, but is usually saying things so new and difficult that he exacts a painful effort of attention. It is not exactly for ease and charm that we turn to these three writers; but we do turn to them for something which perhaps on the whole the Bloomsbury tradition does not offer us, original and creative thought.

Section 5: The New Cambridge Tradition

Bloomsbury itself had its moral roots in Cambridge; but it is of a newer school, of Dr Leavis and Dr Richards, and of disciples of theirs like Mr Empson, that we think when we speak of the Cambridge tradition of criticism now. Of the two greater English universities, Oxford has always been the home of the Tory and Cambridge of the Whig tradition; and in philosophy, Oxford has on the whole been the home of speculation (as with the neo-Hegelian Oxford idealists of the last century), and Cambridge of analysis (as with Sidgwick and Moore). Thus we associate the Oxford of the nineteenth century first with the High Anglicanism of Newman and then with the neo-Hegelianism of Bradley; the associations of Cambridge are rather first with Evangelical Christianity and then with the agnosticism of Leslie Stephen and the analytical approach to ethics of Sidgwick. These broad differences may have something to do with the facts that Greek and Latin literature had traditionally a central place in Oxford studies, mathematics in those of Cambridge. Oxford was the home of faith, imagination, 'lost causes'; Cambridge of 'honest doubt,' the politics of common sense, and hard, dry reasoning. Oxford again was traditionally closely linked with metropolitan culture, with London publishing, politics, and fashionable life; Cambridge was more a world by itself. Yet, paradoxically, in spite or because of these facts, Cambridge rather than Oxford has traditionally been the nursery of English poets: of Milton, Gray, and Wordsworth, to mention no other names. In our own time, the traditional interest in poetry in Cambridge, the prestige there of scientific method, the agnosticism, the unfashionableness (or the proud indifference to fashion), and a certain puritan earnestness in the atmosphere of the place may have all combined to make this city the home of innovations in critical method.

With an expert training in psychology, and a special interest in language as a system of communication, it was, at least, a Cambridge don, Dr I. A. Richards, who first, early in the 1920s, became interested in what light a strictly scientific approach could throw on the nature of poetry. Two questions particularly interested him. Firstly, what is the relationship of the kinds of statement poetry seems to make to the kinds of statement that a scientific student of language believes to be true or possibly true? Secondly, what exactly is the difference, not in terms of the poem itself, but in terms of what happens to us when we read it, between a 'good' poem and a 'bad' one? His answer to the second question was more speculative than his answer to the first. It rested on the idea of the human psyche as a fairly loose self-balancing system of impulses which seeks to satisfy as many of these competing impulses as is logically possible. (An 'impulse' consists of the sort of response to a stimulus which finally transforms itself into overt action.)

A 'satisfactory' balance of 'impulses' is one which allows play to as many as possible, thus producing a sense of well-being, while at the same time leaving the psyche in a free and flexible state, readily responsive to new situations. An 'unsatisfactory' balance is one which owing to a sort of jamming of the machinery at some points – to 'local fixations' – leads in the long run to a sense of ill-being and to a failure to respond except along certain customary channels. A good poem is one which helps to induce a satisfactory balance, or which evokes a satisfactory 'attitude' – an attitude that is not necessarily an attitude *to* anything, or connected with any beliefs about the outer world.

Dr Richards in fact tended to think of the outer universe (as the practising scientist must) as ethically neutral; not a materialist in the ordinary sense, he was not an idealist or a theist either. His problem was how to preserve 'good' states of being when these had lost their traditional theological or metaphysical sanctions; and he did not accept Moore's idea of treating the notion of 'good' itself as a last indefinable non-natural ultimate. It might be, but the job of the suasive psychologist was to describe in rough and general, but in principle at least not in unscientific terms, the kinds of balance of impulse in the psyche that he himself or people generally felt to be 'good' or even merely satisfactory; and whose satisfactoriness had the further positive advantage of leading to readiness to adapt. One difficulty of the theory, as Dr Richards discovered when he tested the responses of undergraduates to poetry, is that it takes a good deal of training of the average reader to induce him either to evoke this 'satisfactory attitude' (to turn, as it were, an unclogged attention to poetry, to read it with a properly directed intelligence and a free yet alert sensibility) and also perhaps to *recognise* it when it is evoked. The first effect of good art on people who are used to commercial art is, as everyone knows, not in fact to make them feel satisfied but to make them feel uncomfortable. Dr Richards's undergraduates, whose responses he records in *Practical Criticism*, were not quite at this level, they had no instinctive hostility to poetry as such; but they projected into their reading their 'local fixations' and their 'stock responses.' Many readers in fact have not enough self-discipline, are not good enough at excluding arbitrary and irrelevant associations, to be able to produce even a schematic summary of what any moderately complex poem is 'about.'

But what *is* a poem 'about'? Here, Dr Richards leaves the field of psychology for that of language as a means of communication. He notices that many mathematicians find it impossible to read poetry because the kind of statements a poet makes for them have no sense; he himself feels sure that poetry does not make sense in the way scientific prose does. Nevertheless we can read poems profitably not so much for what they say to us – not so much for some abstract meaning that they can leave behind, some 'message' – as for what they can do to us. The language of poetry is emotive; it aims not at describing states of affairs and suggesting practical ways of dealing with them but at evoking complex attitudes. The value of these attitudes to us is something quite separate from any beliefs of the poet, about God or the universe, with which they may be associated. With the positivistic bias of his own philosophy, Dr Richards feels that most beliefs poets are likely to have are likely to be false; and he praises Mr Eliot for producing in *The Waste Land* a poem apparently divorced from *all* beliefs. Theologies, mythologies, metaphysical systems, fairy stories – God, the White Goddess, Fate, the witch on her broomstick – are all for him equally metaphorical projections of states of mind. It is within ourselves, quite literally within the surfaces of our own mortal bodies, that Heaven and Hell exist. But the old notions should not be rejected, for all that, as so much unscientific lumber. They are the poet's properties, they are what he uses to do what the scientist cannot do. The scientist can, perhaps, make true general statements – true so far as they go, in a context – about the universe, but they have no emotive value. Our inner emotional states, which we cannot help relating to the outer universe, *are* on the other hand valuable in themselves – as they are rich and coherent, or muddled and frustrating. And poetry by falsely seeming to make a link between these inner states and the nature of the universe can help to produce in us, at a pardonable cost in suspended disbelief or momentary imaginative self-deception, the kind of valuable inner states that the poet himself started with. We must learn to cherish what poetry can do for us while no longer (except perhaps, if it is that sort of poem, while we are reading) expecting the poet to provide us with valid generalisations or true facts. Of course the Moon never kissed Endymion, but what does it matter? Poetry for Dr Richards is thus to some extent a substitute for religion – not for the dogmas but for the practice of religion – in evoking satisfactory conditions of mind; but without linking these up, as religion does, or may do, to misleading notions about the nature of the universe.

There are obvious criticisms to be made both of the theory of the good poem as producing a satisfactory balance of impulses and of the

11

theory of poetic language as mainly, or primarily, emotive. The most obvious criticism of the impulse theory is that it is very pretty but that there is no way, so far, of testing whether it is true. I may have an almost infinite number of impulses – I may be exposed to a thousand tiny stimulations and make or check a thousand tiny unconscious responses to them – every moment of my life. Good poems *may* in fact – it sounds very plausible – produce a satisfactory balance of impulses in the proper reader. There seems, however, to be no way in which we can assure ourselves that they do so. We cannot count our impulses or weigh them up against each other. If a poem pleases us, we *may* be yielding to lazy stock responses or even to vicious habits (the taste for some kinds of poetry, Verlaine perhaps, might be like a taste for liqueurs, and that for some other kinds, like the cruder Kipling, like a taste for raw spirits). If, on the other hand, a poem depresses us or puzzles us, we may, because of some local fixation, be simply failing to apprehend it properly. When we are genuinely in doubt about a poem, we check, at least, our responses by examining *the poem* more carefully; not the poem by examining *our responses*. It is true, of course, as Dr Richards would point out, that we cannot examine the poem *in itself*; but only this instance of ourselves reading it. It remains true, however, that, when we are puzzled, an attention to syntax, to metre, to the relevant application of particular words that worry us in the poem, and perhaps to other poems of a comparable sort, is always more useful than an attention to our own state. Our own state always contains so much that is not relevant.

The question of the primarily emotive nature of poetic language is a more complicated one. Dr Richards seems to be making a distinction between a scientific view of the world, which is knowledge, and various theological, mythological, or metaphysical views which may be very valuable as metaphors expressing obscure truths about ourselves but which are not knowledge but belief (and *as* literal belief, probably false and fantastic). But there is a kind of philosophy like Hume's or Santayana's for which scientific knowledge itself must be based on belief, an 'animal faith' in the existence of the outer universe. We cannot prove logically that the universe exists, or even that our own bodies do. Life might be, what Pascal described it as, a slightly less inconsistent dream. We cannot, certainly, for practical purposes help believing in the reality of the physical world and of human society; but then some theologians might say that we cannot help, either, at least *taking into account* the possibility of the existence of a

God (or of a Transcendent Unconditioned Ground of Being), with all that this possibility logically implies. And the kind of deductions that can be made from that possibility, accepted as a hypothesis, such theologians would describe not as belief but as knowledge, and moreover as a higher kind of knowledge than natural science. Similarly, for other thinkers, the moral philosophers, the world of values, of the good, of evil, of right and wrong, of human freedom and responsibility, is not merely a translation into emotive language of facts about psychological balance but again a matter about which knowledge, though difficult, is possible. And again they would claim it is a higher kind of knowledge than natural science; it is more important to know what is the right thing for a man to do in given circumstances than whether the earth moves round the sun, or the sun round the earth.

Thus the scientist has in a sense to be a believer – in 'this pragmatical, preposterous pig of a world, its farrow that so solid seem'; and the believer, if he tries to think about his beliefs, has to pursue a method that has much in common with that of science – his hypotheses about the nature of God, of the soul, of moral obligation, will, if stated precisely enough, entail consequences as rigorous as any generalisations from laboratory experiments or observation of the natural world. And it may be said also that the picture of the world that science offers us does not seem completely coherent or self-explanatory in itself, but invites us to reason beyond it; however elaborately and accurately we are told that things are so, we can and do still ask, 'Why are they so?' or, 'Is it just or right that they should be so, and why?' It is at least a still unsettled question whether, when we ask the question 'why,' we are not asking a rational question at all but merely seeking to settle some subjective emotional disturbance.

The theory that the language of poetry is mainly emotive can, however, be attacked from another more technical point of view. An emotive statement in the strictest sense would be a statement *merely* aiming at expressing and evoking emotion: an 'O, alas!' or to take a less strict example,

O Sophonisba, Sophonisba O!

The latter example is not 'pure,' because we are presumed to know something about Sophonisba; our emotion is relevant to an imagined situation, and that, in its turn, is typical of a class of real situations. A poem, in fact, generally does provide the reader with information of some sort, even if only information about a fictitious world. And the elements of our fictions, if these are to be communicable, cannot be fundamentally different from the elements of our facts. We can invent centaurs, but we are familiar with men and horses, and we associate the horse with ideas of primitive grace, nobility, and fierceness. The question, so often discussed, about whether we can enjoy Dante if we do not believe in the existence of his Heaven and Hell is a rather futile one. We should have a very sketchy notion of the Christian Hell and Heaven *without* Dante; and so far is the detail of his language from being merely emotive that we can draw a map of his supernatural regions and trace his itinerary through them. Nothing again could be more solidly physical than the Ptolemaic universe, the universe of so much poetry up to and beyond the Renaissance, though it happens not to exist. The poet, in other words, makes imaginative constructions which may be based on ultimate religious beliefs about the universe or premature scientific generalisations about it; but in their detail and structure these must depend on his experience of the world around him. There is nothing else *for* them to depend on. It does not matter very much that the poet's statements about his world are not 'true' as scientific statements are 'true' (though in descriptive poetry about nature, or in analytic poetry about typical states of mind, they may be almost 'true' in this sense). Homer's gods, let us agree, never existed; but it is still true at a higher scientific level than that of physical science (at the level of anthropology, say) that they were taken as existing; and it is true from the literary critic's point of view that their conduct is understandable on a human model, if we can imagine human beings with magical powers of transformation and levitation and exempt from pain and death. Similarly, Dante's Hell may not exist, but if it did, the various kinds of punishment that he invents for various kinds of sin would be dramatically appropriate. The truth of poetry is not a truth to particular ascertained physical facts but a truth to general and profound human experience. Imaginary worlds have their own kind of reality, and this is what it is.

Dr Richards's practice as a critic has, in fact, been strangely at odds with his more general theories. In what is still perhaps his most useful book for young readers, *Practical Criticism*, he does not emphasise either the complexities of inner balance or the emotive nature of poetic language so much as the necessity, if we are to read a poem properly, of attending closely to its sense. One moral of that fine book seems to be that young readers would discriminate better if they read a poem with a detached yet concentrated attention, as they might read a page of philosophy: not seeking directly and primarily for emotional stimulation, but rather for the connection of the poet's thoughts. These thoughts are certainly not the thoughts of the modern physical scientist. The Wild West Wind is not the breath of Autumn's being; Autumn has not, or is not, a 'being' in this sense, and if it had or were 'the breath' is not 'the soul,' and perhaps from Dr Richards's point of view 'the soul' itself, even in man, is a prescientific fiction. Shelley is thinking, or for rhetorical purposes pretending to think, 'primitively.' But it would be wrong to say that he is not thinking at all. All abstract ideas, after all, have their basis in this kind of concrete outer embodiment of inner states. Our words for mental functions are all originally physical metaphors: 'comprehension' is a grasping of things into a set, 'apprehension' a grasping of them towards one. One thing the poet does is to revive in us a gift for making primitive unifying and embodying gestures of this sort. And he does not perhaps either so much directly convey a pure abstract emotion or describe a pure abstract situation (for an abstract emotion is rootless, and an abstact situation is almost by definition one in which we do not feel ourselves emotionally involved) as issue almost a series of commands or directions which enable us, if he is skilful and we are alert enough, to put ourselves through the motions that he has been going through, and feel what he has felt. The language of poetry, compared to all other uses of language, has a kind of peremptory authority. In reading a poem successfully we recreate the 'poetic experience' it embodies (except that it is false to abstract one of these, except at the preliminary stages of our appreciation, from the other).

Thus, poetry, even if its ultimate purpose is some kind of emotional release, some kind of psychic therapy, requires an effort of intellectual attention – an effort, comparable, at a lower level, to the effort required in prayer to exclude irrelevant factors – as intense as any we know. It is wrong to be too eager to get beyond the 'prose sense' of a poem, even if that feels at first dull or fantastic, to the emotional rewards it may offer, just as it is wrong to be too eager to get beyond the strain, the feeling of making a formal or empty offering, the sense almost of dereliction which may accompany prayer, to the sense of spiritual comfort which may succeed prayer. In both cases, the great danger is that of cheating, of providing the emotional rewards or the spiritual comfort (or a simulacrum of them) oneself. A poem causes us to make real to ourselves, or in ourselves, a sequence of spiritual acts, or to embody a situation for ourselves; and that situation must be at once particularised enough to seem at least ideally actual, and sufficiently an instance of a wide and various class of situations to have general human relevance.

It is on this aspect of Dr Richards's teaching, the necessity of close attention to 'what the poem says,' that his most brilliant disciple, Mr William Empson, has concentrated his attention. Mr Empson's first critical book, *Seven Types of Ambiguity*, was an attempt to analyse the kind of statements we find in poems as closely and even as captiously as the historian of thought, for instance, might examine statements by Pascal or Hume. Such examinations of sentences and paragraphs in great thinkers generally aim at discovering some fundamental inconsistency, of which the thinker himself is unaware. Mr Empson was similarly looking for the sort of basic ambivalence in poetic thinking that might display itself, almost unconsciously, in the detail of his language. He noticed that Wordsworth, for instance, torn between a naturalistic pantheism, a more humanistic theory that the 'life' of nature is a projection of our own deep emotions, and the necessity of not saying anything that would conflict too sharply with Christian orthodoxy (for which God infinitely transcends Nature, thus making Wordsworth's apprehension of a unifying spirit *in* Nature a mysticism that has mistaken its object), managed unconsciously, by a tactfully muffled use of language, to mask these divisions from himself and his readers:

> . . . a sense sublime
> Of something far more deeply interfused,
> Whose dwelling is the light of setting suns,
> And the round ocean, and the living air,
> And the blue sky, and *in* the mind of man,
> A motion and a spirit, that impels
> All thinking things, all objects of all thought,
> And rolls through all things.

The key word in that passage is the tiny word, which I have italicised, 'in': the key question is whether we take the phrase, insulated by commas, 'and in the mind of man,' with what precedes it or with what follows it. Mr Empson examines the passage like a lawyer examining a brief. Wordsworth may be contrasting the spirit that *seems to be* immanent in outer nature with the spirit that *is* immanent in man and leads him to project his life into outer nature. But if the 'something far more deeply interfused' dwells indifferently in outer nature and the human mind, 'under this less fortunate arrangement' –

though it does assure Wordsworth that his feelings about Nature are not a hallucination – 'a God who is himself nature subjects us at once to determinism and predestination.' There were critics of Mr Empson who considered this kind of approach to great poetry mean and fussy; but in a sense Mr Empson shows his respect for poets by taking what they say seriously and expecting it to cohere.

Yet a much more coherent point of view than Wordsworth's, the orthodox Christian point of view of the seventeenth century, need not exclude these equivocal effects. Mr Empson quotes from George Herbert's poem about the crucifixion, *The Sacrifice* (the dying Christ on the cross is speaking):

> But now I die; Now, all is finishèd.
> My woe, man's weal; and now I bow my head:
> Only let others say, when I am dead,
>   Never was grief like mine.

The intended sense is almost certainly: 'Let others admit, once I am dead, that there never was such a grief as mine is now.' But because of the ambiguity of indirect speech in English we can also take it: 'Let others as well as myself say, once I am dead, "Never was grief like mine."' Christ is our Judge as well as our Redeemer. Thus the possible secondary meaning is relevant: 'Let those whom even the Redemption will not redeem, whom I came to save but whom I shall have to judge, admit that no fate could be more terrible than theirs!' Another very striking stanza, which Mr Empson quotes without detailed comment, has again, whether consciously or not, the same implications:

> Between two theeves I spend my utmost breath,
> As he that for some robberie suffereth.
> Alas! what have I stolen from you? Death:
>   Was ever grief like mine?

'Death' with that punctuation (I notice that in Mr Auden's and Professor Pearson's *Poets of the English Language*, after 'Death' there is not a colon but the less dramatic full stop) sounds not so much like an answer to a question as like an imprecation. There is bitterness in it. Christ, by dying, has robbed us of death. *Therefore* we are angry with him, we treat him as a robber. For if the death which he has robbed us of shut us out from the hope of bliss it also freed us from the fear of torment. Thus Mr Empson, by what at a first reading might look like a frivolous or trivial attention to verbal niceties, can display the basic ambiguities as reflected in poetry, of a massively coherent human attitude, like that of the orthodox Christian. The poet has his own kind of honesty and cannot help showing us, as the writer of a prose dogmatic treatise or an edifying sermon might not, the reverse of the medal.

Mr Empson's second volume, *Some Versions of Pastoral*, dealt with this kind of ambiguity on a larger scale, as it displays itself in drama or epic. The American title of this volume, *English Pastoral Poetry*, is singularly misleading, for pastoral poetry in the strict sense (Spenser's *Shepherd's Calendar*, or Milton's *Lycidas*, or Pope's pastorals or Thomson's or Arnold's *Thyrsis*) is one of the few subjects on which an extraordinarily widely ranging survey does not touch. The notion of the pastoral mode is used by Mr Empson in a wide and elastic sense to cover every attempt in literature to deal with complex issues through ideal simplification: and the mode also involves a certain nostalgia in those who use it for simplicity, primal energy, or innocence. But the pastoral mode, in this wide sense, may be also used for covert criticism of established values. Thus Falstaff is a pastoral figure who suggests doubts about the heroic values of the action that goes on around him – both about the dashing, short-sighted, attractive heroism of Hotspur and the calculating patriotic machiavellianism of Prince Hal. Milton, asserting that the various classical paradises, which he evokes in long similes with nostalgic vividness, were *less* beautiful than the Garden of Eden expressed the secret hankering of the educated Puritan after Renaissance paganism. Gay, in *The Beggar's Opera*, uses the comic pastoral mode not only for fairly open criticism of contemporary politics (the surly honesty of the permanent Tory opposition), but to express something which the Augustan code could not express more directly – the feeling that though a hero may be a great rogue, still a rogue may be a small hero; and that though both the hero's and the highwayman's use of energy may be socially improper, still in their energy itself there is something we sneakingly admire. Lewis Carroll's Alice, who lays herself so open to Freudian interpretation (an early enthusiasm of Mr Empson's, which he has latterly tended to drop), represents a typically Victorian attempt to combine an intense covert interest in sex with a cult of innocence; and the 'nonsense' of the Alice books may be, much of it, rather sharp hidden satire on Victorian political and university life. Through the pastoral framework Lewis Carroll is able to embody, and to criticise, the complex fantasy of the Victorian compromise.

It is obvious that 'pastoral' here, like 'ambiguity' in the first book, is a conveniently elastic notion. In Mr Empson's third book, *The*

Structure of Complex Words, the theoretical foundations are at once more rigid and more elaborate; and it is not perhaps, to the same degree as the other two, a book which not only stimulates but entertains. Mr Empson takes issue here with the theory of Dr Richards, which we have already considered, that the use of words in poetry is primarily emotive; for he thinks that, though certain words even in ordinary language do acquire a strong emotive value, still that emotive value could ideally be deduced from (and can actually be explained by) the various combinations of their range of primary sense with their social use. Many uses of language in poetry that are thought of as primarily emotive, Mr Empson firmly points out, are not so. When a seventeenth-century poet says that a lady has lips like cherries, he is not expressing a covert, cannibalistic emotion; he means that the lips are fresh, dewy, dark red, and pouting. The cognitive meaning is primary, the secondary meaning emotive. Single words, on the other hand, sometimes have a strong, often pejorative, emotive sense which does not seem to derive from their cognitive sense; that can usually be explained by their social use. The word 'honest' (as in 'honest Iago,' or the Victorian 'honest Jones, my baker') often seems to imply unconscious patronage, almost a sneer. This is not because we do not admire honesty but because above a certain social level we take it for granted; it would be absurd, though much more accurate than in Iago's case, to talk about 'honest Othello.' The word 'native' is similarly felt as offensive because we have been accustomed to apply it to natives of backward and subjected countries, not to natives of our own. Again, in special social contexts, two quite separate senses of the same word can play into each other's hands: 'delicate' means both 'sickly' and 'refined' and in Victorian literature it is sometimes used to imply that a really refined young lady must also be sickly, and therefore that sickliness is a desirable quality. 'Honest,' similarly, means both 'trustworthy' and 'frank.' One could be frank about being untrustworthy. Thus there is a hearty use of the word, which Mr Empson notes, implying, 'At least I am not a hypocrite': 'You never knew a whoremaster, that was not an honest fellow.' There is an earlier instance than this Restoration one in Sir Thomas Wyatt, which Mr Empson missed:

And as I wrote to you last, I mean not that honesty that the common sort calleth an honest man: Trust me that 'honest man' is as common a name as the name of 'good fellow,' that is to say, a drunkard, a tavern haunter, a rioter, a gamer, a waster: so are among the common sort all men honest men that are not known for manifest naughty knaves.

Wyatt was making Mr Empson's essential point that to grasp the emotional values of a word you must consider not only its dictionary meaning but who uses it, where, and when. Words have what Mr Empson calls implications and moods as well as senses; from the implications and moods, from the variations of use and the play between the separate senses, the emotive value of words derives.

This analysis, very crudely summarised here, is probably the most lucid and cogent piece of general argumentation in Mr Empson's works. It will probably lay a heavy but useful load of labour on the backs of future lexicographers. From the point of view of the mere literary critic, however, Mr Empson's 'little bits of machinery' or 'tools' have the disadvantage of *being* tools. A tool is a very useful thing, but it is of its essence that it can perform only a single operation: the carpenter's plane shaves flat, his lathe turns, neither can do anything else. In the essays therefore in *The Structure of Complex Words* in which Mr Empson applies his tools to critical purposes – his examination of *Othello* in terms of Iago's 'honesty,' for instance – we feel that it is not so much his technical approach that enables him to acquire a critical grasp, as his critical grasp that prevents him from using his tools too mechanically. The man is working the machine, not the machine the man. In America, however, where Mr Empson has many disciples, what is called the 'New Criticism' sometimes at least looks like the purely mechanical application of a method: not controlled either by a wide range, like Mr Empson's, of human experience, nor by a depth, like his, of personal sensitivity.

It was probably the fear of the methodological abstractionism that might arise out of Dr Richards's scientific approach that inspired Dr F.R.Leavis, in his critical essays and in his share of the editorship of the Cambridge magazine, *Scrutiny*, to eschew as far as possible all sorts of generalisation and to concentrate on close examination of particular works. Dr Leavis has never claimed to teach, or to practise, a generally applicable 'technique' or 'method' of criticism. Dr Leavis had, of course, as every good critic must have, certain general interests; but these did not touch on psychology, semantics, or the general machinery of communication; they were moral or social rather than scientific interests. They had to do particularly with the problem of the education of a sensitive minority in a commercialised society, in a society in which the traditional cultural framework was decaying. Modern metropolitan culture (whether represented by commercial advertising, popular best-sellers, and political propaganda, or by the 'smart' literary world, by Bloomsbury and the ballet) seemed to Dr Leavis and his colleagues hopelessly corrupt. The last intellectual tradition they wholeheartedly admired was that of the agnostic Puritanism of Victorian Cambridge: the tradition of Sidgwick and Leslie Stephen. They did not feel that such minority culture as survived could, without being so diluted as to destroy itself, receive popular extension. Only a minority at any time were capable of real sensibility. But a larger number of people were perhaps capable of logical thinking, and might be taught at least to distrust advertisements and propaganda, and to recognise the more obvious kinds of literary faking.

The modern writers on whom Dr Leavis and his colleagues concentrated were set by them against this gloomy though not necessarily desperate perspective. D. H. Lawrence saw the general decay of metropolitan culture, the starving of the deep roots of life in our time, but he did not (in a phrase of his that Dr Leavis quotes) 'do dirt' on life itself; Joyce in *Ulysses* seemed to. If *The Waste Land* on the other hand seemed to express almost complete despair, yet its pessimism was not slackly and complacently negative as that of Joyce seemed to Dr Leavis. The *Scrutiny* team could, in fact, be sensitive and receptive to the work of even very minor writers who seemed to them to express their own reverence for life; L. H. Myers was applauded because of his hatred for cleverness and triviality; the rural themes of T. F. Powys and even of Mr Adrian Bell, a pleasant but very slight novelist of village life, suggested that here and there in England at least the tradition of organic community was alive. But the work of either dangerously fashionable writers, like the Sitwells and Mrs Woolf and Mr Aldous Huxley, or of the poets of the 1930s and onwards, from Mr Auden to Dylan Thomas, was on the whole (with some exceptions for Mr Auden's power and promise, and for the early work of Mr Bottrall and, with many more reservations, of Mr Empson) not welcomed. Whether by concentrating on politics, like Mr Auden in his earlier work, or by remaining content with a confused romantic subjectivism, like Mr Barker and Mr Thomas, the poets of the 1930s – and, even more, popular novelists of the 1930s, like Mr Waugh and Mr Greene – must have seemed to the *Scrutiny* critics to be ignoring, as Lawrence and Eliot and Pound had not, the profounder theme of cultural disintegration and the need for getting back to the deep sources of life.

Thus *Scrutiny* to-day represents an influential but isolated point of view: modernist in relation to the older academicism: conservative in relation to most manifestations of 'modernity' over the past twenty years. *Scrutiny* exacts, however, respect even from those who disagree with it by its admirable refusal to act on three principles which are, perhaps, pretty widely diffused throughout the rest of literary journalism: the 'group' principle, the 'personal' principle, and the 'deference' principle. The 'group' principle consists, for instance, of taking Mr Eliot's work very seriously, knowing that Mr Eliot takes the work of the late Charles Williams very seriously, and therefore presuming that one ought to take Williams's work very seriously, too. The 'personal' principle derives from the fact that most metropolitan authors and reviewers know each other reasonably well, like to keep on good terms with each other, and therefore in reviewing each other's work are tempted to pull their punches. The 'deference' principle is that, when on the whole one admires a particular author's work very much, one should treat a book of his which is under notice, even if one feels that it does not represent his highest achievement, with a certain tender forbearance. Dr Leavis's great admiration for the earlier poems of Pound and for very much of Mr Eliot's work does not, however, prevent him from being severe about the *Cantos* or about *The Cocktail Party* and much of Mr Eliot's later prose; the more one respects a writer, he feels, the less deferential one should be, and on the contrary the more unsparing when he falls short of his highest level. What matters is the standards of literature, not the feelings of writers.

Like Matthew Arnold, Dr Leavis takes a special pleasure in finding fastidious reasons for rejecting what has been too carelessly admired. He is as reluctant as Arnold to reduce his ideas to a system, and much more cautious than Arnold about large generalisations. His standards are not yardsticks, to be applied mechanically from without; his 'method,' in so far as he can be said to have anything so crude, is to read with concentration and to try to express precisely, even at the cost of cumbrousness, what he has felt. What he says can always be referred to, and often rises out of, the particular illustrative passages he quotes. He is not interested in form in abstraction from content, in a writer's general intention apart from his detailed presentation, or in that presentation itself apart from the 'quality of life' presented. The quality of life in fact is what he is primarily interested in, but he is a moralist who refuses to generalise. Crudely generalising for him, a reader might say that, in spite of his rather grim severity of tone, what he is always looking for is the embodiment of positive life-enhancing values. His famous case against Milton is based firstly on a feeling that Milton's perceptions are conventional and 'literary' – 'the smooth enamelled green' – and that Milton's thinking about life, for all his claim to 'justify the ways of God to man,' is not sufficiently deep and serious. He finds in Milton what might be called a kind of grand obtuseness. In the same way he looks through a lyric of poor Shelley's, rather as he might look through an essay by an undergraduate, alert for vague undirected enthusiasms and sloppy uses of language. On the other hand, a writer like Swift, for all his vivacity of detail and powers of ruthless organisation, gets bad marks, too: because, however energetically, he seems to express only destructive perceptions and negative values. Similarly, Dr Leavis can forgive the heaviness and clumsiness of much of George Eliot, or the melodramatic literary showmanship that puts a barrier between some readers and Conrad, because of his sense of the aliveness of the material presented and of the author's moral grasp.

It might almost be said that Dr Leavis's final standards, like the intermittent standards in his better moments of Henry Crawford in *Mansfield Park*, are those of 'moral taste.' Not, it should be emphasised, of aesthetic taste. Aesthetic taste for Dr Leavis is by its nature too superficial, not discriminating enough, not sufficiently sincere. Aesthetic critics will, for instance, praise the 'beautiful style' of George Moore, while admitting that they find much of his matter boring; but if there is something wrong with the tenor, there must be something wrong with the vehicle too. An earlier example of a critical attitude rather like Dr Leavis's might be found in the passage in Bagehot, where, dealing with the clumsy and hesitant quality of Bishop Butler's prose, he points out that the very defects of the style add to the impression of total sincerity, so possibly it is not such a bad style after all. More subtly, aesthetic critics will praise the complex organisation of a late novel by Henry James, like *The Ambassadors*; Dr Leavis, though a great admirer of James, finds this novel a bore. James, he feels, has got so lost in abstract problems of construction that the story and characters he started with have lost their crude substance; have become pretexts for merely verbal elaboration. Thus our sense in the end about Dr Leavis (if we can accustom ourselves to the anfractuosities and acerbities of his own prose, and conquer, as some of his colleagues never can, an indignation at what may seem to us an astonishing self-sufficiency and a strangely cavalier treatment of great names) is that his is a mind always enquiring, never resting slackly in its assumptions, probing most remorselessly what it is most drawn to admire; never satisfied with tactful approximations; prickly and combative because of what seems to it the insincerity of more stolid wits; a mind, also, with a touch of mischief in it, taking a faintly malicious pleasure – but also, and probably more profoundly, a public-spirited one – in undermining lazy self-esteem.

What, on the whole, however, has been the effect of the tradition with which Dr Leavis's name is so specially connected on younger writers? The Cambridge tradition still represents a minority influence on English academic life generally, though with a growing number of disciples, or part-disciples, among younger lecturers; in American academic life, it has become almost an orthodoxy, though probably much of the 'New Criticism' there represents an attempt to flatten out, to methodise, to systematise Dr Leavis's original approach (and that of many distinguished colleagues of his, whom space forbids me to mention) in a way which Dr Leavis himself would not approve of. In America, young poets, like Mr Randall Jarrell, have complained that they feel themselves flattened out by the new critical orthodoxy; anything creative they do they feel is 'placed,' and 'placed' with a 'limiting judgment,' by the new critics in advance; and yet in point of fact, as Mr Jarrell points out, it is on the whole more difficult – and more valuable – to write even a 'good minor poem' or a 'good naturalistic short story' than to write a quite ponderous critical essay. The new critics are not so firmly entrenched here, but it does seem true that the Cambridge tradition does tend to have a constipating and intimidating effect on young poets or novelists who come most immediately under its influence. A young man's first efforts in verse or fiction are bound to be crude and immature; if he ever learns to write well, it will be because at one time he has been allowed and even encouraged to write badly. The company of other young men with the same raw ambitions is likely to be more useful to him at this stage than the pervading sense of an ideal he cannot attain to; and there is a danger of his attempting, before he has acquired mature experience, to lay on his writing a pattern of sophistication and complexity from, as it were, above. This would be a fair criticism probably of some of the earlier work in verse of Mr Bottrall, Mr Empson, or Mr Madge; is it necessary or natural to be so clever, oblique, and allusive as that, quite all the time?

But there is a more profound question to be asked. Apart from young creators, may it not be a good thing for young readers sometimes to have passionate and immature admirations? It is a good thing, no doubt, for a young man to be sobered up who has become intoxicated with Shelley; but is it good for any young man never to have passed through the Shelley stage? It was Iago, after all, who said: 'I am nothing if not critical'; and Mr Donald Carne-Ross, in an amusing if unfair polemical article, has recently compared Dr Leavis's view of Othello's character to Iago's own. There is certainly a danger that the Cambridge attitude may breed a habitual suspicion of all kinds of rhetoric, like Othello's or like Milton's (or like Shelley's or like Whitman's), that make an overt claim to nobility. Thus *Scrutiny*, as Mr Carne-Ross noted, has always been a little grudging and cautious in its recognition of that most consciously noble of modern poets, Yeats. And its heroes of thought of the last century, Mill, Stephen, Sidgwick, worthy souls though they all are, are a little on the good, grey side; one wonders sometimes what Dr Leavis would make of a man who wrote so much more beautifully than any of these, and whose mind was in some directions so much more subtle and penetrating, John Henry Newman. . . . Yet, when all these reservations have been made, probably most young writers and critics to-day, of any seriousness of mind, would admit that they owe the Cambridge school a profound debt of gratitude.

Section 6: The Prospects To-Day

Most young critics to-day derive (particularly if they are literary journalists) in some degree from Bloomsbury and (particularly if they are young dons) in some degree from Cambridge; they will also of course have read Eliot and Hulme, if not quite certainly Wyndham Lewis or Pound. No important really new tendency in criticism has developed in this country since the early 1930s. There have been various attempts to harness criticism to religious or political orthodoxies; as by Mr Jack Lindsay or in the 1930s by Mr Philip Henderson to Marxism, and more recently by Brother George Every to Anglican Christianity; but out of mere kindness, the less said about these the better. The young poets of the 1930s, though many of them produced essays or books on literature, did not make the mark on critical thinking that they made on tendencies in verse. Michael Roberts, who helped to provide so many of them with their ideas, will probably be remembered as a brilliant amateur of philosophy and sociology rather than as a literary critic in the strict sense. He stage-managed the first appearances of many of the poets of the 1930s, claiming that they represented a return to Augustan lucidity. Undoubtedly Mr Auden and Mr MacNeice at least had partly such a lucidity in mind. Yet in fact the poetry of the 1930s remains, by any ideal standard, often unnecessarily obscure precisely because of its non-Augustan qualities – the use of a private 'group' mythology rather than a public language, and its use, indeed, as a substitute for a public language which was lacking. Mr Auden's *The Orators*, for instance, has become more and not less obscure with the passage of time; the group that could catch the allusions, and the wider circle in touch with that group who could explain the allusions to the uninitiated, have both dispersed. The poetry of the 1930s is often also obscure because of an extremely elliptical construction (as in some of Mr Auden's earliest poems, put together from surviving fragments which Mr Isherwood had admired out of poems which as wholes Mr Isherwood had rejected); because of deliberate complexity or aloofness, as in the work of Mr Bottrall, Mr Empson, and Mr Madge; and also because of the fundamental ambiguity of attitude that has been noted earlier, the idealisation of the ruled masses from the point of view of the discontented younger sons of the ruling few. Thus Michael Roberts's hopeful remarks about a new Augustanism are typical of the critical writing of the period, which often confidently announces a programme that in point of fact those who adhere to it will not carry out.

In fact, books of propaganda for the poetry of the 1930s, like Mr Day Lewis's *A Hope for Poetry*, tended to minimise, rather than to elucidate, the complexity of the actual situation. Of all the poets of the 1930s, Mr MacNeice had most of the critic's temper; his short book on Yeats is very exact and careful, if not sufficiently profound; but he put most of his critical impulse into his poetry, and his prose is urbane and civilised popularisation rather than an exploring of new ground. Mr Spender's *The Destructive Element* had the odd charm of most of his prose writing – sentences that struggle to express even quite simple ideas with a pleasant angular awkwardness, and that in doing so give an impression of innocent sincerity; but it lacked edge.

Mr Geoffrey Grigson, the editor of *New Verse*, was in a strategic position, if he had wished to do so, to become the leading critic at least of poetry of the 1930s. A volume of essays on contemporary poetry by him was in fact at one time announced, but never appeared.

His opinions have to be sought in the lively files of his own magazine, and very pungent opinions they are. He has published in fact in recent years many anthologies and collections of essays; but the temperament of the critic (or at least of the critic of poetry) has gradually become overgrown in him by the temperament of the naturalist, the traveller, the collector from the past. When he does write to-day about poetry, he finds it easier to indicate what he dislikes and why (the poetry of Miss Sitwell, Mr George Barker, and Mr Dylan Thomas) than to clarify and justify at length, for instance, his admiration for Mr Auden. As an editor, Mr Grigson emphasised the importance of colloquial diction, of a language rational, modulated, and close to life, and of the reporter's eye: the requirements, in fact, of urban poetry. But his deeper taste is for country life, and to-day, in attacking for instance the fantastic and heraldic imagery of Miss Sitwell, he tends to emphasise the importance of precise and loving observation of outward nature. But he hates generalisation, his critical perceptions are immediate and often angry, and he would be the first to admit that his ideas cannot be reduced to a system. What criticism has lost by his ceasing to concentrate on poetry, general literature has perhaps gained; he is the most vivid of our descriptive broadcasters, and, in his talks for instance on a journey across America, can evoke, with his eye for architecture and landscape and the small living details of a scene, a foreign ambience as few other writers can. In his affections and prejudices, in the tart crab-apple savour of his prose, he is extremely English; and stands, perhaps, with such a poet as Mr John Betjeman or such a painter as Mr John Piper, for an insular sensibility which does not bother very much if, by the outsider, it is not understood.

Mr Grigson, in his brief splenetic notices in New Verse, was certainly much closer to at least some of the requirements of criticism than most of the writers in the many 'little magazines' of verse that have succeeded it. Poetry that will last is not a plentiful commodity, and young poets ought to remember the point of view put with satirical exaggeration by Swift:

> Say Britain could you ever boast
> Three Poets in an Age at most?
> Our chilling Climate hardly bears
> A Sprig of Bays in Fifty Years:
> While every fool his Claim alledges,
> As if it grew in common Hedges.

By 'little magazines' a tentative and groping stage in youthful development tends to be prematurely crystallised into a 'style'; and the confusions of very young writers at a given period into a 'movement.' Young writers who stand out a little, but who still must be deeply dissatisfied with their own work, find themselves treated as models. There is, in the criticism in such magazines, a realm of discourse in which perhaps Mr Eliot, Mr Pound, and Yeats represent a 'giant age before the flood'; Mr Auden and the poets of the 1930s will be rather like the eighteenth century for Matthew Arnold, a discredited orthodoxy; and young writers with much to learn, and perhaps with little genuinely in common, will be grouped together as 'growing-points.' A frantic interest in the state of poetry in general, in the rise and fall of its temperature from month to month, replaces cool discrimination about particular poems.

Other factors, also, tend to make the critical articles in little magazines unsatisfactory. One of these is the 'group' factor; those who write for such magazines tend to know each other personally, to write in a sense for each other, and so the magazines are full of private jokes and covert personal allusions. They reflect also the workings of a kind of intellectual stock-exchange: month by month, one discovers that Existentialism is flagging, that Freud is steady but Jung is rising, that there are few buyers of Marx, but that some hardy spirits are risking a belated flutter in Surrealism. One 'little magazine' critic whose occasional very real perceptiveness seems to be often obscured by such congestions of fashionable ideas is Mr Derek Stanford. Another, who obscures his genuine penetration by a fondness for the sly nod and the knowing wink, is Mr Hugh Gordon Porteous. Mr Nicholas Moore, with a pellucid style, a genuine wit, and a quite unusual taste and gift for analysis, seems often to squander these in lengthy and courteous examinations of border-line cases among very minor poets; if he had devoted the same scrupulous attention to writers of some reputation (like the American poets whom he admires, Allen Tate, Wallace Stevens, John Peale Bishop) he would probably now be considered one of our leading younger critics. In *Nine* and *Colonnade*, young writers like Mr Peter Russell, Mr Iain Fletcher, Mr Iain Scott-Kilvert, have shown a longer sense of historical perspective than most 'little magazine' critics, and a more genuine interest in the great poetry of the past; but even these magazines are not free from the *coterie* manner and the *coterie* spirit. Perhaps no small magazine can be; and perhaps if young writers can learn to write in small magazines, the *coterie* spirit there, and the inadequacy of much of the critical writing, does not matter so terribly much. Yet the lack of authoritative and impersonal criticism, the lack of some central organ of literature which is both stabilised and receptive, is in the long run depressing to young writers. It is easy enough for them to get printed, if not to get paid; their friends and their enemies will express opinions on their work; but there seems no source to which they can look either for a firm and final rejection, or for a really inspiriting accolade.

The late George Orwell was almost the only example in the 1940s of the sort of critic whose voice, unlike that of most of the young writers just mentioned, could at once attract the attention of a wide audience. In print, as in life, he was the sort of person whom one stops to listen to. But as a strictly literary critic he suffered from very severe limitations. In a surprising essay on Mr Eliot's *Four Quartets*, which has never been reprinted, he expressed the opinion that *The Waste Land* was a very good poem, because it was about society and threw a light on society, and society was real; but *The Four Quartets* were about religion, and religion was ultimately an escapist illusion, and therefore *The Four Quartets* simply *could* not be so important. Similarly, he honestly admitted that he could not read Mrs Woolf's novels, because there was no story in them, and got far more genuine pleasure out of *Tell England* or *If Winter Comes*. These, and their like, he called 'good bad books'; but in a sense perhaps 'good bad books' were what he liked best. He is at his very best as a critic on works like *Raffles* or the novels of Mr Wodehouse, which, if they are to be counted as literature, are just to be counted so, and no more; they just scrape in. In his essay on Kipling, what fascinates him is not the subtlety of Kipling's short stories, or the queer difference between his really good poems and the ones which, in just as superficially effective a way, are really bad, but Kipling's gift of coining phrases that linger in the vulgar mind. And his essays on subjects that have no literary or artistic interest at all, but a very great sociological interest, like boys' weekly magazines and vulgar comic postcards, have perhaps more genuine relish about them than any purely critical piece he wrote. The one modern writer on whom Orwell has a really interesting essay, Henry Miller, attracts him again chiefly from a sociological point of view: Miller, like Orwell, had been a down-and-out in Paris; he knew the intoxication of hopelessness, the mirages created by hunger, the emancipation from all moralities of the uprooted individual in a disintegrating society. Orwell's essay on Salvador Dali, on the other hand, is not even sociology; it is a hell-fire sermon, a splendid hard-hitting piece of puritan polemics; if art can spring, as Orwell thinks it does in Dali's case, from vice and triviality, from a deliberately perverse attitude, so much the worse for art. What makes Orwell quite unique as a literary critic is, in fact, that he expresses always the plain man's attitude, though with a distinction that the plain man himself can never command; it also makes him at least rather rare among literary critics that he thought purely literary values had a rather low place among all sorts of other more important values of other kinds.

Shakespeare is accessible even to the doctrinaire lowbrow, and Orwell's essay on *King Lear* is a memorable piece of work. His primary interest, even here, however, is moral rather than literary; he is seeking to justify Shakespeare against Tolstoy (whose basic attitude towards literature, in *What Is Art?* was perhaps not profoundly different from Orwell's own); and his case is not based on the poetry of the play, which he barely quotes, nor on any very elaborate examination of theme and structure, but on a conviction that where ultimate moral issues are concerned Shakespeare was harrowingly honest and Tolstoy, in his later days, more than a little of an old unconscious humbug. Thus Orwell was probably not a literary critic in any strict sense; he uses literature, rather, to illustrate what he has to say about social problems and individual morality. The touch of bigotry that sometimes seems a flaw in his own moral attitude comes at least as much perhaps from insensitivity to purely literary qualities as from impatient political passion; as when, in his contribution to the *Partisan Review* controversy over Pound's Bollingen award, he admitted, after quite justifiably attacking Pound's politics, that he had always found Pound's poetry 'bogus.' To take no more controversial instances, the reader who finds Pound's *Cathay* or his *Seafarer* bogus must be lacking in some quite ordinary sensitivity which the common reader who likes poetry, and who never thinks of setting up as a critic, possesses. Orwell, in fact, who wrote with more force and point than any other literary essayist of his generation, might have been a very important critic indeed, if he had ever been able to detach his mind sufficiently from the social struggle to expose it, calmly, to the quality of writing as such. He wrote, as it was, so well that the fact that criticism, in the strict sense, is the one thing he does not offer us perhaps does not matter.

It would be possible to expand the concluding section of this already too extensive survey almost indefinitely. Among younger critics who show promise, one might mention Mr John Wain, who has written an excellent essay on Empson, and who shows himself much influenced by Empson in his own tight, muscular, difficult, and coherent poems; Mr John Heath Stubbs, whose lucid but rather fatigued study of Victorian neglected poets, *The Darkling Plain*, reflects the new interest in the Victorian age also of academic critics like Mr Geoffrey Tillotson, Mr Graham Hough, and Mr Noel Annan; and Mr D. S. Savage, a critic influenced both by Kierkegaard and Hegel, and well-grounded also in the terminology of a Marxism to which he does not adhere. Mr Savage, like Mr Wyndham Lewis, might be said to judge from the point of view of the absolute, though it is an absolute of a different flavour. He tends to dismiss writers of such different types as Mr Forster, Joyce, and Yeats, for fundamentally the same religious reasons: Mr Forster sins against whatever to Mr Savage is the Truth by a shallow agnosticism, Joyce by a rejection of his traditional faith and his failure to discover a new one, except in art, and Yeats by his proud posing and his reactionary politics. Later writers tend to be dismissed as one-sided adherents of 'politicism' or 'aestheticism,' both shallow fallacies. The severe gusto with which Mr Savage sets about his task of universal destruction makes one hope that he will in the long run tell us what the Truth is which he has found, and so many of the rest of us seem to have missed; but so far, in his critical work, the Absolute is assumed rather than expounded. Even on Kafka, a writer whom one would expect to appeal to him, Mr Savage is very severe. Kafka is dismissed as an example of religious cowardice, of the temperament that sees through the hollowness of the world, but cannot pluck up courage finally to renounce it; he is the sinner who wishes to repent but will not do so till he has received an advance guarantee that repentance will bring salvation; or he is the half-awakened man, who is afraid of what he might awake to, and who therefore turns over in bed and tries to go to sleep again. Thus Kafka deserved, and brought upon himself, the dread and anguish which he so poignantly evokes. Readers who do not share Mr Savage's religious or philosophical certainties, and who have their own perhaps humanistic and sentimental notions of what Christian morality implies, may feel that what limits him as a critic (apart from an insensitivity to the detailed qualities of writing) is an almost total lack of charity: he blames writers precisely for being what, in their time and place, and with their temperaments, he would have been himself.

The present state of criticism in England reflects perhaps the fatigue, the uncertainty, the feeling of moral anti-climax, which succeeded the new sense of national unity that arose during the last war. The critic, like the rest of us, wishes that he could see his way forward more clearly; or at the very least that the present ground were firmer under his feet. Our present period, as a recent writer in *The Times Literary Supplement* noted, should be one of consolidation; we should be reaping the fruits of the more than half a century of brilliant experiment in various fields that lies behind us. To the young Eliot, to Pound, to Joyce, to Wyndham Lewis, we should have something of the same relationship as Matthew Arnold had to the great romantics. Our period is certainly no longer, in a literary or artistic sense, an *exciting* period, as the great decade of the 1910s was; it is not a calm period either, but one of diffused anxiety and general inhibition. The young writer is inhibited not only by anxiety over the state of the world (for that has never been secure) but by more practical and intimate difficulties; practical difficulties of finding a publisher, earning a living, making a name; intimate difficulties of sinking roots down to nourishing soil in a shifting and worried metropolitan society. Thus the young men who showed promise in the war years find themselves drifting towards their forties with definite achievement still postponed. Habit and mild distraction dull anxiety. Writers seek in the private life, or in specialised intellectual hobbies, a stimulus which the public situation cannot offer them; but feel, guiltily, that they are thus evading an issue.

There would be no point in pretending, at the end of such a sweeping yet summary survey as this, either that our problems are not serious, or that our responses to them, even at the strictly literary level, are adequate. But when we look back we may feel pride perhaps and also hope. The world has been always full of violence and confusion, of doubt, of dismay; but the spirit of man, as that speaks through great literature, has never in the worst times been wholly silenced. Criticism is in some sense a parasite on more creative literature; but it is also the voice of man perceiving, choosing, pointing a way forward. That criticism has flourished in our century, in spite of apathy and bigotry, is a reason for hopefulness. While we try to discriminate, however many errors we make, we are still alive; when we begin to react mechanically, to drift and let things batter us, we are beginning to die.

We are forced to-day to ask ourselves terrible questions: yet we may find in the end the proper answers and a way forward, if never a way out:

Not fare well,
But fare forward, voyagers.

One's mind, for any peroration, is full of tags. '*Notre histoire est noble et tragique.*' That is true, but this is also true, from a poem out of the Dark Ages, a poem dealing with times as bad as we have gone through, or worse: 'That was overcome: so may this be.' The omens for the immediate future could certainly be more propitious; but while the critical spirit flourishes, civilisation remains actual, and freedom is alive.

INDEX